October 26–31, 2013
Indianapolis, Indiana, USA

Association for Computing Machinery

Advancing Computing as a Science & Profession

SPLASH

SPLASH'13

The Proceedings of the 2013 Companion Publication for Conference on
Systems, Programming, & Applications: Software for Humanity

Sponsored by:
ACM SIGPLAN

Supported by:
Microsoft Research, NSF, Cisco, Oracle Labs, Intel, Google, IBM Research, Purdue University, & Typesafe

**Association for
Computing Machinery**

Advancing Computing as a Science & Profession

The Association for Computing Machinery
2 Penn Plaza, Suite 701
New York, New York 10121-0701

Notice to Past Authors of ACM-Published Articles
ACM intends to create a complete electronic archive of all articles and/or other material previously published by ACM. If you have written a work that has been previously published by ACM in any journal or conference proceedings prior to 1978, or any SIG Newsletter at any time, and you do NOT want this work to appear in the ACM Digital Library, please inform permissions@acm.org, stating the title of the work, the author(s), and where and when published.

ISBN: 978-1-4503-1995-9 (Digital)

ISBN: 978-1-4503-2684-1 (Print)

Additional copies may be ordered prepaid from:

ACM Order Department
PO Box 30777
New York, NY 10087-0777, USA

Phone: 1-800-342-6626 (USA and Canada)
+1-212-626-0500 (Global)
Fax: +1-212-944-1318
E-mail: acmhelp@acm.org
Hours of Operation: 8:30 am – 4:30 pm ET

Printed in the USA

The Fourth Annual ACM International Conference on *Systems, Programming, Languages, and Applications: Software for Humanity*

It is our great pleasure to welcome you to Indianapolis and SPLASH 2013, the umbrella venue for the 28th *OOPSLA*, plus *Onward!*, *Wavefront*, and the *Dynamic Languages Symposium*. Moreover, SPLASH 2013 is proud to host the *ACM SIGPLAN Conference on Generative Programming: Concepts & Experiences* (GPCE), co-locating with the *International Conference on Software Language Engineering* (SLE). SPLASH this year revives the former educator's symposium in its new guise as SPLASH-E, for discussion of Computer Science education uniquely embedded within the culture of visionary research and practice embodied by *OOPSLA*, *Onward!*, and *Wavefront*. SPLASH-E is timely in that it coincides with the finalization of the ACM/IEEE Computer Science Curriculum 2013. This year also sees the return to SPLASH of tutorials and tech-talks, plus a new twist in the form of the synergistic SPLASH-I as a forum for acclaimed speakers from industry, all offered free to SPLASH attendees.

Drawing on the long tradition of *OOPSLA*, and with the addition of *Onward!* and *Wavefront*, SPLASH embraces all aspects of software construction and delivery to make it the premier conference at the intersection of programming, languages, and software engineering. *OOPSLA* was the incubator for CRC cards, CLOS, design patterns, Self, the agile methodologies, service-oriented architectures, wikis, Unified Modeling Language (UML), test driven design (TDD), refactoring, Java, dynamic compilation, and aspect-oriented programming, just to name a few. *Onward!* focuses on everything to do with programming and software: including processes, methods, languages, communities, and applications. *Onward!* is more radical, more visionary, and more open than other conferences to not yet well-proven but well-argued ideas. *Wavefront* is about how industry applies the lessons learned from the software development community in deploying today's software and systems, and how the community can learn from what is happening in the trenches of software engineering. The *Dynamic Languages Symposium* is the place where researchers and practitioners come together to discuss the new crop of wildly successful dynamic languages, their implementation, and their applications.

Guest conferences at SPLASH this year include GPCE and SLE. The *ACM SIGPLAN International Conference on Generative Programming: Concepts & Experiences* (GPCE) is a venue for researchers and practitioners interested in techniques that use program generation, domain-specific languages, and component deployment to increase programmer productivity, improve software quality, and shorten the time-to-market of software products. The *International Conference on Software Language Engineering* (SLE) is devoted to topics related to artificial languages in software engineering. SLE's mission is to encourage and organize communication among communities that have traditionally looked at software languages from different and yet complementary perspectives.

This year we are extremely fortunate to have four keynote speakers who tap into broad and deep SPLASH themes. Kathryn McKinley looks at the impact that heterogeneous hardware is having on the design and implementation of software abstractions for parallelism. Greg Wilson asks why the gap between research and practice remains so wide, and suggests how to narrow it. Molham Aref explores declarative programming for the cloud to combine rapid prototyping with performance in the deployment of large-scale cloud applications. Gilad Bracha ponders the history of innovation in programming languages and what is yet to come, asking how the elegance of Lisp, Simula, Actors, Beta, Smalltalk and Self led to the reality of C++, Java, Javascript, Perl, Python and PHP.

Organizing SPLASH has been a long march, alleviated greatly by the enthusiasm and talent of all those who have volunteered their time to make it a success. We are especially grateful to all the members of the Organizing Committee, comprising the committee chairs of all the conferences and events, and to our corporate supporters for their generosity. All the program chairs, aided by their program committees and reviewers, are to be congratulated on putting together such a strong program of papers and presentations. We thank the authors and presenters for their research, experiences, and valuable insights, which above anything else are the only reason for a conference like SPLASH in the first place. Finally, we thank you, the attendees, for being here to experience the wonder and excitement of SPLASH! We hope that you find the resulting program to be interesting and thought-provoking, and that your interactions at SPLASH with other researchers, educators, students, and practitioners from around the world are stimulating and fruitful.

Antony Hosking
SPLASH'13 General co-Chair
Purdue University, USA

Patrick Eugster
SPLASH'13 General co-Chair
Purdue University, USA

Table of Contents

Panels

Posters

Student Research Competition

Wavefront and Wavefront Experience

Workshops

Author Index

SPLASH INDIANAPOLIS 2013 OCTOBER 26-31

Conference Organizers

General Chairs:	Antony Hosking & Patrick Eugster *(Purdue University, USA)*
OOPSLA Program:	Crista Lopes *(University of California, Irvine, USA)*
OOPSLA Artifacts:	Matthias Hauswirth *(University of Lugano, Switzerland)* Steve Blackburn *(Australian National University, Australia)*
Onward! Program:	Robert Hirschfeld *(Hasso-Plattner-Institut Potsdam, Germany)*
Onward! Essays:	Bernd Brügge *(TU München, Germany)*
Wavefront Program:	Dennis Mancl *(Alcatel Lucent, USA)*
Wavefront Experience:	Eduardo Guerra *(National Institute for Space Research, Brazil)*
DLS Program:	Carl Friedrich Bolz *(Heinrich-Heine U Düsseldorf, Germany)*
SPLASH-E Program:	Kim Bruce *(Pomona College, USA)*
SPLASH-I Program:	Jan Vitek *(Purdue University, USA)*
Tutorials:	Jonathan Aldrich *(Carnegie Mellon University, USA)*
Workshops:	Stephanie Balzer *(Carnegie Mellon University, USA)* Ulrik Schulz *(University of Southern Denmark)*
Panels:	Steven Fraser *(Cisco, USA)*
Demonstrations:	Floréal Morandat *(LaBRI, France)* Igor Peshansky *(Google, USA)*
GPCE Chairs:	Jaakko Järvi *(Texas A&M University, USA)* Christian Kästner *(Carnegie Mellon University, USA)*
SLE Chairs:	Eric Van Wyk *(University of Minnesota, USA)* Martin Erwig *(Oregon State University, USA)* Richard Paige *(University of York, UK)*

Posters:	Emina Torlak *(University of California, Berkeley, USA)*
	K. R. Jayaram *(HP Labs, USA)*
Publicity:	Konstantin Beznosov *(Institute of British Columbia, Canada)*
Doctoral Symposium:	Lukasz Ziarek *(SUNY Buffalo, USA)*
ACM Student Research Competition:	Isil Dillig *(College of William and Mary, USA)*
	Sam Guyer *(Tufts University, USA)*
Proceedings:	Danny Dig *(University of Illinois Urbana-Champaign, USA)*
Web:	Henry Baragar *(Instantiated Software, Canada)*
	Chuck Matthews *(Fifth Generation Systems, Canada)*
	Jan Havel *(Catch Exception, Czech Republic)*
Corporate Support:	Jeff Foster *(University of Maryland, USA)*
	Jan Vitek *(Purdue University, USA)*
Social Media:	Emery Berger *(University of Massachusetts Amherst, USA)*
Local Arrangements:	Rajeev Raje *(IUPUI, USA)*
Steering Committee Chairs:	Crista Lopes *(University of California, Irvine, USA)*
	William Cook *(University of Texas at Austin, USA)*
Conference Management:	Annabel Satin *(PCK, UK)*

Sponsor:  **SIGPLAN**

SPLASH INDIANAPOLIS 2013
OCTOBER 26-31

SPLASH 2013 Supporters

Diamond Supporters:

Microsoft Research

NSF

Silver Supporters:

CISCO

intel Oracle Labs

Friends:

Google

IBM Research

PURDUE UNIVERSITY

Typesafe

The Yin and Yang of Hardware Heterogeneity: Can Software Survive?

Kathryn S. McKinley

Microsoft Research

Abstract

Power and energy constraints are now the driving force in devices from smartphones to servers. Quantitative power, performance, and energy measurements suggest that hardware heterogeneity to match software diversity has the potential to deliver energy efficiency. However, programming heterogeneous hardware directly is a nightmare. We discuss some approaches and results that abstract, choose, and exploit hardware heterogeneity. New programming and system abstractions are essential for establishing a parallel heterogeneous ecosystem in the post-Dennard era.

Categories and Subject Descriptors   Computer Systems Organization: Processor Architectures; Programming Languages

Keywords   Power, Energy, Heterogeneous Hardware, Managed Languages, Virtual Machines

A New Computing Landscape

Over the past fifty years, computer software and hardware erected layers of abstraction to hide complexity and innovate rapidly. As processor speeds increased, the costs of abstraction reduced in each hardware generation. Unfortunately, physical limits in hardware are forcing a disruptive break in this virtuous cycle of innovation, in part by breaking a key abstraction: sequential instruction execution.

Hardware   Moore's law predicts that technology advances will shrink transistors, increasing the number of transistors in the same silicon area. Shrinking transistors lowers their gate delay and until recently translated into faster clock frequencies, as predicted by Dennard scaling. The result was exponential single processor performance gains. Between 2000 and 2010, physical limits of silicon made shrinking transistors harder, in part due to power leakage, which Dennard scaling did not model. The result was the end of clock

scaling. To continue to improve processor capabilities with smaller transistors, hardware vendors turned to parallelism and introduced chip multiprocessors.

Looking forward, physical limits on power, area, and wires will require even more radical solutions. Already emerging from research and industry are heterogeneous processors that improve capabilities using specialized processors and multiple types of general-purpose processors that offer a range of power and performance characteristics. Power constraints also limit memory scaling. Solutions to meeting the ever present demand for more and faster memories are likely to combine non-volatile storage and traditional DRAM. Parallel heterogeneous hardware requires parallel and differentiated software components, exposing software developers to ongoing hardware upheaval.

Software   As in many good partnerships, software encourages, drives, and exploits improving hardware capabilities. Furthermore, hardware capabilities encourage, drive, and exploit substantial software innovations. This ecosystem heralded new ways to sell, deploy, and interact with hardware over the past two decades. The entire computing ecosystem changed to meet demands for portability, reliability, security, correctness, new features, and time-to-market.

These demands drove developers away from native compiled ahead-of-time languages. Developers instead increasingly choose high-level managed programming languages with safe pointer disciplines, garbage collection, extensive standard libraries, and dynamic just-in-time compilation for hardware portability. For example, modern web services deliver software as a service in the browser by combining managed languages, such as JavaScript on the client side and PHP on the server side. In markets as diverse as finance and mobile, Java and C# dominate. This ecosystem produced an explosion of capabilities and an expanding base of developers that continue to change how we live and learn. Improving hardware capabilities hid much of the cost of software abstractions, whereas software virtual machine technologies hid hardware dependence and complexity.

The result was a virtuous cycle with ever more capable and high-level computing systems. However, post-Dennard era processors break this virtuous cycle by changing abstractions and changing assumptions built into hardware and software abstraction layers, as depicted in Figure 1.

SPLASH '13,   October 26–31, 2013, Indianapolis, Indiana, USA.
Copyright © ACM ACM 978-1-4503-1995-9/13/10
http://dx.doi.org/10.1145/2508075.2508188 ... $10.00

Breaks in the Hardware/Software Virtuous Cycle

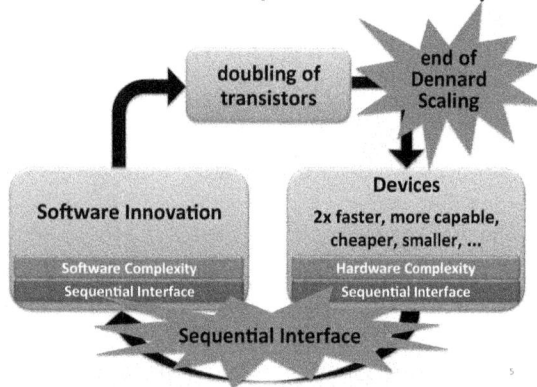

Figure 1. The virtuous cycle of hardware/software innovation is broken by the end of Dennard scaling and the introduction of a new hardware abstraction.

Moving Forward The economics of commodity hardware and the potential for efficiency through specialization create a tension for the designers of future systems. The more specialized the hardware, the higher the potential, but the more likely only a small set of applications will benefit. The less specialized the hardware is, the less the potential improvement, but the more applications that may benefit. At the limits, commodity processors execute every appliation, but are inefficient, whereas an application specific ASIC executes a single application very efficiently. These practical concerns motivate heterogeneous processors that use the same instruction set architectures (ISAs) but have different power and performance characteristics. For example, combining a few big cores with numerous little cores to meet power constraints, where big cores deliver the highest possible performance but are power hungry, and multiple little cores deliver throughput using substantially less power but with less performance. Vendors, such as NVIDIA, TI, and Qualcomm, already are shipping big/little heterogeneous systems.

To create a new virtuous cycle for modern systems ranging from smartphones to data centers requires new abstractions. The best abstractions meet current design goals and capabilities, but ease, encourage, and even create the potential for future innovations. Whereas in the Dennard era, performance was the primary design goal, the post-Dennard era adds power and energy to every market segment, not just mobile and embedded. Optimizing for performance, power, and energy (energy = power × time) is substantially more challenging than optimizing solely for performance.

Creating a new energy-efficient ecosystem requires deep understanding of the power, performance, and energy characteristics of software and optimizing for the hardware transparently. Whereas the programming language, system, and architecture communities understand how to measure and optimize performance, systematic power and energy mea-

surements are not yet common. We show how power measurements lead to new insights about energy efficiency on modern hardware, and the differences between native, managed, parallel, and sequential workloads. With deeper understanding of capabilities in hand, we explore potential ways to optimize, matching software diversity to heterogeneous hardware using existing and new abstractions.

Heterogeneous hardware requires software with differentiated characteristics, parallelism (yes, still!), and ubiquity. We identify and exploit these characteristics to improve energy efficiency in case studies ranging from managed applications to smartphones to interactive services in data centers. For managed applications, we hide overheads from virtual machine services (such as garbage collection and just-in-time compilation), and optimize mapping threads to cores by learning properties such as parallelism, criticality, and sensitivity to core choice. For smartphones, we learn and optimize the tradeoff of responsiveness and battery drain. For interactive cloud services, such as search, we learn and optimize the quality and latency tradeoff, improving performance and energy efficiency. These results offer several insights for optimizing future systems. (1) Dynamically monitoring and adapting to the application is critical to energy efficiency. (2) Although software performance improvements on a particular hardware platform almost always lead to energy efficiency improvements, exploiting tradeoffs in latency and quality of service inherent in many emerging applications, both at design time and on deployed hardware, has the potential to improve energy efficiency more substantially.

These results offer hope that software may perhaps thrive as heterogeneous hardware evolves in the post-Denard era.

Acknowledgments and References My thanks to my collaborators at Microsoft, The University of Texas at Austin, and the Australian National University; and in particular to Steve Blackburn (ANU) and Yuxiong He (Microsoft). My thanks to James Bornholt for comments on this document. For our publications, please see http://research. microsoft.com/en-US/people/mckinley/papers.aspx.

Kathryn S. McKinley is a Principal Researcher at Microsoft Research and served on the faculty of The University of Texas at Austin (2001-2013). She likes to solve programming language implementation problems and make systems programmable, fast, reliable, secure, and energy efficient. Dr. McKinley and her collaborators produced the widely used DaCapo Java Benchmarks, TRIPS Compiler, Hoard memory manager, MMTk garbage collector toolkit, and Immix garbage collector. She is co-Chair of the CRA Committee on the Status of Women in Computing Research, and has testified on how to sustain the information technology innovation ecosystem to the U.S. House Science Committee. Dr. McKinley has graduated 17 PhD students. She is married to artist Scotty Strahan and they have three sons. She is an IEEE Fellow and an ACM Fellow.

Two Solitudes

Greg Wilson

Mozilla Foundation
gvwilson@third-bit.com

Abstract

I have spent much of the last fifteen years trying to build bridges
between the two solitudes of computing: academic researchers on
the one side, and working developers on the other. These efforts
have largely failed, but have done so in interesting ways. This
talk will explore why the wide gulf between research and practice
persists, and outline a new plan for trying to narrow it based on
scurvy, smoking, and statistics.

Categories and Subject Descriptors   D.2.0 [*Sofwtare Engineering*]: General

Keywords   academic-industrial collaboration

SPLASH '13,   October 26–31, 2013, Indianapolis, Indiana, USA.
Copyright is held by the owner/author(s).
ACM 978-1-4503-1995-9/13/10.
http://dx.doi.org/10.1145/2508075.2508189

Declarative Programming for the Cloud

Molham Aref

LogicBlox
molham.aref@logicblox.com

Abstract

I will present the LogicBlox database and describe business applications that use it. The LogicBlox database marries declarative programming (logic-based specifications) with cloud deployment over large datasets. The database is programmed with a variant of the Datalog programming language. The flexibility of declarative programming allows us to integrate both traditional business application development and "probabilistic" applications: machine-learning or search-based solutions, as required by the domain. Our approach aims to eliminate the distance between prototyping and deployed, high-performance implementations. I will discuss real customer applications and actual deployment instances that elastically adapt to several thousands of machines.

Categories and Subject Descriptors   D.1.6 [*Software*]: Programming Techniques—Logic Programming;   H.2.3 [*Information Systems*]: Database Management—Languages;   J.1 [*Computer Applications*]: Administrative Data Processing—Business

Keywords   Logic programming, database, machine-learning, elasticity, scalability

SPLASH '13,   October 26–31, 2013, Indianapolis, Indiana, USA.
Copyright is held by the owner/author(s).
ACM 978-1-4503-1995-9/13/10.
http://dx.doi.org/10.1145/2508075.2508190

Does Thought Crime Pay?

Gilad Bracha

gilad@bracha.org

Abstract

Who controls the past controls the future;
who controls the present controls the past.
– George Orwell [11]

We examine the past, present and future of radical innovation in programming languages. How did Lisp, Simula, Actors, Beta, Smalltalk and Self give us the world of C++, Java, Javascript, Perl, Python and PHP? We'll ponder such questions and speculate what new wonders await us down the road.

Categories and Subject Descriptors   D.3.2 [*Language Classifications*]: Object-oriented languages; Constraint and logic languages. ;   D.3.3 [*Language Constructs and Features*]: Classes and objects; Modules, packages.

Keywords   Programming languages, Objects

1.   Introduction

Thought crime is the thinking of heretical thoughts; thoughts that question the assumptions that the majority never question. Innovation and thought crime are related. If you doubt this point, I refer you to the case of one Galileo Galilei.

Fortunately, today we know better. We live in a golden age of technological innovation. Modern society loves innovators - as long as they don't innovate too much. True innovation also involves questioning the assumptions that almost everyone agrees with. This can sometimes make those of us engaged in research feel a bit like thought criminals.

In my field, programming languages, there is a strong notion of *the mainstream*. We speak of mainstream languages, tools and practices. Of course, no one is going to send inquisitors to our homes to persecute us for disagreeing with the mainstream. However, you can run out of funding very fast.

It was not always so. Once upon a time, programming languages introduced new ways of thinking. Languages like Lisp, APL [9], Simula [5], Smalltalk [8], Prolog, Beta [10], Self [13] and Miranda [12] represented true innovation. Each such language opened a door into a new world, a different way of looking at problems. So did other languages like Forth, SETL, Snobol, Lucid and Esterel.

Today the programming language landscape is dominated by a small number of languages that represent an even smaller number of ideas. Advocating for anything that substantially deviates from the norm is a thought crime. In the words of Dijkstra [7]:

> If the truths are sufficiently impalatable, our audience is psychically incapable of accepting them and we will be written off as totally unrealistic, hopelessly idealistic, dangerously revolutionary, foolishly gullible or what have you.

How did we get here, and is this where we want to be? Some might argue that the languages of today evolved by a process akin to natural selection. Current languages would then represent a refinement of the languages of the past in response to the actual requirements of widespread deployment and industrial scale use.

However, the one thing we can say with confidence is that mainstream programming languages are inadequate in the face of the aforementioned requirements. There is constant stream of new versions of these languages, always adding new features. Yet, no matter how many new features are added, there is always a need for more.

Historically, today's mainstream languages represent a school of thought that constructs languages by agglomeration: specialized constructs are tacked on one by one, each tailored to some specific purpose.

These are the *languages of the present*. As noted above, there is little evidence that this approach ever converges to a satisfactory solution. I argue that we can ill afford to let the present control the future.

There is another school of thought in programming language design. It postulates that a language should have a small set of very general constructs rather than a large number of very specific ones. This approach is exemplified by the APL, Lisp and Smalltalk families of languages. Interestingly, these languages have required remarkably small adaptations over the past 30-50 years. Yet today, such languages tend to be relegated to small niches. These are *the languages of the past*.

Many innovations in implementation technology originally developed for non-mainstream languages have been commandeered by the mainstream. Examples include garbage collection (originating in Lisp), JITs (pioneered in APL and later in Smalltalk) and other aspects of advanced object-oriented runtimes (as introduced in Self and Smalltalk systems).

The mainstream also adopts language ideas from its less popular brethren. Object orientation is the most obvious example, coming from Simula and Smalltalk. In addition to the original class based form, we also have prototypes (Self and others). Other ideas include closures (Scheme), actors ([3]), IDEs (Smalltalk and Lisp), and reflection (Lisp and Smalltalk).

As ideas filter through, they are often attenuated. For example, when Gabriel and Steele et al. debated whether object-orientation had succeeded [6], Gabriel argued that it had failed because the widely adopted version is such a pale shadow of the original ideas. It is small wonder that critics of object orientation are dissatisfied

SPLASH '13,   October 26–31, 2013, Indianapolis, Indiana, USA.
Copyright is held by the owner/author(s).
ACM 978-1-4503-1995-9/13/10.
http://dx.doi.org/10.1145/2508075.2508191

with it; they mistake the dull artifacts of the languages of the present for the real thing.

We can see the wages of sin: thought crime does pay; it just doesn't pay the criminals, it pays the broader society. The innovations of unpopular languages are adopted, albeit often in inferior form, by the popular ones.

Is this a satisfactory situation? Can we afford to to let the present control the past, relegating the most brilliant artifacts in the field of programming languages to the waste basket of history?

Perhaps this is as it should be. After all, aren't the ideas the important thing, not the specific artifacts in which they were first manifested? One problem with this argument that we still need significant new ideas. The mainstream is not a good incubator for new ideas; it is in fact rather toxic to them. As evidence, consider the list of innovations given above, produced by a very small number of people with relatively minimal resources. Compare it to the intellectual contributions of the mainstream, involving orders of magnitude more people and resources.

An example of what passes as innovation in the mainstream is the practice known as *dependency injection*. Dependency injection (DI) is an attempt to address modularity issues that have cropped up in industrial scale programming. Such modularity issues are best addressed at the language level; the designers of some DI frameworks acknowledge this [1].

The languages of the present, the mainstream, do not address the issue of DI, but neither do the languages of the past. We need *languages of the future* to tackle such questions. We can and have found inspiration for such languages by looking into the past. Combining ideas from Smalltalk and Beta, Newspeak shows how a very pure form of objects naturally answers these problems [4]. Combining the idea that everything is an object, with nested classes and the notion that all computation is based on exchanging messages among objects yields a powerful approach to modularity. Arguably it has been staring us in the face for thirty years.

These problems are not hypothetical. Today, we have examples of entire libraries that need to be evolved independently by multiple developers which are distributed geographically and organizationally. Consider the process of evolving web standards such as the DOM. At any given time, there are multiple proposals for distinct extensions to the DOM API. These proposals are prototyped independently by different teams in different places. To evaluate the proposals, others should be able to run the prototypes, both separately and together in various combinations to see how they interact. It is not attractive to build and/or download many versions of a complete web browser to achieve this.

An alternative is to extend and modify entire libraries, and compose the modifications by mixing and matching them in different ways. Javascript enables this through ad hoc and poorly structured modifications to prototypes. Other languages would be even more hard pressed to deal with the situation, but it can be handled gracefully in a language like Newspeak.

Programming tools and environments can also benefit greatly from looking to the past. We are beginning to see a resurgence in this area [2]. Tools that go beyond the view of programs as static source code to support rich interaction with running programs are desperately needed. Tooling needs to be treated as a legitimate area of research, not a thought crime. We need to understand that programming language design should not be divorced from the tools and environments in which these languages are to be used. Even more broadly, research in programming languages needs to re-emphasize the building of complete systems, just as in the glory days of Xerox PARC.

Logic programming is another old idea that is ripe for re-examination. The need to reason about large datasets should prompt us to revisit Prolog and similar languages. Today we have machines that are a thousand times faster than in the 1980s, and the ability to couple thousands of machines together. Not many conclusions are valid across six orders of magnitude; whatever difficulties the field encountered in decades are almost certainly irrelevant.

No doubt I have overlooked important languages and efforts in this brief summary. What is important, however is that we remain cognizant of the history of programming languages. In particular, education is crucial; students need to be aware of a many different ways of programming, lest they reinvent the wheel and reinvent it badly. We must not let the languages of the present obscure our view of the past, because it is the great languages of the past that can lead us to the languages of the future. Only then can we make thought crime really pay.

References

[1] Java on Guice: Guice user's guide. Available at http://code.google.com/p/google-guice/.

[2] First international workshop on live programming, May 2013. Held at ICSE 2013. See http://liveprogramming.github.io/2013/.

[3] G. Agha and C. Hewitt. Actors: A conceptual foundation for concurrent object-oriented programming. In *Research Directions in Object-Oriented Programming*, pages 49–74. MIT Press, 1987.

[4] G. Bracha, P. von der Ahé, V. Bykov, Y. Kashai, W. Maddox, and E. Miranda. Modules as objects in Newspeak. In *European Conference on Object-Oriented Programming*, June 2010.

[5] O.-J. Dahl and K. Nygaard. Simula: An Algol-based simulation language. *Communications of the ACM*, 9:671–678, 1966.

[6] M. Devos, B. Foote, R. Gabriel, and J. N. G. Steele. Debate at OOPSLA 2002. See http://www.oopsla.org/2002/ap/files/pan-1.html. See also http://www.dreamsongs.com/Essays.html.

[7] E. Dijkstra. How do we tell truths that might hurt? In *Selected Writings on Computing: A Personal Perspective*. 1975.

[8] A. Goldberg and D. Robson. *Smalltalk-80: the Language and Its Implementation*. Addison-Wesley, 1983.

[9] K. Iverson. *A programming language*. Wiley, 1962. URL http://books.google.com/books?id=zR81AAAAIAAJ.

[10] O. L. Madsen, B. Møller-Pedersen, and K. Nygaard. *Object-Oriented Programming in the Beta Programming Language*. Addison-Wesley, 1993.

[11] G. Orwell. *1984*. 1949.

[12] D. Turner. Miranda: A non-strict functional language with polymorphic types. volume 201 of *Lecture Notes in Computer Science*, pages 1–16. Springer-Verlag, 1985.

[13] D. Ungar and R. Smith. SELF: The power of simplicity. In *Proc. of the ACM Conf. on Object-Oriented Programming, Systems, Languages and Applications*, Oct. 1987.

Welcome Message from the Demonstrations Chairs

Welcome to the SPLASH 2013 Demonstrations track. We all know that it's better to see something once than to hear about it a hundred times. Live demonstrations show the impact of software innovation in a dynamic and highly interactive setting. This track is an excellent opportunity for companies and universities to share their latest work with an experienced and technically savvy audience – you.

We have received many interesting and diverse demonstration submissions from both industry and academia, and have compiled an exciting demonstration program consisting of tools, applications, and languages in various stages of development – from prototypes and proofs of concept to mature tools and systems. Each of them contains interesting and relevant technology and should appeal to the SPLASH community.

These demonstrations are not product sales pitches, but rather an opportunity for the authors to highlight, explain, and present interesting technical aspects of running applications. The sessions are intended to be two-way interactions with the audience, which has the opportunity to share ideas, interact with the authors in a small scale venue, and learn techniques used in developing innovative and high quality software. Presenters are encouraged to actively solicit feedback from the audience, which should lead to very interesting and entertaining demonstration sessions.

We would like to thank this year's demonstration presenters for their hard work in bringing live demonstrations to SPLASH 2013. We are also grateful to this year's demonstrations subcommittee for their efforts to shape the 2013 demonstrations program.

Demonstrations Committee Members:

Nicolas Geoffray (**Google**, Denmark)

Christoph Reichenbach (Goethe-Universität Frankfurt am Main, Germany)

Michel Zam (Karmic Soft, France)

Igor Peshansky	**Floréal Morandat**
Google, USA	*LaBRI, France*

Client-Aware Checking and Information Hiding in Interface Specifications with JML/ajmlc

Henrique Rebêlo[λ], Gary T. Leavens[θ], Ricardo Lima[λ]

[λ]Universidade Federal de Pernambuco, PE, Brazil
{hemr, rmfl, phmb}@cin.ufpe.br

[θ]University of Central Florida, Orlando, FL, USA
leavens@eecs.ucf.edu

Abstract

Information hiding controls which parts of a module are visible to different clients. This aids maintenance because hidden implementation details can be changed without affecting clients. The benefits of information hiding apply not only to code but also to other artifacts, such as specifications.

In this demonstration we show how our client-aware checking (CAC) technique, which is implemented by our JML/ajmlc compiler and freely available online, use the privacy information in specifications to promote information hiding. We demonstrate the benefits of CAC over existing runtime assertion checkers (RACs) of contemporary interface specification languages.

Client-aware checking allows runtime assertion checking and error reporting based solely on specifications visible to clients. This avoids exposing hidden implementation or specification details that cannot be understood by non-privileged clients.

This demonstration will proceed by discussing the goals of the CAC technique by means of realistic examples. Attendees will mainly see JML specifications, including pre- and postconditions for methods. They will learn how to use the JML/ajmlc compiler, which also provides information hiding capabilities. In addition, they will learn how to use model fields to hide the actual field declarations in classes, and how model fields play an important role in achieving information hiding. We will conclude with pointers to ongoing work on design, implementation and runtime checking of Java programs with CAC-based JML/ajmlc.

Categories and Subject Descriptors D.2.4 [*Software*]: Program Verification—Programming by contract; F.3.1 [*Specifying and Verifying and Reasoning about Programs*]: Assertions, Invariant, Pre- and postconditions, Specification techniques

General Terms Languages, Verification

Keywords Information hiding, interface specification languages, design by contract, runtime assertion checking, Java Modeling Language (JML)

SPLASH '13, October 26–31, 2013, Indianapolis, Indiana, USA.
Copyright is held by the owner/author(s).
ACM 978-1-4503-1995-9/13/10.
http://dx.doi.org/10.1145/2508075.2514569

1. Background and Problem Statement

Information hiding [11] (also known as black-box abstraction) is a widely-accepted principle that aids software development. It advocates that a module should expose its functionality but hide its implementation behind an interface. This supports modular reasoning and independent evolution/maintenance of the hidden parts of a module. If programmers have carefully chosen to hide those parts "most likely" to change [11], most changes, in the hidden implementation details, do not affect module clients.

Information hiding and its benefits apply not only to code but also to other artifacts, such as documentation and specifications [8]. Leavens and Müller [8] present rules for information hiding in specifications for Java-like languages. Following Meyer's book [10], Leavens and Müller's Rule 1 [8] says that specifications should not expose hidden members. This implies that postconditions (visible to public clients) of a public method must not mention the existing private members, such as fields and methods. In this sense, the specification language JML [7] provides syntax for visibility modifiers [8] that is applied to various specification constructs. As with Java visibility modifiers, these JML modifiers allow one to specify a class's public (non-privileged client), protected (subclass), package (friend), and private (implementation) interfaces.

Although there is a set of rules for information hiding in specifications [8] and although JML [7] supports visibility modifiers, existing runtime assertion checker (RAC) tools violate those information hiding rules during runtime assertion checking and error reporting.

The problem is the way contemporary RACs implement runtime assertion checks for method calls. Such RAC compilers operate by injecting code at the supplier side, thus checking each method's precondition at the beginning of its code, and injecting code to check the method's postcondition at the end of its code. Since supplier-side checks do not take into account what kind of client (i.e., privileged or non-privileged) is calling a method, a RAC checks all the specifications regardless of visibility. Therefore, we say that a RAC that checks all the specifications at supplier side as *overly-dynamic*.

Overly-dynamic checking mentions hidden members in its error reporting. The problem is that such error reports, involving hidden members, are not meaningful to all clients. As a consequence, clients confront an issue that the interface claimed to hide [6].

In this demonstration, we focus on formal interface specifications and their runtime assertion checking (RAC) tools. Formal interface specifications include contracts written in Eiffel [9], the Java Modeling Language (JML) [7], Spec# [2], and Code Contracts [4].

2. Client-Aware Checking (CAC)

Our goal is to ease proper checking of visibility rules in a RAC. We call our technique for doing this client-aware checking (CAC). CAC aims to runtime check contracts from the client's view.

The most important feature of CAC is that it checks method specifications on the client side [5] of each call (i.e., at the call site). Doing this allows CAC to be consistent with information hiding rules, by checking only the visible pre- and postconditions for each call. This also avoids the not meaningfull error reporting that may arise from overly-dynamic RACs.

To see how these checks are made, we use the proof rule for method calls that allows one to derive

$$\{pre_m^T[\vec{a}/\vec{f}]\} \; p.m(\vec{a}) \; \{post_m^T[\vec{a}/\vec{f}]\}$$

from a specification $(T \triangleright pre_m^T, post_m^T)$ associated with the receiver p's the static type T. (The notation $[\vec{a}/\vec{f}]$ means the substitution of the actual parameters $\vec{a}$ for m's formals $\vec{f}$.) An automated static verifier that uses weakest precondition semantics can modularly replaces a call $p.m(\vec{a})$ by the sequence of "**assert** $pre_m^T[\vec{a}/\vec{f}]$; **assume** $post_m^T[\vec{a}/\vec{f}]$" [1].

A RAC will do runtime checks at each **assert** and **assume** statement. That is, in the CAC technique, a RAC injects runtime checks around each method call to check the pre- and postconditions of the statically-visible specifications for the call.

A private postcondition should be omitted from the error reporting since specifications of wider visibility should be refined by their counterparts of narrower visibility (hence public method preconditions should imply private preconditions, and private postconditions should be implied by public postconditions, when the public preconditions hold [3]). The reason for this is that a client would be surprised if they encountered assertion violation errors due to invisible assertions.

3. Benefits and Demonstration Overview

We begin our demonstration with an overview of the Java Modeling Language (JML) [7]. JML is used to specify and check the behavior of Java modules. The CAC technique we explain in this demo is implemented in the JML/ajmlc compiler [12, 13].

The first benefit by attending our demo sessions will be the explicit recognition of the visibility problems that plague contemporary RACs due to their overly-dynamic checking in compromising information hiding rules. Attendees will see examples of information hiding violation in Code Contracts [4], JML [7], and Eiffel [9].

Second, the attendees will see an improved form of runtime checking consistent with information hiding. Hence, we will introduce the concept of *client-aware checking* (CAC), and show how it checks pre- and postconditions for OO programs in a way that is respects information hiding. At this stage, the examples will be given in JML [7], since our CAC is implemented in the JML/ajmlc compiler [13]. They will realize our CAC technique works by injecting code to check pre- and postcondition into clients at method call sites. Because code is injected at the site of each method call, it properly uses the visible specifications associated with the clients.

We believe that these benefits are important for the software engineering community as they can aid in further improving information hiding in specifications and runtime assertion checking.

4. CAC Infrastructure

We implemented the CAC technique in the Aspect-JML RAC compiler (ajmlc) [12, 13] which is available online at:
http://www.cin.ufpe.br/~hemr/JMLAOP/ajmlc.htm.
This is the first RAC to support CAC.

5. Presenter Biography

Henrique Rebêlo is one of the three original authors and creators of the CAC technique. He has extensive experience in separation of concerns and design by contract techniques. He is the main developer of the aspect-oriented JML compiler known as ajmlc [12, 13]. This compiler uses aspect-oriented programming (AOP) for enforcing JML contracts at runtime. He was a researcher intern in 2010 at Microsoft Research working on program analysis and program verification. He has given talks on design by contract and AOP at prestigious venues like SEKE'11, FTFJP'11, SAVCBS'09, ICST'08, and SAC'08.

6. Acknowledgments

We thank Rustan Leino, Mike Barnett, Peter Müller, Shuvendu Lahiri, and Tom Ball for discussions about these topics. Mike Barnett also gave us a demo of Code Contracts at MSR.

Special thanks to Mira Mezini and Ralf Lämmel for detailed discussions and for comments on an earlier version of these ideas.

We would like to thank David Naumann and Bertrand Meyer for interesting discussions during CBSoft 2012 (Natal/Brazil).

References

[1] M. Barnett and K. R. M. Leino. Weakest-precondition of unstructured programs. *SIGSOFT Softw. Eng. Notes*, 31:82–87, September 2005.

[2] M. Barnett, K. R. M. Leino, and W. Schulte. The Spec# programming system: an overview. In G. Barthe, L. Burdy, M. Huisman, J.-L. Lanet, and T. Muntean, editors, *Post Conference Proceedings of CASSIS: Construction and Analysis of Safe, Secure and Interoperable Smart devices, Marseille*, volume 3362 of *LNCS*. Springer-Verlag, 2005.

[3] K. K. Dhara and G. T. Leavens. Forcing behavioral subtyping through specification inheritance. In *Proceedings of the 18th International Conference on Software Engineering, Berlin, Germany*, pages 258–267. IEEE Computer Society Press, Mar. 1996. A corrected version is ISU CS TR #95-20c, http://tinyurl.com/s2krg.

[4] M. Fähndrich, M. Barnett, and F. Logozzo. Embedded contract languages. In *Proceedings of the 2010 ACM Symposium on Applied Computing*, SAC '10. ACM, 2010.

[5] R. B. Findler and M. Felleisen. Contract soundness for object-oriented languages. In *Proceedings of the 16th ACM SIGPLAN conference on Object-oriented programming, systems, languages, and applications*, OOPSLA '01, pages 1–15, New York, NY, USA, 2001. ACM.

[6] G. Kiczales. Beyond the black box: Open implementation. *IEEE Softw.*, 13(1):8–11, Jan. 1996.

[7] G. T. Leavens, A. L. Baker, and C. Ruby. Preliminary design of JML: A behavioral interface specification language for Java. *ACM SIGSOFT Software Engineering Notes*, 2006.

[8] G. T. Leavens and P. Müller. Information hiding and visibility in interface specifications. In *International Conference on Software Engineering (ICSE)*, pages 385–395. IEEE, May 2007.

[9] B. Meyer. *Eiffel: the language*. Prentice-Hall, Inc., Upper Saddle River, NJ, USA, 1992.

[10] B. Meyer. *Object-oriented software construction (2nd ed.)*. Prentice-Hall, Inc., Upper Saddle River, NJ, USA, 1997.

[11] D. L. Parnas. On the criteria to be used in decomposing systems into modules. *Commun. ACM*, 15:1053–1058, December 1972.

[12] H. Rebêlo, R. Lima, G. T. Leavens, M. Cornélio, A. Mota, and C. Oliveira. Optimizing generated aspect-oriented assertion checking code for jml using program transformations: An empirical study. *Science of Computer Programming*, 78(8):1137 – 1156, 2013.

[13] H. Rebêlo, S. Soares, R. Lima, L. Ferreira, and M. Cornélio. Implementing Java modeling language contracts with AspectJ. In *Proceedings of the 2008 ACM symposium on Applied computing*, SAC '08, pages 228–233, New York, NY, USA, 2008. ACM.

Mining Source Code Repositories with Boa

Robert Dyer   Hoan Anh Nguyen   Hridesh Rajan   Tien N. Nguyen

Iowa State University

{rdyer,hoan,hridesh,tien}@iastate.edu

Abstract

Mining source code has become a common task for researchers and yielded significant benefits for the software engineering community. Mining source code however is a very difficult and time consuming task. The *Boa* language and infrastructure was designed to ease mining of project and revision metadata. Recently *Boa* was extended to support mining source code and currently contains source code for over 23k Java projects, including full revision histories.

In this demonstration we pose source code mining tasks and give solutions using *Boa*. We then execute these programs via our web-based infrastructure and show how to easily make the results available for future researchers.

Categories and Subject Descriptors   D.3.3 [*PROGRAMMING LANGUAGES*]: Language Constructs and Features

Keywords   MapReduce; software repository mining

1. Background

Source code repositories such as SourceForge, GitHub, and Google Code contain a vast wealth of information. Researchers are interested in mining this source code to gain insights into problems and test hypotheses. Mining this source code is a difficult task requiring, at a minimum: 1) substantial knowledge about how to access the source code data; 2) knowledge about how to mine the source code data, including parsing; and 3) analyzing a large quantity of data, typically requiring additional complexity and knowledge of how to parallelize the mining task.

Consider a relatively simple example that wishes to answer the question "how many null checks are there in Java programs?" A typical approach to solve this task would write a program that does (at a minimum) the following: downloads/scrapes project metadata from the repository, parses

this metadata, determines which projects are Java projects, accesses the source code repository to download the source code, parses the source code, mines the parsed code for null checks, and accumulates the results into a final answer. Such a solution would require using several libraries (e.g. to parse the metadata, access the repository, parse the code). This analysis would also take a significant amount of time as it runs sequentially and accesses thousands of remote repositories. Minimizing this time would require additional complexity and knowledge of distributed programming.

2. Boa

To solve these issues, we present the *Boa* language and supporting infrastructure [3, 4]. *Boa* provides several domain-specific types to ease software mining tasks. These types abstract the details of how to mine repositories and represent the data from the repository. *Boa* also abstracts away the details of its underlying MapReduce framework [2], allowing *Boa* programs to run efficiently in a distributed environment without requiring users to explicitly define parallelism in their code.

```
1   p: Project = input;
2   NullChecks: output sum of int;

3   nullVisitor := visitor {
4     before node: Expression ->
5       if ((node.kind == ExpressionKind.EQ ||
            node.kind == ExpressionKind.NEQ)
6           && (isliteral(node.expressions[0], "null") ||
               isliteral(node.expressions[1], "null")))
7         NullChecks << 1;
8   };

9   ifVisitor := visitor {
10    before node: Statement ->
11      if (node.kind == StatementKind.IF)
12        visit(node.expression, nullVisitor);
13  };

14  exists (i: int; p.programming_languages[i] == "Java")
15    visit(p, ifVisitor);
```

Figure 1. Program in *Boa* answering "How many null checks are there in Java programs?"

An example program is shown in Figure 1 which answers the previous question of how many null checks are there in Java programs. Note how simple this code is - it is only 15 lines of code! There is also no notion of mining the software

SPLASH '13,   October 26–31, 2013, Indianapolis, Indiana, USA.
Copyright is held by the owner/author(s).
ACM 978-1-4503-1995-9/13/10.
http://dx.doi.org/10.1145/2508075.2514570

repository or parallelizing the code, as these are completely abstracted from the user.

To run such programs, our infrastructure builds on the Sizzle compiler [5], which generates programs that run on the Hadoop MapReduce framework [1]. We add support for our domain-specific types as well as several language features not previously implemented, such as quantifiers. These statements allow easily filtering, e.g. Figure 1 on line 14 for selecting only Java projects.

The language also provides syntax based on the object-oriented visitor pattern to ease source code mining tasks. This allows easily querying for `if` statements (lines 9–13) that contain a comparison to `null` (lines 3–8).

Output is then sent to a table (line 7). The table provides an aggregation function (several are built into the language, such as *sum, mean, min/max*, etc.) to collect the results and reduce them to a final answer.

3. Benefits of Boa

Boa aims to lower the barrier to entry for researchers wishing to perform software mining tasks. It also aims to provide efficient support for performing these tasks on a very large scale. In summary, *Boa* provides the following key benefits:

- Simple programs,
- details of repository mining abstracted away,
- no libraries needed to perform repository mining,
- extremely efficient and scalable - automatically runs in a fraction of the time of standard approaches, and
- queries a very large set of data (project and revision metadata for all projects on SourceForge and all Java source code with full histories).

4. Demonstration Overview

This demonstration gives several simple mining tasks and uses the *Boa* language to solve those tasks. These *Boa* programs are then submitted to the web-based infrastructure [4] (see Figure 2) for execution and the query output downloaded. Additionally, we demonstrate how researchers can use *Boa* to answer their hypotheses and then publish their results to allow easy reproduction by other researchers.

5. Presenter Biographies

Robert Dyer and Hridesh Rajan have prior experience in developing new programming languages. Rajan developed the Ptolemy event-based language as well as the aspect-oriented language Eos. Dyer worked on the implementations and evaluation of the Ptolemy language. They have successfully given previous demonstrations at AOSD'10, FSE'10, ECOOP'11, SPLASH'11, and SPLASH'12.

Hoan Nguyen and Tien Nguyen are experts in software evolution and mining software repositories. Their work includes mining research in clone and API usage evolution,

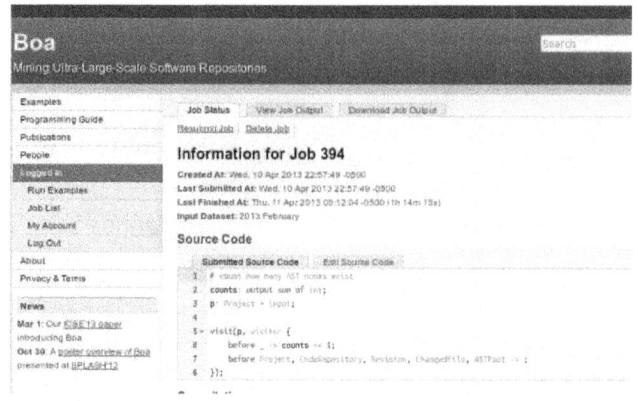

Figure 2. *Boa*'s web-based interface [4] for submitting and executing programs and retrieving their results

bug prediction and localization, and traceability link recovery. They are also experts in version control systems with work on novel infrastructures for semantics-based version control and configuration management.

All four authors worked on the design of the *Boa* language and infrastructure. Robert Dyer and Hoan Nguyen also developed the supporting infrastructure. Robert Dyer has previously given a demo of an early version of *Boa* at SPLASH'12 and a demo during the ICSE'13 presentation.

Acknowledgments

Dyer and Rajan are funded in part by NSF grants CCF-10-17334, CCF-11-17937, and CCF-08-46059. Tien Nguyen and Hoan Nguyen are funded in part by NSF grants CCF-10-18600 and CNS-12-23828.

References

[1] Apache Software Foundation. Hadoop: Open source implementation of MapReduce. http://hadoop.apache.org/.

[2] J. Dean and S. Ghemawat. MapReduce: simplified data processing on large clusters. In *Proceedings of the Symposium on Opearting Systems Design & Implementation - Volume 6*, OSDI'04, 2004.

[3] R. Dyer, H. A. Nguyen, H. Rajan, and T. N. Nguyen. Boa: A language and infrastructure for analyzing ultra-large-scale software repositories. In *Proceedings of the International Conference on Software Engineering*, ICSE'13, pages 422–431, 2013.

[4] H. Rajan, T. N. Nguyen, R. Dyer, and H. A. Nguyen. Boa website. http://boa.cs.iastate.edu/, 2012.

[5] A. Urso. Sizzle: A compiler and runtime for Sawzall, optimized for Hadoop. https://github.com/anthonyu/Sizzle.

NitroGen: Rapid Development of Mobile Applications

Aharon Abadi[1], Yael Dubinsky[1], Andrei Kirshin[1], Yossi Mesika[1], Idan Ben-Harrush[1], Uzy Hadad[2]

[1] IBM Research – Haifa
[2] The Academic College of Tel Aviv-Yaffo
{aharona,dubinsky,kirshin,mesika,idanb}@il.ibm.com, uzy.hadad@gmail.com

Abstract

Constructing a mobile application is expensive and time consuming. In this paper, we present NitroGen which is a platform independent tool that provides a consumable integrated set of capabilities to construct mobile solutions aiming at reducing development and maintenance costs. NitroGen is a visual, mostly codeless, cloud-based platform to construct mobile applications. It can easily connect to back-end services thus enable fast and facile development in enterprises. Evaluating NitroGen, we found among others, that participants learned it fast and found it simple and suitable for mobile applications development.

Categories and Subject Descriptors   D.2.2 [**Design Tools and Techniques**]: *User interfaces;* D.2.6 [**Programming Environments**]: *Graphical environments*

Keywords   Mobile development, rapid application construction.

1. Presenter

Aharon Abadi's main research focus is on mobile software engineering. He belongs to the research group developing Nitrogen. He performed the evaluation of Nitrogen. His current research focuses on analysis and optimizations of Nitrogen applications. He joined IBM in 2007. His work has been included in IBM products. Aharon was awarded the IBM Research Division award (RDA) and the IBM Outstanding Innovation Award (OIA). He is the main author of more than 15 patents. He is the main organizer and the PC chair of the DeMobile 2013 workshop at FSE and MobileDeLi 2013 workshop at SPLASH.

2. Introduction

Building a mobile application is complex and expensive. Based on a study performed by Propelics [1] on the average of deployed mobile applications, there is an estimate of 1 week of effort per screen for a simple baseline, i.e for a simple 8-screen application the baseline is 8 weeks of effort, application visualization and prototype (2 weeks), development, unit testing, (4 weeks), quality assurance, user acceptance testing (2 weeks).

Developing an application involves obsessing over vast amounts of technical details due to today's fragmented and proprietary mobile market [2]. The proprietary programming languages, tools, models, and device variability cause a significant increase in development and maintenance costs. The development process becomes complicated for enterprises as there are critical decision points

SPLASH '13,   October 26–31, 2013, Indianapolis, Indiana, USA.
ACM 978-1-4503-1995-9/13/10.
http://dx.doi.org/10.1145/2508075.2514571

along the way that need broad technical perspective, as they significantly impact the developed application.

Finding an easy way to build client-side service-oriented applications is still a challenge. The existing state-of-the-art requires a deep understanding of technologies and internals, and the mobile aspect is adding a new set of challenges such as security, connectivity, and state synchronization. There are known existing development environments and frameworks for mobile, among them Xcode, ADT, Titanium, PhoneGap. These environments are for developers and require deep knowledge of the targeted technology. Further, these are no cloud-based and code-less environment. Most important, these environments do not provide easy access to back-end services. We suggest that there is a need to define new models that focus on the goal of the application itself, provide interface for non-developers and enable facile connectivity with the enterprise services.

Based on previous work [3], we present the NitroGen tool (see NitroGen screencast at https://ibm.biz/BdxLnu). NitroGen is a visual, mostly codeless (drag and drop), cloud based environment to construct mobile applications. The tool uses enterprise managed interfaces and provides a consumable, high-level integrated approach to building mobile applications that are not specific to any single platform or device. NitroGen allows solutions to be quickly constructed from customizable templates, instead of developing them from scratch. This solution accelerates mobile application construction, lowers the costs, and simplifies the development process by eliminating the need for heroic efforts or deep technical skills.

3. NitroGen Architecture

IBM Mobile Foundation® delivers a range of application development, connectivity and management capabilities that support a wide variety of mobile devices and mobile app types. However, a great deal of mobile application development skills is still required to construct a mobile application. These skills include, but not limited to: programming languages (Objective C, Java, C#, HTML, JavaScript, CSS), development environments (XCode, Eclipse, ADT, Visual Studio), platform specific APIs, frameworks (Dojo, jQuery, Backbone.js), communication with back-end, mobile specific user experience. NitroGen aims to eliminate technical skills that are required to develop mobile applications and extends IBM Mobile Foundation capabilities. It aims at making it easier for enterprise employees to create line of business applications that use and create data within their enterprise.

NitroGen is composed of design time components and runtime components. With respect to design time components, IBM WebSphere Cast Iron® is a graphical tool that enables users to integrate cloud and on-premise applications. The results are exposed to mobile applications in a form of services. Our contribution is based on IBM Forms Experience Builder®. With the help of this tool users of all skill levels can rapidly build and deploy data intensive web applications. NitroGen extends the tool for designing mobile applications. Services defined in Cast Iron are dynamically discovered and bound to the application data fields. NitroGen allows the user to quickly preview the application in browser exactly as it will look like on a real device (various platforms are available). Then Nitro-Gen generates the application code and publishes it to the IBM Worklight® for validation and testing on actual mobile devices. As for runtime components, tested applications are hosted and distributed using IBM Worklight. Applications securely communicate with Cast Iron via Worklight server. Cast Iron in its turn brings together the data from various sources.

4. Application Abstraction

To deal with the complexity associated with mobile application development, we have defined an abstract application model that represents a mobile application. The user designs the application with the help of a simple and intuitive web based Integrated Development Environment (IDE) never seeing any of the underlying models. Our runtime then interprets the application model providing the best user experience on different mobile platforms and form factors. While the created application is a true Model, View, Controller (MVC) type of application, the user of the IDE is unaware of this. She simply works with the user interface (UI) and connects the backend data to the UI. The user is unaware of how the application connects to the backend data as the IDE uses meta-data about the various backend data sources to generate the needed Worklight artifacts for this.

An application is a set of forms (screens), each having a sequence of fields that show application data. Fields are of different kinds, such as text, telephone, date, and image. Fields can be either read-only to present data or editable to collect data. Table is a special kind of field for showing repetitive data. Buttons and table rows are used for navigation between forms. Under the covers these UI artifacts are bound to a data model that is extracted from the UI designed by the user.

Services transfer data between the application and back-end. For example, the *Pre-population* service is automatically invoked when a form opens to fetch the needed data; the *Save* service is used to save form's data and its existence causes automatically add a save button to the UI in runtime. The NitroGen IDE's server has an extendable method for discovering data sources available to the user when creating the application. This process provides information such as connectivity and data fields available enabling an easy way to connect to the needed backend data sources.

The integration with the backend services in NitroGen is relevant in two stages of the application lifetime: design and runtime. At design time the application developer is binding the services to the application. The Cast Iron as a backend system provides SOAP based Application Program Interface (API) to query for available services and description of each service in a Web Service Definition Language (WSDL) format. The result of this discovery is a set of structured service description documents that contains the relevant information needed for the service binding. NitroGen platform use these service descriptors at design time to create the mapping dialog where developer is able to select the service and map fields to and from the service.

The same service descriptor is being used for generating the required adapters for the invocation of the service at runtime. Each adapter is configured to communicate with a specific backend system and acts as the mediator between the mobile application and the backend service. The main advantage of using an adapter is to take out the complexity of the integration from the client side to the server side. The use of an adapter is also crucial for overcoming security issues where the mobile application is not allowed to directly communicate with a backend service.

5. Evaluating NitroGen

We studied the functionality and usability of NitroGen with CS-major students in their third year of graduation who take the 'Developing Web Applications' course in The Academic College of Tel Aviv-Yaffo. In the first evaluation stage, participants were asked to fill in a pre-experiment questionnaire (10 minutes); In the second stage, they learned NitroGen while using the tool according to written tasks (90 minutes); and in the third stage they reflected on and shared their experience (10 minutes). In what follows, we present some of the findings.

Learning about their skills level using the pre-experiment questionnaire (36 participants' answers), we found that participants are knowledgeable with tools and techniques for developing web applications still do not have experience with development of mobile applications. In the second half of this questionnaire, we introduced a scenario to be developed as a mobile application and we asked participants to estimate the amount of time they need for the development of such a mobile application. The answers varied from 2 days to 3 months. We further asked about the most problematic issue in this application development. 11 participants indicated that developing the user interface is the most problematic issue, and 10 participants mentioned different features of the application. Only few (3 participants) refer to the database, to the suitability to different platforms (2 participants), or suggested that there are no problems (3 participants).

In the second stage, we presented the basic concepts of NitroGen to the participants, divided the class to groups (pairs and triplets), and provided a movie on developing using NitroGen and 9-tasks exercise that led step by step the development of a mobile application using NitroGen. We checked NitroGen server for the completion status of the different groups. 5 groups completed the exercise. 9 groups completed till a certain point among them 4 groups left at the early tasks and 5 groups stopped in the advanced part. It took 46 minutes for the first group to complete the exercise. After 75 minutes 5 groups completed the exercise.

In the last stage we asked participants to reflect on their development activity filling in a post-experiment questionnaire using close and open questions. Only 15 participants filled in the questionnaire, all of them are part of groups that completed the task. We found that participants like NitroGen features and found it not difficult to work with. In the last part of the questionnaire, we iterate the question on the estimation to develop the scenario. Answers ranged between 1 hour and 1 week. This is a significant change in how participants perceived of mobile application development. Since the scenario is relatively comprehensive and a small-scale application was developed in less than one hour, participants changed the way they estimated such a development.

We noticed that NitroGen is intuitive and easy to learn, and that no significant barrier was reported.

References

[1] Propelics, How to Size a Mobile App Development Effort, 2013 [online] http://www.slideshare.net/propelics/how-to-size-a-mobile-app-development-effort.

[2] Gavalas,D.,Economou,D.,Development platforms for mobile applications: status and trends. IEEE Software 28(1),2011.

[3] Shachor, G., Rubin, Y., Guy, N., Dubinsky, Y., Barnea, M., Kallner, S., Landau, A. What You See And Do Is What You Get: A Human-Centric Design Approach to Human-Centric Process, Business Process Design (BPD) in BPM, 2010.

ZipPy on Truffle: A Fast and Simple Implementation of Python

Christian Wimmer

Oracle Labs

christian.wimmer@oracle.com

Stefan Brunthaler

University of California, Irvine

s.brunthaler@uci.edu

Abstract

Building high-performance virtual machines is a complex and expensive undertaking; many popular languages still have low-performance implementations. We present a new approach to virtual machine (VM) construction that amortizes much of the effort in initial construction by allowing new languages to be implemented with modest additional effort. The approach (named *Truffle*) relies on tree-rewriting abstract syntax tree (AST) interpretation, together with an optimizing compiler (named *Graal*) that exploits the structure of the interpreter. The compiler uses speculative assumptions and deoptimization in order to produce efficient machine code. We illustrate the concepts of Truffle by the means of our open-source implementation of Python (named *ZipPy*). To show that Truffle supports a variety of programming language paradigms, we also present prototype implementations of other languages.

Categories and Subject Descriptors D.3.4 [*Programming Languages*]: Processors—Run-time environments

Keywords Java; JavaScript; R; Truffle; Graal; dynamic languages; virtual machine; language implementation

1. Introduction

An abstract syntax tree (AST) interpreter is a simple and natural way to implement a programming language. However, it is usually also considered the slowest approach because of the high overhead of virtual method dispatch. Language implementers therefore define bytecodes to speed up interpretation, followed by a just-in-time compiler that is needed to reach excellent peak performance. In addition, a high-performance garbage collector is necessary for automatic memory management, together with a runtime system to form a complete virtual machine (VM). The algorithms for all these compo-

nents are well known. However, VM code is rarely reused when implementing a VM for a new language. This makes the process of developing new high-performance languages expensive and tedious.

Truffle is a novel approach to implement AST interpreters in which the syntax tree is modified during interpretation to incorporate type feedback. In a previous demonstration, we introduced the basic concepts of Truffle [5]. Since then, we have improved the performance and stability of implementation, and published our approach in detail [6]. Other research groups and we have advanced prototype of several languages: Python [2], JavaScript, Ruby, R [1], and J.

Truffle and Graal are available as open source in an OpenJDK project [4]. ZipPy is available as open source from [2].

2. System Structure

We propose a layered approach where a *guest VM* is running on top of a *host VM*. The *guest language* is the language that we want to define and write our application in, while the *host language* is the language that we write our guest VM in, i.e., the language that the host VM executes.

This layered approach has several advantages that simplify the implementation of a guest language. The host VM provides many services such as automatic memory management, exception handling, threads, synchronization primitives, and a well-defined memory model that can be leveraged by the guest VM. It is not necessary to implement a complete VM, allowing the language designer to focus on the execution semantics of the language. However, the benefits of the layering must not sacrifice peak performance of the guest language. The execution speed of the guest language application is usually the most important metric that end users care about. Dynamic compilation of guest language code to machine code is therefore essential. The key steps of our language implementation and optimization strategy are as follows:

- The guest language implementation is written as an AST interpreter. We believe that implementing an AST interpreter for a language is a simple and intuitive way of describing the semantics of a language. Whether through formal operational semantics or informal specifications, a language's behavior is typically defined by specifying the behavior of its constituent expressions independently.

SPLASH '13, October 26–31, 2013, Indianapolis, Indiana, USA.
Copyright is held by the owner/author(s).
ACM 978-1-4503-1995-9/13/10.
http://dx.doi.org/10.1145/2508075.2514572

- Tree rewriting in the interpreter captures dynamic type information and profiling information. The AST is rewritten during interpretation, thus incorporating profiling feedback. Counters measure execution frequencies and AST stability.

- When the compiler is invoked to compile a part of the application, it uses the extant ASTs (with type and frequency information) to perform an automatic partial evaluation of the AST interpreter. For this, the AST is assumed to be in a *stable* state where subsequent rewrites are unlikely, although not prohibited. Partial evaluation, i.e., compilation with aggressive method inlining, eliminates the interpreter dispatch code and produces optimized machine code for the guest language.

- The parts of the interpreter code responsible for tree rewriting are omitted from compilation. Branches that perform rewriting are not compiled, but instead cause *deoptimization* [3]. This results in machine code that is aggressively specialized for the types encountered during interpretation.

- In case that a specialization subsequently fails, *deoptimization* discards the optimized machine code and reverts execution back to the AST interpreter. The AST interpreter then performs the necessary tree rewrites to incorporate revised type information into the tree, which can be compiled again using partial evaluation.

Note that at no point was the dynamic compiler modified to understand the semantics of the guest language; these exist solely in the high-level code of the interpreter and runtime. A guest language developer who operates within our interpretation framework gets a high-performance language implementation, with no need to understand dynamic compilation.

3. Demonstration Outline

- Motivation for a modular language framework and re-use of VM components.

- System architecture: Truffle runs on the Graal VM, a modified version of the Java HotSpot VM with the Graal JIT compiler.

- Overview of Truffle: core classes that form the AST and the framework for AST rewriting. This includes the handling of frames for local variables.

- Overview of the ZipPy, the implementation of Python using the Truffle framework.

- AST interpreter best practices: AST interpreter design patterns that proved to be useful in our implementations of Python, JavaScript, and Ruby.

4. Presenters

Christian Wimmer is a researcher at Oracle Labs, working on the Maxine VM, the Graal compiler, the Truffle dynamic language infrastructure, as well as on other projects that involve dynamic compilation and optimizations. His research interests span from compilers, virtual machines, and secure systems to component-based software architectures. He received a Dr. techn. degree in computer science (advisor: Prof. Hanspeter Mössenböck) from the Johannes Kepler University Linz, Austria.

Stefan Brunthaler is a postdoctoral researcher at the University of California, Irvine, working with Prof. Michael Franz. His primary research interest is programming languages design and implementation. He is interested in compilation, interpretation, analysis, optimization and verification. He received a Dr. techn. degree in computer science from the Vienna University of Technology (advisor: Prof. Jens Knoop).

Acknowledgments

Truffle and Graal would not be possible without the efforts of our academic collaborators, especially the Institute for System Software at the Johannes Kepler University Linz. Oracle and Java are registered trademarks of Oracle and/or its affiliates. Other names may be trademarks of their respective owners.

This material is based upon work partially supported by the Defense Advanced Research Projects Agency (DARPA) under contracts D11PC20024 and N660001-1-2-4014, and by the National Science Foundation (NSF) under grant No. CCF-1117162. Any opinions, findings, and conclusions or recommendations expressed in this material are those of the authors and do not necessarily reflect the views of the Defense Advanced Research Projects Agency (DARPA), its Contracting Agents, the National Science Foundation, or any other agency of the U.S. Government.

References

[1] FastR, 2013. URL https://github.com/allr/fastr/.

[2] ZipPy, 2013. URL https://bitbucket.org/ssllab/zippy/.

[3] U. Hölzle, C. Chambers, and D. Ungar. Debugging optimized code with dynamic deoptimization. In *Proceedings of the ACM SIGPLAN Conference on Programming Language Design and Implementation*, pages 32–43. ACM Press, 1992. doi: 10.1145/143095.143114.

[4] OpenJDK. Graal project, 2013. URL http://openjdk.java.net/projects/graal.

[5] C. Wimmer and T. Würthinger. Truffle: A self-optimizing runtime system. In *Demonstration at Systems, Programming, Languages and Applications: Software for Humanity*, pages 13–14. ACM Press, 2012. doi: 10.1145/2384716.2384723.

[6] T. Würthinger, C. Wimmer, A. Wöß, L. Stadler, G. Duboscq, C. Humer, G. Richards, D. Simon, and M. Wolczko. One VM to rule them all. In *Proceedings of Onward!* ACM Press, 2013. doi: 10.1145/2509578.2509581.

Panini: a Capsule-oriented Programming Language for Implicitly Concurrent Program Design

Eric Lin   Hridesh Rajan

Iowa State University
Ames IA, USA
{eylin, hridesh}@iastate.edu

Abstract

This demonstration will present Panini, a new programming language designed with an objective to help programmers with concurrent programming. Current abstractions for concurrency fall into two categories: explicit abstractions for concurrency such as threads, and implicit abstractions for concurrency such as actors. Explicit concurrency abstractions are hard to use, reason about, and error prone. Implicit abstractions like actors help solve these problems, but they require programmers to adapt to the asynchronous style of programming. Many programmers find this adaptation hard. We will demonstrate the notion of *capsules* in Panini. A capsule is an implicit abstraction for concurrency that has many properties of actors, but provides a logically synchronous programming model to programmers. Main technical challenge in realizing capsules was to maximize concurrency while minimizing overhead and abstracting away all the details of concurrency from the Panini programmer. We will also demonstrate scalability benefits of Panini programs without writing a single line of explicitly parallel code, and compile-time checking of concurrency-related properties such as confinement violation, and sequential consistency.

Categories and Subject Descriptors   D.3.3 [*Language Constructs and Features*]: Concurrent programming structures

Keywords   capsules, implicit concurrency, modularity, synergy

1. Problem: Concurrent Programming is Hard

Concurrent programming is hard. Most programmers find it difficult to write concurrent programs. Moreover, a large number of programmers are used to thinking sequentially about their programs. This makes the task of reasoning about a concurrent program even more difficult because it requires reasoning about interleaving of concurrent tasks. On top of that, to ensure concurrency safety, the concurrency construct applied in the program often obscures the logic flow of the program, resulting in difficulty understanding both the logic of the program and the concurrency constructs.

As an example, Figure 1 is a simple concurrent program in which a number of "worker" tasks execute a Monte Carlo approx-

SPLASH '13,   October 26–31, 2013, Indianapolis, Indiana, USA.
Copyright is held by the owner/author(s).
ACM 978-1-4503-1995-9/13/10.
http://dx.doi.org/10.1145/2508075.2514573

imation of π concurrently; a "master" task combines the results as the workers finish. Figure 1, left shows an explicitly concurrent implementation of this program in Java. The explicitly concurrent Java program has the application's concerns tangled with two concurrency concerns: creation and starting of new threads, and synchronization between these threads. This makes it harder to write, test, reason about, and evolve this concurrent program.

2. Solution: Eliminate Concurrent Programming

Capsule-oriented programming is a new style designed to address these challenges of concurrent programming [1]. The first objective of capsule-oriented programming is to allow programmers to design and implement more modular programs, and in doing so expose implicit concurrency in program design. To achieve this goal, we have developed a new abstraction called *capsule*. A capsule is like a process, it encapsulates objects stored in its local region of memory and provides public operations that can be called by other capsules. A significant difference between capsules and similar abstraction *actor* is that inter-capsule calls are logically synchronous, and the topology of capsule-oriented can be statically determined. These differences decrease the impedance mismatch between capsule-oriented programming model and the mainstream imperative programming model, and makes it easier to design polynomial-time algorithms for analyzing capsule-oriented programs that can be integrated into industry-strength compilers.

To illustrate, consider a capsule-oriented implementation of our motivating example in Figure 1, right. This program has two capsules that are combined to form a static topology in the design block on lines 13-16. As in the Java program, a "Master" task combines the results as the workers finish, but all of the concurrency details are hidden from the programmer. Each call to `compute` on line 21 executes asynchronously in an instance of a `Worker` capsule; the returned `Number` object is transparently replaced by a future for the eventual result. The futures provide an implicit barrier; that is, in the call to `value` on line 22, the execution of the `run` procedure in master capsule blocks until the corresponding *Worker* has finished computing its result.

The explicitly concurrent Java program has the applications's concerns tangled with the concurrency concerns, whereas the Panini program abstracts away the details of concurrency. As Figure 1 shows, the performance of the Panini program is comparable to that of the thread-based program. A more significant potential benefit is that the Panini compiler can be employed to guard against race conditions when parallelism is introduced into an application.

The Panini language and associated tools are made available as an open source project under Mozilla Public License 1.1. The source code and examples, as well as pre-built binaries, are available for download from http://www.paninij.org/.

Java program with threads and synchronization to compute π

```
1  class Worker implements Runnable {
2    long num;
3    private final CountDownLatch doneSignal;
4    Worker(long num, CountDownLatch doneSignal) {
5      this.num = num;
6      this.doneSignal = doneSignal;
7    }
8    Number _circleCount = null; //Emulates return value of worker
9    Number getCircleCount() { return _circleCount; }
10   public void run() {
11     _circleCount = new Number(0);
12     for (long j = 0; j < num; j++) {
13       double x = Math.random();
14       double y = Math.random();
15       if ((x * x + y * y) < 1) _circleCount.incr ();
16     }
17     doneSignal.countDown();
18   }
19 }
20 class Master {
21   void assign(long totalCount, int numWorkers) {
22     CountDownLatch l = new CountDownLatch(numWorkers);
23     Worker[] workers = new Worker[numWorkers];
24     for (int i = 0; i < numWorkers; ++i) {
25       workers[i] = new Worker(totalCount/numWorkers, l);
26       new Thread(workers[i]).start ();
27     }
28     try {
29       l.await ();
30     } catch (InterruptedException e) { /* Error recovery */ }
31     Number[] results = new Number[numWorkers];
32     for (int i=0; i< numWorkers; i++)
33       results [i] = workers[i]. getCircleCount();
34     long total = 0;
35     for (Number result: results)  total += result.value();
36     double pi = 4.0 * total / totalCount;
37   }
38 }
39 public class Pi {
40   public static void main(String[] args) {
41     Master master = new Master();
42     master.assign(50000000,10);
43   }
44 }
```

Panini program to compute π

```
1  capsule Worker {              // Capsule declaration
2      Number compute(int num) {      // Capsule procedure
3          Number _circleCount = new Number(0);
4          for (int j = 0; j < num; j++) {
5              double x = Math.random();
6              double y = Math.random();
7              if ((x * x + y * y) < 1) _circleCount.incr ();
8          }
9          return _circleCount;
10     }
11 }
12 capsule Master {
13     design {
14         Worker workers[5000000]; //Capsule arraydeclaration
16     }
17     void run(){
18         Number[] results = new Number[workers.length];
19         for (int i = 0; i < workers.length; i++)
20             results [i] = workers[i]. compute(50000000);
21         // Inter-capsule procedure
                  calls  long total = 0;
22         for (Number result: results)  total += result.value();
23
24         double pi = 4.0 * total / 50000000;
25     }
   }
```

Performance results

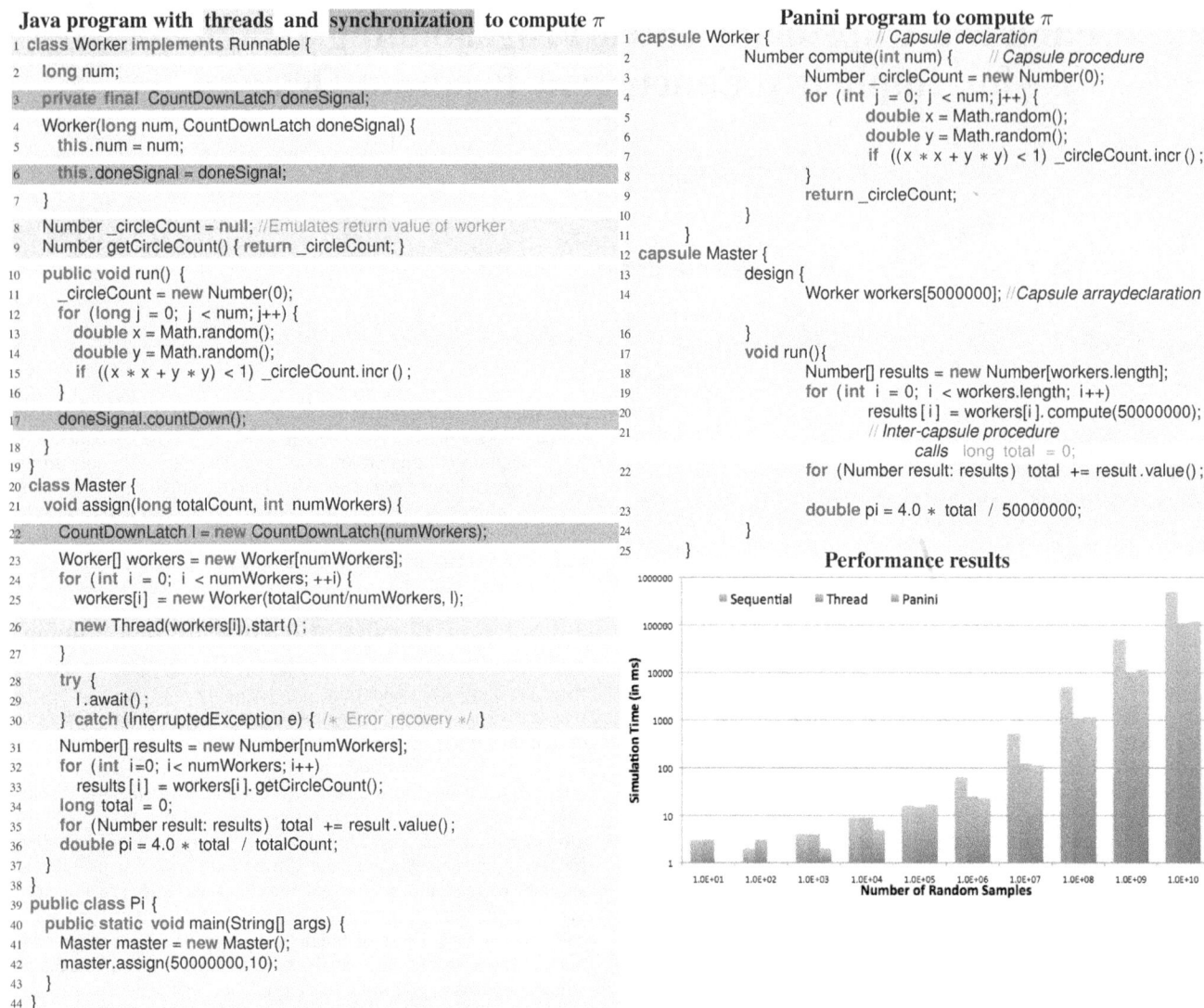

Figure 1. Panini programs are shorter, get speedup, and don't have 2 type of bugs: sequential inconsistencies and data races due to sharing.

3. Demonstration Description

We will present the key features of the Panini Language through several examples. In particular, we will show a comparison of an example with a traditional approach of using explicitly concurrent language features, and the same example in Panini for contrast. We will demonstrate installation of the Panini compiler, compilation, and profiling process for Panini programs. The Panini compiler is built on top of the standard OpenJDK Java compiler (javac) and is fully backwards compatible with pure Java programs.

Acknowledgements This work has been supported in part by the US National Science Foundation (NSF) under grants CCF-11-17937, CCF-10-17334, and CCF-08-46059.

References

[1] H. Rajan, S. M. Kautz, E. Lin, S. Kabala, G. Upadhyaya, Y. Long, R. Fernando, and L. Szakács. Capsule-oriented programming. Technical Report 13-01, Iowa State U., Computer Sc., 2013.

Biographies This demonstration will be carried out by Eric Lin and Hridesh Rajan. *Eric Lin* is a graduate student in the department of computer science at Iowa State University. He earned his undergraduate degree in Computer Science from Iowa State University in 2012. Eric has worked on the frontend and the backend of the OpenJDK-based Panini compiler, focusing on code transformation strategies and type-checking. *Hridesh Rajan* has extensive experience in developing new languages. He developed the Panini language. Prior to that, he developed the Boa language, a language for data-mining large software repositories. He has also developed the Ptolemy language, an event-based language for advanced separation of concerns and the aspect-oriented language Eos. Rajan has successfully given multiple tutorials and demonstrations on other topics at AOSD'10, FSE'10, ECOOP'11, AOSD'11, and ASE'11.

Target Audience The target audience for this demonstration is intermediate level developers and researchers. Participants will need a working knowledge of Java and object-oriented development. The demonstration will provide any additional background material.

Finding Architectural Flaws in Android Apps Is Easy

Radu Vanciu   Marwan Abi-Antoun

Department of Computer Science, Wayne State University
{radu, mabiantoun}@wayne.edu

Abstract

Mobile devices store confidential information. As a result, security vulnerabilities such as information disclosure in mobile apps can have serious consequences. To build secure apps, developers are expected to follow security policies that are described only informally. Some policies target architectural flaws, rather than coding defects, and are not easily checked or enforced with existing tools.

Scoria is a prototype tool that allows architects to write security policies as machine-checkable constraints that are executed against a program abstraction that is a hierarchy of abstract objects with dataflow communication edges. Using Scoria, architects reason not only about the presence or absence of communication, but also about object provenance, hierarchy and reachability. We show how Scoria can find information disclosure in an open-source Android app.

Categories and Subject Descriptors   D.2.11 [*Software Engineering*]: Software Architectures—Data abstraction

Keywords   architectural risk analysis; security architecture

1. Introduction

We propose a semi-automatic approach, Scoria, to find architectural flaws such as information disclosure. One requirement of security analyses that find architectural flaws is to use a runtime architecture [2]. Previous work approximates a runtime architecture by a sound, hierarchical, Ownership Object Graph (OOG) that a static analysis extracts from code with annotations [3]. The OOG has nodes that represent abstract objects and groups of abstract objects, and edges that represent relations between objects. In an object hierarchy, an object does not have child objects directly. Instead, an object contains groups of objects (domains). A points-to edge is a relation between two abstract objects due to a

field reference. A dataflow communication between two abstract objects is due to a method invocation, field read or field write [3]. Similarly, a creation edge is due to an object allocation expression. Both a dataflow edge and a creation edge refer to an abstract object.

Scoria uses a security graph that is an OOG enriched with security properties and queries (SecGraph). Architects understand a runtime structure as needed and assign values for the security properties of abstract objects and edges using queries. A query returns a set of abstract objects or edges. A constraint is a predicate on the result of the query, such as the set is empty. The architects use Scoria to convert informally-specified security policies into machine-checkable constraints.

2. Description

The main contribution of Scoria is queries that capture the thought process of how an architect can reason about the communication of objects in a runtime architecture. For example, to find information disclosure, the architect assigns security properties to objects and finds a confidential object that flows into an untrusted destination. One consequence of representing dataflow as an object is that an architect can use object identity to reason about the information content available from an object. The dataflow object may not be confidential, but a confidential object could be reachable from it or be contained within its substructure.

Scoria automatically considers object ancestors and descendants, transitive communication, and reachability. Such information allows the architect to reason about the object provenance. That is, an architect can reason about "what" object a dataflow communication refers to, and "how" other objects are using the same dataflow object. Scoria also enables architects to query indirect communication through object hierarchy and reachability. Architects may miss such communication if they were to reason based on a diagram alone, because it requires computing transitive information.

The demonstration starts with examples of queries that architects can use to assign values to properties of objects in the SecGraph. Next, architects use constraints based on object provenance and indirect communication queries to find architectural flaws as suspicious dataflow communication edges. A SecGraph also provides traceability information

SPLASH '13,   October 26–31, 2013, Indianapolis, Indiana, USA.
Copyright is held by the owner/author(s).
ACM 978-1-4503-1995-9/13/10.
http://dx.doi.org/10.1145/2508075.2514574

```
void insecureIntents() {
  SecGraph g = loadGraph();
  Property[] snkP = {TrustLevelType.Untrusted};
  Property[] flwP = {IsConfidential.True};
  g.assignProperty(snkP, new InstanceOf("Intent"));
  g.assignProperty(flwP,
    new IsChildOf("AccountInformation","String"));
  Set<SecEdge> se = g.getFlowSink(snkP,flwP);
  Assert.assertTrue(se.size()>0);
}
```

Figure 1. A constraint implemented as a JUnit test to find information disclosure in objects of type `Intent`

such that architects can trace from a suspicious edge directly to the code and investigate the vulnerability. Scoria works as follows: architects add annotations to code; the static analysis extracts SecGraph; architects assign security properties to abstract objects and edges using SecGraph queries; architects write and execute constraints and finds suspicious edges; architects trace to code from suspicious edges and inspect potential vulnerabilities.

Example of a found architectural flaw. We illustrate using Scoria to find information disclosure in UPMA, an open-source Android application for managing passwords. During the demonstration, we will assume that the OOG has been already extracted and focus on the process of assigning security properties and writing constraints.

Android security policy dictates that confidential information should not be disclosed to objects of type `Intent`, since other applications can access it. We implement this policy as the *insecureIntents* constraint (Fig. 1) that is then executed against the UPMA SecGraph. First, the constraint assigns the Untrusted property to all objects of type `Intent`. Objects of the same type can have different property values. Scoria allows the architect to assign the IsConfidential property to those objects of type `String` that have a parent of type `AccountInformation`. Next, the constraint finds an information disclosure in the `ViewAccountDetails` class through a creation edge (Fig. 3). The password is exposed indirectly being a child of the `AccountInformation` object that is referred by the `ViewAccountDetails` object. In addition, Scoria finds a second vulnerability in the `AccountsList` class where the unencrypted password is disclosed to the Android clipboard through a dataflow edge. Since the clipboard is accessible to any other app, passwords stored by UPMA are vulnerable to eavesdropping.

Implementation. Scoria is based on a typechecker, an extraction analysis, and a constraint checker. The typechecker and the extraction of OOG with points-to edges were previously demonstrated [1]. In this demonstration, we focus on extracting dataflow edges [3] and on implementing security policies as constraints. Although the demonstration will focus on Android apps, tools are suitable for any Java system.

The extraction analysis is implemented using the Crystal framework as an Eclipse plugin. Constraints are implemented as SecGraph queries, such that architects can write

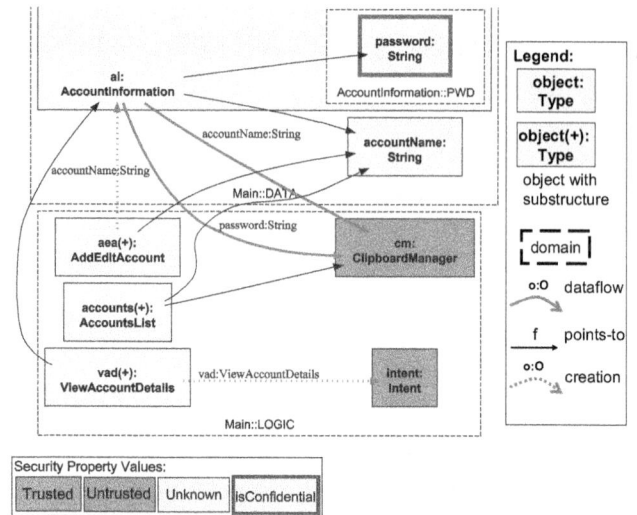

Figure 2. Indirect communication of `password:String` to `intent:Intent`, and a direct communication of `password:String` to `cm:ClipboardManager`

```
class ViewAccountDetails{
  public static AccountInformation account;
  void onOptionsItemSelected(...) {
    // password exposed into Intent
    intent = new Intent(this,...);
  }
}
class AccountInformation {
  private String accountName;
  private String password;
}
class AccountsList{
  void onContextItemSelected(...){
    // password exposed into clipboard
    p = getPassword(getAccount(targetView));
    setClipboardText(p);
  }
  String getPassword(AccountInformation account) {
    return new String(account.getPassword());
  }
}
```

Figure 3. UPMA code that introduce vulnerabilities

and execute constraints as JUnit tests. From the query results, Scoria can trace to AST nodes, such that the architect locates the vulnerability in the code. To debug queries, Scoria also includes a visualization of the SecGraph (Fig. 2).

References

[1] M. Abi-Antoun and J. Aldrich. Tool Support for the Static Extraction of Sound Hierarchical Representations of Runtime Object Graphs (Tool Demo). In *OOPSLA*, 2008.

[2] F. Swiderski and W. Snyder. *Threat Modeling*. Microsoft Press, 2004.

[3] R. Vanciu and M. Abi-Antoun. Ownership Object Graphs with Dataflow Edges. In *WCRE*, pages 267–276, 2012.

Finding the Missing Eclipse Perspective: the Runtime Perspective

Andrew Giang   Marwan Abi-Antoun

Department of Computer Science, Wayne State University, Detroit, Michigan, USA
{andrewgiang, mabiantoun}@wayne.edu

Abstract

When evolving object-oriented code, developers need to understand both the code structure and the runtime structure. However, Integrated Development Environments such as Eclipse still predominantly emphasize the code structure. We propose to add to Eclipse a *Runtime Perspective* to complement the existing perspectives such as the Java *code* perspective and the *debugging* perspective, and to present to developers a hierarchical abstract runtime structure in terms of abstract objects and relations between them.

Categories and Subject Descriptors D.2.3 [*Software Engineering*]: Coding Tools and Techniques—Object-oriented programming

Keywords Object structure; Object diagrams

1. Introduction

Today's Integrated Development Environments (IDEs) still do *not* present to *object*-oriented developers a view of the *objects* in the system! Instead, IDEs seem to emphasize a *class*- oriented view of the system at design-time. This is particularly challenging for beginner programmers while they learn object-oriented design patterns and frameworks.

For example, the popular Eclipse IDE presents to developers a *hierarchy of classes* where classes are organized by packages, as in the Package Explorer. Eclipse also shows a *type hierarchy* that shows the inheritance hierarchy of the selected classes and interfaces. If developers want to understand the objects in a system, they have to either mentally visualize them, or run the system and use the *debug* perspective in Eclipse and wade through a heap of *concrete objects* in the debugger, examining *specific instances*. There are often too many specific instances. For some coding tasks that require knowing how many instances of a class are created,

a debugger is crucial. But for many program comprehension tasks, *specific* instances may not matter.

In previous work, Abi-Antoun and Aldrich developed a static analysis to extract from a program with annotations an approximation of the runtime structure as a global, hierarchical, Ownership Object Graph (OOG) [1]. A controlled experiment found that developers who have access to a hierarchy of *abstract objects* make code modifications faster and browse less irrelevant code [2]. The previous tool, however, was not well integrated with the Eclipse IDE and lacked several features. In this work, we add to Eclipse a novel, *Runtime Perspective*, to complement the current perspectives.

2. High-Level Description

The Runtime Perspective (Fig. 1) is integrated with various features in Eclipse such as the Javadoc viewer and the Package Explorer and has several views that are based on information from the abstract runtime structure. The abstract runtime structure is extracted by another tool and stored in a file. The Runtime Perspective loads the file and uses the information to populate the various views. In the abstract object hierarchy, the objects that are architecturally relevant are higher in the hierarchy than low-level implementation details such as data structures.

The **Abstract Object Tree (1)** displays a hierarchy of abstract objects. From a selected abstract object, the **Abstract Stack (2)** shows the nested abstract interpretation contexts that lead to the creation of the selected abstract object. Ultimately, each abstract object is due to an object creation expression in the code. Several creation expressions, scattered across several Java classes, may be represented by the same abstract object. Moreover, one object creation expression may create several abstract objects that are in different contexts. Furthermore, the Abstract Stack View has a traceability feature: when the developer double-clicks on an entry, the tool selects the corresponding lines of code. This is similar to the stack in the debug perspective.

The **Summary View (3)** shows the list of the Most Important Classes (MICs), the Most Important Related Classes to a class (MIRCs), and the Most Important Methods of a class (MIMs). The Summary View suggests the MICs for the open project. When a developer picks a class C from the MICs, the Summary View automatically opens the class in

SPLASH '13, October 26–31, 2013, Indianapolis, Indiana, USA.
Copyright is held by the owner/author(s).
ACM 978-1-4503-1995-9/13/10.
http://dx.doi.org/10.1145/2508075.2514575

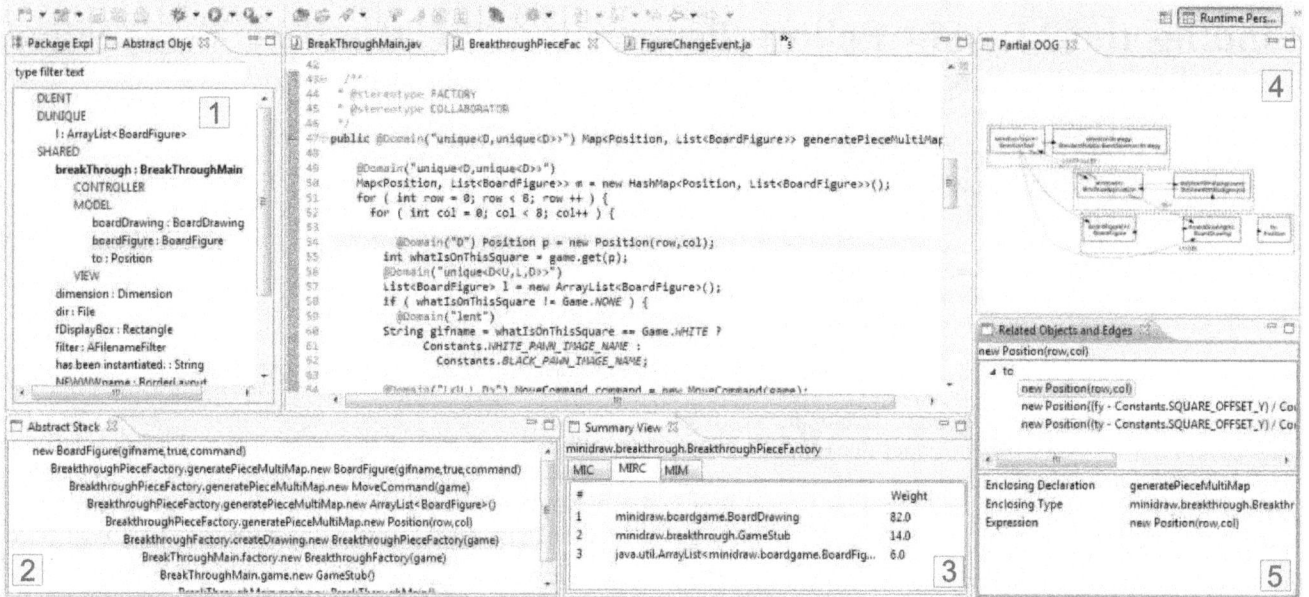

Figure 1. The Eclipse *Runtime Perspective*.

the Eclipse Java editor. As the developer navigates to a class C in the project or using the Package Explorer, the tool automatically displays the list of MIRCs or MIMs related to C. While browsing classes and methods in the IDE, when a developer selects a field declaration that is of an interface, the Runtime Perspective automatically shows the Most Important Classes behind an Interface (MCBIs) as a Quick Fix in Eclipse. The **Graph View (4)** displays a partial OOG that shows only the nodes and edges OOG that are related to the class that the developer is working on.

If the developer selects some code elements in the Java editor, the **Related Objects/Edges View (5)** displays a list of related objects and edges that the selected code element maps to in the abstract runtime structure. The developer can expand each related object or edge and go to the corresponding lines of code in the Eclipse project.

3. Description of the Summary View

The demonstration will illustrate how the Summary View works using a small system, MiniDraw, a pedagogical object-oriented framework. In the demonstration, the audience will see how a developer completes a code modification task. The task given to the developer is to validate the movement of a piece on a boardgame [2].

The Summary View lifts the information about architectural relevance back to the types. For example, the Summary View considers the MICs to be the classes of the objects at the top level of the hierarchy. All the top-level objects are included in the MICs, then ranked based on the number of filtered edges. To f nd the MIRCs for a given class C, the strategy traverses the set of filtered edges and collects the union of edges that have a source or a destination that is of type C or a subtype of C. To find the MIMs for a given class C, the Summary View ranks the methods by the number of

edges they create. To f nd the MCBIs, for a given interface, the Summary View finds all the classes that implement the interface, then ranks these classes using a similar strategy.

One Summary View strategy uses the number of incoming, outgoing, and self edges from an abstract object to rank the corresponding classes and methods. Using the MICs tab in the Summary View, the developer determines which of the most important classes may implement movement or drawing items to the board. Since the Summary View shows a ranked subset of classes, it is easier for a developer to decide which classes are important and where to begin. From the list of MICs, there are two classes that stand out for our task: BoardDrawing and BoardFigure. From here, the developer can start to look at the MIRCs and the MIMs of these classes. The search ends when the developer f nds the method move in GameStub, the first method listed in the MIMs of GameStub.

When encountering a field declaration that is of an interface type, the developer typically uses the Eclipse Type Hierarchy to find all possible classes behind the interface. This list can be potentially long, and does not rank these classes in any way except using the depth of the inheritance tree. Since they are based on the abstract runtime structure, the MCBIs in the Runtime Perspective are often a smaller, more precise set of possible concrete types.

References

[1] M. Abi-Antoun and J. Aldrich. Static Extraction and Conformance Analysis of Hierarchical Runtime Architectural Structure using Annotations. In *OOPSLA*, pages 321–340, 2009.

[2] N. Ammar and M. Abi-Antoun. Empirical Evaluation of Diagrams of the Run-time Structure for Coding Tasks. In *WCRE*, pages 367–376, 2012.

Objektgraph: Why Code When MVC Applications Can Be Generated With UML-based Diagrams?

Duane Buck

Otterbein University
Westerville, Ohio
dbuck@otterbein.edu

Ira Diethelm

Carl von Ossietzky University
Oldenburg, Germany
ira.diethelm@uni-oldenburg.de

Stephen Sheneman

Otterbein University
Westerville, Ohio
stephen.sheneman@otterbein.edu

Abstract

Objektgraph is an integrated development environment (IDE) for generating applications. Unlike other Unified Modeling Language (UML) based tools, it comprehensively supports implementation. Instantiable object diagrams eliminate the need for start-up code, both for domain model structures and the user interface. Objektgraph enables a complete model-view-controller (MVC) based application with model persistence to be developed entirely with diagrams: no conventional coding is required, although it is supported. The motivation for developing Objektgraph was to support pedagogy, however it is robust and may prove useful in other contexts. Its goal is to simultaneously lower the frustration level and raise the level of abstraction to permit novices to experience what it might be like to have a career in software development.

Categories and Subject Descriptors D.2.2 [Software Engineering]: Computer-aided software engineering.

Keywords Unified Modelling Language; Generative Programming.

1. Introduction

Important features of Objektgraph will be explored in a pedagogical usage scenario. This will include the use of object diagrams to (1) create the class diagram as a side-effect, (2) document use-cases for both development and testing, and (3) instantiate within an implementation. Instantiated domain objects and graphical user-interface (GUI) objects will then be connected by cross-diagram model-view-controller (MVC) references. A complete application will be developed and demonstrated.

2. Features

Objektgraph facilitates the construction of an object diagram before a class diagram is constructed. In a curricular setting, the student first models several small concrete situations with object diagrams, while the class diagram is created by the tool as a side-effect. Then the student may study the more abstract class diagram and readily comprehend its meaning, having just created

SPLASH '13, October 26–31, 2013, Indianapolis, Indiana, USA.
ACM 978-1-4503-1995-9/13/10.
http://dx.doi.org/10.1145/2508075.2514576

instance structures that it describes. Although intended for pedagogy, this feature may prove useful in other contexts.

A key feature of Objektgraph is its extended semantics for object diagrams. An object diagram may be instantiated, either interactively or programmatically. Using this capability, an application's initial runtime object structure may be constructed by creating instantiations of one or more object diagrams and connecting them using interactive method invocations (see Figure 1). The GUI is also implemented by creating an object diagram of GUI objects (Java Swing-based GUIs are currently supported). It is then augmented with MVC references to domain objects. The GUI is instantiated and linked with the domain objects at runtime.

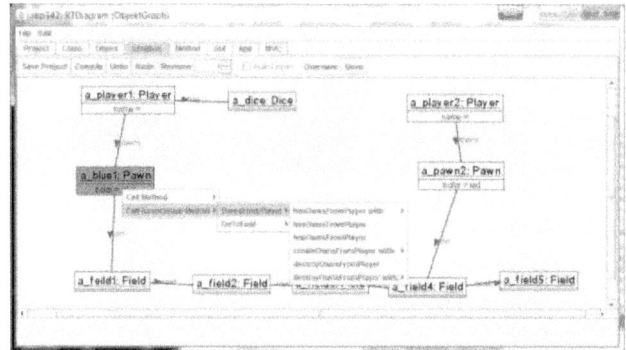

Figure 1. The Sandbox tab showing an instantiated object diagram with a context menu opened to invoke a method.

Objektgraph's support for UML semantics is comprehensive, including support for bi-directional many-to-many associations. Association links are given permanent identifiers and persisted in the same way that objects are. Care has been taken to provide an efficient runtime implementation.

Although Objektgraph eliminates the need for most methods, those that deal with queries or transformations of the domain model must be constructed. Another of Objektgraph's pedagogical features enables concrete method invocation within an object structure to aid in method development. This parallels object diagram editing aiding class diagram construction. In a curricular setting, the student carries out the steps of a method on method-specific concrete use-cases to guide the development of methods that query and update the domain object structure.

During method implementation, the 'sandbox' panel showing a runtime object structure and the method design panel are displayed side-by-side to assist the development process. The sandbox is loaded with the previously developed 'before' situation of a method-specific concrete use-case. When the "method" is invoked, the student plays the role of the method, traversing associations to bind variables and invoking other methods as needed to carry out the task. Objects bound in the current context are dynamically highlighted in the sandbox.

Because textbooks often introduce control structures using flowcharts, it is apparent that many educators believe flowcharts are readily understood by beginners. For this and other reasons, classical flowcharts with diamond decision nodes, rectangular process nodes, and flow-lines were chosen for method implementation. To impose a degree of structure similar to that imposed by a traditional structured language (one that excludes 'go to,' like Java), the 'method diagram' is statically checked as it is edited to ensure that no loop has multiple entry points.

As the student caries out the steps of a method specific use-case, each method invocation is reflected in the sandbox object structure and, as a side-effect, creates a flowchart node in the method diagram panel. The student may edit the flowchart at any time. The sandbox has its own undo/redo system so that the student may easily recreate a particular situation. The flowchart diagram may be invoked repeatedly for testing, and single-stepped. Repeating this process on a variation of the use-case informs the student of differences. When a difference is found, a decision node may be created (for instance, by invoking a Boolean method) and linked into the flowchart. The student edits the flowchart as required and again tests against each case. This methodology is similar to test-driven development (TDD).

Some features of Objektgraph are motivated simply by the need to support novices. For example, its undo/redo system maintains each revision when an edit is made during an undo, rather than permanently discarding revisions that are undone. Although it does not alter the typical undo/redo behavior, it makes all revisions accessible with a widget that spins through revisions in the order the edits were made. In addition, the undo/redo history is maintained across multiple program invocations.

3. Implementation
Implementation techniques used within Objektgraph and its generated applications will be discussed during the demonstration. One of those is a strongly typed identifier system that allows permanent identifiers to quickly be resolved to references at runtime, with robust compiler support for type consistency. The implementation consists mostly of boilerplate code for each class. The identifiers are easily obtained and dereferenced as needed.

To simplify pedagogical use of Objektgraph, a single project file holds all artifacts used within the project. It does this by persisting the object structures in what is essentially an object-oriented database, keyed by the permanent object identifiers.

Objektgraph is implemented in Java, and currently the generated applications also require Java. However, the design is language independent and other target platforms, such as Android and Google Web Toolkit (GWT), are anticipated.

4. Curriculum and Tool
Objektgraph supports a curricular approach pioneered in Germany by Ira Diethelm [3], and was given a German name in recognition of its roots ('Objektgraph' translates as 'object diagram'). The curriculum is based on *explicit object-oriented modeling*, which is defined here as creating a model where meaning arises primarily from associations, not attributes. Rather than using lists or arrays, an explicit object model typically exhibits a recursive object structure, which is closer to natural language. Objektgraph supports a curriculum that brings explicit object-oriented modeling and implementation to the front of the curriculum, often as the first experience.

A counterintuitive outcome has been observed when employing curricula based on explicit object modeling. The students most experienced with programming tend to struggle the most to create good object models. Because those students have successfully implemented assignments without creating explicit models, they may fail to appreciate the importance of modeling and instead consider it unnecessary busywork. Although projects assigned in this curriculum are complex, virtually requiring explicit models to enable their completion, some of the procedurally oriented students "don't get it" and resist explicit models even as they struggle. This also occurred when German high school teachers were being trained in a related curriculum. [3] The phenomenon could potentially be useful to facilitate diversity within the major.

5. Presenters
Duane Buck earned a master's degree in computer science and went into industry where he eventually held the titles 'systems analyst' and 'supervising analyst.' He developed an early framework for GUI applications; later he received an enthusiastic demo by a devotee unaware of its origin! He returned to academia where he earned a PhD. in computer science. He currently holds the rank Professor of Computer Science at Otterbein University, where he has developed previous pedagogical tools [1, 2]. He is the originator of the Objektgraph project and is its architect.

Professor Ira Diethelm currently directs the computer science education department and is vice-director of the school of education at Oldenburg University in Germany. She is the originator of the curriculum approach described here [4] and currently plays a consulting role in the project.

Stephen Sheneman is a senior computer science major at Otterbein University and has been working in the Objektgraph project for two years. He has coded a significant amount of its implementation, and has recently taken a broader design role.

6. References

[1] Duane Buck. GUIGraph: Editing live object diagrams for GUI generation enables new pedagogy in CS1/2. In Proceedings of the 16th joint conference on Innovation and technology in computer science education, ITiCSE '11, pages 193–197, New York, NY, USA, 2011. ACM.

[2] Duane Buck and David J. Stucki. JKarelRobot: A case study in supporting levels of cognitive development in the computer science curriculum. Proceedings of the 32nd symposium on Computer Science Education, SIGCSE '01, pages 16–20, New York, NY, USA, 2001. ACM.

[3] Ira Diethelm, Leif Geiger, and Albert Zündorf. "What's a Good Model and How to Teach It? – Introducing object oriented modeling by using scenarios." In *LYICT 2008, Joint Open and Working IFIP Conference: ICT and Learning for the next generation*, Kuala Lumpur, Malaysia, 2008. URL http://dl.ifip.org/index.php/ifip/article/download/13584/510.

[4] Ira Diethelm, (Strictly) Models and Objects First – Unterrichtskonzept und -methodik für objektorientierte Modellierung im Informatikunterricht. Dissertation. University of Kassel, Germany. 2007 (in German).

Welcome Message from the Doctoral Symposium Chair

It is our great pleasure to welcome you to Indianapolis and the 2013 Doctoral Symposium! This year's symposium continues the tradition of providing students with an opportunity for additional feedback and suggestions on their dissertation work, contacts for further interaction, and experience in communicating with other professionals in their field of study. The SPLASH Doctoral Symposium provides students with useful guidance for completing their dissertation research and beginning their research careers.

We are happy to report that the overall quality of this year's submissions was high. Out of a total of 9 proposer applications, the program committee accepted 9 proposals whose topics range from trustworthy computing and Android security to testing in the classroom, scripting languages, distributed systems, and energy efficient optimization.

Beyond the formal program, we hope this year's doctoral symposium will, like its predecessors, be a valuable forum for sharing ideas on the students' research. We are happy that you are able to join us for this exciting doctoral symposium, and hope that the ideas you take home with you will enrich the experience of your students and provide valuable feedback as they prepare to defend their dissertation work. Thank you for being part of this exciting community, and once again, welcome!

Lukasz Ziarek
SUNY Buffalo
lziarek@buffalo.edu

VM-Level Memory Monitoring for Resolving Performance Problems

Philipp Lengauer

Christian Doppler Laboratory for Monitoring and Evolution of Very-Large-Scale Software Systems,
Johannes Kepler University Linz
philipp.lengauer@jku.at

Abstract

Memory anomalies, such as memory leaks, floating garbage, and excessive garbage collection pauses, impact application performance considerably. Sadly, these anomalies often remain inexplicable as detecting and locating them is a tedious task for which only little automated tool support exists. We propose to design a Java virtual machine extension that exposes parts of its internal memory state and allows memory monitoring tools to access this state at runtime. Furthermore our goal is to automate the tuning of the Java virtual machine to counteract memory anomalies. Together with domain experts from our industrial partner, Compuware Austria, we plan to validate our approach on real-world applications.

Categories and Subject Descriptors C.4 [*Performance of Systems*]: Measurements; D.2.8 [*Software Engineering*]: Metrics—Performance measures

General Terms Measurements, Performance

Keywords Memory monitoring, memory anomalies, garbage collection

1. Introduction and Motivation

The way how applications allocate objects and manage object references greatly impacts their performance. While this is obviously true for applications that use unmanaged memory, it is also true for applications that use garbage-collected memory. We research memory anomalies, such as leaking memory, floating garbage, and spikes in garbage collection times, which cause performance problems that are hard to locate and even harder to resolve.

In unmanaged applications, a *memory leak* occurs if the programmer clears all references to an object without freeing it explicitly. Although in managed memory the garbage collector automatically detects unreferenced objects and reclaims the occupied memory, a memory leak can still occur; namely if an application falsely continues to reference objects that it actually does not use anymore, the garbage collector cannot free them. As memory leaks can accumulate during execution, the garbage collector compromises performance by wasting more and more time scanning unused mem-

ory. An additional (and even worse) problem is that eventually the application will run out of memory and crash.

Floating garbage are objects that are no longer referenced, but have not yet been collected. This happens if a dead object lives in a heap space A, and another dead object, which keeps a reference to it, lives in a heap space B, and both heap spaces are collected independently. During a collection of heap space A, the dead object cannot be freed. Only after the dead object in heap space B has been collected, the floating garbage in A can be collected as well. The time spent to unnecessarily scan floating garbage degrades performance. Floating garbage makes out-of-memory scenarios more frequent, thus more garbage collection cycles are necessary, degrading performance even more.

During garbage collection an application must be suspended, thus *excessive garbage collection times* make an application unresponsive. Possible reasons for such spikes are full heaps, garbage collection algorithms that are unsuited for the given heap content, or badly configured garbage collectors for the application's allocation behavior. However, choosing a suitable garbage collector and configuring it properly is by no means trivial, particularly without exhaustively trying them all.

This paper presents our research goals in locating and resolving memory anomalies in applications with garbage-collected memory. We propose a Java virtual machine extension, enabling external tools to detect and locate memory anomalies. Furthermore we intend to build a knowledge base for recommending an application-tailored garbage collector configuration.

We conduct our research in cooperation with Compuware Austria GmbH. Compuware develops leading-edge performance monitoring tools for multi-tier Java and .NET applications. In applications of their customers, sporadically occurring high GC times and permanently increasing memory consumption are problems that currently cannot be resolved with Compuwares' tools.

2. State of the Art

Memory leaks are a well-researched area: Xu et al. [1] propose to annotate coarse-grained transactions in the source code that define the life time of associated objects. Their tool monitors the program execution and detects objects that exceed the life time defined by the transaction; such objects are considered to be memory leaks. The sound partition of a program into transactions, although critical for good results, is left to the programmer. Aftandilian et al. [2] propose programmer-written assertions to declare when objects are supposedly dead. At run time their modified garbage collector checks the assertions and reports violations. This approach requires programmers to specify object lifetimes, which partly takes away the convenience of using automatic memory management in the first place. Xu et al. [3] propose a profiler that instruments calls

SPLASH '13, October 26–31, 2013, Indianapolis, IN, USA.
Copyright is held by the owner/author(s).
ACM 978-1-4503-1995-9/13/10.
http://dx.doi.org/10.1145/2508075.2508076

to Java's collection classes in order to track unused data objects. During garbage collection their tool calculates leakage confidence values based on the time at which an object was last retrieved from the collection. This approach is limited to objects stored in standard library collections and likely will produce false positives, as it solely relies on the last time of retrieval, which is typically influenced by user input. Printezis et al. [4] describe an architectural framework that helps tracking memory leaks by visualizing large heaps as well as changes of the heap. The framework can easily be adapted to any technology and memory manager.

In contrast to memory leaks, there is only little research about floating garbage and spikes in GC times, however, there is some research that covers allocation behavior and GC performance in general. For example, Singer et al. [5] worked on how to chose the proper heap size for an application. This is relevant for our research, because choosing an improper heap size can cause spikes in GC times. Dieckmann and Hölzle [9] analyzed the allocation behavior and object properties of the SPECjvm98 benchmarks and proposed optimizations based on their observations. Blackburn et al. [11] describe the garbage collection costs as a function of the heap size and identify key algorithmic features influencing performance.

Singer et al. [8] determine application-specific garbage collectors for a particular program without exhaustively profiling the program. They use machine learning techniques to build a prediction model and recommend a garbage collector based on a single profiling run of the program. However, they only recommend the garbage collector itself, but no configuration (e.g., heap size) for it.

Other research, partly relevant for our work, is about memory anomalies in a more general way: Chis et al. [6] define eleven patterns of inefficient memory use in Java programs, e.g., boxed primitive types in collections, sparsely populated collections, nested collections instead of flat collections. Their analysis framework monitors the execution of a Java program and counts how often the patterns occur. Pauw and Sevitsky [7] provide a tool that visualizes large heaps with relatively small graphs, making it easy to locate the root reference of a memory leak.

Some proprietary Java virtual machines (i.e., JRockit [10] and IBM JVM) are shipped with tools to retrieve and visualize statistics, e.g., garbage collection pause times, allocated bytes for each thread and memory usage of individual spaces. They are able to visualize object statistics, such as number of bytes and number of objects for each type, and suggest heap sizes tailored to the exact needs of a given application. However, most of the object statistics are gathered by suspending the virtual machine and snapshotting the heap, which considerably decreases performance.

3. Problem and Research Questions

We derived the following research questions (see Figure 1) based on the problems described in Section 1:

(1) Which monitoring capabilities are needed in Java virtual machines to support locating and resolving performance degradations in garbage-collected memory? Current Java virtual machines expose a native interface for debuggers and profilers: the Java Virtual Machine Tool Interface (JVMTI). This interface partly exposes the internal state of the executed Java application and of the virtual machine itself, e.g., the state of all objects, all threads and their according call stacks, and loaded classes. However, JVMTI does not expose other information that is required to detect memory anomalies, such as the actual layout of all objects on the heap, statistical data about garbage collection (e.g., number and age of objects collected, number of objects promoted, and total number of objects survived), nor reasons for garbage collector decisions (e.g., why objects have been not collected although they are dead or why a garbage collection was necessary). Our goal is to specify a richer tool interface that exposes the memory and the garbage collector.

(2) How can we methodically detect and locate memory anomalies that degrade performance in garbage-collected memory? As our industrial partner reports, detecting memory anomalies is a tedious task which involves labor-intensive manual analysis, with only little automated tool support available. Our goal is to define run-time metrics (measurable with the richer tool interface), such as live objects aggregated by allocation site, that indicate performance-degrading memory anomalies and help locating their cause (e.g., the allocation site, the root object, or the source line). Furthermore, we want to provide tool automation for detecting and locating memory anomalies.

(3) How can we reduce the performance impact of garbage collection by recommending garbage collection settings tailored to a given application? Current Java virtual machines support a variety of garbage collector algorithms, which can be individually configured. Some configuration options are common to all garbage collectors, but others are individual for specific ones. Finding a well-suited configuration (i.e., choosing a garbage collector and selecting a configuration from all parameter combinations) for a given application is difficult. Singer et al. [8] propose a method for selecting a garbage collector based on a single profiling run of an application. Our goal is to additionally recommend a configuration for the garbage collector that is well-suited for a given application, because we expect further performance improvements from that.

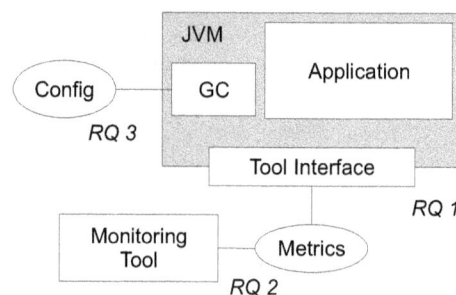

Figure 1. Key Elements and Research Questions (RQ)

4. Approach

Our approach is to define and measure run-time metrics that reflect the memory and garbage collector behavior and to compare the measurements of programs with and without memory anomalies. Based on these measurements, we plan to detect memory anomalies, locate their cause, and recommend steps to resolve them. In detail we plan the following steps:

1) Identify run-time metrics that describe the memory usage of an application. We plan to monitor object allocation and garbage collection, and thereby measure metrics that allow classifying applications by their memory usage behavior, e.g., number of objects allocated and freed, object lifetime and size, number of references traversed, and number of objects survived or promoted.

2) Specify and implement a Java virtual machine extension that exposes the data necessary to calculate the run-time metrics. We plan to extend the Java virtual machine tool interface by creating a custom virtual machine, based on the OpenJDK 8. Our extensions focus on exposing statistical heap and garbage collector data.

3) Find correlations between measurements and memory anomalies. We plan to find statistical correlations between the measurements and the existence of memory anomalies.

We plan the following additional steps for resarch question 3:

4) Measure garbage collector performance and run-time metrics for real-world applications with different garbage collector configurations. The Hotspot Java Virtual Machine (JVM) provides four different collectors with a multitude of configuration options. We

plan to define and measure reasonable combinations, e.g., the scavenging collector with varying tenuring thresholds, survivor ratios, and space resizing policies.

5) Build a knowledge base by mapping the measured performance together with run-time metrics to the according garbage collector configuration. We plan to use machine learning techniques (e.g., k-nearest neighbors, binary decisions trees, or support vector machines) to build a knowledge base from real-world applications and make it publicly available. We plan to include applications from our industrial partner and other third-parties as well, and widely used benchmarks.

6) Recommend a garbage collector configuration for a given application by measuring its run-time metrics and retrieving the best configuration of similar applications from the knowledge base.

5. Research Methodology and Evaluation

We use an iterative approach: (1) we analyze the problem together with domain experts from our industrial partner; (2) develop a prototype, and (3) evaluate the prototype with benchmarks and real-world case studies from our industrial partner.

We plan to evaluate research questions 1 and 2 from Section 3 in an laboratory experiment where developers apply our method in order to detect and locate prior-known memory anomalies in real-world applications. Moreover, we will measure run-time metrics in applications with and without memory anomalies. In applications with known memory anomalies, we will locate and fix the anomaly manually, so that we can compare two versions of the same application, one with the anomaly and one without it.

For research question 3, we plan to use two application sets, a training set and an evaluation set. We will train our recommender system on the training set and evaluate the recommendation by means of the evaluation set. In order to rate the recommendation, we will compare the run time of the recommended configuration with a reasonable amount of alternate configurations as well as a configuration from a domain expert.

6. Ongoing Research

In the last few months, we have been working on a transactional memory leak detector. Transactions are key for our industrial partner, as our partner's monitoring software aggregates most data on transactions, e.g., on a customer checkout in a web shop application. A transaction comprises a set of activities (possibly in parallel) in reaction to a user input. The start and end of a transaction is automatically detected when methods (specified by the operator) are entered, e.g., a method representing the customer checkout, or a web request is received. We observed that in such applications some transactions leak memory whereas others do not. Our prototypical transactional memory leak detector can spot such transactions, which our industrial partners monitoring software could not. In order to develop the detector, we defined a set of run-time metrics (e.g., allocated and freed objects per class and per transaction) extended the tool interface of the OpenJDK 8 virtual machine (VM) so that it provides our run- time metrics, and implemented an agent that retrieves and processes the metrics.

Our modified VM collects these metrics as follows: it adjusts the necessary counters whenever an object is allocated or freed by the garbage collector. When an object is allocated, the VM checks if a transaction is currently active and adjusts the allocation counter for the respective transaction and class. It stores the transaction in the object header, which we extended to carry the additional information. As soon as the garbage collector frees the object, the VM uses the information stored in the object header to identify the allocating transaction and to adjust the corresponding free counter. When a transaction completes, our agent detects potential memory

leaks by checking the allocation and free counters for each class in order to determine how many objects have survived. For transactions with survivors, the agent locates the surviving objects on the heap and retrieves their allocation site so that the user can decide which survivors comprise an actual memory leak. As our solution involves the garbage collector, the user must wait for the next collection cycle in order to get accurate results for a transaction.

As we progress with our research of correlations between metrics and memory anomalies, we plan to include the other metrics that our VM already provides in the detector.

7. Conclusion

This paper presented our planned and ongoing research on detecting and locating memory anomalies such as memory leaks, floating garbage, and garbage collection spikes, which we consider open research issues. We propose a virtual machine extension that provides run-time metrics reflecting the memory usage and the heap content of applications. We intend to measure these metrics in applications with known memory anomalies and to find correlations between the measurements and memory anomalies. Furthermore, we propose building a knowledge base for recommending application-tailored garbage collector configurations.

Acknowledgments

This work has been supported by the Christian Doppler Forschungsgesellschaft, Austria, and Compuware Austria GmbH.

References

[1] G. Xu, M. D. Bond, F. Qin, and A. Rountev, *LeakChaser: Helping Programmers Narrow Down Causes of Memory Leaks*, Proceedings of the 32nd Conference on Programming Language Design and Implementation, 270 - 282, 2011

[2] E. E. Aftandilian and S. Z. Guyer, *GC Assertions: Using the Garbage Collector to Check Heap Properties*, Proceedings of the 2009 Conference on Programming language Design and Implementation, 235 - 244, 2009

[3] G. Xu and A. Rountev, *Precise Memory Leak Detection for Java Software Using Container Profiling*, Proceedings of the 30th International Conference on Software Engineering, 151 - 160, 2008

[4] T. Printezis and R. Jones, *GCspy: an Adaptable Heap Visualization Framework*, Proceedings of the 17th Conference on Object-oriented Programming, Systems, Languages, and Applications, 343 - 358, 2002

[5] J. Singer, R. E. Jones, G. Brown, and M. Lujn, *The Economics of Garbage Collection*, Proceedings of the 2010 International Symposium on Memory Management, 103 - 112, 2010

[6] A. E. Chis, N. Mitchel, E. Schonberg, G. Sevitsky, P. O'Sullivan, T. Parsons, and J. Murphy, *Patterns of Memory Inefficiency*, Proceedings of the 25th European Conference on Object-oriented Programming, 383 - 407, 2011

[7] W. D. Pauw and G. Sevitsky, *Visualizing Reference Patterns for Solving Memory Leaks in Java*, Proceedings of the European Conference on Object-oriented Programming, 1999

[8] J. Singer, G. Brown, I. Watson, and J. Cavazos, *Intelligent Selection of Application-specific Garbage Collectors*, Proceedings of the 6th International Symposium on Memory Management, 91 - 102, 2007

[9] S. Dieckmann and Urs Hölzle, *A Study of Allocation Behavior of the SPECjvm98 Java Benchmarks*, Proceedings of European Conference on Object-oriented Programming, 1999

[10] M. Hirt and M. Lagergren *Oracle JRockit - The Definitive Guide*, ISBN 978-1-847198-06-8, 2010

[11] S. M. Blackburn, P. Cheng, and K. S. McKinley *Myths and Realities: the Performance Impact of Garbage Collection*, Proceedings of the Joint International Conference on Measurement and Modelling of Computer Systems, 25 - 36, 2004

TruSSCom – Proposal for Trustworthy Service Representation, Selection and Negotiation for Integrating Software Systems

Lahiru S. Gallege

Department of Computer and Information Science,
Indiana University-Purdue University Indianapolis (IUPUI), Indianapolis, IN, USA.
Email: lspileth@cs.iupui.edu

Abstract

Integrating a distributed software system using publically available software services saves effort, time, and cost. One key step in this process is the service selection which identifies a relevant set of services for this integration. In an open service marketplace, it is hard to judge the trust of software services using a static view (consisting of service specifications) published by their developers. Instead, the concepts of trust in the context of services needs to be properly quantified, specified, negotiated, and then used in the selection process. Prevalent service selection and negotiation approaches do not consider the trust aspect of services. Trustworthy service representation, selection, and negotiation are challenging tasks due to the subjective and temporal nature of trust, lack of standards, and associated uncertainty. This proposal defines the trust of a service, quantifies the trust by monitoring and aggregating various evidences, represents the trust in the service specification and improves the service selection and negotiation process using this representation. Publically available software objects (from Java collection framework library) and mobile app services (from the Android marketplace) are used as datasets to empirically evaluate this proposal.

Categories and Subject Descriptors K.6.3 [**Management of Computing and Information Systems**]: Software Management - software selection.

Keywords : Trust; Service Representation; Service Selection; Service Negotiation; Software Services.

1. Motivation

Proper reuse of software services helps complex software projects to meet budgets and deadlines. The Service Oriented Architecture (SOA) provides concepts of reusing software services to integrate software systems. For example, consider a distributed tracking system that tracks the location of an object (of interest) using publically available sensor services such as Camera, Wi-Fi, and GPS. Such reuse of software services demands an establishment of trust between independent venders and consumers at the time of service selection [1]. Our previous survey [2] confirmed that the trust aspects of software entities (e.g., software objects, libraries, modules, services, etc.) in the context of publically hosted software services are yet to be standardized and that increases the complexity of software service reuse.

SPLASH '13, October 26–31, 2013, Indianapolis, Indiana, USA.
ACM 978-1-4503-1995-9/13/10.
http://dx.doi.org/10.1145/2508075.2508077

Publically available software services, along with associated information, are typically hosted in a cloud – Android market place is one such example. These marketplaces still follow the traditional way of representing the trust of a service, which is to indicate it as a quality of service (QoS) attribute (e.g., numerical star ratings). This naive quantification (or representation) has limited usage at the time of service selection, as it does not reflect important information such as, how the trust value was aggregated and its fluctuations over time. During the lifetime of a service, it is expected that the trust of a service deviates due to various factors such as, changes in operating conditions, new revisions, and feature updates. Hence, a fairly rudimentary and static way of providing a star rating for a publically available service is not a comprehensive solution. Instead there is a need for new approaches to define, represent trust aspects of software services and also to select and negotiate attributes of them based on their trustworthiness.

2. Problem Statement

The focus of this proposal is to *"provide a software framework and associated algorithmic modifications to perform trustworthy service representation, selection and negotiation in the context of service marketplaces.* The goal of this effort is to facilitate effective service reuse while integrating distributed software systems. To achieve this goal, the framework should identify the complete spectrum of the trust of a service at the time of service selection. It should also track and record fluctuations associated with both the service and its environment. This additional information provided by the framework will enhance the service selection process by basing its decision on the trustworthiness of the service. Proposing a software framework for service selection based on the trust of a service is a challenging task due to the disagreements about the definition of trust of a service, the subjective and temporal nature of trust, the heterogeneity associated with available evidences, and the complexity associated with aggregation and evolution of the trust-related aspects of services.

3. Our Approach

This proposal, therefore, focuses on tackling the above mentioned problems of the quantification and representation of trust in the context of software services and its usage in the service selection and negotiation processes. The proposed work is based on our preliminary efforts reported in [1, 2, 3, 4]. This paper initially presents our definition and quantification of the trust associated with a software service. Then it describes the preliminary trust model which helps to monitor and aggregate relevant evidences using suitable operators. Finally, the algorithmic modifications necessary to perform trustworthy service selection and negotiation using the model defined are briefly discussed along with proposed empirical validation scenarios.

3.1 Trustworthy Service Representation

Our formal definition of the trust of a service is based on the definition proposed by the Trusted Computing Group [5] (i.e., "An entity can be trusted if it always behaves in the expected manner for the intended purpose"). Hence, we define the trust of a software service as the "degree of conformance of its behaviour to its published specification."

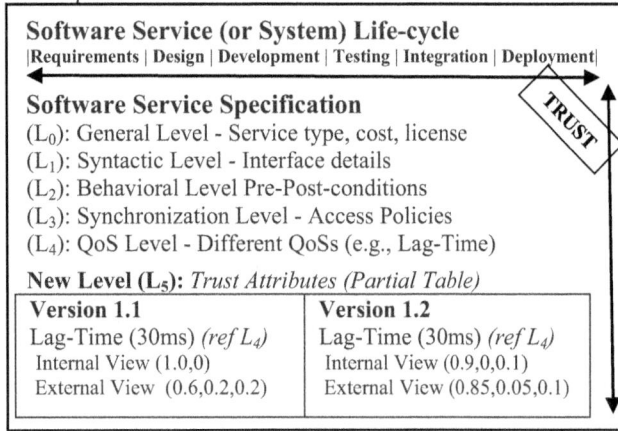

Software Service (or System) Life-cycle
|Requirements | Design | Development | Testing | Integration | Deployment|

Software Service Specification
(L_0): General Level - Service type, cost, license
(L_1): Syntactic Level - Interface details
(L_2): Behavioral Level Pre-Post-conditions
(L_3): Synchronization Level - Access Policies
(L_4): QoS Level - Different QoSs (e.g., Lag-Time)

New Level (L_5): *Trust Attributes (Partial Table)*

Version 1.1	Version 1.2
Lag-Time (30ms) *(ref L_4)*	Lag-Time (30ms) *(ref L_4)*
Internal View (1.0,0)	Internal View (0.9,0,0.1)
External View (0.6,0.2,0.2)	External View (0.85,0.05,0.1)

Figure 1. Trust aspects of the multi-level service specification [3]

The trust aspect, due to its definition, crosscuts the entire software lifecycle (Figure 1). At the same time, the software specification is structured as a collection of contracts at each level. Therefore, our trust model [1] focuses on different artefacts (i.e., conceptual or physical outcomes of a particular phase of the lifecycle) and their associated evidences. These evidences are also produced at each phase of software lifecycle of a service (e.g., test cases during the testing phase). For a particular artefact, the evaluations done by the developers indicate its internal view, while the evaluations done by the users/reviewers indicate its external view. These two views provide the necessary mechanisms for quantifying and representing trust of a service. The formal quantification of trust that we used is based on the theory of evidence [6] and theory of subjective logic [7]. Using these theories, our model associates a numerical tuple of Belief, Disbelief, and Uncertainty (B, D, U) to indicate the trust about each evidence. The numerical values of the B, D, and U are between 0 and 1 and their sum equals to 1. This BDU-based quantification is selected because of its inherent ability to capture the subjectiveness of the associated evidences and a lack of complete information (as represented by the "U" part) about evidences.

In general, the service selection process evaluates the service meta-data which are publically available via the service specifications. For example, a multi-level structure is proposed by Beugnard et al. [8] has four levels in the service specification (syntax, semantics, synchronization, and QoS (Figure 1 - L_{1-4})). However, most prevalent approaches do not include trust aspects as a part of the specification. We have modified our previous version [9], an enhancement of the Beugard et al.'s specification (with L_0 indicating the inherent attributes), also to include trust aspects of a service (Figure 1 - L_5). The trust crosscuts all levels hence, the BDU tuples are computed for all the levels for each attribute. These values are computed as a reference to another level attribute (e.g., BDU of Lag-Time is referring to QoS attribute) and placed as a part of trust contract according to an agreed temporal aspect (e.g., versions). The calculation of the BDU tuples are done in both internal (i.e., developers) and external (i.e., users) perspectives with respective to that particular attribute of the specification [1, 3, 4]. The aggregation of these individual BDU tuples (represent each evidences with respect to a certain attribute in the specification) is done by subjective logic operators such as the conjunction and consensus [4, 7]. For example, when multiple opinions are present, such as (e.g., consistent or conflicting user reviews about Lag-Time of a data service) then the consensus operator is used to aggregate these opinions.

3.2 Trustworthy Service Selection

Prevalent service specifications do not include a separate trust-related section. The existing selection schemes also do not use operators which are needed for matching trust-attributes. According to the above scheme (Section 3.1), when the trust contracts are created for services, they are also used to perform the selection process. We have abstracted the generic structure (i.e., Table 1 without the terms with *) behind the prevalent service selection algorithms (such as [9]). Additionally, we propose the following modifications to this abstracted structure (shown in Table 1 with *) to perform trustworthy service selection [4].

The off-line phase of the service selection algorithm periodically collects the evidences about trust attributes published by a service contract. The time frame of the aggregation can be hourly, daily, or based on versions. Figure 1 shows the trust aggregation of one attribute (i.e., Lag-Time of a data service) based on versioning. A significant divergence between the B, D, U tuples for the attribute in Version 1.1 is noted with then a convergence between the views in Version 1.2. Possible reason for such a change of opinion between versions is that, in the former version the developers have not considered the external opinions and later updated the service in the next version by considering them. These progressions of trust views provide additional information to the on-line service selection phase. In this phase, the service selection process requires additional matching operators such as conjunction and ordering [4, 7] to match new information available through the proposed trust contract. Having these trust related aggregations collected over a period of time provides additional knowledge to the service selection process.

Table 1. Service selection algorithm modifications	
Service Query	List of service (*trust**) requirements
Off-Line Phase	Periodically aggregate (*trust**) attributes of services
Online Phase	Perform (*trustworthy**) service matching
Output	Ordered list of Services (*based on trustworthiness**)

3.3 Trustworthy Service Negotiation

As indicated earlier, most prevalent service selection schemes do not include a trust establishment based on mutual evaluations between the service vendors and consumers. Hence, these service negotiation schemes operate only based on quality of service agreements such as, service level agreements (SLAs). Online services are affected by the change of the environment conditions, which result in the fluctuations of the quality of service offered. Therefore, we propose a negotiation establishment based on the trust between vendors and consumers at the time of service selection. These establishments are based on the aggregated views of a trust of the services (Figure 1) and their future rules of engagements to address the fluctuations. For example, trust aspects of the negotiation contact should include information about which evidences to consider in quantifying the effects of a service outage. Considering the prevalent negotiation strategies, we are currently investigating on how the algorithms can be modified based on two phases (as described in Table 2). An active phase of negotiation is initiated at the end of the service selection. This is based on the current views of the trust of that service which establishes a mutual agreement of negotiation for current and future variations. After selection process is completed, as new evidences are available (such as new feature updates and releases), the passive phase periodically monitors the agreement. If any violations are noted then the negotiation switches back to the active phase.

Table 2. Service negotiation algorithms modifications

Active Phase	Initiates the trust establishments during service selection.
	Agreements on future fluctuations in trust establishments.
Passive Phase	Periodically monitors the trust establishments after selection.
	Updates trust establishments (both vendors and consumers).

4. Evaluation Methodology

To evaluate the above approach, we propose to use two datasets namely, the Java Collection Framework and Android Marketplace. Selected objects from the collection framework and selected apps from the marketplace are assumed to behave as services within our prototypical (TruSSCom) environment.

4.1 Case Study using the Android Marketplace

We evaluated, as a preliminary study, a subset of Android apps in relation to a trip planning case scenario [4]. External reviews available about these apps are mainly considered for aggregating evidences over time. The selected service dataset includes 36204 apps and 1108343 reviews. We used a default value for the internal view of a service because the evidences are not available. When a service query is submitted, the prototype displays a list of possible instances (for each type of service needed, e.g., travel related services). This process includes the prevalent selection process plus the above described trustworthy service selection.

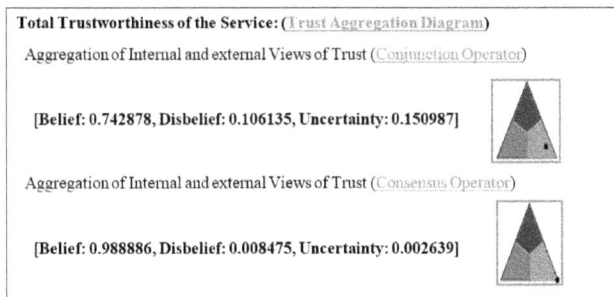

Total Trustworthiness of the Service: (Trust Aggregation Diagram)

Aggregation of Internal and external Views of Trust (Conjunction Operator)

[Belief: 0.742878, Disbelief: 0.106135, Uncertainty: 0.150987]

Aggregation of Internal and external Views of Trust (Consensus Operator)

[Belief: 0.988886, Disbelief: 0.008475, Uncertainty: 0.002639]

Figure 2. Total trustworthyness of a service is presented usig two operators (conjunction and consensus).

The TruSSCom prototype calculates the trustworthiness of each service based on associated evidences. It also tracks the progression of trust for that service based on temporal intervals (i.e., versions, weeks). It can switch the algorithms which calculates the trust of services and compare different selection results. For example, the current algorithm used to compute the trust tuple is based on the external reviews about a service. It is calculated using the services': 1) average user star ratings, 2) each review, using a suitable techniques (such as keyword counting or term-frequency-inverse document frequency), 3) the reputation of the reviewer by using the recommendation operator from [7], and 4) the expiration of the reivew using the distence to the review date from today. The consensus operator is used to aggregate these different views of the service to obtain a single quantification of the trust of the service. Figure 2 presents a screencapture of the prototype indicating the computed trust value of a selected service. The prototype follows two methods for calculating the total trustworthiness of a service (Figure 2). The consensus operator is preferred when the evaluated views fall within a range. Otherwise the conjunction operator is preferred. Final aggregation values are displayed using both numerical and graphical representations. We also use a BDU

triangle which is simmlar to the visual representation used by Josang et al. in [7].

4.2 Case Study using the Java Collection Framework

Currently we are evaluating a subset of classes from the Java Collection Framework. We run them in different virtual machines to simulate as services hosted in marketplaces. In our experiment, the serializable interfaces of the objects together with their JavaDoc are treated as their service specifications. The scenario is assumed to be the selection of data services (e.g., data structure operations related to List, Queue, Set, Vector and Map). We base our study from the start of the collection framework (i.e., from pre-JDK 1.2 libraries) to the new Java-7 libraries. Our first goal is to identify the limitations of the initial versions of the operations by investigating bugs and features reported by users. Naturally, they are fixed and updated in later releases. Our trust evaluations are based on those evidences and we experiment the service selection negotiation algorithms against them. Since the collection framework is defined as a hierarchy of interfaces, we can study the effects of service substitution (e.g., super class operation – Sub class operation) based negotiation and their effect in the trust of the integrated system.

5. Conclusion and Future Work

Based on the concepts of theory of evidence and multi-level specifications, the trust aggregation of services using a contract improves the service selection process. Future directions include: further experimentation of the TruSSCom prototype and find ways to improve the certainty in predicting trust values of services.

Acknowledgments

This work is supported in part by the US Air Force Research Laboratory (AFRL) through the Security and Software Engineering Research Center (S^2ERC). Our research group members are Dimuthu U. Gamage, Dr. James H. Hill, and Dr. Rajeev R. Raje.

References

[1] L. S. Gallege, D. U. Gamage, J. H. Hill, and R. R. Raje, "Towards a comprehensive method for integrating trust into enterprise DRE systems," in *Proceedings of the Embedded and Real-Time Computing Systems and Applications (RTCSA)*, IEEE Computer Society, 2011.

[2] L. S. Gallege, D. U. Gamage, J. H. Hill, and R. R. Raje, "A Study of Trust in Distributed Systems," Department of Computer and Information Science Technical Report (TR-CIS-0420-03), 2012.

[3] L. S. Gallege, D. U. Gamage, J. H. Hill, and R. R. Raje, "Trust contract of a service and its role in service selection for distributed software systems," in *Proceedings of 8th Cyber Security Information Intelligence Research Workshop (CSIIRW '13)*, ACM, 2013.

[4] L. S. Gallege, D. U. Gamage, J. H. Hill, and R. R. Raje, "Trustworthy service selection using long-term monitoring of trust contract," to appear in *Proceedings of 17th EDOC Conference*, IEEE, 2013.

[5] S. Pearson, "Trusted Computing Platforms: TCPA Technology in Context," Prentice Hall PTR, Upper Saddle River, NJ, USA. 2002.

[6] G. Shafer, A Mathematical Theory of Evidence. Princeton University Press, Princeton, 1976.

[7] A. Jøsang, "Artificial Reasoning with Subjective Logic," in *Proceedings of the Second Australian Workshop on Common-sense Reasoning*, Perth, Australia, 1997.

[8] A. Beugnard, J. M. Jezequel, N. Plouzeau, and D. Watkins, "Making components contract aware," *IEEE Computer*, pp (32), July 1999.

[9] L. S. Gallege, K. Pradhan, and R. R. Raje, "Experiments with a multi-level discovery system," in *Proceedings of the International Conference in Computing (ICC)*, New Delhi, India, 2010.

Automated Assessment of Students' Testing Skills for Improving Correctness of Their Code

Zalia Shams
Virginia Tech
2202 Kraft Drive
Blacksburg
VA-24060,USA
zalia18@cs.vt.edu

ABSTRACT

Although software testing is included as a regular part of many programming courses, current assessment techniques used in automated grading tools for evaluating student-written software tests are imperfect. Code coverage measures are typically used in practice, but that approach does not assess how much of the expected behavior is checked by the tests and sometimes, overestimates the true quality of the tests. Two robust and thorough measures for evaluating student-written tests are running each students' tests against others' solutions(known as all-pairs testing) and injecting artificial bugs to determine if tests can detect them (also known as mutation analysis). Even though they are better indicators of test quality, both of them posed a number of practical obstacles to classroom use. This proposal describes technical obstacles behind using these two approaches in automated grading. We propose novel and practical solutions to apply all-pairs testing and mutation analysis of student-written tests, especially in the context of classroom grading tools. Experimental results of applying our techniques in eight CS1 and CS2 assignments submitted by 147 students show the feasibility of our solution. Finally, we discuss our plan to combine the approaches to evaluate tests of assignments having variable amounts of design freedom and explain their evaluation method.

Categories and Subject Descriptors

K.3.2 [**Computers and Education**]: Computer and Information Science Education; D.1.5 [**Programming Techniques**]: Object oriented Programming; D.2.5 [**Software Engineering**]: Testing and Debugging—testing tools.

Keywords

Test driven development, automated grading, mutation testing, software testing,test coverage, reflection, bytecode transformation.

1. INTRODUCTION

Testing is an inaugural part of software development. Even though it accounts for 50% cost of software development, practitioners perceive testing as a tedious, uncreative, boring work and less than 15% of them ever receive any formal training in the subject [12]. Students are not accustomed to test their code. They

Permission to make digital or hard copies of part or all of this work for personal or classroom use is granted without fee provided that copies are not made or distributed for profit or commercial advantage and that copies bear this notice and the full citation on the first page. Copyrights for third-party components of this work must be honored. For all other uses, contact the owner/author(s).
Copyright is held by the author/owner(s).
SPLASH'13, October 26–31, 2013, Indianapolis, Indiana, USA.
ACM 978-1-4503-1995-9/13/10.
http://dx.doi.org/10.1145/2508075.2508078

usually focus on output correctness on instructor's sample data [5] and do less testing on their own [4]. Considering the necessity of testing, more educators are including software tests [3] in programming and software engineering courses [5, 8]. To support software testing as a part of regular programming assignments, current classroom assessment systems (e.g.,Web-CAT, ASSYST, Marmoset) allow students to turn in their programs along with tests. These automated grading tools evaluate student-written tests using coverage metrics. Code coverage measures the percentage of code—e.g., statements or branches—that is executed by running tests. The rationale behind code coverage is: the more code executed during testing the higher the chance of finding flaws in them. However, code coverage may falsely indicate test quality as it does not check if the executed code has been tested against expected behavior [1, 9]. Moreover a students' solution may be incomplete or incorrect. Large percentage execution of an incomplete solution will result in high code coverage missing all the omissions.

Two robust and thorough mechanisms for evaluating student written tests are: 1) *all-pairs* student testing, and 2) *mutation testing*. Even though they are strong indicators of test quality and adequacy, because of technical difficulties they are rarely used for assessing student-written tests, especially when programs are written in object-oriented languages such as Java. All-pairs testing [7] involve running every student's tests against the others' programs. This mechanism gives students a greater realization of the density of bugs in their code and their ability to write tests that find defects in others' solutions. However, implementation of this all-pairs model of executing tests is rare because student-written tests, such as JUnit tests written for Java programs, depend on individual aspects of the author's solution and may not compile against another student's program. Automated grading systems face similar issues when running instructor-provided JUnit-style reference tests against student submissions. Student solutions that fail to conform to the all requirements of the assignment cannot be compiled or assessed using reference tests. As a result, partial or incomplete submissions would have no results against reference tests, and most grading systems would assign no credit for the corresponding portion of the assignment grade. Thus, to run each student's tests against every other student's solution, a way must be devised to ensure a uniform interface against which tests can be executed regardless of differences between solutions or divergence from the assignment requirements. The other mechanism, mutation testing, seeds artificial errors into code (generating buggy versions called mutants) and then checks whether a test suite can detect them. Mutant score is computed from the number of mutants detected vs. number of mutant generated, and is used to indicate adequacy of test suites. Mutation testing is difficult to use in an educational setting for three main reasons [1]. First, mutation testing is computationally expensive and time consuming as it involves a manual determination process of whether an injected error is a true bug or an innocuous solution. Second, mutants must be generated from a solution that is presumably correct and complete. A student solution is not a reliable candidate for mutant generation as it may be incorrect or partial. Third, students' tests may have dependencies on their own solutions and may fail to compile against mutants. Thus, to use mutation testing for assessment of student written tests and provide students immediate feedbacks, mutants should be generated from a solution that covers all the aspects of the assignment, they must be classified into true bugs or equivalent of an original solution using an automated efficient mechanism, and the mutants must run against students' tests irrespective of the tests' internal structure.

Application of all-pairs testing and mutation analysis will give students a deeper realization on the quality of their tests, which will help them thoroughly test their own code. As a result, they will learn to write software having fewer bugs.

2. PROBLEM
Automated grading tools allow students to turn in software tests along with their solutions. Assessment of the quality of student-written tests helps students learning software testing and programming at the same time. These grading tools evaluate their tests using code coverage which may overestimate test quality as it does not assess how much of the expected behavior has been checked correctly. Therefore, to assess true quality of students' tests we must identify: **Which test quality measures actually assess how much of the expected behavior is checked by the tests**?

Even though some test quality measures may work well in an industry setting, they may not be practical for evaluating students tests for three main reasons: 1) students should have varying amount of design freedom to learn mapping requirements to software modules, 2) they must get immediate feedback on their work, and 3) no formal tracking system for bugs or code changes is available for small class assignments. Therefore, we need to find out: **What are the practical obstacles of using identified test quality measures in an educational setting**? Once we identify the main problems, we will devise: **How can we resolve the obstacles to apply the measures in classroom tools**?

Since students have varying amounts of design freedom in their assignments, we will investigate: **Which approach is more appropriate for open-ended assignments, and what measure works better for close-ended assignments**? Finally, we will determine: **What combination of the approaches works well as a hybrid measure to separately evaluate tests of the assignments having variable amounts of design freedom**?

3. APPROACH
All-pairs testing and mutation analysis are two robust measures to evaluate the quality of student written tests. The main obstacle of using all-pairs testing is the compile-time dependency of the tests on its author's solution. In object-oriented languages, such as Java, tests are written as a part of the solution and may refer to any visible or public feature of the solution. For example, a student may decide to add a helper method in his solution to assist some computation. If a student tests such components that arise from his personal design decisions, and are not present in others' code, then his tests will not compile against others' solutions. A novel way to resolve this issue in Java is to transform the student-

written tests so that they use reflection to defer binding to specific features of a solution until run-time. Test sets that depend on the internal details on one particular solution can be compiled against the particular solution they were written for. For example, one student's tests will compile against his or her own code, if they compile at all, and so we need not worry about syntactically invalid test sets. Similarly, instructors typically provide their own implementation to double-check reference test sets, so the reference tests will compile against the implementation. We transform the byte-code of the compiled test sets into reflective forms so that they use late binding. Reflection is a feature of Java that is used to reduce compile time dependency between code components. Hence, the byte-codes of the test cases are transformed using Javassist [2] into purely reflective forms. Java reflection can be complicated and error-prone to use, but we use ReflectionSupport [10], a library of methods that completely encapsulates the details of using reflection underneath a powerful, streamlined interface ideal for writing test actions. As a result, test cases written using this library will have no compile-time dependencies on the software under test.

The purely reflective test cases will compile and run against any student submission. Individual test cases that depend on features that are missing or indirectly declared in the student's work fail at run-time, while other test cases run normally. Therefore, the test-sets will run against all solutions, even if some of them are incomplete. Finally, we collect how many bugs a student-written test has revealed to assess its robustness.

The second approach, mutation testing, injects artificial bugs in the code and checks if test-cases can detect the bugs. Mutants (buggy versions) must be generated from a correct and complete solution. Usually instructors provide a reference solution, which is presumably correct and includes all the required features of the assignment, to an automated grader. We choose the reference solution to generate mutants. Mutant generation also takes time. If mutants are generated from a reference solution available when an assignment is created, it is possible to pre-generate the full set of mutants from the reference solution ahead of time, so that mutant generation will not slow down analysis of student-written tests. Later, student-written test-cases are transformed to remove compile-time dependencies so they will run against any mutants. Afterwards, we validate students' tests against the reference solution and run mutants against only the valid tests. Mutants that produce different results from the original solution are considered as bugs. Our conservative process reduces computational overhead of manual differentiation, determining whether injected faults in a mutant are true bugs or a behavioral equivalent of an innocuous solution. Then, we evaluate the quality of a student's test from how many mutants it has detected.

All-pairs testing evaluates robustness and mutation analysis measures adequacy of the tests. The approaches may need some modification to evaluate open-ended assignments where large percentage of test-cases examines student-specific features. For example, to evaluate student-specific tests, we can use mutants generated from the same author's solution. Finally, using massive test-suites collected from all students' tests with the same assignments in different semesters, we determine if students are producing fewer bugs than they used to using code coverage, after getting feedback from all-pairs testing and mutation analysis.

4. EVALUATION METHODOLOGY

We identified that all-pairs testing and mutation analysis are better indicators of test quality than code coverage. Then, we investigated obstacles for using them in automated grading systems, and devised novel solutions to resolve the problems. We applied our solution for all-pairs testing in one CS1 and one CS2 assignments to evaluate our primary hypothesis.

The CS1 assignment had 46 submissions with 46 test sets consisting of 463 test cases. We removed compile-time dependencies from the test-cases and screened them against the reference solution. This resulted in a total of 18,225 individual tests after removing invalid or student-specific test cases. Every test case was passed by at least 65% of the programs and 63% of the submissions passed every test case written by every student. Keeping in mind that it was the first assignment for the beginners, we consider that students were able to write 35% effective tests that did uncover defects in many other submissions. The CS2 assignment had 101 student submissions with 101 test sets consisting of 2155 test cases. We used byte code translator to convert the test sets to their reflective versions like before. After validating them against an instructor-provided reference solution we got 2001 (92.9%) valid test cases and ran them against 101 solutions. The performance of the programs was representative of a more challenging assignment. The average portion of the test cases passed by a solution was 83.5%. Only five student programs passed all valid test cases, and it shows that students on the whole are quite capable of writing test cases that will reveal bugs. Unlike the CS1 assignment, there were *no* test cases that were passed by every program. Also, *no* transformed test suite failed to compile or run because of their dependency on the author's solution. To our knowledge, we are the first to successfully apply all-pairs testing [6] in automated grading.

To evaluate the practicality of our solution for mutation analysis, we applied it to six CS1 and CS2 assignments, where students were required to write their own software tests for each of their solutions. We pre-generated mutants from the reference solution, removed compile-time dependencies from students' tests, validated the tests against the reference solution, automatically detected mutants from the valid tests, and computed mutant detection ratio of the tests. Among the six assignments, three were from CS1 where the number of mutants varied from 42-47. The other three CS2 assignments had 147, 109 and 305 mutants. Total number of valid test cases from the CS1 assignments was 672, where 42 among 47students completed all the assignments. In the CS2, 107 students completed assignments where valid student test cases were 2224. In all the assignments, the mutant detection ratio (M = 42.2% ~ 87.2%, sd = 13.5%~ 25.9%) was significantly lower (Wilcoxon signed rank test, 855.5+, p < 0.0001) than the test coverage achieved (M = 93.8%~96.9%, sd = 17.2%~7.7%). From this result, it is clear that achieving a higher mutation score (better bug-revealing capability) was harder than achieving higher test coverage, supporting the belief that mutation analysis provides a better evaluation of test quality. However, we found that when students have larger design freedom in assignments, significant number of their tests examine components related to their personal design decisions. Such student-specific tests could not be evaluated against mutants generated from the reference solution. Outcome of our mutation analysis is published [11] in ICER, 2013. We are researching effective ways of generating feedback from the two approaches without revealing reference solutions or other students' solutions. Afterwards, we will develop a hybrid approach of all-pair testing and mutation analysis to evaluate student-written tests having variable amounts of design freedom.

Finally, to evaluate our secondary hypothesis we will create massive test-suites collecting all the students' tests over different semesters with the same assignments where students will receive feedback from three different measures: code coverage, all-pairs testing, and mutation analysis. We will analyze defect density, the number of bugs per thousands non-commented line of code, of students' solutions when they receive feedback from the three different approaches.

Our research outcome will provide educators and students insight into the quality of students' testing skills. Implementation of our solution to remove compile-time dependencies from the test cases will enable automated graders to evaluate partial solutions. Application of all-pairs testing and mutation analysis will encourage students to practice testing skills in many classes and will give them concrete feedback on their testing performance. As a result, students will learn to test their code well which will improve accuracy of their solution.

5. REFERENCES

[1] Aaltonen, K. *et al.* 2010. Mutation analysis vs. code coverage in automated assessment of students' testing skills, *Proc. of OOPSLA*, pp. 153-160, Nevada, USA.

[2] Chiba, S., and Nishizawa, M. 2003. An easy-to-use toolkit for efficient Java bytecode translators, *Proc. of the 2nd international conference on Generative programming and component engineering*, Erfurt, Germany.

[3] Desai, C. *et al.* 2009. Implications of integrating test-driven development into CS1/CS2 curricula, *SIGCSE Bull.,* vol. 41, pp. 148-152.

[4] Edwards, S. H. 2003. Using test-driven development in the classroom: Providing students with concrete feedback . *Proc. of the International Conference on Education and Information Systems: Technologies and Applications.*

[5] Edwards, S. H. 2004. Using software testing to move students from trial-and-error to reflection-in-action. *SIGCSE Bull.,* vol. 36, pp. 26-30.

[6] Edwards, S. H. *et al.* 2012. Running students' software tests against each others' code: new life for an old "gimmick". *Proc. of SIGCSE'12* , pp. 221-226, Raleigh, NC, USA.

[7] Goldwasser, M. H. 2002. A gimmick to integrate software testing throughout the curriculum. *SIGCSE Bull.,* vol. 34, pp. 271- 275.

[8] Janzen, D. S. and H. Saiedian. 2006. Test-driven learning: intrinsic integration of testing into the cs/se curriculum. *SIGCSE Bull.,* vol. 38, pp. 254–258.

[9] Schuler, D. and Zeller, A. 2011. Assessing Oracle Quality with Checked Coverage. *Proc. of ICST'11*, pp. 90-99.

[10] Shams, Z. and Edwards, S. H. 2013. ReflectionSupport: Java Refection Made Easy. to appear at *The Open Software Engineering Journal, TOSEJ.*

[11] Shams, Z., and Edwards, S. H. 2013. Toward Practical Mutation Analysis for Evaluating the Quality of Student-Written Software Tests. *Proc. of ICER*, pp. 53-58.

[12] Wilson, R. C. 1995. *UNIX test tools and benchmarks: methods and tools to design, develop, and execute functional, structural, reliability, and regression tests*: Prentice-Hall, Inc.

PyLOM: An Interpreted Language for Planning Applications

Scotty Smith

The George Washington University
cssmith@gwmail.gwu.edu

Abstract

Controlling software systems autonomously has been a challenging research area. Modern autonomous systems are guided by a plan, which is a sequence of actions to take to achieve a goal. Many planning algorithms exist today to produce plans given a problem definition and goal. To ease programmability of autonomous systems, many languages have been developed for defining problems and goals. However, planning algorithms tend to need to be customized not only for the problem definition language, but also for the problem definition itself. This work presents a new problem definition language called *PyLOM*, an interpreted, object-oriented language. The PyLOM run-time system uses generic algorithms, which do not need to be customized for each problem definition. Thus, PyLOM separates problem definitions from planning algorithms to ease programmability and software reuse. The choice of an object-oriented language also is intended to aid programmability, since prior problem definition languages adopt a functional programming style.

Categories and Subject Descriptors D.3.2 [*Programming Languages*]: Language Classifications—Object-oriented languages; D.3.0 [*Programming Languages*]: General

1. Problem

Creating software to autonomously control other software systems has been the focus of research since the 1960's. *Planning* is the act of computing a sequence of actions that accomplish some defined goal. Many general planning algorithms have been developed, such as A*[7], GraphPlan[4], and SATPlan[9]. These algorithms take a specially formatted problem definition and goal as inputs, and produce a sequence of actions, or plan, as outputs.

Planning algorithms do not specify how to formulate problem definitions. Programmers can use any mechanism for defining the problem, as long as the algorithm implementation is expecting that formulation. Research has worked towards developing generic problem definition languages, such as PDDL [10], NDDL [2], and MDLe [8]. These languages help to define planning problems.

Usually, planning algorithms are embedded in the applications that use the plan. This embedding adds complexity to the development of autonomous systems, since a planning algorithm must be implemented in each system that needs one. While object-oriented

abstractions such as classes and components have reduced this complexity slightly, many high-profile, successful autonomous systems still customize the planning algorithm for each problem definitions.

This research proposes a new problem definition language known as *PyLOM*[1]. PyLOM is a Python-based, interpreted, object oriented language that supports defining planning problems. The PyLOM run-time environment allows for using generic planning algorithms in a simple fashion. The run-time also allows for execution of plans outside of the PyLOM system.

2. Prior Work and Motivation

Early algorithms for planning were developed in the late $1960's$. STRIPS was developed at Stanford in 1968 as a definition language and planning engine, with a focus on solving simple, robotics based problems [6]. To this day, STRIPS acts as a basis for many problem definition languages.

Heavily influenced by STRIPS, PDDL is the de facto standard planning problem definition language. PDDL is a functional language that allows definition of objects and Boolean predicates involving those objects. Planners can be written to interpret these definitions, to produce a plan. However, planners often have to be configured to interpret PDDL, and may need to be configured specifically for the problem definition.

Many of the high-profile, successfully planned systems have come from NASA. In 1998, NASA launched the Deep Space 1 probe, the first mission in The New Millennium program [11]. This probe was launched in order to test out advanced technologies for future space flight missions. One of the advanced technologies being used was the Remote Agent autonomous system [1]. This system receives high-level goals from ground control, and autonomously generate a plan to achieve the specified goals. The goal of the system was to reduce the cost of robotic space flight missions by allowing actions to be planned and executed remotely, as opposed to being tele-operated from the ground.

The Spirit and Opportunity Martian Exploration Rovers were planned using a system known as Europa [2]. Europa is a Java-based framework for planning robotic missions that is partially based on the Remote Agent. Europa uses NDDL as the problem and robot definition languages. NDDL is a declarative language that borrows syntax from C++ and Java. The programmer must write not only the NDDL definitions, but also write planners specific to the problem definitions. The Mars Exploration Rovers use custom planning algorithms.

Bernardini and Smith [3] developed a custom state space search algorithm for problems defined using NDDL. Their approach is a guided depth-first search, using generic distance measurements as heuristics to guide the depth-first search. Their research also includes a custom control strategy, which allows for the execution

SPLASH '13,   October 26–31, 2013, Indianapolis, Indiana, USA.
Copyright is held by the owner/author(s).
ACM 978-1-4503-1995-9/13/10.
http://dx.doi.org/10.1145/2508075.2508079

---

[1] PyLOM stands for Python-based Language for Object Modeling

of plans generated by their system. Using their planning algorithm requires restrictions to how the problem is formulated, to facilitate the use of their custom built search algorithms.

In prior work, custom software must be produced to facilitate the use of the planning algorithm. PyLOM brings object orientation to problem definition languages to ease programmability and reduce the amount of custom code needed to use general planning algorithms.

3. Approach

At its core, PyLOM is heavily based on the Python syntax. Python 2.5 syntax has been modified to add several tokens to the language, necessary to determine the searchable state space. One of the core added features to PyLOM is a rudimentary typing system, which allows for the reduction of the state space. The PyLOM interpreter takes the problem as defined, and produces two separate Python files: one for the planners, and one for the plannable object that executes the plans produced by the PyLOM system.

Figure 3 shows a definition of the classical Towers of Hanoi problem. For the towers problem, three classes are defined: Tower, Disk, and Bottom. Class definitions work much the same way as normal class definitions in Python, with two major differences.

The first difference is that class attributes that are used in planning must be defined outside of the __init__ method. These attributes define what makes up the "state" of the object instance. They are defined outside __init__ for ease of extraction, and allows for typing information to be added. For example, the Disk class has three attributes to define its state: the size of the disk, the disk that it rests upon, and the tower it belongs to. The attributes are of type integer, Disk, and Tower respectively. The typing system extends to the parameter lists as well, which facilitates quick expansion of an operator to all possible actions that can be executed on that class.

The second difference pertains to how methods are defined for the classes. In addition to the traditional **def** keyword, three new keywords are used to distinguish between the methods that are defined for the planning algorithms, and the methods that are used for controlling of the planned system.

Note that the class Disk in Figure 3 has functions, predicates, and operators. Operators, such as Move, are used by the planning algorithms as actions that update the planner's state. Functions define how the system executes a planned action. Predicates are boolean functions that simplify specification of operators and functions.

Operators are of the form *if pre-conditions: post-conditions*, which follows traditional pre- and post-condition syntax of problem definition languages.

Functions are associated by name and parameter list to a defined operator, except for the __init__ function, which is included in both the planner file, and the execution file. Binding function and operator names allows for the PyLOM runtime to execute a plan directly by invoking functions in place of operations.

The PyLOM run-time environment facilitates the planning and execution of plans. The PyLOM run-time is influenced by the work on the Titan Executive system, co-developed by MIT and the Applied Physics Laboratory at Johns Hopkins University [5]. A high level overview can be seen in Figure 3. The PyLOM compiler is responsible for reading a specification file, and producing the two separate files that go to the planning and execution engines. The execution file can be run within the PyLOM engine as a simulation, or executed directly on an external system.

PyLOM defines a suite of generic planning algorithms that can be used. Currently, only A* is implemented to work with the system. Information from the problem definition files gets propagated to the planners by way of a programmer written translator. This translator is responsible for converting complex problem definitions to a form that the planner can understand and for translating

```
1   class Disk:
2       int size
3       Disk on
4       Tower t
5
6       function __init__(self, int size, Tower t, Disk on):
7           self.t = t
8           self.size = size
9           self.on = on
10
11      predicate smaller(self, Disk D2):
12          return self.size < D2.size
13
14      operator Move(self, Tower t2):
15          if(self.t.top == self and self.smaller(t2.top)):
16              self.t.top = self.on
17              self.on = t2.top
18              t2.top = self
19
20      function Move(self, Tower t2):
21          print("Move Disk " + self.size +
22              " from tower " + self.t +
23              " to " + t2)
24
25
26      predicate __eq__(self, other):
27          return (self.size == other.size
28              and self.on == other.on)
29
30  class Bottom(Disk):
31      function __init__(self, Tower t):
32          Disk.__init__(self, float("inf"), None, t)
33
34  class Tower:
35      Disk top
36      int id
37
38      function __init__(self, id):
39          self.top = Bottom(self)
40          self.id = id
41
42  class init:
43      Tower t1 = Tower(1)
44      Tower t2 = Tower(2)
45      Tower t3 = Tower(3)
46      Disk d4 = Disk(4, t1, t1.top)
47      Disk d3 = Disk(3, t1, d4)
48      Disk d2 = Disk(2, t1, d3)
49      Disk d1 = Disk(1, t1, d2)
50
51      function __init__(self):
52          d4.on = t1.top
53          d3.on = d4
54          d2.on = d3
55          d1.on = d2
56          t1.top = d1
```

Figure 1. The PyLOM definition of the Towers of Hanoi objects.

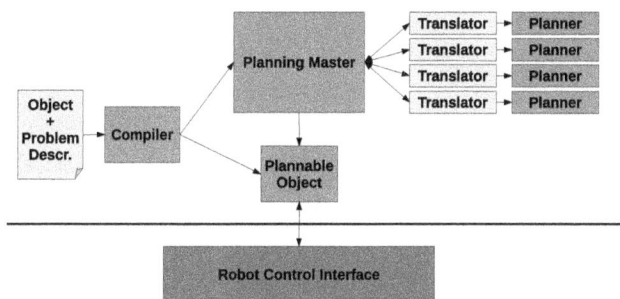

Figure 2. A high level view of the PyLOM Runtime.

plans back to executable actions for the plannable objects. Most problem def nitions can use an included generic translator. The translator mechanisms may be needed for more complex problem domains.

PyLOM delegates control between the planners, and the plannable objects. Plannable objects communicate to the PyLOM run-time via sockets, which allows for the plannable object to either execute as part of the PyLOM run-time, or externally on the system that is being planned for, such as a robotic system. The `init` class def nes what plannable objects are created at run-time, and only objects which def ne operations have plannable objects generated.

4. Evaluation Methodology

PyLOM brings object oriented programming to the domain of problem def nition languages in order to reduce the complexity of def ning problems, interfacing with planners, and executing plans. Although problem def nition lines of code (LOC) seems like an intuitive metric for success, LOC does not account for all of the bene-f ts of object oriented programming. At current time, PyLOM def-initions tend to be slightly larger than PDDL def nitions, partially because PyLOM def nitions contain some information relevant for the planning and execution that PDDL def nitions lack.

I have created a couple of simulated environments for full evaluation of the PyLOM system. The f rst simulated environment is known as GridWorld. GridWorld is a 32×27 grid based 2-d environment. Each grid location can be set as occupied, or unoccupied. Occupied grid locations cannot be traversed, and are essentially obstacles in this environment. GridWorld provides one class, called "robots", which are the "actionable" entities. The robots in grid world are two-wheeled, with an eight-way sensor array that uses simulated laser range sensors that originate from the center of the robot. The robots can be controlled in two separate modes: discrete and continuous. In the discrete mode, the robot can be turned right or left, or move forward. In continuous mode, each wheel can have a speed set independently.

GridWorld has targets that can be placed in any unoccupied grid location. These targets can be picked up by the robot, and placed in any unoccupied grid location orthogonally adjacent to the current location of the robot. These targets act as goals for the robots to achieve. Typical scenarios in GridWorld are target acquisition and target fetch and return. The GridWorld simulator allows for varying environment parameters, such as sensor and actuation noise. Grid World also allows for the specif cation of "Monster" robots, which currently use very simple algorithms in an attempt to provide temporal environmental changes.

Another simulator we have developed is a simulator for a multi-link arm problem. The environment is a 2-d continuous environment that allows for the manipulation of an arm, which is represented by a series of nodes joined by rigid links. Each node, with

the exception of the nodes at the two ends of the arm, can be un-folded to extend the reach of the arm. In this scenario, a target is placed in the environment, and several rectangular shaped objects can be specif ed to occupy the environment. The goal of the simulation is to unfold the arm into a conf guration where the f nal node intersects the target.

For evaluation, we plan on comparing PDDL and a custom planner against PyLOM for several working scenarios in both simulators. Using these setups, we will compare the LOC and run-time performance of a full PDDL plan and execute system against PyLOM using the same planning algorithm.

5. Conclusions

This paper introduced PyLOM, an object-oriented language for planning problem def nition and execution. With the simulators described in Section 4, I plan on quantitatively evaluating the benef ts of bringing the object-oriented abstractions to the domain of problem def nition languages. Through comparisons against PDDL, the de facto standard for planning problem def nitions, I strive to determine what aspects of PyLOM provide the greatest advantages to the programmer.

Future evaluations include comparisons against other problem def nition languages, specif cally NDDL. I also want to connect to more in-depth simulated environments, such as those included with ROS.

References

[1] Remote agent. NASA, May 1999. http://ti.arc.nasa.gov/tech/asr/planning-and-scheduling/remote-agent/.

[2] T. Bedrax-Weiss, J. Frank, A. Jónsson, and C. McGann. Europa2: Plan database services for planning and scheduling applications. 2004.

[3] S. Bernardini and D. E. Smith. Developing domain-independent search control for europa2. In *Proc. of the Workshop on Heuristics for Domain-independent Planning, 17th Int. Conference on Automated Planning and Scheduling (ICAPS07)*, 2007.

[4] A. L. Blum and M. L. Furst. Fast planning through planning graph analysis. *ARTIFICIAL INTELLIGENCE*, 90(1):1636–1642, 1995.

[5] L. Fesq, M. Ingham, M. Pekala, J. V. Eepoel, D. Watson, and B. Williams. Model-based autonomy for the next generation of robotic spacecraft, 2002.

[6] R. E. Fikes and N. J. Nilsson. Strips: A new approach to the application of theorem proving to problem solving. *Artif cial Intelligence*, 2(34): 189 – 208, 1971. ISSN 0004-3702. .

[7] P. Hart, N. Nilsson, and B. Raphael. A formal basis for the heuristic determination of minimum cost paths. *Systems Science and Cybernetics, IEEE Transactions on*, 4(2):100–107, 1968.

[8] D. Hristu-Varsakelis, M. Egerstedt, and P. S. Krishnaprasad. On the structural complexity of the motion description language mdle. In *Decision and Control, 2003. Proceedings. 42nd IEEE Conference on*, volume 4, pages 3360–3365 vol.4, 2003.

[9] H. Kautz and B. Selman. Planning as satisf ability. In *Tenth European Conference on Artif cial Intelligence*, 1992. Vienna, Austria.

[10] D. McDermott, M. Ghallab, A. Howe, C. Knoblock, A. Ram, M. Veloso, D. Weld, and D. Wilkins. Pddl-the planning domain def-nition language. 1998.

[11] M. D. Rayman, P. Varghese, D. H. Lehman, and L. L. Livesay. Results from the deep space 1 technology validation mission. *Acta Astronautica*, 47(2):475–487, 2000.

Implementing A Scripting Language Parser with Self-Extensible Syntax

Masahiro Ide

Yokohama National University, Japan
ide@konohascript.org

Abstract

Today, many developers try to create a new scripting language to provide scripting features to their own application domain. We proposed The DeSugar parser that provides a flexible means of extending the user-defined syntax by scripting. The goal of the DeSugar parser is to make it easier for users to adopt the language syntax to their own application domain. This paper presents Konoha, which is fully integrated with the DeSugar parser, and which allows users to extend its own syntax through the DeSugar parser scripting interfaces.

Categories and Subject Descriptors   D.3.4 [*Programming Languages*]: Processors-parsing

General Terms   Languages

Keywords   Scripting Language, Syntax Sugar

1. Introduction

Many scripting languages are embedded in software as a means of extending the functionality of their hosted software. Typical examples are emacs lisp (shown in Emacs) and JavaScript (in Web browsers). As shown in these examples, embedded scripts play an integral role in improving the usability of hosted software. The idea we present in this paper is on the same line; we attempt to use a scripting language as a means to extend its own syntax and programming features.

An arising question is why a scripting language with self-extensible syntax is necessary. To answer this question, we would like to argue why a new language is necessary. The usage of a scripting language is spreading from web programming and system administration to a new problem domains, such as embedded and high performance computing[3]. Adapting the existing popular scripting languages, such as Python and Ruby, to new domains is not easy, because the requirement for programming varies from domain to domain. For example, floating point numbers are not necessary in many embedded computing cases[1, 4]. Thus, many developers try to create a new scripting language to provide scripting features to their own application domain.

SPLASH '13,   October 26–31, 2013, Indianapolis, Indiana, USA.
Copyright is held by the owner/author(s).
ACM 978-1-4503-1995-9/13/10.
http://dx.doi.org/10.1145/2508075.2508080

Our goal is implementing a scripting language core that can be easier adapted to variety domains of programming. The approach we present is the extensible parser by scripting. We call our scripting language core, Konoha. And we call our proposed parser, DeSugar parser. Here is a list of the extension points that the Desugar parser provided:

- Tokenizer (for any letters)
- Syntax pattern matcher (for any patterns)
- Type Checker

Recently, existing approaches to provide syntactically extending a programming language within the language such as Scala and SugarJ[2] have appeared. Unlike these compilers, scripting languages need to integrate the parser into the runtime system. Since the syntax extension requires in part the functionality of some parser generators, such as lex and yacc, the compactness of implementing such a parser is one of key challenges. We achieve the compactness by introducing token patterns that are flexible gateway for script functions. Konoha is an open source software and readers can download from the following site:
Konoha is an open source software and the readers can download from the following site:

https://github.com/konoha-project/konoha3

2. Related Work

There is much work that is related to our approach including other extensible programming languages.

SugarJ[2] is an extension of Java and SugarJ supports the definition of syntactic sugar within libraries. Each syntactic sugar specified a transformation from the extended syntax into the base syntax. In Konoha, users can redefine a syntax and can extend extend the rule of type checking including Konoha's pre-defined syntax.

In contrast to SugarJ and similar to Lisp, Racket[7] and Honu[6] provide facilities for adapting its lexical syntax using reader macro. In Racket, the capability of the syntactically extension is limited to the host language syntax. To support a syntax unconstrained by parentheses, Honu adds a parsing step for converting a flat stream of tokens into an S-expression-like tree. In Konoha, users can extend the class of tokens through the API for extending lexical analysis. In contrast, Racket and Honu does not contain a mechanism for extending its lexical analysis of the raw input data.

Polyglot[5] provides language extensions through extensible compiler. Unlike Konoha, Polygot uses a meta-language to provide language extension. Consequently, users cannot develop extensions with the extension that already exisiting because the extended language is different from the meta-language.

3. Desugar parser

The DeSugar parser is a flexible parser that is controlled by scripting. It provides users with programmable interfaces to its tokenizer, AST constructor, and type checker. This section shows the overview of the DeSugar parser.

3.1 Overview

DeSugar parser provides a range of features for syntactic extension, which can be added written by a scripting. In the same way as a parser without syntactic extensibility, DeSugar performs lexical analysis, syntax analysis, and type checking and code generation. From the viewpoint of syntactic extensibility, DeSugar parser provides hook points in each stage of parsing, which consist of three stages: in tokenizing, in syntax analyzing and in typing. Note that the parser of the built-in syntax on Konoha uses hook points. By inserting functions that intercept parsing, we can easily extend the definition of syntax. Figure 1 shows the architecture of DeSugar parser. It read source code and then generates executable code on a target system.

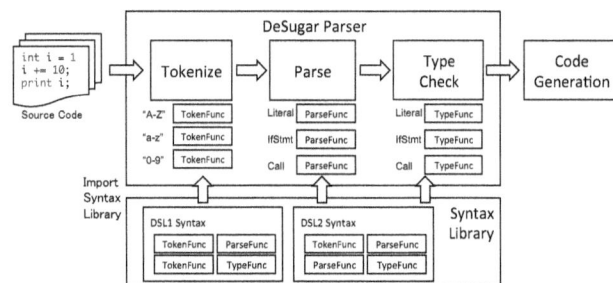

Figure 1. Overview of Desugar Parser

In the following sections, to illustrate the concept of the DeSugar parser, we take a running example: the extension of the while statement. The syntax of the while statement is defined with the sugar statement:

```
sugar $while "where" "(" $expr ")" $block
```

The sugar statement is a built-in statement to define a syntax rule. A syntax rule is a sequential pattern of tokens, specified by keywords and patterns. Keywords, such as "while" and "(", are means that exactly the same token is required. "$block" and $expr are token patterns, which are used as a part of more complex pattern of sequences.

3.2 Tokenizer

Tokenizing is the first stage of Desugar parser. Desugar parser splits source code into tokens. Each character has one and more **TokenFunc** functions that are set in the hook point and intercepts tokenizing. TokenFunc has following interface:

```
int TokenFunc (Token token, String src);
```

If a TokenFunc cannot tokenize source code, next TokenFunc function will be called until it succeeds. Taking the character "/" as a simple example, it might be valid for comment ("//") or division sign. Thus, function that tokenizes both comment and division sign are relevant to the character "/". Programmer can customize tokenizer with how to cut out the token by defining the tokenize function for the character class.

3.3 Syntax Matcher

Parsing is the second stage of DeSugar parser. DeSugar parser makes abstract syntax tree (AST) from token sequence. Syntax analyzing proceeds by the use of backtracking, since various functions

are inserted into hook point. We use a **ParseFunc** function to transform a sequence of tokens to an AST form. The ParseFunc function has the following interface.

```
UntypedAST ParseFunc (Token [] toks,
      int start, int end);
```

Each pattern is associated with one and more ParseFunc functions. If a pattern function matches with some input tokens (given by token arrays toks[start,end]), the part of the statement stmt is updated with the parsed result. Since the while statement defined in the sugar statement has $expr and $block parts, the following input:

```
while(a < 100) {
  System.println(a)
}
```

is parsed to an AST form :

```
stmt "while" {
  $expr := (< a 100)
  $block := [
    stmt "$expr" {
      $expr := (println System a)
    }
  ]
}
```

Note that for readability we use S-Expression to denote parsed expressions. The blocks are a list of statements. The statements are key-value data, as defined by the sugar statement. In addition, An AST specified by extended syntax (Ext-AST) exists along with an AST originally specified by Konoha (Host-AST).

3.4 Type Checker

Type Checking is the third stage of Desugar parser. An untyped AST generated on the previous stage is verified by static type-checking. Type Checker performs the name resolution and grants type information to AST (we call this Typed-AST). After typed AST passes through type-checking, Ext-AST will be replaced with the combination of Host-AST. Finally, a code generator translates Host-AST into a target code.

4. Imprementation

Konoha is a small (and hopefully minimalistic) language is designed to allow the users to program the TokenFunc, the ParseFunc, and type checkers described in the previous section. In addition, Konoha has an integrated sugar parser, which means that its syntax can be extended by itself.

Many of language features are removed, including class declaration, object-oriented operations, type inference, and the while statement. These features could be extendable by the sugar parser with the user-defined syntax. Main features remaining are:

- C-style grammar (subset of C)
- static typing
- types: boolean, int, String, Array, Func(function)
- method definition/method call
- if statement, return statement

All of functionalities the DeSugar parser are controlled by programmable interfaces (called Sugar API). The Sugar API is provided for Konoha (as an external library and available by importing:

```
Import("DeSugar");
```

Figure 2 shows how to integrate the syntax of JavaScript Object Notation (JSON) [1] using update scheme of the syntax association.

---

[1] http://json.org/

```
Import("DeSugar");                                    ⎫ Importing Already
Import("Common.String");                              ⎬ Defined Syntax
Import("Common.Number");                              ⎭

sugar $JSON    = "{"$Members "}" / "{" "}" {…}        ⎫
sugar $Members = $Pair* {…}                           ⎪
sugar $Pair    = $Common.String ":" Value {…}         ⎪
sugar $Value   = $Common.String / $Common.Number /    ⎪
                 $JSON / $Array / "true" / "false" / "null" ⎪
{                                                     ⎪
       // Make AST from token sequence                ⎪
    UntypedAST AST = new UntypedAST ();               ⎪
    AST.SetProperty("Value", $0);                     ⎪
}                                                     ⎬ Definition of
                                                      ⎪ JSON Syntax
@Typecheck $Value = function(UntypedAST AST) {        ⎪
       // Type check                                  ⎪
    TypedAST Value = AST.TypeCheck("Value");          ⎪
    if(Value.isValid() == false)                      ⎪
       return new ErrorAST("Type Error at Value");    ⎪
    return Value;                                     ⎪
}                                                     ⎪
@Typecheck $JSON  = function(UntypedAST node){…}      ⎪
}                                                     ⎭

JSON Json = {"Key" : "Value"};                        ⎫ Host language with
String[] a = Json.Keys();                             ⎬ JSON Syntax
                                                      ⎭
```

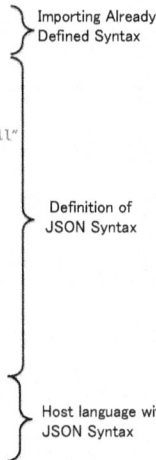

Figure 2. Definition of JSON syntax in Konoha

Import function is a function for loading the syntax definition from already defined syntax. After loading "Common.String" and "Common.Number" syntax, JSON syntax module would be able to use Tokenizer for numbers and strings. Each syntax pattern starts with "sugar" keyword. Desugar parser uses these de-sugared syntax patterns to make AST from token sequence. Function definition with @Typecheck annotations indicates type checker for AST. Using the function set of these definitions, Desugar parser is able to parse JSON.

5. Evaluation Methodology

A prototype has been developed to understand the feasibility of our approach.

Our primary hypothesis is that it is that minimized built-in syntax does not lose programmability and does not affect the runtime. To evaluate our hypotheses, we re-implementing existed DSLs and other approaches and compare processing speed and memory usage to reveal what kind of the processing affect the performance.

Another secondary hypothesis is that the DeSugar parser provides the ability to express syntax equal to existing approaches and syntax definition formalisms. To evaluate this hypothesis, we will also develop a translator that converts a syntax defined by DeSugar API to other syntax definition formalism (e.g., Parsing Expression Grammar (PEG)) and we compare to verify our approach.

6. Conclusion

In this paper, we proposed Desugar parser that provides a flexible means of extending the user-defined syntax by scripting. To adopt Desugar parser into scripting languages, we minimized built-in syntax and simple-hook point base extensible parser. Using Desugar parser, the users can adopt syntax and its underlying language features to their own application domain.

Acknowledgments

The work is founded by Japan Science and Technology Agency: CREST "Dependable Embedded Operating System for Practical Use". The author would like to thank the OOPSLA anonymous reviewers for their helpful comments.

References

[1] A. Dunkels. A low-overhead script language for tiny networked embedded systems, 2006.

[2] S. Erdweg, T. Rendel, C. Kästner, and M. Ostermann. Sugarj: library-based syntactic language extensibility. In *Proceedings of the 2011 ACM international conference on Object oriented programming systems languages and applications*, OOPSLA '11, pages 391–406, New York, NY, USA, 2011. ACM. ISBN 978-1-4503-0940-0. . URL http://doi.acm.org/10.1145/2048066.2048099.

[3] P. Liggesmeyer and M. Trapp. Trends in embedded software engineering. *IEEE Softw.*, 26(3):19–25, May 2009. ISSN 0740-7459. . URL http://dx.doi.org/10.1109/MS.2009.80.

[4] R. Müller, G. Alonso, and D. Kossmann. A virtual machine for sensor networks. In *Proceedings of the 2nd ACM SIGOPS/EuroSys European Conference on Computer Systems 2007*, EuroSys '07, pages 145–158, New York, NY, USA, 2007. ACM. ISBN 978-1-59593-636-3. . URL http://doi.acm.org/10.1145/1272996.1273013.

[5] N. Nystrom, M. R. Clarkson, and A. C. Myers. Polyglot: an extensible compiler framework for java. In *Proceedings of the 12th international conference on Compiler construction*, CC'03, pages 138–152, Berlin, Heidelberg, 2003. Springer-Verlag. ISBN 3-540-00904-3. URL http://dl.acm.org/citation.cfm?id=1765931.1765947.

[6] J. Rafkind and M. Flatt. Honu: syntactic extension for algebraic notation through enforestation. In *Proceedings of the 11th International Conference on Generative Programming and Component Engineering*, GPCE '12, pages 122–131, New York, NY, USA, 2012. ACM. ISBN 978-1-4503-1129-8. . URL http://doi.acm.org/10.1145/2371401.2371420.

[7] S. Tobin-Hochstadt, V. St-Amour, R. Culpepper, M. Flatt, and M. Felleisen. Languages as libraries. In *Proceedings of the 32nd ACM SIGPLAN conference on Programming language design and implementation*, PLDI '11, pages 132–141, New York, NY, USA, 2011. ACM. ISBN 978-1-4503-0663-8. . URL http://doi.acm.org/10.1145/1993498.1993514.

Program Transformation Techniques Applied to Languages Used in High Performance Computing

Songqing Yue

Department of Computer Science
University of Alabama
Tuscaloosa
Alabama 35401, USA
syue@cs.ua.edu

Abstract

Meta-programming has shown much promise for improving the quality of software. A system that supports meta-programming is able to generate or manipulate other programs to extend their behaviour. Thus far, the power of meta-programming has not been explored deeply in the area of High Performance Computing (HPC). We propose to bring the power of meta-programming to languages that may be used in HPC to help to solve various problems in HPC software related to efficiency, scalability, and adaptation. In our initial efforts we have implemented a meta-programming framework called OpenFortran to build arbitrary source-to-source program transformation libraries for Fortran programs. The design focus of OpenFortran is to enable program transformation in a manner that is transparent to application programmers. Similarly, we have also built a framework for C called OpenC. In this doctoral symposium summary, we present the idea of building a generalized meta-programming framework suitable for extending an arbitrary programming language, which would allow source-to-source program transformation. We also describe the possibility of solving problems emerging in HPC software via program transformation.

Categories and Subject Descriptors D.3.4 [**Programming Languages**]: Translator writing systems and compiler generators.

General Terms Design, Languages.

Keywords Program Transformation; High Performance Computing

1. Motivation for Transforming HPC Software

Meta-programming refers to the technique of writing programs that generate or manipulate other programs. Meta-programming can be used to improve the quality of software by offering programming language techniques to address issues of modularity, reusability, maintainability, and extensibility. A meta-object protocol (MOP) enables the extension or redefinition of a program's semantics to make it open and extensible [1]. A MOP is a powerful tool that provides meta-programming by means of object-oriented and reflective techniques [1]. A MOP provides an interface that can be used to modify the internal implementation of a program. Through the interface, programmers can incrementally change the implementation and the behaviour of a program to better suit their needs. Compared with Aspect-Oriented programming (AOP), the MOP-based approach is able to overcome the limitations imposed by AOP by providing a richer interface that can be used to deal with a wider range of transformation challenges that are not limited to crosscutting concerns in more diverse scenarios.

MOPs have been implemented for a few mainstream object-oriented languages, for example OpenC++ [2] for C++ and OpenJava [3] for Java. However, there are no MOPs existing for Fortran and C, which are two programming languages widely used in High Performance Computing (HPC). There is a vast body of legacy code written in Fortran and C that has been written to address HPC concerns, where both Fortran and C remain the preferred programming languages in HPC [4][5]. In addition, it is often very expensive to make changes to legacy code on a large scale [6]. The procedural paradigm and lower-level programming constructs make Fortran or C applications even more difficult to maintain and evolve.

In order to facilitate software maintenance and evolution in HPC systems, we introduce the power of meta-programming to Fortran and C by the means of a MOP. At the initial stage of our research, we have implemented OpenFortran for Fortran and OpenC for C. With OpenFortran and OpenC, source-to-source program transformation libraries can be built and then applied in a manner that is transparent, whereby application programmers only need to add a simple annotation, while removing the need to know the details on how the transformations are performed. We have used OpenFortran to build a simple profiling tool and a code coverage analysis tool for Fortran programs. Our experience has shown that the MOP mechanism, as a form of program extension, can be used to address a wide range of problems by facilitating the implementation of source-to-source program translators, especially suitable for those dealing with crosscutting issues like logging, profiling and checkpointing.

In this doctoral symposium summary, we describe our use of MOPs to address problems in HPC by identifying new requirements on HPC software imposed by evolution in the hardware and by the ever-increasing user demands. There is a lack of infrastructure support for language extension in the way of building a MOP for an arbitrary language. Therefore, we also propose to build a generalized framework, named OpenFoo, suitable for extending an arbitrary programming language by

SPLASH'13, October 26–31, 2013, Indianapolis, Indiana, USA.
ACM 978-1-4503-1995-9/13/10.

creating a MOP for the language. The design goal is to allow end-users to specify source-to-source transformation to programs written in the language. In addition, we will simplify the use of OpenFoo by building a DSL on top of OpenFoo (working on the meta-meta-level) to achieve the abstraction for expressing program transformations.

2. Challenge Problems for HPC Software

HPC aims at providing solutions to problems that require massive computational power. Rapid advances in hardware architectures for HPC have been observed recently [7], which implies higher requirements on HPC software. However, the software development and evolution for HPC often is not as mature as the hardware. We have surveyed several strategies dealing with different problems in HPC software. However, many issues are raised when attempting to integrate those strategies into practical applications. One major problem involves flexibility; for example, transparency, ease of use and reusability of existing strategies to derive new ones. Another problem is caused by the fact that most systems in HPC are computationally sensitive and thus the performance should not be impaired by applying a strategy.

Meta-programming has shown initial promise in many contexts, such as in the design of development environments, language extension, and the dynamic, unanticipated adaptation of running systems. Additionally, meta-programming can separate the base concerns of the application from other orthogonal concerns. Therefore, we are investigating the possibility of applying meta-programming techniques to implement software development and maintenance tools that are able address issues with the following characteristics [8]: 1) adaptive – being adapted automatically to problem characteristics or environmental restrictions, 2) easy to use – being able to provide efficient and portable libraries, and 3) secure and accountable – very critical to maintaining the correctness and to enhance fault tolerance and robustness of HPC systems [9]. This is particularly true for systems with clusters or grids where computational nodes are distributed physically and connected through high-speed links.

3. Research Approach

In this session, we will first introduce the preliminary results of our research about the implementation of the OpenFortran framework. Then, we will outline the proposed research plans.

3.1 OpenFortran Design

To facilitate software maintenance and evolution in systems coded in Fortran, we developed a MOP for Fortran, named OpenFortran. Similar to Open C++ [2], OpenFotran is mainly a mechanism for library developers who are responsible for developing transformation libraries with the facilities provided by OpenFortran. The libraries that work at the meta-level are able to inspect and modify the static internal data structures of base-level programs, as well as to intercept function calls and variable accesses to add new behaviour to base-level programs written in Fortran.

The benefit of OpenFortran to scientists and application programmers writing HPC software is that they can use the libraries to translate the application code in a transparent and repeated way. By their nature, most HPC systems are computationally sensitive and thus the performance should not be impaired by applying transformations. Therefore, we pursued an implementation of OpenFortran that offers control over compilation rather than over the run-time execution to avoid run-time penalties.

In the infrastructure shown in Figure 1, the base-level program is Fortran source code including annotations. The meta-level program refers to the libraries developed to perform transformations on the base-level code. OpenFortran takes the meta-level transformation libraries and base-level Fortran code as input and generates the extended Fortran code. The extended Fortran code is composed of both the original and newly generated Fortran code and can be compiled by a traditional Fortran compiler. In our approach, the low-level transformation is achieved by an open source compiler infrastructure ROSE [10] to which the Open Fortran Parser (OFP) [11] is used as a front-end to support Fortran.

The top-level entities in Fortran, such as modules and functions, are represented by meta-objects in OpenFortran that can be manipulated to control the behaviour of the program. The working mechanism of OpenFortran can be described as source-to-source translation performed in the following steps:

1. The base-level Fortran source code is parsed and the top-level definitions are identified.

2. The parse tree is traversed and, for any interested top-level definitions, a corresponding meta-object is constructed.

3. A member function of the meta-object is called to modify the abstract syntax tree (AST) to perform transformations.

4. The parse trees created by all meta-objects are synthesized and transformed back to Fortran code, which is then processed by a general Fortran compiler.

3.2 Research Plan

To build a generalized framework that is able to accommodate an arbitrary programming language by creating a meta-object protocol for the language, we propose the following approach as illustrated in Figure 2. To make usage of MOP facilities more natural and concise, we are working on a new DSL, named PTOF, that sits on top of OpenFoo (working on the meta-meta-level) to achieve the abstraction for expressing program transformations. The design focus is to make PTOF easy to learn and use and thus increase the productivity of developing transformation libraries. End-users can specify translation for their code by using the constructs provided by PTOF. A code generator accepts transformation specification in PTOF as input and generates the actual transformation code. OpenFoo is responsible for carrying out the specified transformations on application code. PTOF will provide grammars to identify and create language constructs, such as a variable, a statement, a function, etc. and grammars to customize these constructs with several attributes.

To provide an OpenFoo instance for a new programming language, a transformation tool is required either to integrate a full front-end for the language or to provide some mechanism to

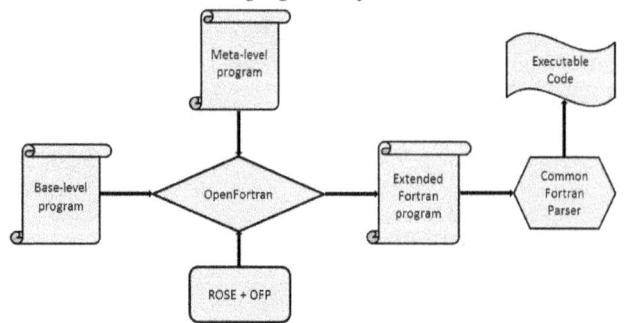

Figure 1. Overview of the OpenFortran transformation process

take as input a grammar description that is used to automatically parse inputs in the language defined by the grammar. OpenFoo integrates ANTLR [12] as the language recognition tool that takes as input a context-free grammar in Extended Backus-Naur Form (EBNF) defining the language and generates as output a recognizer for that language. Besides lexers and parsers, ANTLR can generate tree parsers used to process abstract syntax trees that can be produced by parsers [12].

In our future efforts, we will utilize OpenFoo to extend the languages used in HPC software, which may be a general-purpose language or a domain-specific language. With the MOP extension, we will implement transformation tools to address the following three problems in HPC:

1. Profiling is a technique that is able to provide a general view on source locations where time is consumed [13]. It is very useful for developers to understand the performance characteristics of the computing elements. We have implemented a very simple profiling library that is able to compute the time spent on each procedure during execution in a project with OpenFortran. One goal is to extend the profiling library to make it more powerful in dealing with different issues of performance measurement, easier to use and more portable for platforms using different programming languages. One important future need is support for HPC applications using MPI or OpenMP, which are standards that are used widely in the HPC community.

2. Checkpointing is a technique that provides fault-tolerance to HPC systems by saving a snapshot of the current system state and then utilizing it to restart the execution in case of failure [14]. We plan to add a checkpointing capability to applications in the way of auto-transformation that allows implementing application-level checkpointing. In our solution, we provide the clients the control over choosing: a) What to save and the tool is able to identify the right place to do checkpointing, and b) How often to save, that is the optimal checkpoint placement interval for their own systems based on the analysis of historical data concerning system failures, which is essential in performance sensitive systems.

3. Code coverage analysis is a means of determining the quantitative measure of the extent to which the source code of a program is covered by running a test suite. Our solution will support both statement coverage and branch coverage analysis across different scope and granularities. Through OpenFoo, client users will be able to switch meta-objects easily to achieve the desired coverage information. The coverage tool will be highly configurable to perform code coverage analysis in different scenarios by utilizing different keywords.

4. Evaluation

To assess potential influence of our research, we will perform a series of experimental evaluations using various experimental techniques, primarily from case studies derived from the challenges mentioned. We will investigate the impact on case studies by applying transformation libraries developed with OpenFoo to a few known benchmark applications in HPC. Comparison will be made to show how efficient and accurate OpenFoo can be used to perform program transformations.

5. Conclusion

In summary, we first presented our efforts in building a MOP framework for Fortran. Inspired by our initial work, we propose to generalize the OpenFoo framework to make it suitable for generating a MOP, not only for Fortran, but also for other programming languages. In order to simplify the usage of an Open-Foo instance, we plan to create a DSL, called PTOF, on top of OpenFoo (working on the meta-meta-level) to achieve the abstraction for expressing program transformations. We will continue to investigate the possibility of using OpenFoo to implement libraries that are able to address real issues in HPC, such as profiling, checkpointing and code coverage.

References

[1] Kiczales, G., Rivieres, J., and Bobrow, D., "The Art of the Metaobject Protocol," The MIT Press, 1991.

[2] Chiba, S., "A Metaobject Protocol for C++," *Conference on Object-Oriented Programming Systems, Languages, and Applications*, Austin, TX, October 1995, pp. 285-299.

[3] Tatsubori, M., Chiba, S., Killijian, M., and Itano, K., "OpenJava: A Class-Based Macro System for Java," *Reflection and Software Engineering*, Denver, CO, November 1999, pp. 117-133.

[4] Ceruzzi, P. E., "A History of Modern Computing," MIT Press, Cambridge, MA, 1998.

[5] Loh, E., (2010). "The Ideal HPC Programming Language," *Commun. ACM*, 53(7), 42-47.

[6] Bennett, K. H., & Rajlich, V. T. (2000, May). Software maintenance and evolution: a roadmap. In *Proceedings of the Conference on the Future of Software Engineering* (pp. 73-87). ACM..

[7] Bell, G., Gray, J., "What's next in high-performance computing," *Communications of the ACM*, Volume 45 Issue 2, Feb. 2002

[8] Trefethen, A., Higham, N., Duff, I., & Coveney, P. (2009). "Developing a high performance computing/numerical analysis roadmap." *International Journal of High Performance Computing Applications*, 23(4), 423-426.

[9] Yue, S., & Xiao, Y. (2010, December). "Building global view with log files in a distributed/network system," In *Global Telecommunications Conference* (GLOBECOM 2010), 2010 IEEE (pp. 1-5). IEEE.

[10] ROSE, http://rosecompiler.org/

[11] Open Fortran Parser, http://fortran-parser.sourceforge.net/

[12] Parr, Terence (May 17, 2007), The Definitive Antlr Reference: Building Domain-Specific Languages (1st ed.), Pragmatic Bookshelf, p. 376.

[13] Fürlinger, K., & Gerndt, M. (2008). ompP: A profiling tool for OpenMP, In *OpenMP Shared Memory Parallel Programming* (pp. 15-23). Springer Berlin Heidelberg.

[14] Elnozahy, E. N., Alvisi, L., Wang, Y. M., & Johnson, D. B. (2002). "A survey of rollback-recovery protocols in message-passing systems," *ACM Computing Surveys* (CSUR), 34(3), 375-408.

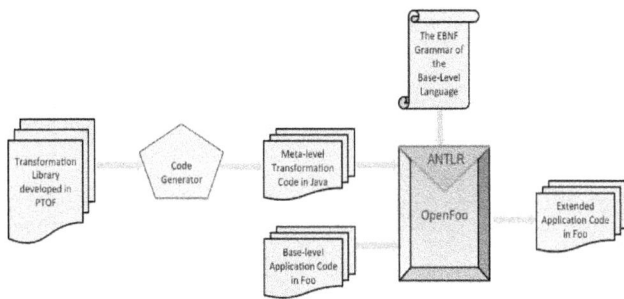

Figure 2. Program transformation process using OpenFoo

Effective Fusion and Separation of Distribution, Fault-Tolerance, and Energy-Efficiency Concerns

Young-Woo Kwon

Software Innovations Lab, Virginia Tech
ywkwon@cs.vt.edu

Abstract

As modern software applications are becoming increasingly distributed and mobile, their design and implementation are characterized by distributed software architectures, possibility of faults, and the need for energy awareness. Thus, software developers should be able to simultaneously reason about and handle the concerns of distribution, fault-tolerance, and energy efficiency. Being closely intertwined, these concerns can introduce significant complexity into the design and implementation of modern software. Thus, to develop reliable and energy efficient applications, software developers must understand how distribution, fault-tolerance, and energy efficiency interplay with each other and how to implement these concerns while keeping the complexity in check. This paper studies these concerns and their interaction; it also develops novel approaches, techniques, and tools that effectively fuse and separate these concerns as required by particular software development scenarios.

Categories and Subject Descriptors   C.2.4 [*Distributed Systems*]: Distributed applications

General Terms   Language, Design, Experimentation

Keywords   Distribution; fault-tolerance; energy-efficiency; middleware; cloud computing

1. Introduction

A combination of naïve implementation practices and the extreme heterogeneity of mobile computing platforms makes it hard to ensure that distributed mobile applications are always reliable and energy efficient. Because centralized and distributed applications have different failure modes, simply rendering a subset of a centralized application remote does not preserve the original semantics. Distributed applications are subject to partial failure, in which its different components (client, server, or network) may fail independently from each other. Although one cannot handle all the possible failures in a distributed application, some failures have well-known handling strategies. Thus, to better preserve the original execution semantics, programmers must change code to transition applications to use cloud-based services and add proper fault

handling functionality to any application that invokes services remotely. Moreover, most distributed applications coordinate the execution of multiple remote processes through middleware, which provides programming and runtime support for one process to execute functionality in a different process. Because network communication is one of the largest sources of energy consumption [11], the choice and parameterization of middleware can reduce the amount of energy consumed by a distributed application.

This research enhances the current state of the art in developing distributed mobile software through innovations in automated program transformations and distributed programming abstractions, making the following contributions:

- **Automated program transformations for the transitioning to distributed applications**: A set of refactoring techniques facilitate the process of transforming centralized applications to use remote services. These techniques automate the program transformations required to render portions of functionality of a centralized applications as remote services and re-target the application to access the remote functionality.

- **Hardening distributed applications with resiliency against partial failures** [7]: A declarative approach for hardening distributed applications with resiliency against partial failures—we introduce a domain-specific language for describing both failures and the hardening strategies to eliminate them.

- **Energy-efficient distributed execution through offloading** [4, 6]: An effective energy consumption optimization approach efficiently and fault-tolerantly synchronizes execution state between the mobile device and remote server to provide energy-efficient and reliable mobile execution.

- **Middleware with dynamic adaptation capabilities:** Energy-aware adaptive middleware enables the programmer to express how to dynamically adapt middleware execution patterns in the presence of volatile mobile networks, so as to reduce the mobile application's energy consumption.

- **Systematic assessment of distributed applications across middleware** [5, 8]: A novel mechanism can accurately assess the performance, conciseness, complexity, reliability, and energy consumption of distributed applications across middleware for accessing remote functionality.

- **An empirical evaluation**: We will apply our approach to a set of benchmarks and third-party mobile applications to show how to effectively reduce the energy consumed by the applications.

2. Research Overview

A refactoring—a semantics preserving program transformation performed under programmer control [3]—has become a popular

SPLASH '13,   October 26–31, 2013, Indianapolis, Indiana, USA.
Copyright is held by the owner/author(s).
ACM 978-1-4503-1995-9/13/10.
http://dx.doi.org/10.1145/2508075.2508082

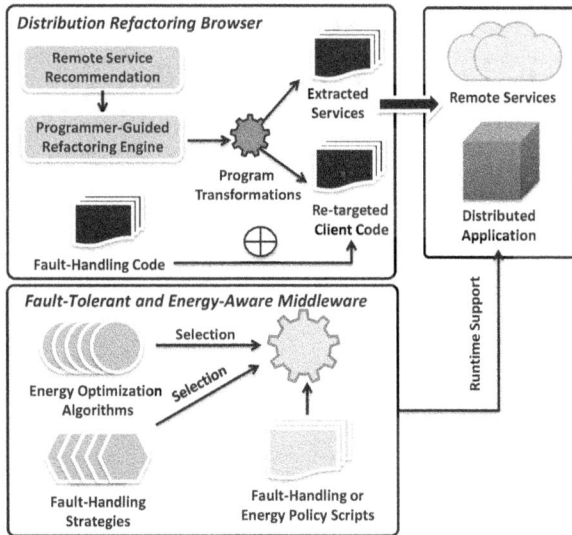

Figure 1. Transitioning to Distributed Applications.

technique in modern software development. *Distribution Refactoring*—transforming a program into distinct, distributed components communicating across a network–is used both to migrate centralized applications to the cloud to take advantage of cloud computing and to offload energy-intensive client functionality to the energy consumed by mobile devices. Specifically, using cloud-based services has become a common avenue for leveraging cloud computing resources, with the benefits that include reduced costs, increased automation, greater flexibility, and enhanced mobility [1]. Furthermore, to reduce energy consumption, *Distribution Refactoring* can partition a mobile application into local and remote parts, so that energy intensive functionality is executed remotely in the cloud.

This research addresses the deep conceptual challenges of reengineering an existing centralized application for fault-tolerant and energy-efficient distributed execution. Figure 1 shows how *Distribution Refactoring* can transform a centralized application and render the transformed application fault-tolerant and energy-efficient. In particular, we focus on three software re-engineering goals. The first goal involves moving some of a centralized application's functionality to the cloud and adding fault-handling code to the client. The second goal involves handling the faults raised during the invocation of a cloud-based service via fault-tolerant middleware. The third goal involves optimizing the energy consumption in a distributed application by flexibly adapting its execution patterns at runtime based on the execution environment, as specified by programmers. In the following discussion, we describe our approach's individual parts.

2.1 Refactoring Centralized Applications

The first goal is to alleviate the code transformation hurdles involved in adapting existing applications to take advantage of cloud-based services. To reduce development efforts/costs and increase programmer productivity, we will express as refactorings several common program transformations that programmers perform when adapting applications to use cloud computing resources. Although the approach is not fully automatic, programmers only determine if the source code should be transformed. The actual transformations are performed by a refactoring engine. However, because centralized and distributed applications have different failure modes,

transformed applications are subject to partial failure. Thus, the enhanced refactoring will add the ability to handle partial failures. Then, detected partial failures will be handled by fault-tolerant middleware, which will be accomplished through the second goal.

The proposed approach focuses on common program transformations occurring when using cloud-based services that are well-amenable to be expressed as a refactoring. In particular, we will explore a set of refactoring techniques that facilitate the process of transforming centralized applications to use cloud-based services. These techniques will automate the program transformations required to 1) rewrite a class making all its methods into remote service methods, 2) partition class methods into service methods and regular methods, rewriting all the communication between the two into remote service calls, 3) re-target all clients of the original class to access its functionality in the cloud by means of remote service calls, and 4) add fault handling code to the client.

The refactoring browser depicted in Figure 1 shows how the constituent components of our approach fit together. The two main parts of our approach are *Recommendation Engine* and *Refactoring Engine*. The recommendation engine uses program analysis techniques to infer class coupling; this optional component can inform the programmer about which classes can be converted into a remote service. The refactoring engine then transforms the given methods into remote service methods, leaves the remaining methods on the client, and rewrites all communication between the original and remote methods into remote service calls. Furthermore, the distribution refactoring can be used for the energy efficiency of mobile applications by offloading their energy-intensive functionality to the cloud. In this case, the refactoring browser does not transform selected class methods into remote service methods because offloading operations are tightly coupled with a certain execution state. Instead, we provide a novel offloading framework to synchronize two different execution states between the client and server.

2.2 Hardening Distributed Applications

Refactoring an existing centralized program for distributed executions should preserve its original execution behavior, so that a distributed application would provide the same or equivalent functionality to the user as the original centralized version. In other words, distributing an application should not only improve its performance, availability, scalability, and efficiency, but also furnish the original functionality to the user. One of the most significant impediments to this goal is that centralized and distributed applications have drastically different failure modes. Distributed applications are subject to partial failure, where components of a distributed system can fail independently of each other. An example of partial failure is *network volatility*, when a network suffers an outage and then shortly becomes operational again. Despite its temporary nature, network volatility is disruptive and detrimental to the user experience. Many cases of partial failure are application specific and require an expert to handle properly. The proposed approach aims at accommodating programmers who may not possess deep expertise in failure handling.

The proposed approach focuses on *application-level failure handling* as compared to all the multiple system level approaches to achieve fault tolerance. The enhanced distribution refactoring will add the ability to operate partial failures, and then fault-tolerant middleware will manage failure handling strategies, service components integrated with distributed applications. The failure handling strategies will be rendered as reusable software components, which can be developed by third-party programmers for a variety of distributed applications. Refactored into a distributed application, these components will harden it against network volatility.

The fault-tolerant middleware depicted in Figure 1 shows how the constituent components of our approach fit together. Because in the presence of partial failures, mainstream middleware mechanisms cannot dynamically handle them, we will innovate middleware by means of a fault diagnosis module and a strategy manager. The programmer can specify and configure the fault tolerance strategies to apply by means of a domain-specific language. The fault diagnosis module catches raised exceptions or failures. The strategy manager associates raised exceptions with fault handling strategies. In response to detecting an exception, the middleware initiate the fault handling strategy as configured by a given script written in the domain-specific language. A strategy implementation is simply a sequence of corrective actions whose execution counteracts the effect of experiencing the fault.

2.3 Leveraging Static and Dynamic Energy Optimizations

Network communication commonly constitutes one of the largest sources of energy consumption in mobile applications [10]. Many mobile applications are operated across a variety of mobile networks (WiFi, 3G, and 4G), whose conditions (e.g., bandwidth, delay, etc) often fluctuate continuously. Networks and their conditions can significantly affect how much energy is consumed by a mobile application. However, mainstream middleware mechanisms cannot flexibly adapt their execution patterns to minimize energy consumption in mobile execution environments, in which an application often switches between mobile networks with different bandwidth/latency characteristics [9]. The focus of mainstream middleware mechanisms is on facilitating distributed communication and improving performance. They lack runtime supports and programming mechanisms that can be engaged to reduce the energy consumed by distributed interactions over networks.

As the final goal, this research will close the knowledge gap on how the choice, parameterization, and optimization of middleware impact the overall energy budget of a distributed mobile application. We will first identify optimization opportunities with respect to energy consumption for a variety of mobile applications running on different hardware capacities and network conditions. Although several prior approaches focus on identifying how mobile applications consume energy [10, 11], none of these studies have specifically focused on middleware. Therefore, our goal is to understand which portions of distributed communication incur the highest energy costs. Then, we will create a novel middleware mechanism, *energy-aware adaptive middleware*, which features dynamic adaptation capabilities as well as a declarative domain-specific language that enables the programmer to express a rich set of middleware energy optimizations and the runtime conditions under which these optimizations should be applied. In designing the new language, we pursued the goals of expressiveness, extensibility, and reusability. In our language, energy policies apply to a given distributed execution. Figure 2 shows the initial design of policy language.

Energy-aware adaptive middleware depicted in Figure 1 shows how the amount of energy consumed by a mobile device can be reduced via advanced, dynamic optimizations. Enabling these optimizations will require innovation in runtime support and expressiveness. A dynamic adaptation mechanism selects an optimal execution patterns at runtime by leveraging the information provided by various system components, thereby enabling the middleware to optimize the energy consumption of software systems [2]. Specifically, the middleware runtime system will select a strategy to use, and will dynamically switch strategies in response to the changes in the execution environment. With the programmer provided energy optimization strategies and the runtime deploying them based on the conditions in place, the proposed approach has the potential to reach the energy efficiency levels not achievable through static energy optimization approaches.

```
policy [name] {
    execution [remote API] of [address];
    energyStrategy [name] ((and|or) [name])*;
    energyCriteria (energy|performance|epr);
    faultStrategy [name] ((and|or) [name])*;
    faultCriteria (energy|performance|recovery); }

strategy [name] {
    join (before|around|after); }
```

Figure 2. Policy language construct.

3. Future Work and Conclusion

We plan to (1) leverage static and dynamic energy optimizations via a novel middleware architecture, (2) enhance the distribution refactoring via a novel program analysis and transformation to achieve adaptive cloud offloading, and (3) integrate the distribution refactoring with a modern IDE to help the programmer easily produce fault-tolerant and energy-efficient distributed applications. As our evaluation, we will apply the described techniques to a series of benchmarks and centralized Java applications. The expected results will indicate that our approach can effectively handle partial failures and reduce energy consumption of distributed applications.

Acknowledgments

This research is supported by the National Science Foundation through the Grant CCF-1116565.

References

[1] R. Buyya, C. Yeo, S. Venugopal, J. Broberg, and I. Brandic. Cloud computing and emerging IT platforms: Vision, hype, and reality for delivering computing as the 5th utility. *Future Generation Computer Systems*, 25(6):599–616, 2009.

[2] J. Flinn, S. Park, and M. Satyanarayanan. Balancing performance, energy, and quality in pervasive computing. In *Proceedings of the 22nd International Conference on Dist. Computing Systems*, 2002.

[3] M. Fowler. *Refactoring: Improving the Design of Existing Code*. Addison-Wesley, Boston, MA, USA, 1999.

[4] Y.-W. Kwon and E. Tilevich. Energy-efficient and fault-tolerant distributed mobile execution. In *Proceedings of the 32nd International Conference on Distributed Computing Systems*, 2012.

[5] Y.-W. Kwon and E. Tilevich. The impact of distributed programming abstractions on application energy consumption. *Information and Software Technology*, 55(9):1602–1613, 2013.

[6] Y.-W. Kwon and E. Tilevich. Reducing the energy consumption of mobile applications behind the scenes. In *Proceedings of the 29th IEEE International Conference on Software Maintenance*, 2013.

[7] Y.-W. Kwon, E. Tilevich, and T. Apiwattanapong. DR-OSGi: Hardening distributed components with network volatility resiliency. In *Proceedings of the ACM/IFIP/USENIX 10th International Middleware Conference*, 2009.

[8] Y.-W. Kwon, E. Tilevich, and W. Cook. Which middleware platform should you choose for your next remote service? *Service Oriented Computing and Applications*, 5:61–70, 2011.

[9] A. Miettinen and J. Nurminen. Energy efficiency of mobile clients in cloud computing. In *Proceedings of the 2nd USENIX conference on Hot Topics in Cloud Computing*, 2010.

[10] A. Pathak, Y. Hu, and M. Zhang. Where is the energy spent inside my app?: fine grained energy accounting on smartphones with eprof. In *Proceedings of the 7th ACM European Conference on Computer Systems*, 2012.

[11] F. Qian, Z. Wang, A. Gerber, Z. Mao, S. Sen, and O. Spatscheck. Profiling resource usage for mobile applications: a cross-layer approach. In *Proceedings of the 9th International Conference on Mobile Systems, Applications, and Services*, 2011.

A Secure Play Store for Android

Feng Shen

University at Buffalo, The State University of New York
fengshen@buffalo.edu

Abstract

As Android becomes popular, Android security acquires more and more attentions. This paper proposes a new system design strategy for dissemination of high fidelity applications. We propose to use static and dynamic data flow analysis on Android applications to detect about how the apps leverage users'/enterprises' sensitive data. Also, we plan to build up a cloud-based backend to safeguard mobile devices. The new secure sytem framework will not only analyze an individual app isolately, but also analyze the correlation between apps.

Categories and Subject Descriptors   D.3.4 [*Processors*]: Compilers; C.5.3 [*Microcomputers*]: Portable devices; F.3.2 [*Semantics of Programming Languages*]: Program analysis

Keywords   Android; Permissions; Information Flow

1. Motivation

Portable consumer electronics are pervasive in our society, being used both for personal enjoyment as well as business. The sheer amount of sensitive data, both personal and business oriented, is staggering. As such, the safety and integrity of these devices is paramount. This is especially true for government entities, the medical profession, banking, and law, as for such enterprises a security vulnerability can result in large financial losses, violation of privacy laws, or even impact national security. For convenience and demand, more and more enterprises allow their employees to use their personal devices to access privileged company information (so-called the "Bring Your Own Device" policy). For example, IBM reports that out of their 400,000 employees, 80,000 emplyees use their own devices to access IBM's internal network. In this case, there is a tangible need for a new enterprise-oriented application store design for dissemination of high fidelity applications. The existing solutions' focus is on the immediately addressable problem of enabling remote administration for security and control. Thus, current solutions seek to answer questions such as, how to create a Web storefront, how to remotely install, uninstall, or block an app, how to monitor an app's behavior, how to remotely delete certain data. To address this limitation, we aim to go beyond the question of remote administration and seek to answer a more fundamental

SPLASH '13,   October 26–31, 2013, Indianapolis, Indiana, USA.
Copyright is held by the owner/author(s).
ACM 978-1-4503-1995-9/13/10.
http://dx.doi.org/10.1145/2508075.2508083

question for an enterprise app store — "Is this app safe to deploy on an employee's device?"

2. Problem Statement

To answer the above question, my research goal is to build a new mobile application store for dissemination of high fidelity applications. Unlike existing mobile application stores designed for end-users such as Apple's App Store and Google's Play Store, our focus is on enterprises that have a large number of mobile devices used by their employees.

The main challenge is protecting the sensitive data of an enterprise from insecure applications installed on employees' devices. The source of the problem is not the pervasive availability of mobile devices in the workplace, but the equally pervasive availability of applications for such devices (known colloquially as "apps"). Although self-published software has always been available, providing such software through a centralized app store such as Apple's App Store and Google's Play Store not only makes the software easily and always available but also imparts a sense of implicit validity to the software for the uniformed user. As such, we are faced with large volumes of code, which have not been appropriately validated and contain un-tested interactions with other software applications, present on portable devices that contain sensitive information. For example, TaintDroid [4] has revealed that there are many apps that leak private information to the network; ComDroid [3] has shown that mobile apps can use IPC mechanisms to bypass access control policies; in addition, numerous security websites continually report the discovery of new mobile malware.

3. Approach

Our approach is to perform continuous app validation and analysis through our proposed enterprise app store. This continuous validation and analysis includes static and dynamic analyses at all stages of an app's life cycle, i.e., submission, deployment, execution, and maintenance:

- **Submission Stage:** When an app is submitted to our enterprise app store, it goes through a rigorous static analysis process and ultimately gets transformed into a more secure version of the app. We propose a new compiler to achieve this purpose.

- **Deployment Stage:** When serving a download request from a user for an app, our enterprise app store analyzes the app against all apps already installed on the user's device; this is to ensure that there is no malicious interaction among the apps. We propose new cross-app analysis techniques to achieve this goal.

- **Execution Stage:** When an app is running on the device, it continuously interacts with a cloud service running as part of our enterprise app store. We propose runtime analysis techniques to further improve the safety of the app.

- **Maintenance Stage:** New versions of the app will be submitted to the store and undergo the same validation and analysis techniques. Meta-data on all versions of the app will be stored by the cloud service.

To achieve the outlined goals, we are building a new system framework. It consists of a new compiler that implements a suite of analysis techniques, a cloud backend that safeguards mobile devices from harmful conditions, and new group testing strategies that test not only a single mobile app in isolation, but a group of apps together. In addition to these components, we plan to release the analysis framework we develop and the dataset we collect for this research as an open service for the research community; this service will enable external researchers to submit their analysis code to evaluate the effectiveness of their techniques against previously proposed techniques in a standardized fashion. We briefly outline our research topics as follows:

- **Permissions Based on Information Flow** Although Android has a rather comprehensive permission mechanism, it still has significant limitations. For example, Android's permission mechanism is a "take-it-or-leave-it" approach — installing an app requires that a user grants all the permissions requested. In addition, most users do not understand what each permission means and simply grant all of them without paying much attention. Studies have shown that the existing Android permission mechanism is not effective and is weak as a protection mechanism. To tackle this problem, we design a new permission system specifically for providing transparency with respect to what data is used and how it is used. Our permission mechanism is based on information ow. For example, if an app reads contacts information and sends it over the Internet, there is a flow of information from the device through the app and to the Internet. Therefore, the developer of the app must explicitly request permission for the "contacts-to-Internet" information flow. This will be discussed in detail in Section 4.

- **D2D Compiler** We are building a new compiler called the Dex to Dex (D2D) compiler that takes an unmodified Android app in the Dex format (the default bytecode executable format for Android) and transforms it into an analyzed, instrumented version with added security guarantees.

- **Integration Testing and Cross-App Analysis** The research literature on smartphone app analysis has focused entirely on single app analysis in isolation, with an exception of ComDroid [3]; ComDroid can analyze whether an app exposes any channel for a different app to gain unauthorized access to protected resources. However, ComDroid still analyzes an app in isolation, and thus cannot determine if any app actually exploits such channels. We propose a set of analysis techniques with a focus on analyzing groups of apps together.

- **Cloud Backend for Safeguarding Smartphones** Our system will also leverage a secure, private cloud-based service to drive the app store itself and to avoid costly computation on the phones themselves (i.e., dynamic analysis/slicing). The secure enterprise app store assumes the availability of a secure business cloud. This cloud should be securely deployed on the internal network of the business itself and will provide the necessary services to power the app store. Specifically, the cloud infrastructure will be responsible for performing dynamic analysis, integration testing, as well as meta-analysis and IPC. In addition, the cloud will need to store computed results of various analyses to power meta-analysis.

- **Open Analysis Service with a Standardized Dataset** Static and dynamic analysis for Android is becoming increasingly more important as the platform grows in its popularity. How-

ever, the evaluation of a new technique is largely ad-hoc; each research group selects a small subset of applications available using their own criteria, making it difficult to properly compare different approaches. Recognizing this difficulty, we plan to release our analysis framework and the dataset we collect for this research as an open service. This service will allow external researchers to upload their analysis code to our server and perform the analysis against the dataset that we have. This will allow proper comparison between different approaches as well as reproduce previous results done over our dataset.

4. Current Work

Here, we discuss the current state of our research. As mentioned above, the current Android permission machnism is insufficient because it does not provide detail information about how the user's data is deployed by apps. Our current work focus on a flow based extention of current Android permission mechanism, called Flow Permissions [5]. Additional information and performance results are available at: http://blueseal.cse.buffalo.edu.

To motivate the necessity of extending the current Android permission mechanism, we examine four apps in detail: My-Calendar, MySpace, Blackmoon File Browser, and Gmail. My-Calendar (com.kfactormedia.mycalendarmobile) is a third-party calendar app, MySpace (com.myspace.android) is a social networking app with multimedia support, Blackmoon File Browser (com.blackmoonit.android.FileBrowser) is a popular file manager, and Gmail (com.google.android.gm) is a well-known email app from Google. Although these apps have widely varying functionalities, MyCalendar and MySpace request similar permissions.

A partial and stylized set of permissions each app requests is given in Table 1. Notice that MyCalendar and MySpace both request PHONE CALLS and NETWORK. The PHONE CALLS permission grants the app a set of more fine grained permissions, which we omit for brevity, including permission to read the phone number, device ID, and the phone state. Similarly, the permission NETWORK allows the app to access the internet, either through wifi or cellular networking.

Savvy users may notice that by granting permissions to read from the phone's log and phone state as well as access to the internet, they are also implicitly granting permission to transmit data stored within the call log and phone state over the internet to an external source. Once the app has permission to read from a given piece of data stored on the phone (*i.e.* a data *source*) as well as permission to send data outside of the app (*i.e.* a data *sink*), the app also *implicitly* has permission to export the source data via the sink. Importantly, the permissions offer no insight if the apps leverage the APIs to ex-filtrate data.

4.1 Flows as Permissions

The goal of the Flow Permission mechanism is to show whether or not an app contains a *flow* between a source and a sink. The general structure of a Flow Permission is of: *source* → *sink*. From Table 2, we can see that, even though MyCalendar and MySpace are granted the same permissions (PHONE CALLS and NETWORK), MyCalendar is augmented by our tool to contain the Flow Permission: PHONE NUMBER → NETWORK. This Flow Permission indicates that data read from the stored phone number was subsequently exported through the use of the network. Additionally, we can deduce that MySpace does not contain such a flow as it does not report such a permission. The MySpace app does, however, transmit the International Mobile Equipment Identity (IMEI) number of the device, which is indicated by the IMEI NUMBER → NETWORK Flow Permission.

In this manner, Flow Permissions provide the user additional context on how the standard Android permissions and the resources/data they protect are leveraged by the apps. Nevertheless,

Table 1. Table listing Android apps and their requested permission examples.

Android App	Permissions Requested
MyCalendar	NETWORK
	PHONE CALLS
MySpace	NETWORK
	PHONE CALLS
Blackmoon File Browser	STORAGE
Gmail	NETWORK
	STORAGE

Table 2. Table listing Android apps and their requested permissions along with our proposed Flow Permission extensions.

Android App	Flow Permissions
MyCalendar	PHONE NUMBER → NETWORK
MySpace	IMEI NUMBER → NETWORK
Blackmoon File Browser	STORAGE → NETWORK

it is up to the user to decide if these behaviors should be allowed or not. The existence of a flow does *not* indicate that the app is necessarily malicious. For example, a social networking app might be expected to contain a flow from the IMEI number to the network as this provides the app a mechanism to uniquely identify the device for analytics. However, some users may not be comfortable providing such information to the app developer, as other mechanisms (*e.g.* manual login screens) can be used without exposing such data. In contrast, a calendar app should not have such a flow. We do note, that certain Flow Permissions should never be granted, namely exposure of the user's International Mobile Subscriber Identity [1] (IMSI) number from the SIM card.

4.2 Interaction Between Apps

Consider a more complicated case that highlights how multiple apps can expose data sources and sinks to one another, thereby acquiring additional implicit permissions. The Blackmoon File Browser app includes functionality to send a file as an email attachment. However, the app cannot access the network to send an email as it does not have the NETWORK permission. Instead, the Blackmoon File Browser leverages Gmail's public interface to send files over the network. In other words, the Blackmoon File Browser is implicitly granted permission, if Gmail is also installed, to use the network without overtly requesting such a permission. Flow Permissions, on the other hand, highlight the flow between the Blackmoon File Browser and the network, accomplished through the RPC mechanism leveraged to transmit the file, as shown in Table 2.

5. Evaluation Plan

To test the validity of our approach, we tested our system tool on 600 of the top rated free apps availiable on the Google Play Store and on 1,200 known malicious apps identified by the MalGenome-Project 6 [8]. In the future, we are plan to run more related apps to test the validity.

To test the correctness of our implementation we compared against TaintDroid-a custom Android OS that performs a dynamic taint analysis for identifying malicious flows. We have manually

compared our Flow Permissions to TaintDroid's dynamically discovered taints on over thirty apps. Each app was excuted for 15 minutes and fed random key-presses. For every taint reported by TaintDroid while using the app, we checked that a corresponding Flow Permissions was synthesized by our system tool. Thus far we have not discovered any taints reported by TaintDroid for which Blue Seal does not gurantee a corresponding Flow Permission.o

In the past few years, one of our research labs has been focusing on developing a proper evaluation platform for systems research involving smartphones. The result is an open, public testbed, called PhoneLab [1]. The PhoneLab team has distributed 200 Android phones in August, 2012 to the undergraduates in SUNY Buffalo and will eventually distribute the total of 700 phones with the goal of providing a large-scale, realistic platform for smartphone research. Our research will use PhoneLab as an evaluation platform. Although PhoneLab is an open testbed, having it locally and operating it ourselves will give an unmatched opportunity for the evaluation of this research.

6. Related Work

The growing popularity of Android has resulted in many tools, case studies, and analysis engine. One of the most closely related work to ours is CHEX [6], which provides a tool for detecting highjack enabling flows with an app. It is the first tool to tackle analysis of Android's constructs such as async tasks and handlers, though it uses a brute force permutation approach for disambiguation.

Soot [7], a framework for optimizing Java bytecode, is implemented in Java and supports the intermediate representations for representing Java bytecode. It provides a tool, called Dexpler [2], which can convert Android Dalvik bytecode to Soot intermediate representation for static analysis. In our research, we deploy Soot as our compiler engine.

References

[1] Phonelab: A large-scale participatory smartphone testbed.

[2] A. Bartel, J. Klein, M. Monperrus, and Y. Le Traon. Dexpler: Converting android dalvik bytecode to jimple for static analysis with soot. In *Proceedings of the International Workshop on the State Of the Art in Java Program Analysis (SOAP'2012)*, 2012.

[3] E. Chin, A. P. Felt, K. Greenwood, and D. Wagner. Analyzing inter-application communication in android. In *Proceedings of the 9th international conference on Mobile systems, applications, and services*, MobiSys '11, pages 239–252, New York, NY, USA, 2011. ACM.

[4] W. Enck, P. Gilbert, B.-G. Chun, L. P. Cox, J. Jung, P. McDaniel, and A. N. Sheth. Taintdroid: an information-flow tracking system for realtime privacy monitoring on smartphones. In *Proceedings of the 9th USENIX conference on Operating systems design and implementation*, OSDI'10, pages 1–6, Berkeley, CA, USA, 2010. USENIX Association.

[5] S. Holavanalli, D. Manuel, V. Nanjundaswamy, B. Rosenberg, F. Shen, S. Y. Ko, and L. Ziarek. Flow permissions for android. In *Proceedings of the 28th IEEE/ACM International Conference on Automated Software Engineering*, ASE 2013. ACM, 2013.

[6] L. Lu, Z. Li, Z. Wu, W. Lee, and G. Jiang. Chex: statically vetting android apps for component hijacking vulnerabilities. In *Proceedings of the 2012 ACM conference on Computer and communications security*, CCS '12, pages 229–240, New York, NY, USA, 2012. ACM.

[7] R. Vallée-Rai, P. Co, E. Gagnon, L. Hendren, P. Lam, and V. Sundaresan. Soot - a java bytecode optimization framework. In *Proceedings of the 1999 conference of the Centre for Advanced Studies on Collaborative research*, CASCON '99, pages 13–. IBM Press, 1999.

[8] Y. Zhou and X. Jiang. Dissecting android malware: Characterization and evolution. In *Security and Privacy (Oakland), 2012 IEEE Symposium on*, 2012.

---

[1] This number is used to uniquely identify the user, phone, and subscription plan. Networks use this to establish roaming policies and charges associated with non local network usage.

Refactoring Multicore Applications Towards Energy Efficiency

Gustavo Pinto

Informatics Center
Federal University of Pernambuco
Recife, PE, Brazil
ghlp@cin.ufpe.br

Abstract

Great strides have been made to increase the energy efficiency of hardware, data center facilities, and network infrastructure. However, in any computer system, it is software that directs much of the activity of the hardware. Moreover, multicore processors have become ubiquitous, mainly because their multiple benefits, especially enhanced performance for multi-threaded and compute-intensive applications. Nonetheless, there are few studies addressing the topic of restructuring multicore applications to consume less energy and even fewer that leverage developer expertise to achieve that goal. In this thesis we present a brief background study for refactoring multicore applications in order to improve both performance and energy consumption. The idea consists in proposing a catalog of refactorings targeting some languages of the JVM platform.

Categories and Subject Descriptors   D.2.7 [*Software Engineering*]: Restructuring, reverse engineering, and reengineering;   D.1.3 [*Programming Techniques*]: Concurrent Programming, Parallel Programming

Keywords   Refactoring, Concurrent/Parallel Programming, Energy Consumption

1. Motivation

In spite of advances in many areas, IT energy consumption keeps rising steeply [1], which indicates that rising demand is outpacing efficiency improvement. Nonetheless, for many years, research that connects computing and energy efficiency has concentrated on the hardware layer. These studies are motivated by the assumption that only hardware dissipates power, not software. However, there are studies that show that this assumption does not capture the whole picture [2, 8]. That would be analogous to postulating that only automobiles are responsible for burning gasoline, not the people who drive them and the way they are used. In any computer system, it is software that directs much of the activity of the hardware. Consequently, software can have a substantial impact on power consumption.

SPLASH '13,   October 26–31, 2013, Indianapolis, Indiana, USA.
Copyright is held by the owner/author(s).
ACM 978-1-4503-1995-9/13/10.
http://dx.doi.org/10.1145/2508075.2514880

Software solutions for improving energy efficiency of computer systems can work at different levels, ranging from machine code level to end-user applications. Notwithstanding, concerns about energy usage were left for compiler writers, operating system designers and hardware engineers. Nonetheless, energy efficiency for higher layers of the software stack, in particular at the application level, is a subject that has been the target of only few studies [3, 9, 13].

Measuring the energy consumption of high level applications and understanding where the energy usage lies provides new opportunities for energy savings. In order to understand the complexities of this approach, we specifically look at multi-threaded applications, since multicore processors have become ubiquitous. The performance of the existing constructs for concurrently[1] execution is reasonably well-understood [10, 14], but little is known about its energy efficiency. Furthermore, since concurrent/parallel programming enables programmers to run their applications faster, a common belief is that this application will also consume less energy [4]. Nonetheless, some researchers [7, 12] have shown that it is not necessarily true. This contradiction poses a challenge, creating the need of new research with deeper analysis.

In order to reduce the energy consumed, many communities can benefit from the results of this work: (i) large corporations which spend too much money on energy consumption derived from software applications; (ii) tool vendors could also benefit, because they can increase their products' value by implementing the refactorings described in this work; and (iii) indirectly, every software user could be benefit, since their favorite applications will be able to run faster, resulting in an overall decrease of energy, besides showing a better user-experience.

2. Problem

Considering the great number of concurrent applications currently in use, existing software systems should be refactored to consumes less energy. Hitherto, however, there are only few studies addressing the topic of restructuring existing concurrent high level applications to consume less energy [4], and even fewer that leverage developer expertise to achieve that goal. Fortunately, there is opportunity for substantial reductions in the energy consumption of existing applications.

Thus, the overall aim of this study is twofold: (i) To better understand the relationship between concurrent programming and energy consumption, and (ii) to derive a refactoring catalog of energy code smells for concurrent software. The first task is currently on development and preliminary results can be found in [7]. The general conclusion we can draw from it is that the trade-off between

---

[1] Throughout the paper, we often employ the terms "concurrent" and "parallel". Since the Java language does not have specific constructs for each abstraction, we use these terms interchangeably.

performance and energy consumption in multicore applications is not obvious, besides be very difficult to generalize. However, more experiments are planned to be conducted. The results of these experiments will be used as an input for a second study. Then, derive a catalog is currently the most important task and it presents the exact problem that the author will address.

The knowledge gained from these experiments will then be applied in the form of guidelines to programmers, in order to educate application programmers to safely restructure their applications to both improve performance and energy consumption.

2.1 Refactoring for Multicore and Energy Efficiency: Opportunities and Challenges

Refactoring an application to use concurrent constructs with the goal of improving performance does not necessarily imply on energy savings, even if there is a reduction in the execution time of the application [12]. Using the Java language as an example, programmers have at their disposal numerous constructs to create and manage concurrent/parallel applications.

Nevertheless, each one of them has its own advantages and disadvantages. For instance, the Thread class is the primary, and the simplest, construct to create a new thread [11]. If a programmer chooses to use these constructs, it will be necessary to worry about a number of tasks, such as (i) to manage thread creation and termination, and related operations; (ii) to choose the number of threads that should be initialized, which can vary with the number of available CPUs; (iii) to decide at what moment they should be initialized; (iv) to implement sophisticated mechanisms to reuse threads; and (v) to control access shared resources. As a consequence of having perform all the tasks, programmers often misuse concurrent constructs, which may result in wast of energy resources, and/or deterioration in the application's performance (i.e. code runs sequentially instead of concurrently [6]).

On the other hand, developers could choose enhanced threading constructs, such as those provided by the java.util.concurrent (j.u.c) library, available since version 1.5 of the language. Using high-level constructs instead of low-level threads has many benefits: not only are they less error-prone, but they also have better performance in some situations, at the expense of being less general. Moreover, recently was released the new version (1.7) of the j.u.c. library, with some improvements and new concurrent constructs, such as the ForkJoin framework [5]. Furthermore, the Java Virtual Machine also offer others concurrent-friendly programming languages, such as Scala. The Scala language is a highly productive programing language combining functional and object-oriented programming. It incorporates ground-breaking features supporting asynchronous programming.

To the best of our knowledge, there is no work in the literature that assesses the energy efficiency of the concurrent/parallel constructs of the Java Virtual Machine platform, considering more than one language. In addiction, to the best of our knowledge, there is an absence of any refactoring cookbook that supports developers in using different constructs, based on the performance and the power consumption requirements of an application.

3. Approach

This study aims to identify new methods, techniques and tools for refactoring programs in order to improve the energy consumption and still achieve a better performance on multi-core platforms. Its main expected outcome is a catalog of refactorings targeting two languages of the Java Virtual Machine platform: Java and Scala. More specifically, the set of refactorings that we intend to propose will support developers in employing different techniques to manage the execution of units of work that can be performed in parallel.

For example, a typical example of a refactoring to energy efficiency is between Thread and tasks from ForkJoin framework. It is well-known that Thread has high overhead (creating, scheduling, destroying, etc) which might outperform the useful computation. On the other hand, the ForkJoin is a lighter-weight thread-like entity, which could host a large number of tasks in a pool of small number of threads. Nonetheless, given the nature of divide-and-conquer algorithms, tasks that run in parallel should have the following characteristics: (i) are CPU-bound, not IO-bound; (ii) depending on the sequential threshold, and (iii) only need to synchronize when waiting for subtasks to complete. If the above conditions are satisfied, the refactoring could be applied.

Another, similar example is the refactoring between Thread and Scala Actors. However, as we reported elsewhere, a number of factors could impact these refactorings. We intend to investigate each case fully to determine if the refactoring will be beneficial.

Thus, to better understand the open problems of this area, that is, the refactoring approaches that could be derived, the author initially carried out a literature review to fully understand current issues within concurrent programming, as well as the energy consumption of high level application. The findings from this review are discussed in section 1 and 2 above, and highlight the importance of this topic.

An initial investigation was carried out to understand the various concurrent construct under several workloads. Previous results show that it is not as straightforward as it would seem. One reason to this, is because each language construct has its pros and cons. For instance, the ForkJoin framework, which is highly indicated to fine-grained parallelism, should be avoided in applications that make use of synchronized methods or blocks, or other blocking synchronization apart from joining other tasks and when performing blocking IO. To understanding which scenario a given transformation could achieve better results, for both performance and energy, is part of this work.

This study focus on two mainstream languages that are part of the Java Virtual machine platform: Java and Scala. The Java language was chosen because it is widespread in both academia and industry. Moreover, Java offers several high-level libraries that implement complex concurrent algorithms, besides the traditional model based on threads and shared data. On the other hand, Scala is a mixed object-functional language, which is very interesting to use to solve problems concurrently, since Scala can eliminate side-effects, and thus, problems like race conditions. Scala also has its own interesting properties for concurrent programming. One simple way to write concurrent programs is with Scala actors. The general approach is to create actors that represent the computation that you want to run asynchronously, and then start these computations by using one of the triggering functions. One key thing about the actors programming model is that it provides primitives that are scalable and you can be use for both CPU and I/O computations.

4. Evaluation Methodology

The author is currently in the process of assessment of the energy efficiency of concurrent constructs. A number of experiments have been done, and few more experiments should be conducted.

4.1 Hypothesis

This study has two hypotheses. The primary hypothesis is that it is possible to generalize the relationship between performance and energy consumption in concurrent programs. The secondary hypothesis is that programmers can safely refactor their applications in order to improve both performance and energy efficiency. Our benefits include: (i) a better understanding of the energy efficiency of concurrent constructs in the JVM; (ii) a set of factors that could also imply on the energy efficiency of a given application, and (iii) a catalog of refactorings that will help application programmers to better use energy resource.

4.2 Experiment Setup

The experiment setup of this study will be conducted by performing the following activities:

- Measurement: To assess the energy efficiency of the most common concurrent programming constructs. For example, in the Java language, `Thread` and `Runnable` classes are the most important concurrent constructs [11]. Initially, experiments to measure the energy efficiency of these constructs targeted programs from a set of benchmarks, since it provides a wide range of concurrent applications that employ varied constructs.

  Preliminary experiments have been executed and show that it is possible to switch from one technique to another in order to consume less energy [7]. Nonetheless, we also conclude that it is very hard to identify which technique is the better for a given scenario. Moreover, our experiments show that factors such as the nature of the problem to be solved, the technique used to manage concurrent execution, the CPU clock frequency, and the JVM implementation can create variations. For example, for a CPU-bound problem, the `ForkJoin` framework can perform better while using less energy. At the same time for a heavily IO-bound problem, it can consume about 10% more energy than a sequential implementation, although still 30% faster. We also noticed that the choice of the JVM implementation can increase the energy consumption in more than 10%.

- Study Design: The refactorings from the catalogue are accordingly organized in three groups, each focusing on one of the refactoring phases. Their phases are (i) identify code which actually runs concurrently; (ii) identify which constructs could be replaced in order to improve performance and energy efficiency; (iii) extract code into the new concurrent construct.

- Evaluation by specialists: To assess the generality of the refactoring catalog, the refactorings will be applied to an existing system by a specialist. We will document the scenarios where the refactorings can not be applied and use this information to analyze whether they need to be more general and, if so, how that goal can be achieved.

- Evaluation by controlled experiments: Controlled experiments with graduate and undergraduate students. These studies will compare the performance of students explicitly instructed in the use of the transformations against students performing ad-hoc restructuring. Performance will be measured in terms of the time to complete the assignment and the number and nature of the bugs in the code, if any.

5. Future Work

As future work, we are planning to implement a tool in order to to aim programmer to refactoring their application automatically. This tool should be integrated with well-known IDE, such as Eclipse and InteliJ. Moreover, we need to adapt our approach to use other JVM-languages. Thus, this allows us to go beyond the traditional refactoring approach in order to propose refactorings between languages. We also intend to investigate how this approach can be used to improve the battery life of Android phones.

6. Acknowledgments

I would like to thank Professor Fernando Castor (my supervisor) for the fruitful discussions we had about the ideas of my PhD thesis proposal, Francisco Neto-Soares for the valuable reviews, and the OOPSLA anonymous reviewers for their helpful comments. This work is supported by Brazilian funding agencies. Gustavo is supported by CAPES and Fernando is supported by CNPq (306619/2011- 3), FACEPE (APQ-1367-1.03/12), and by INES (CNPq 573964/2008-4 and FACEPE APQ-1037- 1.03/08).

References

[1] J. Asafu-Adjaye. The relationship between energy consumption, energy prices and economic growth: time series evidence from asian developing countries. *Energy Economics*, 22(6):615 – 625, 2000. ISSN 0140-9883. .

[2] M. Cohen, H. S. Zhu, E. E. Senem, and .Y. D. Liu. Energy types. In *Proceedings of the 13th OOPSLA*, pages 831–850, 2012.

[3] M. G., M. J., J. J., and A. W. Removing energy code smells with reengineering services. In *Beitragsband der 42. Jahrestagung der Gesellschaft fr Informatik e.V. (GI)*, volume 208, pages 441–455. Bonner Kllen Verlag, 2012.

[4] J. Jelschen, M. Gottschalk, M. Josefiok, C. Pitu, and A. Winter. Towards applying reengineering services to energy-efficient applications. In *CSMR*, pages 353–358, 2012.

[5] D. Lea. A java fork/join framework. In *Java Grande*, pages 36–43, 2000.

[6] S. Okur and D. Dig. How do developers use parallel libraries. In *Proceedings of the 21st ACM SIGSOFT Symposium on Foundations of Software Engineering*, 2012.

[7] G. Pinto and F. Castor. On the implications of language constructs for concurrent execution in the energy efficiency of multicore applications. In *OOPSLA Companion*, 2013. to appear.

[8] A. S., W. D., E. F., D. G., L. C., and D. G. Enerj: approximate data types for safe and general low-power computation. In *Proceedings of the 32nd*, PLDI '11, pages 164–174, 2011. ISBN 978-1-4503-0663-8.

[9] C. Sahin, F. Cayci, I. Gutiérrez, J. Clause, F. Kiamilev, L. Pollock, and K. Winbladh. Initial explorations on design pattern energy usage. In *GREENS*, pages 55–61, 2012.

[10] L. A. Smith, J. M. Bull, and J. Obdržálek. A parallel java grande benchmark suite. In *Proceedings of the 2001 ACM/IEEE conference on Supercomputing (CDROM)*, Supercomputing '01, pages 8–8, New York, NY, USA, 2001. ACM. ISBN 1-58113-293-X.

[11] W. Torres, G. Pinto, B. Fernandes, J. a. P. Oliveira, F. A. Ximenes, and F. Castor. Are java programmers transitioning to multicore?: a large scale study of java floss. In *Proceedings of the Transitioning to multicore (TMC'11)*, SPLASH '11, pages 123–128. ACM, 2011.

[12] A. Trefethen and J. Thiyagalingam. Energy-aware software: Challenges, opportunities and strategies. *Journal of Computational Science*, 1(0):–, 2013. ISSN 1877-7503. .

[13] Y. Zhang, G. Huang, X. Liu, W. Zhang, H. Mei, and S. Yang. Refactoring android java code for on-demand computation offloading. In *OOPSLA*, pages 233–248, 2012.

[14] W. Zhu, J. del Cuvillo, and G. R. Gao. Performance characteristics of openmp language constructs on a many-core-on-a-chip architecture. In *IWOMP*, pages 230–241, 2006.

SPLASH INDIANAPOLIS 2013 OCTOBER 26-31

Welcome Message from the Panels Chair

Greetings,

As the ACM's SPLASH'2013 Panels Chair - Welcome to this year's panels program!

Panels come in many formats - ranging from debates e.g. OOPSLA's 1996 "Translation: Myth or Reality?" to special events including: the "Show Trial Of The Gang Of Four" (OOPSLA'99) and "No Silver Bullet - Reloaded" (OOPSLA'07). The common element shared by all these "panels" was your participation - both for education and entertainment.

This year the program features two panels - one is a debate: "Should Software Conferences Respect Software?" and the second is the continuation of a dialogue first begun in the IEEE's ICSE (International Conference on Software Engineering) community and continued as a 2013 SPLASH Workshop on: "Technical Debt: From Source to Mitigation".

You are invited to attend and participate in these SPLASH'13 panel events and contribute your questions, perspectives, and passion. Please keep in mind that panels aren't a series of mini-presentations - but rather a live event that demands your participation and interaction to be relevant and meaningful.

Looking forward to seeing you in Indianapolis!

Steven D. Fraser
Cisco Systems Inc., USA

Panel

Technical Debt:
From Source to Mitigation

Steven Fraser
Director
Cisco Research Center
Cisco Systems, San Jose
sdfraser@acm.org

Dennis Mancl
Distinguished Member
of Technical Staff
Alcatel-Lucent
Murray Hill, NJ, USA
dennis.mancl@alcatel-lucent.com

Bill Opdyke
Architecture Lead
Corporate Internet Group
JPMorgan Chase, Chicago
opdyke@acm.org

Judith Bishop
Director of Computer Science
Microsoft Research
Redmond, WA USA
jbishop@microsoft.com

Pradeep Kathail
Chief Network Architect
Cisco Systems, San Jose
pkathail@cisco.com

Junilu Lacar
Technical Leader
Cisco Systems, Ohio
jlacar@cisco.com

Ipek Ozkaya
Senior Member, Technical Staff
Software Engineering Institute
ozkaya@sei.cmu.edu

Alexandra Szynkarski
Research Associate
CAST Software Research Labs
a.szynkarski@castsoftware.com

Abstract

The term "Technical Debt" was coined over 20 years ago by Ward Cunningham in a 1992 OOPSLA experience report. Ward used "Technical debt" to describe the trade-offs between delivering the most appropriate – albeit likely immature – product, in the shortest time possible. Since then, the repercussions of "technical debt" have become more visible, though not necessarily more widely understood. This SPLASH panel will bring together practitioners to discuss and debate "Technical Debt".

Categories and Subject Descriptors   K.0 [**Computing Milieux**]: General

General Terms   Management, Design, Economics, Experimentation, Standardization.

Keywords   tools; process; research

1. Steven Fraser – *Panel Impresario*

STEVEN FRASER joined the Cisco Research Center as Director in July 2007. His responsibilities include: fostering Cisco-university research collaborations, coordinating PhD/Post-Doc recruiting, and nurturing technology transfer, e.g. as General Chair of the CTech Forum. Prior to joining Cisco, Steven was a Senior Staff member of Qualcomm's Learning Center in San Diego, leading software learning programs and creating the corporation's internal technical conference (the QTech Forum). Steven formerly held a variety of technology strategy roles at Bell-Northern Research (BNR) and Nortel including: Process Architect, Senior Manager

(Disruptive Technology and Global External Research), Advisor (Design Process Engineering), and General Chair of the BNR/NT Design Forum. In 1994 he spent a year as a Visiting Scientist at the Software Engineering Institute (SEI) collaborating with the "Application of Software Models" project on the development of team-based domain analysis software reuse) techniques. Fraser has been a panel "impresario" for more than a dozen conferences including serving as Panel Chair of ACM's OOPSLA (SPLASH) in 2003 and 2013, and the Panel Chair for the European series of XP conferences. He is the Publicity Chair for ESEC 2013. Previously he was the Corporate Support Chair for OOPSLA'08 and OOPSLA'09. He was the Tutorial Chair for XP2008 and the Tutorial Co-Chair for ICSE'09. Fraser holds a doctorate in Electrical Engineering (software engineering) from McGill University in Montréal and is a senior member of the ACM and the IEEE.

This panel will leverage discussions earlier this year at ICSE 2013's "Software Engineering in Practice" (SEIP) track in San Francisco and XP2013 in Vienna. The panel will follow the SPLASH Technical Debt Workshop organized by Mancl, Fraser, and Opdyke. Panel topics and questions as a catalyst for discussion may include:

- Anticipated impact on software, on the user and on the software engineering practitioner communities
- Measures, models and tools for analyzing, assessing, and communicating levels of Technical Debt
- Strategies for educating: software developers, managers, executives, organizations, and customers
- Strategies for mitigating Technical Debt ("debt relief")
- Utility of Technical Debt as a mechanism to increase the stickiness of software best practices
- What (if any) are the parallels between Technical Debt and other aspects of software engineering, e.g. "security" (something that customers often take for granted, but are unwilling to fund)?
- Where will Technical Debt fit into the arsenal of software engineering concepts 20 years from now?

- Who should learn about Technical Debt – and why?

While the above topics/questions will be used to initiate panel conversations, it will be up to the SPLASH audience to be inquisitive and to ask challenging questions.

2. Dennis Mancl – *Panel Co-Facilitator*

DENNIS MANCL works for Alcatel-Lucent, where he is involved in technologies to support the development of high-quality software: applying software modeling approaches, agile development practices, and legacy software development techniques to the development of large telecom systems.

Both software developers and leaders need to be aware of technical debt. One recurring task for software developers needs to be reducing technical debt in legacy code modules. Any long-lived software product will have some modules that evolve from release to release, and if debt reduction activities can slow the build-up of accidental complexity, everyone can save time and money.

Technical debt is caused by many forces in a big software project. Leaders need to watch out for the impact of intense schedule pressure, excessive requirements churn, lack of experience of the development team in the problem domain, and the use unfamiliar programming languages and tools. Effective software development is a process that involves on-going learning, and leaders need to manage the learning cycles as much as their project deliverables and milestones.

3. Bill Opdyke

BILL OPDYKE has spent much of his career focusing on the technical and organizational issues related to software engineering, particularly focusing on large scale evolving systems. He is currently an architecture lead at JPMorgan Chase. Previously, at Motorola he was part of a team focusing on improving productivity and reducing costs of software developments. While at Bell Labs, Bill was technical lead for several advanced development projects where he gained a keen appreciation for the challenges in extending existing products to meet emerging market needs. He also spent several years as a faculty member at North Central College. His doctoral research in object-oriented refactoring (University of Illinois) focused on techniques for supporting the process of change to object-oriented software, including structural changes that reduce technical debt.

4. Judith Bishop

JUDITH BISHOP is Director - Computer Science at Microsoft Research, based in Redmond, USA. Her role is to create strong links between Microsoft's research groups and universities globally, through encouraging projects, supporting conferences and engaging directly in research. Her expertise is in programming languages and distributed systems, with a strong practical bias and an interest in compilers and design patterns. She initiated the Software Innovation Foundation (SEIF) and is currently investigating aspects of running programs in browsers (particularly F# and TouchDevelop). Judith is active in IFIP WG2.4 and the ACM, where she has responsibility for the Student Research Competition. Judith received her PhD from the University of Southampton in 1977 and has a distinguished background in academia.

Debt: how do we get into it and how do we get out of it? Good citizens don't get into unreasonable debt and neither should good companies. But there are traumatic circumstances that can cause a change in fortunes such as a stock market crash or an earthquake. The equivalent in the case of technical debt for a software company would be an unanticipated or one-off change in direction caused by outside forces. For example, the world witnessed an unprecedented investment in software change for the turn of the millennium (Y2K) and in Microsoft, the rise of worms and viruses caused a security lockdown in 2002. At the moment we are still working with the effects on software of the changes wrought by hardware, especially display resolution, and touch and pen input. Systems have been written that rely entirely on one kind of input-output systems and now have to be upgraded to another. That is a debt that was not foreseen.

In order to create systems that are as amenable to change as possible, we need to gaze into the crystal ball in order to put the company's effort and funding where it will be best leveraged later. Working with the results of past software investments helps. We can measure past changes, their impact, the company's readiness and the speed with which it could react. For older systems, it might be worth inserting a clean framework that handles change well, but doing so could be too costly and by the time it is done, it could be out of date.

Given the choice of living with technical debt (and unwieldy code) and getting rid of the debt (by means of a partial rewrite), the latter has more going for it. The reason is due to the human resources that will be involved in the project. They can bring the latest technology to bear, and also add ownership, both of which are factors that can be shown to increase stability and performance.

5. Pradeep Kathail

PRADEEP KATHAIL is the Chief Network Architect for the Network Operating Systems Technical Group (NOSTG) and is responsible for technology and standards strategy, next-generation enterprise architecture and innovation. He leads a team to promote and incubate innovation within ENG and is part of Cisco's DE/Fellow Technology Fund steering team. Prior to his current assignment, he held the CTO position in Unified Access Business Unit and Network Systems and Solution Technology Group, responsible for technology strategy and software architecture. As a Cisco Distinguished Engineer, Pradeep led many large scale OS infrastructure and system development projects such as IOS componentization, Modular IOS (ION) and IOS/ENA (predecessor to IOS-XR). Prior to Cisco, Pradeep held various technology management jobs at Apple, Novell, SITA and IBM designing, developing and maintaining large or ultra large scale systems.

6. Junilu Lacar

JUNILU LACAR is a technical leader in the Cisco Services Technology Group and is responsible for the development of business-critical applications that support the management of Cisco's security intelligence assets and research operations. He is an original member of the Cisco Agile Coaches Network and has helped drive adoption of agile development practices at Cisco since 2006. His interests lie mainly in agile technical practices such as Test-Driven Development and extend to successful strategies for large-scale agile transformations. Prior to Cisco, Junilu held various senior development positions at JP Morgan Chase and Compuware. Junilu's experience spans over two decades, multiple industries, and several countries including the Philippines, Singapore, Malaysia, and Hong Kong.

As agile adoption continues its march into mainstream development organizations, the term "technical debt" becomes increasingly subject to "semantic diffusion," a term coined by Martin Fowler to describe how the spreading acceptance of a term can change its definition and weaken its usefulness (http://martinfowler.com/bliki/SemanticDiffusion.html). Robert

Martin's 2009 article hints at this on-going semantic diffusion. (https://sites.google.com/site/unclebobconsultingllc/a-mess-is-not-a-technical-debt).

Despite its continuously evolving meaning, technical debt is still a useful metaphor that helps us think about a class of problems. As with financial debt, technical debt can be addressed both at micro levels and macro levels of development organizations. At the lower levels, technical debt is best addressed with more education for those who make the day-to-day decisions that cause debt to be incurred in the first place. At the higher levels, management should provide infrastructure and services that help stimulate and sustain the flow of development. Just as governments and financial institutions use various indicators to gauge the health of the economy, management can also use technical debt as an indicator of the health of their development organizations. Management should provide guidelines and policies that help steer decisions and behaviors for managing technical debt in the right direction, just as governments and financial institutions define macroeconomic policies to steer the economy. Management should be careful not to impose guidelines and policies that are so restrictive as to inhibit creativity and innovation.

7. Ipek Ozkaya

IPEK OZKAYA is a senior member of the technical staff at the Carnegie Mellon Software Engineering Institute (SEI). With her team at the SEI, she works to develop methods for improving software development efficiency and system evolution with a focus on software architecture practices, software economics, and requirements management. Her latest publications include multiple articles on these subjects focusing on agile architecting, dependency management, and architectural technical debt. She also serves as the chair of the advisory board of the IEEE Software magazine and as an adjunct faculty member for the Master of Software Engineering Program at CMU. Ipek holds a doctorate from CMU in Pittsburgh.

The concept of technical debt has been around for over two decades (W. Cunningham, "The WyCash Portfolio Management System" in *OOPSLA'92*. Vancouver, 1992.); however, understanding what technical debt is and developing/using practices towards its management has gained increased interest both from research and developer communities in the past few years (*International Workshops on Managing Technical Debt*, http://www.sei.cmu.edu/community/td2013esem/previous/?location=secondary-nav&source=723401). Unfortunately, increased interest resulted in a tendency to label all kinds of software ills as technical debt. This tendency to label all ills as technical debt results in a) a confusion on the basic definition of what technical debt is, b) diminishes the value of defining and sharing practices that can enable managing design trade-off strategically to better handle technical debt, c) hinders progress on research that focus on quantifying design decisions and software quality towards understanding technical debt.

The software engineering community should focus less on re-inventing a definition and focus on practices for managing technical debt and research that help better guide quantitative decision making (Philippe Kruchten, Robert L. Nord, Ipek Ozkaya, Davide Falessi. "Technical Debt: Towards a Crisper Definition: Report on the 4th International Workshop on Managing Technical Debt," held at ICSE 2013. *SIGSOFT Software Engineering Notes*, ACM, September 2013). Steve McConnell offers a clear technical debt definition S. McConnell, "Managing technical debt (slides)," in Workshop on Managing Technical Debt (part of ICSE 2013, IEEE, 2013): "A design or construction approach that's expedient in the short term but that creates a technical context in which the same work will cost more to do later than it would cost to do now (including increased cost over time)." What is clear in McConnell's definition is a focus on the design and construction approach that can potentially bear technical debt and the impact of time on the resources spent.

We now have considerable material from small and large industries about technical debt, how they perceive it and manage it (Philippe Kruchten, Robert L. Nord, Ipek Ozkaya: "Technical Debt: From Metaphor to Theory and Practice." *IEEE Software* 29(6): 18-21 (2012)). This includes companies such as IBM, Cisco, Siemens, Google, Lockheed-Martin, and so on. We have reports from companies who have a different interest at stake, selling tools or services pertaining to technical debt: Cast Software, Software Improvement Group, ThoughtWorks, Cutter Consortium, and so on.

The increasing industry interest and emergence of organization specific practices can be seen as an early indication that industry needs a clearly defined practical managing-technical-debt practice to deal with issues such as evolution, strategic resource management and bridging the stakeholder communication gap that has been on the forefront of research as well. While often the impact of technical debt is seen as the inevitable consequences of "death by a thousand cuts" understanding the key contributors and deciding whether managing them as debt would help is an important first step. Organizations that have embraced technical debt as part of their iteration planning practices achieve success as a result of the following actions:

- making technical debt visible,
- differentiating strategic structural technical debt from technical debt that emerges from low code quality,
- using the elicited technical debt as a means for bridging the gap between the business and technical sides,
- integrating technical debt into planning,
- associating technical debt with future risk to identify a payback strategy.

8. Alexandra Szynkarski

ALEXANDRA SZYNKARSKI is a research associate at CAST Research Labs, New York. Her research interests include industry benchmarks on structural software quality and software performance and productivity measurement on the global application development community. Szynkarski participated in the ICSE 2013 Technical Debt Panel (Technical Debt: Past, Present, Future). She currently works with Bill Curtis on putting together a benchmarking repository of structural quality data. She also participates in creating an online community through the platform www.ontechnicaldebt.com with the goal of raising awareness on the topic and making sure the industry and research community have access to the latest and most accurate information on the topic. Szynkarski received an MS in international business administration from the Institut Administration des Entreprises de Nice, France.

I have had the opportunity to work with the world's largest repository of structural quality data: more than 1,300 applications and over 350 million lines of code. Over the past 3 years, I have studied this repository publishing global trends in the structural quality of business software applications. Working alongside Bill Curtis (Vice President and Chief Scientist at CAST), we were able to put together a calculation of Technical Debt based on violations of good architectural coding practices as well as discover the average amount of Technical Debt that exists within a typical business application.

The debate on the definition of Technical Debt is a difficult one to tackle. The concept has evolved since it was coined by

Ward Cunningham in 1992 to include more components and originally anticipated. With little reference data on the topic, I believe that each company has their own definition of what should or should not be included as Technical Debt. At CAST we define Technical Debt as the effort required to fix violations of good architectural and coding practices that remain in the code when an application is released. Technical Debt is still an emerging concept and the term tends to be loosely thrown around. It is therefore important to be able to quantify and measure Technical Debt as it provides a framework to understanding the state of our business applications and will push the metaphor to another level of research. The CAST benchmarking repository of structural quality data provided a unique opportunity for us to do just this: calculate Technical Debt across different technologies, based on the number of engineering flaws and violations of good architectural and coding practices in the source code.

Automated static code analysis tools can help play an initial role in calculating and managing Technical Debt. It is unfortunate and undeniable that many tools to not provide the complete scope needed to deal tackle the issue. However, certain tools will be able to provide useful quantification of Technical Debt, as well as help improve the structural quality of code. I believe that quality of our code matters. And in order for the Technical Debt term to move forward we need to start measuring software quality and understanding the Technical Debt's implications to quality.

Should Software Conferences Respect Software?

A SPLASH Panel

Shriram Krishnamurthi

Brown University

sk@cs.brown.edu

James Noble

Victoria University of Wellington

kjx@ecs.vuw.ac.nz

Jan Vitek

Purdue University

jv@cs.purdue.edu

Abstract

A new trend in software engineering and programming language conferences is to investigate the reproducibility of research results. This trend has led to the creation of Artifact Evaluation Committees at several conferences, including OOPSLA this year. What is the motive behind these committees? How should they be structured? Do they help? Can they hurt? And should software be given more respect, at least at conferences devoted to the study of software, or should papers remain supreme? These are some of the questions that addressed in this panel. Shriram Krishanamurthi argues in favor of the new process and James Noble plays devil's advocate. The panel is moderated by Jan Vitek.

Categories and Subject Descriptors D. 1.0 [*Software*]: General

Keywords Software artifact

1. Shriram Krishnamurthi

The software sciences are rich in artifacts: programs, yes, but also datasets, tests, execution logs, models, and more. Yet, our research is evaluated entirely on the content of bitmapped encodings of partial views of these artifacts. In reality, the work is embodied at least as much in this constellation of artifacts as in the paper that describes them. It's time artifacts got their due.

How did we arrive at the current state of affairs? Decades ago, our discipline made the important step from the specific to the general: one could no longer publish a paper merely for having built something, but rather needed to learn something from the experience, and distill what they learned into packaged, reusable scientific knowledge. This was an important, necessary step for the discipline. This shift, however, devalued the artifacts that embody and lead to that knowledge. We must restore this missing balance.

Naturally, not every paper needs to be accompanied by an artifact. In particular, entirely theoretical or speculative ideas are as valuable as ever. However, an artifact-driven paper that is not accompanied by an artifact that can be evaluated independently should perhaps rightly be regarded with some suspicion. It remains – as it already is – the responsibility of program committees to assess these submissions. Formalizing artifact evaluation merely forces authors to be clear on what type of paper they are claiming to submit, so program committees can arrive at more informed decisions.

What might we learn from evaluating artifacts? The most negative interpretation is that they increase honesty and decrease outright fraud. More neutrally, they help reviewers form a fuller picture of what a paper accomplishes: for instance, where the artifacts are executable, reviewers can experiment with new inputs, building a better understanding of what the system does. In the best case, the process can even teach reviewers new things that the papers did not cover.

The beauty and power of the peer review process is, by applying diverse viewpoints to an effort, it raises questions the initial authors did not consider. The more inputs the reviewers have to work with, the better they can function.

2. James Noble

Science is about knowledge. Engineering is about products. We should not confuse the two, but artifact evaluation is based in this confusion. Ideas, algorithms, and studies should not be accepted based on how easy they are to obtain, install, run, or how much memory you need to start a VM.

Artifact evaluation is biased against many kinds of research. Good human ethics research practice requires confidentiality or anonymity. Companies often need to keep their code (and especially their customers' code) in house. Double blind artifact evaluation is biased against large and complex systems of systems: how can you evaluate a web-based system without leaking identity (other than virtualizing the entire infrastructure?) Under some qualitative research methods (such as ground theory) it simply does not make sense to re-analyze data – reproducibility requires new studies.

Finally, artifact evaluation discourages innovation and encourages rent seeking. Toolsmiths have vested interests in encouraging researchers to build upon their mature tools, rather than hacking together quick prototypes, or just working things out on paper. New programs, languages, systems, applications, and proof techniques will obviously be more fragile that more established methods. In no other research discipline are papers evaluated upon how easily experimental equipment can be packaged up and moved into other labs, rather than on the quality of the results, descriptions, and analyses.

OOPSLA '13, October 26–31, 2013, Indianapolis, IN, USA.
Copyright is held by the owner/author(s).
ACM 978-1-4503-1995-9/13/10.
http://dx.doi.org/10.1145/2508075.2516928

SPLASH INDIANAPOLIS 2013 OCTOBER 26-31

Welcome Message from the Posters Chairs

It is our great pleasure to welcome you to the SPLASH 2013 Posters session! This session provides an excellent forum for authors to present their recent or ongoing projects in a highly interactive setting, and receive feedback from the community. It is held early in the conference, to promote continued discussion among interested parties.

This year's Posters session includes both independent poster presentations and posters on papers that were accepted to SPLASH 2013 conferences and workshops. We hope that all of these posters lead to many interesting and lively discussions. On the following pages, you will find the extended abstracts for the independent presentations, which cover a wide range of exciting topics in programming, systems, languages and applications.

We would like to thank all Posters authors and attendees for their participation. We would also like to extend special thanks to the Posters committee, Ademola Adejokun (Lockheed Martin Aeronautics) and Nick Sumner (Purdue University), for helping review the submissions and offering valuable feedback to the authors.

K. R. Jayaram　　　　　**Emina Torlak**
HP Labs, USA　　　　　*U.C. Berkeley, USA*

The Poor Man's Proof Assistant

Using Prolog to Develop Formal Language Theoretic Proofs

Joey Eremondi

University of Saskatchewan

joey.eremondi@usask.ca

Abstract

While proving a theorem from a set of axioms is undecidable in first order logic, recent development has produced several tools which serve as automated theorem provers. However, often these systems are too complex for a given problem. Their usefulness is outweighed by the difficulty of learning a new tool or translating results into computer-readable form.

I describe tools developed in Prolog to partially characterize the shuffle-inclusion problem. These tools allowed for rapid development of proofs with little intellectual overhead. While focused around a specific problem, the techniques described are general, and well suited to many problems on discrete structures.

Categories and Subject Descriptors D.1.6 [*PROGRAMMING TECHNIQUES*]: Logic programming

Keywords Prolog; shuffle; proof assistant

1. Problem and Motivation

This paper shows how logic languages such as Prolog provide a fast and easy way to develop assistive tools in theorem proving. As a case study, I use the characterization of the shuffle inclusion problem.

The shuffle operator, which represents the set of all ways of "merging" two strings, has received much attention in recent research. Its main application is in modelling parallelism [10]. Moreover, it represents a fundamental operation on strings, so researching it contributes to a greater understanding of the theory underlying computation.

I examined shuffle inclusion, the question of whether one shuffle set was a subset of another. The search tools I developed for this problem serve as an example of how logic languages can be used to facilitate the development of proofs in formal languages and discrete mathematics.

2. Background and Related Work

2.1 The Prolog Language

A detailed introduction to Prolog can be found in [6]. There are three features which are particularly relevant here. *Unification* al-

lows logical predicates to generate answers, rather than simply test conditions, by leaving some variables *unbound*. Roughly, Prolog searches for a value causing a goal to succeed. *Nondeterminism* allows for multiple definitions of a predicate. These are each tried in sequence when proving a goal, allowing queries to return multiple answers. The *Definite Clause Grammar* (DCG) feature provides tools for string parsing and generation. While based on context-free grammars, they can be mixed with arbitrary Prolog code for context-sensitve testing.

2.2 Shuffle Inclusion

I use Σ^* to denote the set of all (possibly empty) words over the alphabet Σ, and $|w|$ to denote the length of a word w. The shuffle operator $\sqcup\!\sqcup$ denotes all ways of interleaving the letters from two words while preserving their order relative to the original words. It maps two strings to a finite set of strings, and is formally defined in [3] as follows:

$$u \sqcup\!\sqcup v = \{u_1 v_1 \cdots u_n v_n \mid u = u_1 \cdots u_n, v = v_1 \cdots v_n,$$
$$u_i \in \Sigma^*, v_i \in \Sigma^*, 1 \le i \le n\}$$

In [3] and [2] it was shown that $u \sqcup\!\sqcup v = x \sqcup\!\sqcup y \iff \{u,v\} = \{x,y\}$ when u and v contain at least two distinct letters. When equality is so easily described, it is natural to ask a similar question about the inclusion problem, and to examine when $u \sqcup\!\sqcup v \subseteq x \sqcup\!\sqcup y$.

2.3 Proof Assistants

Despite the undecidability of first-order logic [5], many successful proof-assistants exist. HOL [9] is based on higher-order logic. Coq uses dependent types, and was used to verify proof of the four color theorem [8]. Several of these languages have counter-example search packages, such as Nitpick [4] and Kodkod [11]. The Alloy Analyzer provides counter-example search with SAT-solvers, with a focus on specifying Object-Oriented systems [1]. However, these languages can be challenging to learn, and translating statements into computer-readable code is difficult and tedious. Some Prolog tools, such as PFLAT [12] have been developed for formal language work, but these are geared more towards education rather than real theorem proving.

3. Approach and Uniqueness

My approach to the inclusion problem was to find a complete characterization of cases when the subset relation holds. For example, $xwy \sqcup\!\sqcup w \subseteq xw \sqcup\!\sqcup wy$ for all $w,x,y \in \Sigma^*$. My research followed a cyclic approach. Initially, a list of all u,v,x,y fulfilling $u \sqcup\!\sqcup v \subseteq x \sqcup\!\sqcup y$ and $|uv| \le k$ was generated. I examined this list to find patterns and develop hypotheses about the subset relation. Once a conjecture was formulated, I would use a search framework to search for counter-examples of length k. If no counter-example was found, I attempted a pen-and-paper formal proof, then wrote a

SPLASH '13, October 26–31, 2013, Indianapolis, Indiana, USA.
Copyright © 2013 ACM 978-1-4503-1995-9/13/10... $15.00.
http://dx.doi.org/10.1145/2508075.2508088

predicate to test which strings matched its pattern. The process was repeated, but strings matching previously proved theorems were filtered out. Thus I could gauge the completeness of my characterization, continually narrowing the list of strings I examined.

3.1 Enumeration

Since strings are discrete objects, it is possible to enumerate all cases where $u \shuffle v \subseteq x \shuffle y$ with bounds on $|uv|$. In order to help find patterns, my program printed all such u, v, x, y of a given length. With Prolog's nondeterminism and unification, the predicate specifying such u, v, x, y also served to enumerate them. This predicate declared a list with unbound members, then declared u, v as a partition of that list. Another predicate, `hasSameParikh`, selected a number of a's and b's for uv to have, then unified x, y with words having the same number of each letter. Finally, x, y were unified with words fulfilling the subset relation. Once a theorem was proved and added to the characterization, any u, v, x, y which fulfilled the conditions of the theorem were filtered out. This enumeration allowed me to experimentally prove that my characterization was complete up to length 8.

3.2 Counter-example Search and Hypothesis Testing

The hypothesis-testing tool generated strings u, v, x, y matching a hypothesis' conditions with $|uv| = k$, then tested if $u \shuffle v \subseteq x \shuffle y$. Two k-element lists were declared with unbound contents. Then u, v and x, y were declared as a partitioning of these lists.

The search called a rule `counterCond` which unified a query u, v, x, y with strings matching my hypothesis. The rule was rewritten for each conjecture being tested, usually using DCG clauses.

By passing an unbound list to `counterCond`, the predicate generated strings that matched the hypothesis condition. This was more efficient than generating every pair of strings of a given length and testing if they matched the hypothesis condition. The logic-programming approach meant that no additional code was written to perform this optimization.

Restricting search to a given length was necessary, since recursion on unbound-length strings caused infinite loops. Continually increasing k led to an iterative-deepening search, ensuring that the search would halt and find a counter-example of length k if it existed.

3.3 Definite clause grammars

The task of matching a set of strings against a given "pattern" arose frequently. DCG's provided a useful tool for expressing such patterns. Regularly used clauses were written, such as `aToMbToN` to match $a^m b^n$, $m, n \in \mathbb{N}_0$. These could be combined and composed. For example, `concatStr` concatenated strings matching different DCG clauses. Likewise, calling `concatStr` on two different words could then be used to test for a common infix between them. By using Prolog's DCG tool, patterns and conditions could be coded in an easily readable form without requiring a parser or generator to be written.

3.4 Inductive queries

Prolog is designed to have programs run interactively from a console, rather than compiled to an executable. This allowed my framework to answer queries without having to write any sort of user interface. A common usage of this feature was querying which discovered patterns, if any, proved $u \shuffle v \subseteq x \shuffle y$ for a given u, v, x, y. Many of the proofs that patterns held were based on induction, constructing new relations from ones I had already proved. While these proofs were completed manually, the process was made much easier with the ability to query previously-proved theorems.

4. Results and Contribution

Using the techniques described above, I found a list of over 40 patterns which completely characterize when $u \shuffle v \subseteq x \shuffle y$, with $uv \in \{a, b\}^*$, $|uv| \le 8$. For example, $w \shuffle xwy \subseteq xw \shuffle wy$, and $a^p w b^k \shuffle a^q w b^l \subseteq a^{p+q} w \shuffle w b^{k+l}$.

While human-developed proofs verified the correctness of each subset relation, their completeness for length 8 was verified using my search tools. The development of pen-and-paper proofs was made easier with the use of my assistive tools. The full list of patterns, as well as proof of each pattern's correctness, can be found in [7]. The techniques used here can be generalized to other problems. In particular, the counter-example search could be used to test any hypothesis involving a finite number of discrete structures.

5. Conclusion

I presented Prolog tools for assisting with proofs and formal language-theoretic research. These demonstrate how software can help automate the proof developing process, and how Prolog's unique feature-set allows for rapid development and interactive use of such software. While more complete tools exist, my framework provided a shallower learning curve better suited to the day-to-day challenges of formal language research. My success in partially characterizing the shuffle inclusion problem provides a strong example of both the ease and effectiveness of these tools.

Acknowledgments

The author was supervised by Dr. Ian McQuillan and supported by the Natural Sciences and Engineering Research Council of Canada.

References

[1] K. Anastasakis, B. Bordbar, G. Georg, and I. Ray. On challenges of model transformation from uml to alloy. *Software & Systems Modeling*, 9(1):69–86, 2010. ISSN 1619-1366. .

[2] J. Berstel and L. Boasson. Shuffle factorization is unique. *Theoretical Computer Science*, 273:47–67, 2002.

[3] F. Biegler, M. Daley, M. Holzer, and I. McQuillan. On the uniqueness of shuffle on words and finite languages. *Theoretical Computer Science*, 410:3711–3724, 2009.

[4] J. Blanchette and T. Nipkow. Nitpick: A counterexample generator for higher-order logic based on a relational model finder. In M. Kaufmann and L. Paulson, editors, *Interactive Theorem Proving*, volume 6172 of *Lecture Notes in Computer Science*, pages 131–146. Springer Berlin Heidelberg, 2010. ISBN 978-3-642-14051-8. .

[5] A. Church. A note on the entscheidungsproblem. *J. Symb. Log.*, 1(1): 40–41, 1936.

[6] W. F. Clocksin and C. S. Mellish. *Programming in Prolog: Using the ISO Standard.* Springer, 5th edition, 9 2003. ISBN 9783540006787.

[7] J. Eremondi and I. McQuillan. A Partial Characterization of the Shuffle Inclusion Problem on Words. Manuscript in preparation, 2013.

[8] G. Gonthier. Formal proof the four-color theorem. *Notices of the AMS*, 55(11):1382–1393, 2008.

[9] M. J. C. Gordon and T. F. Melham, editors. *Introduction to HOL: a theorem proving environment for higher order logic.* Cambridge University Press, New York, NY, USA, 1993. ISBN 0-521-44189-7.

[10] A. Mateescu, G. Rozenberg, and A. Salomaa. Shuffle on trajectories: Syntactic constraints. *Theoretical Computer Science*, 197(1–2):1–56, 1998.

[11] E. Torlak and D. Jackson. Kodkod: A relational model finder. *Tools and Algorithms for the Construction and . . .*, pages 632–647, 2007.

[12] M. Wermelinger and A. M. Dias. A prolog toolkit for formal languages and automata. *SIGCSE Bull.*, 37(3):330–334, June 2005. ISSN 0097-8418. .

Dictionary-Based Query Recommendation
for Local Code Search *

Xi Ge

NC State University, Raleigh, NC, USA

xge@ncsu.edu

Abstract

Local code search tools help developers efficiently find code snippets in the code base under development. The quality of the retrieved code largely depends on the quality of queries provided by developers. Manually synthesizing high-quality queries is a nontrivial task, partially because it places a cognitive burden on developers by requiring them memorize words used in the code base under search. To help developers synthesize better queries, this paper proposes a recommendation technique called MultiD that uses multiple dictionaries. We also report an ongoing study to evaluate the effectiveness of MultiD.

Categories and Subject Descriptors   D.2.3 [*Software Engineering*]: Coding Tools and Techniques

General Terms   Design, Languages

Keywords   search, navigation, tool, recommender, IDE

1. Introduction

Software is probably the most complex system that human beings have ever made. Due to the complexity of software systems, developers' working on them are never easy. One cause of this hardness is that a developer needs to collect enough information before she can work properly; while collecting the information is both arduous and labor-intensive. Existing study shows that collecting information is an unavoidable step for software maintenance tasks [3]. To help developers meet with their information need, researchers proposed local code search (LCS) tools that assist developers efficiently locate the intended code snippets in the code base under development [7].

The effectiveness of using LCS tools largely depends on the quality of queries. A high-quality query should contain terms that are both informative and relevant. Being informative means that a term does not happen too often in the code base under search ("a" is not informative, for instance); being relevant suggests that the term exists at least somewhere in the code base under search. Synthesizing highly relevant queries is especially hard, partially because

---

* Work during the author's internship at ABB Inc.

SPLASH '13,   October 26–31, 2013, Indianapolis, Indiana, USA.
Copyright is held by the owner/author(s).
ACM 978-1-4503-1995-9/13/10.
http://dx.doi.org/10.1145/2508075.2508089

it places a cognitive burden on developers. For instance, to synthesize a relevant query, a developer needs to remember the exact words that are used in the code base under search, even though those words used are sub-optimal. For instance, if the code base under search uses "instantiate" to describe the action of creating an object, the developer's searching of "create" may lead to no useful results.

Conventional techniques to find synonyms, such as by using WordNet [5], may solve this problem. However, these techniques fail to consider the context of the code base under search; hence they may lead to the synonyms that generally make sense in the English language, but are not relevant to the code base under search. For example, WordNet can suggest multiple synonyms of "create", but most of these synonyms may not exist in the code base under search. To make things even worse, WordNet, as a general English dictionary, does not consider that "instantiate" is a synonym of "create", in spite of the fact that developers typically do. To solve this problem, we propose a query recommendation technique that uses multiple dictionaries. In summary, we make the following contributions:

- A query recommendation technique called MultiD that uses multiple dictionaries to help developers correct and improve queries on LCS tools. MultiD takes an original query from the developer as input, outputs a set of recommended queries.

- An implementation of the technique as an extension to a state-of-the-practice LCS tool called Sando [7].

2. Approach

In this section, we detail the MultiD implementation. We first present the different dictionaries used by MultiD, next explain the query improvement algorithm by using these dictionaries.

2.1 Dictionaries

Currently, MultiD uses three different dictionaries that vary in terms of the amount of the information contained and their relevance to the code base under search. Although we start at these three dictionaries, we may later add more to the technique.

Level I: project-specific dictionary. Level I dictionary is the lowest level of dictionaries in MultiD. This dictionary contains terms that appear in the project under search. To collect these terms, MultiD needs to traverse the project under search. Fortunately, LCS tools such as Sando usually index source code documents before developers can use them. Taking advantage of this process, MultiD builds the level I dictionary by reusing the terms collected during the indexing.

After collecting the terms, the level I dictionary represents these terms through two ways. The first way is a binary search tree of these terms to facilitate looking for a specific term. The second way is a co-occurrence matrix that records the counts of every two terms occur together. Building the term co-occurrence matrix is equally easy. Initialized as every cell being 0, for each pair of terms $[t_1, t_2]$ that occurs together in a source document, the dictionary builder increments the current value of the cell at $[t_1, t_2]$ by one. MultiD uses the co-occurrence matrix to sort recommended queries, as illustrated in Section 2.2.

Level II: software-engineering-specific thesaurus. Level II dictionary is a thesaurus of terms that are frequently used in software development. As a field with fast growth, software development has evolved its own set of terms, synonyms and abbreviations that do not exist in the conventional English. Simply reusing a general dictionary cannot get the field-specific information, or even be detrimental to client software tools [2]. To build a field-specific thesaurus, we reuse Gupta and colleagues' work that mines the relationship between different words in source code, generating 1724 pairs of semantically related terms, among which 91% are synonyms specific to the field of software development [2]. Several examples of these field-specific synonyms are "execute"–"invoke", "load"–"initialize" and "instantiate"–"create".

level III: General English thesaurus. The highest level of dictionaries used in our technique is a general English thesaurus. To build this thesaurus, we reused Miller's lexical database called WordNet [5]. WordNet groups English words by their meanings, therefore finding synonyms by using WordNet is trivial. Although WordNet obtains a complete set of English words, using it directly is costly in memory. Hence, we reduced the size of WordNet by only including the $50k$ most frequently used words in English [1], partially because $50k$ is the upper bound of the vocabulary size for an average individual [6]. We queried WordNet to collect the synonyms of these frequent words and saved them to a file. MultiD uses this file as a general English thesaurus.

2.2 Recommendation Algorithms

We next present the algorithm to generate recommended queries by using these dictionaries. The goal of this algorithm is to transform the original query to a set of queries that consist of terms in the Level I dictionary. Supposing the original query having several space-separated words, MultiD first queries the level I dictionary to decide whether each word exists in the code base. If a word does, MultiD does not transform the word; otherwise our technique tries to use the following three steps to transform the word.

Word splitting. Firstly, MultiD greedily extracts the parts of the word that exist in the Level I dictionary. More specifically, for a given word, MultiD tries to find its longest prefix and suffix that exist the level I dictionary; next, the technique recursively splits the middle part of the word until no in-dictionary prefix or suffix can be found. For instance, supposing the level I dictionary only contains the terms of "get" and "name", splitting the word of "getelementname" leads to three new words which are "get", "element", and "name".

Word recommendation. After splitting, if the query still contains words that are not in the level I dictionary, MultiD tries to find their synonyms in the dictionaries of higher levels as recommendations. Our technique starts with the level II dictionary due to its higher relevance. If no synonyms in the level II dictionary are found, MultiD tries to find synonyms in the level III dictionary. After retrieving the synonyms, the technique next excludes those synonyms that are not in the level I dictionary. The remaining synonyms are recommended to the developer as the replacements to the original word. If finding multiple synonyms to recommend, MultiD uses the co-occurrence matrix stated in Section 2.1 to rank them. The synonyms that occur more frequently with the rest part of the input query rank higher.

Word correction. For those words that neither exist in the level I dictionary by themselves nor have synonyms in the dictionaries of higher levels, our technique considers them as the typos of the terms in the level I dictionary. Therefore, MultiD uses the terms in the level I dictionary to correct them. The algorithm for correction adopts 2-gram indexing to quickly find the terms that spell similarly with a given typo [4].

3. Evaluation

Although we have implemented MultiD as an extension to Sando [7], the evaluation of MultiD is an ongoing work. While a developers is using Sando, a data collector running in the background of Sando logs usage information of the search tool, including the queries the developer provided, the recommendations she reviewed and the search results she examined. By investigating the collected data, we can measure whether MultiD can help developers synthesize high-quality queries. In addition, we also plan to distribute a survey among Sando users to collect their subjective opinions towards MultiD recommendations. In summary, we plan to answer the following three research questions: (1) what is the percentage of queries recommended by MultiD that are actually adopted by developers? (2) How much can the MultiD-recommended queries improve search results in terms of recall and precision? (3) According to Sando users' subjective opinions, how can we improve MultiD?

4. Conclusion

In this extended abstract, we introduce a dictionary-based technique to assist developers improve the queries they put in LCS tools. Our technique uses multiple levels of dictionaries that vary in terms of the amount of information contained and their relevance to the code base under search. By using these dictionaries, our technique recommends developers queries that are potentially more promising in retrieving useful results.

Acknowledgment

This work is under mentoring of Dr. David Shepherd from ABB Inc. I thank the comments from Dr. Emerson Murphy-Hill.

References

[1] Frequent Word Lists. http://invokeit.wordpress.com/frequency-word-lists/, 2013.

[2] S. Gupta, S. Malik, L. Pollock, and K. Vijay-Shanker. Part-of-speech tagging of program identifiers for improved text-based software engineering tool. In *Proc. ICPC*. IEEE, 2013.

[3] A. J. Ko, B. A. Myers, M. J. Coblenz, and H. H. Aung. An exploratory study of how developers seek, relate, and collect relevant information during software maintenance tasks. *TSE*, 32(12):971–987, 2006.

[4] K. Kukich. Techniques for automatically correcting words in text. *ACM Computing Surveys*, 24(4):377–439, 1992.

[5] George A. M. Wordnet: A lexical database for english. *Communications of the ACM*, 38:39–41, 1995.

[6] S. Pinker. *The language instinct.* New York: W. Morrow, 1994.

[7] D. Shepherd, K. Damevski, B. Ropski, and T. Fritz. Sando: an extensible local code search framework. In *Proc. FSE*, pages 15:1–15:2, 2012.

A Screen-Oriented Representation for Mobile Applications

Aharon Abadi

IBM Research – Haifa
aharona@il.ibm.com

Yishai A. Feldman

IBM Research – Haifa
yishai@il.ibm.com

Konstantin Shagin

IBM Research – Haifa
konst@il.ibm.com

Abstract

Program analysis plays an important role in a variety of software engineering processes, such as automated code refactoring, compiler optimizations, and program slicing. The internal program representation used by the program analysis algorithm affects the power and efficiency of the analysis. In particular, representations that contain data-flow information alongside control flow are known to be especially useful. While there are many popular internal program representations with data-flow information for traditional languages and platforms, few specifically target mobile applications. In this paper, we propose a new data-flow-enabled representation that addresses the screen-oriented nature of a mobile application and explores its potential. We consider a mobile application to be a reactive system whose states are the screens, and whose events are user actions, incoming communication, or anything else that causes transition from one screen to another. The resulting representation is a finite state machine extended with data-flow information. We suggest that this representation can greatly contribute to optimization, refactoring, and understanding of mobile applications.

Categories and Subject Descriptors D.2.2 [*Software Engineering*]: Design Tools and Techniques—State diagrams

General Terms Algorithms, Design

Keywords Mobile, analysis, optimization, refactoring

1. Introduction and Motivating Example

Contemporary compilers and IDEs make extensive use of program analysis in a variety of tasks, including optimization, refactoring, and validation. The more useful and more sophisticated tasks require the internal program representation produced by the program analysis algorithm to contain data-flow information. There are many existing program representations that meet this requirement and yield excellent results for traditional programming languages and platforms, including the program-dependence graph (PDG) [2], static single assignment (SSA) form [1], and the plan calculus [3].

The growing popularity of smart mobile devices has given rise to new GUI-centered programming paradigms. The main control

SPLASH '13, October 26–31, 2013, Indianapolis, Indiana, USA.
Copyright is held by the owner/author(s).
ACM 978-1-4503-1995-9/13/10.
http://dx.doi.org/10.1145/2508075.2508090

of an information-based mobile application is defined by the application screens and the transitions between them. This information can greatly enhance program analysis in this domain.

In this paper, we propose a novel data-flow-enabled program representation for mobile applications that takes their screen-oriented nature into account. In this representation, the application screens are the states of a finite state machine, while events such as user actions and communication-related triggers cause transitions between the states. In addition to the control-flow edges, which indicate state transitions, the application graph contains unidirectional data-flow edges. The extended FSM representation is analogous to the SSA form [1]; whenever there is more than one incoming data-flow edge into the same state labeled with the same variable, there is a data-flow join similar to an SSA ϕ function.

As an example, consider the eBay mobile application, which, like the eBay web site, allows the user to search for, buy, and sell various items. Figure 1 depicts two control flow paths of this application. The item search path spans screens 1–4. The search query is fed in screen (1). Screen (2) presents the search results. If the user touches one of the items, the item is presented in screen (3). Then, if the user touhes the item's picture, screen (4) shows a larger picture.

The second control path shown deals with feedback. Screen (5) appears when the *Reminders* button on screen (1) is touched. When *Leave feedback* is touched on screen (5), screen (6) appears, and presents the purchased items for which feedback has not yet been submitted. When one of the purchases is touched, screen (7) presents the chosen item. If the *Leave feedback* button, located at the bottom of screen (7), is pressed, screen (8) enables user feedback. Note that screens (3) and (7) are very likely implemented using the same piece of code.

Figure 2 shows the data and control flow of this part of the eBay application. The *entry* state is a virtual initial state; it does not represent a screen. The dashed arrows represent control flow, and the solid arrows represent the data flow. Data-flow arrows are labeled with the transmitted data item. The *cDB* and *iDB* labels represent the databases containing customer and item information, respectively. The *id*, *search*, and *item* labels represent the customer identification number, the search string, and the chosen item, respectively.

The user identification *id* is set or changed on screen (1), where the user logs in, and flows from there to all other screens that need it. The search string flows from screen (1) to (2), and the specific item chosen from screens (2) and (6), where it is set, to the others that need it. The item database *iDB* cannot change via any user actions, so it flows from the entry state to the others. However, the customer database *cDB* can change as a result of adding user feedback. It therefore has two sources, the initial value in the entry state, and the modified value in screen (8). Screens (1) and (5) serve as join points for this value. For screen (5) this happens since it determines whether the value comes from (1), when control flows from there, or from (8), when control flows from (6). The reasoning

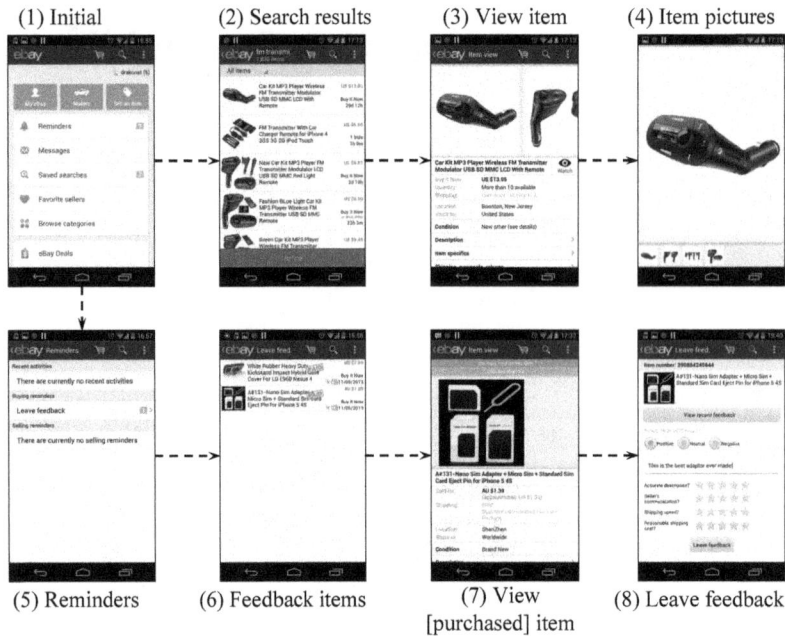

Figure 1. An excerpt from the eBay application.

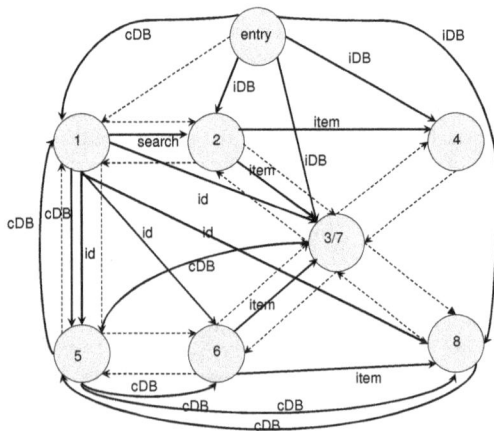

Figure 2. Internal representation of the eBay application.

for screen (1) is similar. It should be noted that we chose to unify the states for screens (3) and (7), because (we assume) they are implemented by the same code.

2. Applications

Reducing server access is crucial for the efficiency of mobile applications. The extended FSM representation can be used to perform this analysis at the abstraction level of the states. If data computed in a single state is not used in that state and does not flow to any other state, its computation can be eliminated. This cleanly separates the intra- and inter-state analysis. The analysis on the extended FSM can be carried out by performing a slice starting from all user-visible elements in all screens, as described next.

A (backward) program slice is a meaningful executable subprogram that computes the same values as the original program for a given set of variable occurrences. A common algorithm for computing program slices uses the notions of data and control dependence [4]. The data-flow edges in the extended FSM immediatley provide the data-dependence relationship: a state that receives data from another state has a data dependence on it. Starting from a set of screens (or screen elements), the slicing algorithm recursively traces data relationships backwards to collect the slice.

Consider the slice from screen (8), the feedback form. It has data dependences on screen (6) through the variable *item*, since the choice of which item to give feedback on is made there; on screen (5) through the variable *cDB*, since the choice of where this variables comes from (screen (1) or a previous visit to screen (8)) is made there; and on screen (1) though *id*. There are no new dependences from these screens, and the slice of screen (8) therefore contains screens (1), (5), (6), and (8) itself.

An interesting conclusion from this analysis is that screen (8) does not really depend on screen (7). This is in fact true, since the purpose of screen (7) is just to show more details about the product, but no decision is made there. It might therefore be reasonable to eliminate this extra step, and go directly from screen (6) to (8), or merge the feedback functionality into screen (6). This refactoring that eliminates a screen, is naturally defined in terms of the extended FSM representation. This change has several constraints. In particular, it must be the case that the data used in screen (8) is not changed; that is, data dependences must not change. This is easily verified using the data-flow part of the representation.

References

[1] R. Cytron, J. Ferrante, B. K. Rosen, M. N. Wegman, and F. K. Zadeck. Efficiently computing static single assignment form and the control dependence graph. *ACM Trans. Prog. Lang. Syst.*, 13(4):451–490, Oct. 1991.

[2] J. Ferrante, K. J. Ottenstein, and J. D. Warren. The program dependence graph and its use in optimization. *ACM Trans. Program. Lang. Syst.*, 9 (3):319–349, 1987.

[3] C. Rich and R. C. Waters. *The Programmer's Apprentice*. ACM Press and Addison Wesley, 1990.

[4] F. Tip. A survey of program slicing techniques. *J. Programming Languages*, 3:121–189, 1995.

Hardware and Software Support for Fine-Grained Memory Access Control and Encapsulation in C++ *

Eugen Leontie   Gedare Bloom   Rahul Simha

The George Washington University

eugen@gwu.edu   gedare@gwu.edu   simha@gwu.edu

Abstract

Object-oriented programming (OOP) encapsulates object implementations with access specifiers like *public* and *private*. Compilers can verify that code adheres to specifiers, but verification can be broken in languages like C++ by unchecked pointers. Thus, C++ programmers are taught that "private is not secure." The lack of isolation between objects frustrates memory protection in OOP code. We propose hardware and software support to confine memory accesses in fine-grained memory regions that isolate within and between objects so that C++ programs can enforce encapsulation and prevent pointer-based exploits. Such support makes *private* secure. Although we target C++, our approach handles generic techniques like inheritance, polymorphism, dynamic dispatch, dynamic binding, and encapsulation.

Categories and Subject Descriptors   Security and privacy [*Security in hardware*]: Hardware security implementation

Keywords   hardware containers, encapsulation

1. Introduction

Objects are the natural boundary for protection in an OOP application. Memory protection can isolate between and within objects (inter- and intra-object protection). Although researchers have studied memory protection extensively for unsafe languages like C, OOP languages like C++ present new challenges including inheritance and composition, polymorphism, constructors/destructors, exception handling, friend classes, casting, and stack-instantiated objects. Even Java can violate language-based memory protection with reflection and the Java Native Interface.

* Work supported by NSF CNS-0934725 and AFOSR FA9550-09-1-0194.

Commodity memory protection works at the granularity of page and process, which is little help for object protection. For such *process-oriented memory protection*, isolating code modules requires dividing an application into processes and replacing function calls with inter-process communication, which imposes development and runtime costs.

In prior work, we introduced *containers*, hardware support for fine-grained memory protection [1]. In this paper, we discuss adopting containers to support inter- and intra-object protection in C++. Our approach aligns well with object interactions without artificial processes. Our contribution is a platform that secures direct memory access with OOP. Our solution improves on the related work by being the first to address private member runtime protection for C++.

2. Hardware Containers

A container is a set of bounded, contiguous ranges of instructions that is given permission to access memory regions. Containers do not overlap instruction ranges, and each container has a unique *container identifier* (cid). Code that belongs to the same container shares a cid. In OOP a method is a useful unitary container. Methods in the same library or class can be combined into a larger container for efficiency.

The *container manager (CM)* is a hardware reference monitor that enforces permissions using content-addressable memory to avoid affecting processor path delays [1]. The CM enforces memory permissions—read, write, execute, and delegate—on all memory regions. Delegate permission controls permission propagation between containers. The compiler infers permissions on arguments and automatic variables. Permissions for dynamically-allocated memory that the compiler is unable to resolve are granted programmatically by permission-granting ALLOW instructions. *ALLOW* enables permissions on dynamic memory, and the ALLOWM variant supports linked data structures [1]. A call/return to another container causes a *security context switch*, which pushes/pops the dynamic permissions onto a permission stack mirroring the call stack. This stack obviates permission naming, lookup, and revocation.

2.1 Containers for C++

OOP features can cause problems for the CM: permissions for private data must exist for object methods; exceptions circumvent the call stack and access object fields, locals, and global structures; inheritance and composition fragment object memory layout; virtual functions and polymorphism require dynamic execution control flow and dynamic type information; and `friend` classes require permission to access private fields. `const`, casts, and placement new are straightforward, but containers alone is insufficient for serialization.

To support `private` data we add ownership transfer of memory regions with ALLOWD, and persistent private access rights with ALLOWP. ALLOWD revokes access from one container and delegates access to another. ALLOWP creates a dynamic permission that a container with a specified cid can use—cid 0 gives permission for any container. Allocators execute ALLOWD to pass ownership rights over private memory to class constructors, which use ALLOWP on private data with the cid of each member method, and with cid 0 for public data. Adversarial code could use a derived class to access `protected` members, so the compiler and CM treat protected like private, and instances of the base class are not affected by (malicious) derived objects. Inheritance and composition affect performance of delegating permissions because compilers split object memory layouts so that a child (front-end) class cannot access private members of ancestor (back-end) classes. Splitting the memory range fragments the object representation and increases the overhead of permission management, because the CM needs to manage permissions for each private region of an object.

We have also identified solutions to problematic areas of C++ but not yet implemented our solutions. For *exception handling*, we propose to compartmentalize global state, remove trusted access from exception handling code, and subject exception handling to the same memory protection as other code. We identify three necessary modifications: (1) each container needs methods for stack unwinding and compensation code; (2) global tables need to be divided into per-container tables; (3) global lists must be placed in containers to confine operations done on these lists. *Virtual functions and polymorphism* require inserting extra ALLOW instructions to handle dynamic binding, and dynamic permissions may be needed for fields in a derived class that are not present in the base class. Such permissions may be derived by extending virtual tables with object permission layout information similar to runtime type identification (RTTI). The same kind of RTTI can be applied to disambiguate *multiple inheritance*. Containers can support *friend classes* if constructors create private permissions for all friends, which is not a problem because classes already declare friends. The compiler can extend the *const attribute* to CM enforcement by using read-only permission on `const` data, but `const` casts will not change the read-only permission. Other *cast operators* can work directly. *Placement new* allows a pro-

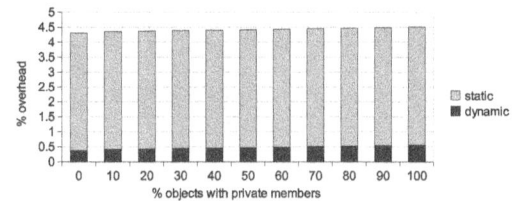

Figure 1. Overhead for heap-allocated objects.

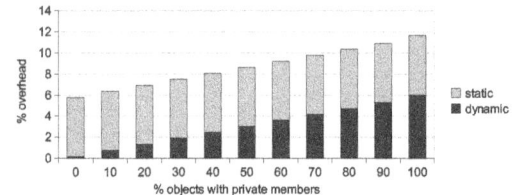

Figure 2. Overhead for stack-allocated objects.

grammer to place an object at a predetermined memory location, which bypasses heap allocation, but otherwise uses the same permission delegation as `new`—execute ALLOWD to relinquish ownership of object memory. *Serialization* enables object storage and transmission and requires additional trusted code in the C++ runtime and kernel I/O.

3. Experiments and Results

We implemented our approach using GEMS/Opal [2] and evaluate it using C++ microbenchmarks designed to stress performance. Our microbenchmark mimics C program workloads and adds C++ object creation, access of private/public members, and object destruction. We have not been able to measure real applications due to time constraints. Results show the percent overhead of execution time using our approach compared with the baseline: smaller is better.

Figures 1 and 2 show the costs for object creation and destruction on the heap and stack respectively for 1000 objects and a varying percent of objects using private data. Memory allocation, rather than permissions management, dominates the performance for heap objects. For stack objects, overhead reaches 11.68% when all objects have private data.

4. Conclusion

We demonstrated that fine-grained memory protection can support OOP languages like C++. Future work can implement and evaluate more OOP features and real applications.

References

[1] E. Leontie, G. Bloom, B. Narahari, and R. Simha. No principal too small: Memory access control for fine-grained protection domains. *15th Euromicro Conference on Digital System Design(DSD)*, September 2012.

[2] M. M. K. Martin, D. J. Sorin, B. M. Beckmann, M. R. Marty, M. Xu, A. R. Alameldeen, K. E. Moore, M. D. Hill, and D. A. Wood. Multifacet's general execution-driven multiprocessor simulator (gems) toolset. *SIGARCH Comput. Archit. News*, 33 (4):92–99, 2005. ISSN 0163-5964.

Source Code Management for Projectional Editing

David H. Lorenz[1]

[1]Open University of Israel,
1 University Rd., P.O.Box 808, Raanana 43107
Israel
lorenz@openu.ac.il

Boaz Rosenan[1,2]

[2]University of Haifa,
Mount Carmel, Haifa 31905
Israel
brosenan@cslab.openu.ac.il

Abstract

Traditionally, Source Code Management (SCM) tools rely on the source code being text. In Projectional Editing (PE), however, the source code is an opaque model, rendering traditional SCM support ineffective. In this work we present an effective approach to enabling SCM for PE.

Categories and Subject Descriptors   D.2.3 [*Software Engineering*]: Coding Tools and Techniques—Program editors; D.3.4 [*Programming Languages*]: Processors—Projectional editing.

General Terms   Design, Languages.

Keywords   Projectional editing (PE); Source Code Management (SCM); Language-oriented programming (LOP); Domain-specific languages (DSL).

1.   Introduction

Projectional Editing (PE) is a programming language implementation approach based on the Model/View/Controller (MVC) architecture. With PE, source code is stored as an opaque *model*. To allow editing, the model is projected to a *view*. The user edits the view to modify the model. These changes are then projected back to the view to provide feedback to the user. PE is defined in contrast to the traditional *Textual Editing (TE)* approach, where the source code is stored in the form of textual files and edited as such.

The main challenge in using *Source Code Management (SCM)* tools in the context of PE is that PE does not provide a well defined way to merge two versions of a model, and at the event of merge conflicts, does not provide a way to mark the conflicts. Some PE implementations come with their own

SPLASH '13,   October 26–31, 2013, Indianapolis, Indiana, USA.
Copyright is held by the owner/author(s).
ACM 978-1-4503-1995-9/13/10.
http://dx.doi.org/10.1145/2508075.2508092

internal SCM (one example is MS Word). However, these SCM tools are often limited in capabilities (e.g., MS Word is not always able to show differences between versions). Even if the internal SCM is powerful enough, it is stand-alone, meaning that in an organization that releases software based on both PE and TE languages, or even different PE tools, the code cannot be versioned as a whole.

2.   Approach

The key to SCM support for PE, is the ability to automatically merge non-conflicting models. There are three fundamental approaches to doing so in PE: (1) merging based on textual diff on models that are stored in a textual format (e.g., in XML); (2) merging based on a tree-diff algorithm (such as *change distilling* by Fluri *et al.* [2]) applied to the model; and (3) recording history within the model, and merging based on it.

The first approach is the simplest to use, and allows the use of any off-the-shelf SCM tool. Its main disadvantage is regarding conflict handling. First, a textual merge is more prone to find false conflicts, since it is based on text lines, and not model nodes. Second, when a conflict is found, the format agnostic SCM tool will mark the conflicts in a way that will typically break its format, i.e., create an invalid model file. Third, resolution of the conflicts is done in the raw format (e.g., XML), with a representation unfamiliar to the developer.

The second approach is better than the first. It provides a more precise way to differentiate models, and a better way to mark conflicts. Its model-aware nature allows conflict markers to be embedded in the model, allowing the projectional editor to be used to resolve them. The main disadvantage of this approach is that like any diff algorithm, tree-diff algorithms find *a* sequence of operations that can transform one version into the other, not necessarily *the* sequence of operations that were actually used. The result could be finding conflicts on none-conflicting changes, or finding conflicts that do not actually represent the changes made by the user and are thus not familiar to them. This approach is used by MPS [4].

```
{"xxxx": ["compound", "a", 2],
 "xxxx-A": {"v": "yyyy", "h": {}},
 "xxxx-B": {"v": "zzzz", "h": {}},
 "yyyy": ["string", "b"],
 "zzzz": ["number", 7]}
```

Figure 1. JSON representation of a possible model for $a(\text{``}b\text{''}, 7)$

```
{"xxxx": ["compound", "a", 2],
 "xxxx-A": {"v": "yyyy", "h": {}},
 "xxxx-B": {"v": "wwww", "h": {"zzzz":1}},
 "yyyy": ["string", "b"],
 "zzzz": ["number", 7],
 "wwww": ["number", 8]}
```

Figure 2. JSON representation of a possible model for $a(\text{``}b\text{''}, 8)$

The third approach addresses the limitations of the second one, by using one of PE's core features: the opacity of the model. Thanks to that, the model's representation can be chosen in such a way that will store not only the current state, but also enough history to allow merging. By recording history in the model, we do not need a diff algorithm to "guess" the sequence of editing operations made on our model. We simply "know it." This makes the merge more accurate, assuring that only real conflicts are marked as such. This approach is used by the Cedalion WebBench – a Web-based projectional editor for the Cedalion programming language [3].

3. Design and Implementation

Any PE implementation needs to start by defining a model representation. Other than the obvious need for being able to represent the model (i.e., a compound Cedalion term [3, Section 3.2]), we had two requirements for the representation: (1) providing unique identifiers to nodes, ones that are resilient to editing. If, e.g., a node is inserted between two existing nodes, the existing nodes' IDs must stay the same, and (2) support for fast and accurate merge of two versions of a model.

We chose a flat JSON object, containing key/value pairs representing the different *model nodes* and their *relationships*. *Model nodes* are keyed by unique identifiers. We use strings representing over 128 random bits, to avoid collisions at the event that different users are editing different versions of the same model independently. The content of such entries includes information on the node, such as what language construct it represents (e.g., name/arity pairs for compound terms or the values of literals). *Relationships* are keyed by the parent node's unique identifier, followed by a dash and a character representing the position of the child node with respect to the parent ('A' represents the first child, 'B' the second and so forth). The content of such entries is an object containing the unique identifier of the child node, and a history with all previous values. For example, the term $a(\text{``}b\text{''}, 7)$ can be represented by a model similar to the one in Figure 1 (we omitted some details to improve readability).

The use of random unique identifier strings to represent nodes helps support the above requirements, by making sure nodes can be stored in the model unchanged, forever. Changes to the model are only reflected in the relationship entries, with history tracked (in the "h" field). This field records the previous values held by this relationship (as keys, for fast access). For example, when editing the model in Figure 1, by changing it from $a(\text{``}b\text{''}, 7)$ to $a(\text{``}b\text{''}, 8)$, the model changes to, e.g., the one depicted in Figure 2.

With history recording, merging two models is easy, and is done in a single pass through the keys of one of them, moving items to the other as appropriate. Conflicts are marked by placing new conflict marker nodes in the target model, with two children: the two conflicting versions.

The above merging algorithm can be plugged into any SCM that supports custom merge tools (e.g., Git, as done by Völter [4]). However, since ours is a Web-based editor, we opted to use CouchDB [1], as our SCM infrastructure. The use of CouchDB as an SCM tool is somewhat unconventional, but for a Web-based development environment it makes sense, for the following reasons: (1) its replication mechanism allows synchronization of entire repositories between databases and servers, and (2) it has a mechanism for identifying conflicts that our merge algorithm can resolve.

With CouchDB, the operations of pulling, pushing, branching and merging can therefore be performed using replication (with conflict resolution as appropriate). Databases represent repositories and branches, and labeling can be simulated using snapshots.

Acknowledgment

This research was supported in part by the *Israel Science Foundation (ISF)* under grant No. 926/08.

References

[1] C. Anderson. Apache CouchDB: The definitive guide. 2009. http://guide.couchdb.org/.

[2] B. Fluri, M. Wursch, M. Pinzger, and H. Gall. Change distilling: Tree differencing for fine-grained source code change extraction. *Software Engineering, IEEE Transactions on*, 33(11):725–743, 2007.

[3] D. H. Lorenz and B. Rosenan. Cedalion: A language for language oriented programming. In *Proceedings of the 26th Annual ACM SIGPLAN Conference on Object-Oriented Programming Systems, Languages, and Applications (OOPSLA'11)*, pages 733–752, Portland, Oregon, USA, October 2011. ACM.

[4] M. Völter. Working with MPS and git, 2011. http://confluence.jetbrains.com/display/MPSD25/HowTo+-+MPS+and+Git.

Migration from Deprecated API in Java

Roman Štrobl

Faculty of Information Technology
Czech Technical University in Prague
Czech Republic
stroblr@fit.cvut.cz

Zdeněk Troníček

Faculty of Information Technology
Czech Technical University in Prague
Czech Republic
tronicek@fit.cvut.cz

Abstract

When software components evolve, they change interfaces. Members that are obsolete are marked as deprecated and new members are added. We deal with the problem of migration from deprecated members to their replacement. We implemented two tools: Java Source Code Update Tool, which updates the source code based on a configuration file, and a generator, which heuristically figures out how to migrate from deprecated members and generates the configuration file. We evaluated these tools on five open source projects and the results are very encouraging.

Categories and Subject Descriptors   D.2.3 [Software Engineering]: Coding Tools and Techniques; D.2.7 [Software Engineering]: Distribution, Maintenance, and Enhancement

Keywords   Component upgrade, software evolution, Java, deprecated API, migration

1.   Introduction

We deal with a problem related to the evolution of Java component-based software. When a component evolves, it may change its interface (Application Programming Interface, API). For instance, a class can be renamed or a method can change its signature. Since these changes can break component clients, they are usually introduced gradually: first, obsolete API members are deprecated and new API members are introduced, and then, after some time, these deprecated members are removed. When an API member is deprecated, clients are expected to migrate to its replacement. In this paper, we address the problem of migration from deprecated API members to non-deprecated ones.

SPLASH '13,   October 26–31, 2013, Indianapolis, Indiana, USA.
ACM 978-1-4503-1995-9/13/10.
http://dx.doi.org/10.1145/2508075.2508093

2.   JaSCUT

In order to facilitate migration, we implemented Java Source Code Update Tool (JaSCUT) [1], which is able to transform the Java source code based on a configuration file. For instance, a change from `enable()` to `setEnabled(true)` in `java.awt.Component` is described in the configuration file as follows:

```
<change-method-signature>
  <type>java.awt.Component</type>
  <method-orig>enable</method-orig>
  <args-orig/>
  <method-new>setEnabled</method-new>
  <args-new>
    <arg>
      <name>b</name>
      <type>boolean</type>
      <value kind="literal">true</value>
    </arg>
  </args-new>
</change-method-signature>
```

The following refactorings are supported in JaSCUT: rename method, move static method, change method signature, rename type, move type, rename field, move static field, replace constructor call with a factory method call, replace a field reference with a method call, and combinations of these refactorings.

3.   Generator

Since preparing the configuration file for JaSCUT manually can be tedious, we implemented a desktop application that parses component source code and heuristically searches for replacements of deprecated API members. We use the following heuristics:

- Deprecated Javadoc heuristic
- Delegation heuristic
- Header similarity heuristic
- Type pairing heuristic
- Transitive deprecation heuristic

The Deprecated Javadoc heuristic analyzes the text in the @deprecated Javadoc tag and searches for known patterns such as "replaced by {@link …}". If such pattern is found, the heuristic extracts the value specified in the link, and stores it as a replacement of the deprecated API member. We use the patterns as follows:

1. replaced by [the] {@link ...}
2. use [the] {@link ...}
3. see [the] {@link ...}
4. access [the] {@link ...}
5. {@link ...} (only at the beginning of the @deprecated tag)
6. replaced by [the] <code>...</code>
7. use [the] <code>...</code>
8. use [the] <a href='...'>...</a>
9. replaced by [free text]
10. use [free text]

The Delegation heuristic looks into the body of a deprecated method and if the body contains a single method call, the called method is considered as a replacement for the deprecated method. A similar approach is used for fields.

The Header similarity heuristic detects small changes in method and field names. We use the Damerau-Levenshtein string distance to measure the similarity of strings. The Type pairing heuristic creates pairs from members of renamed types. For example, if A is deprecated and replaced with B, the members of A are paired with members of B. The Transitive deprecation heuristic is used when a replacement is also deprecated. The heuristic finds the first non-deprecated member in a chain of replacements.

All these heuristics are combined and their results are merged based on weights. If the replacement found by the generator is uncertain, the rule is marked for review and the user is expected to either confirm or edit the rule.

4. Evaluation

We used five open source projects for the evaluation: Apache Http Client, OpenJDK, Joda Time, Bouncy Castle, and Apache PDFBox. In each project, we identified deprecated members and manually searched for their replacements. In case a hint was present in the Javadoc which said how to migrate from the deprecated member, we considered this migration rule as manually resolvable. We distinguished between regular rules and pairing rules. Regular rules are related to members that have either the @deprecated Javadoc tag or the @Deprecated annotation. Pairing rules are used for members that are not explicitly deprecated but they are inside of a deprecated type, and thus they must be migrated as well. Then we let the generator generate the migration rules, and we manually checked whether they are correct. We classified each rule in the following way: true positive (TP) if the API member can be resolved and the generator provides the same rule as manual resolution, true negative (TN) if the API member cannot be resolved and the generator marks the member as unresolvable, false negative (FN) if the API member can be

resolved manually but the generator marks the member as unresolvable, and false positive (FP) if the generator provides incorrect resolution. Then we used this classification to count accuracy, precision, and recall as follows: accuracy = (TP + TN)/(TP + TN + FP + FN), precision = TP/(TP + FP), recall = TP/(TP + FN).

Table 1: Evaluation of automated migration

Project	Accuracy	Precision	Recall
Apache Http Client	86%	95%	74%
OpenJDK	83%	92%	66%
Joda Time	97%	100%	78%
Bouncy Castle	69%	100%	49%
Apache PDFBox	79%	100%	71%

5. Related Work

Perkins [3] proposed a technique, called *method inlining*, for refactoring client code in response to changes in library API. The technique is based on a simple idea: calls to deprecated methods are replaced by their bodies.

We are not aware of any tool developed specifically for migration from deprecated API, but the problem is similar to the problem of migration to an alternative API, which was investigated by several researchers. Henkel and Diwan [4] described the CatchUp! tool, which records refactorings when the component evolves and enables to replay them later. The same idea was implemented in the Eclipse IDE [5]. It could presumably be used for migration from deprecated API provided that we prepare the configuration file manually; however, its use in the Eclipse IDE is limited only to migration of a JAR file.

6. Conclusion

We evaluated the possibility of automated migration from deprecated API members to their replacements. The evaluation shows that the migration can be partially automated for most Java APIs.

References

[1] JaSCUT. http://java.net/projects/jascut

[2] JaSCUT Config Generator. http://java.net/projects/jascutconf

[3] J. H. Perkins. Automatically generating refactorings to support API evolution, *ACM SIGPLAN-SIGSOFT Workshop on Program Analysis for Software Tools and Engineering*, pp. 111–114, 2005.

[4] J. Henkel and A. Diwan. CatchUp!: capturing and replaying refactorings to support API evolution, *International Conference on Software Engineering*, pp. 274–283, 2005.

[5] Eclipse IDE. http://www.eclipse.org

[6] R. Štrobl. *Generator of a configuration file for JaSCUT: Master's thesis.* Czech Technical University in Prague, Faculty of Information Technology, 2013.

On Testing the Source Compatibility in Java

Jan Hýbl

Faculty of Information Technology
Czech Technical University in Prague
Czech Republic
hybljan2@fit.cvut.cz

Zdeněk Troníček

Faculty of Information Technology
Czech Technical University in Prague
Czech Republic
tronicek@fit.cvut.cz

Abstract

When software components evolve, they change interfaces, which may break backward compatibility. We present a tool that facilitates checking whether a new version of component is source compatible with a previous version. This tool figures out the component interface and generates the client code that uses the component interface to maximum extent. If the generated client compiles against the new component interface, those two versions are more or less compatible. The tool can be useful for API authors.

Categories and Subject Descriptors   D.2.3 [Software Engineering]: Coding Tools and Techniques; D.2.7 [Software Engineering]: Distribution, Maintenance, and Enhancement

Keywords   Software evolution, Java, API evolution, source compatibility

1. Introduction

When a change in application programming interface (API) causes that a client that compiled against the previous API version does not compile against the new API version, we say that the change breaks source compatibility [1] and call it the breaking change. For instance, if a class has the method

`Class<?> loadClass(String codebase, String name);`

and a new version of this class adds the method

`Class<?> loadClass(URL codebase, String name);`

the calls of the method with the first argument `null` do not compile against the new version because the call is ambiguous. We identified the following breaking changes:

1. The `final` modifier added to a class, a field, or a method

2. The `static` modifier added to or removed from a class, a field, or a method
3. The access modifier changed on a class, a field, or a method (only changes from `protected` to `public` and from `public` to `protected` are relevant; for instance, a change from `public` to `private` is considered as an API member removal)
4. A class added, deleted, renamed, or moved
5. The superclass of a class changed
6. The interfaces implemented by a class changed
7. A method added, deleted, renamed, or moved
8. The method parameters changed
9. The method return type changed
10. The exceptions thrown from a method changed
11. A field deleted, renamed, or moved
12. The field type changed
13. The annotation target changed
14. The annotation elements changed
15. The default value of an annotation element deleted
16. An enum value added, deleted, or renamed

We take into account all breaking changes but two for compatibility testing. We do not consider "a class added" as a breaking change because it happens very often (any new class may break a client) and the situation when a client is broken is rare. For the same reason we do not consider "an enum value added".

2. JASCC

In order to facilitate checking of source compatibility of two APIs, we implemented a tool called Java API Source Compatibility Checker (JASCC) [2]. The tool first figures out the component API by scanning either the source code or the bytecode. The source code scanner is based on javac and the bytecode scanner exploits reflection. The gathered information is then used to generate a code of a "complete" API user and a "complete" API extender. The complete API user of a tested class C calls every constructor and every method of C and accesses every field in C. The structure of the API user is as follows:

`public class TestedClassUser {`

SPLASH '13,   October 26–31, 2013, Indianapolis, Indiana, USA.
ACM 978-1-4503-1995-9/13/10.
http://dx.doi.org/10.1145/2508075.2508094

```
// constructors tests
// methods tests
// fields tests
// ancestors tests
}
```

In addition to common constructor and method calls with arguments of appropriate types, the API user also contains calls with null arguments, so that we are able to detect constructor and method overloading in a next API version. If a constructor or method throws exceptions, we catch them at the call site. For instance, if the `play` method throws `IOException` and `InterruptedException`, the generated API user contains the method as follows:

```
public void play(C instance, int speed) {
    try {
        instance.play(speed);
    } catch (IOException e) {
    } catch (InterruptedException e) {
    }
}
```

The complete API extender of a class D declares a subclass of D that overrides every protected and public method in D and accesses every protected and public field in D. The structure of the generated API extender is as follows:

```
public class TestedClassExtender extends
    TestedClass {
    // constructors tests
    // methods tests
    // fields tests
    // unimplemented methods
}
```

If the API class contains abstract methods, the extender implements them so that we are able to catch changes in them.

3. Evaluation

We evaluated the tool on five open source projects: Google Gson, Apache HttpClient, Apache PDFBox, Apache log4j, and Joda Time. For each project, we performed the steps as follows:

1. We downloaded the source codes of several versions of the project

2. For each version,

a) we used JASCC to generate the API clients

b) we compiled the API clients against the selected version

c) we compiled the API clients against the next version; this either succeeded (when there are no breaking changes) or failed

d) if the compilation failed, we blacklisted in the configuration file of JASCC all the API members that caused compilation failure and repeated steps c and d until compilation succeeded

e) we manually investigated the API changes found in previous steps and classified them as either refactorings or non-refactorings

The changes on existing API members are classified as refactorings based on assumption that the semantics of API members is stable. The changes that add new API members (New abstract method, Overloaded method) are classified as non-refactorings.

Table 1: The counts of breaking changes (#ver. is the number of investigated versions, Total is the number of all changes)

Project	#ver.	Refactorings	Total	%
Gson	9	53	55	96%
Apache HttpClient	3	5	7	71%
Apache PDFBox	9	135	153	88%
Apache log4j	13	169	174	97%
Joda Time	14	45	49	92%

4. Related Work

To the best of our knowledge, there is no tool similar to JASCC. Concerning the API evolution, we found several works. Dig and Johnson [3] presented a study on API evolution, which is similar to ours; however, their approach was different: they selected always two versions of five components, manually analyzed the API changes, and then double-checked the result by a tool and heuristics.

The studies on API evolution are motivated by effort to build a tool for automatic migration between two versions of a component. Henkel and Diwan [4] described the CatchUp! tool, which records refactorings when the component evolves and enables to replay them later. The same idea has been implemented in the Eclipse IDE [5].

5. Conclusion

The differences in the counts of breaking changes of investigated projects are large. On projects log4j and Joda Time we can see that the number of breaking changes does not depend on the size of the project. Either of them has between 60 and 70 kLOC and the counts of breaking changes are very different.

References

[1] https://blogs.oracle.com/darcy/entry/kinds_of_compatibility.

[2] Java API Source Compatibility Checker (JASCC). http://java.net/projects/jascc.

[3] D. Dig and R. Johnson. How do APIs evolve? A story of refactoring, *Journal of Software Maintenance and Evolution: Research and Practice*, Vol. 18, Issue 2, 2006, pp. 83-107.

[4] J. Henkel and A. Diwan. CatchUp!: capturing and replaying refactorings to support API evolution, *International Conference on Software Engineering*, pp. 274–283, 2005.

[5] Eclipse IDE. http://www.eclipse.org

[6] J. Hýbl. *Code generator for testing of compatibility of API: Master's thesis*. Czech Technical University in Prague, Faculty of Information Technology, 2013.

Concurrent Object-Oriented Programming with Agents

Alessandro Ricci

University of Bologna, Italy
a.ricci@unibo.it

Andrea Santi

University of Bologna, Italy
a.santi@unibo.it

Abstract

ALOO is a novel approach to Concurrent Object-Oriented Programming, integrating plain old objects with concurrency through the adoption of *agent-oriented* first-class abstractions.

Categories and Subject Descriptors D.3.3 [*Programming Languages*]: Language Constructs and Features; D.1.3 [*Programming Techniques*]: Concurrent Programming

Keywords Concurrent Object-Oriented Programming; Agents

1. Introduction

The conceptual integration of OOP with concurrency [2] – including asynchronous and event-driven programming – is still an issue, both from a conceptual and practical point of view. Proposals in the state-of-the-art can be broadly classified in two opposite families. On one extreme we have those proposals that keep essentially the good old "mainstream" OOP with a support for multi-threading and add *ad hoc* abstractions and mechanisms to simplify multi-threaded and asynchronous programming. On the other extreme we have proposals that revise the foundations, injecting concurrency at the core of the object model. A main example is given by *actors* [1] and related approaches like concurrent/active objects [6]. Each family has some pros and cons and this leads developers to mix different concurrent models in practice, for instance integrating actors, passive objects, and threads [5]. This makes programming quite tricky and often leads to solutions with a poor design.

In this work we introduce a novel approach to Concurrent Object-Oriented Programming based on a simple conceptual model integrating plain old objects with *agents*, introduced as first-class abstraction for modeling the active parts of the program. The model is implemented in a language/platform called ALOO[1]. and is based on previous work done in the context of the simpAL project [3]—where agent-oriented abstractions were introduced but without being integrated with objects. The ALOO name is the short version of simpAL-OO.

A program (system) in ALOO is modelled as an *organization* of task-driven autonomous agents that work together inside a shared

---

[1] On ALOO web site (http://aloo.sourceforge.net) the interested readers can find a technical report providing details about the language, as well as a first prototype of the platform with simple examples.

SPLASH '13,   October 26–31, 2013, Indianapolis, Indiana, USA.
ACM 978-1-4503-1995-9/13/10.
http://dx.doi.org/10.1145/2508075.2508095

environment represented by a set of objects, that they cooperatively use, observe, create. The organization abstraction is used to explicitly define a collection of agents and objects, structured in *workspaces*. Workspaces are logical containers defining a notion of locality–in the case of organizations distributed over multiple network nodes. In the simple example shown in Figure 1, the program is given by a couple of Worker agents working inside a main workspace, doing cooperatively a Counting task, sharing a Count object. Classes implementing the interfaces are not reported.

The background metaphor underlying the approach is given by human organizations where people (agents) work cooperatively by exploiting resources and tools (objects), representing either instruments or the results of their job.

On the one side, the approach shares some key features of the actor model—decoupling of logical and physical concurrency, strong encapsulation (of control) and modularity, abstraction level avoiding locks and related low-level mechanisms, event-driven programming without inversion of control. On the other side, it allows for also exploiting features such as safe (without races) sharing and use of passive objects, synchronous communication and coordination without deadlocks due to wrong use of locks. Besides, the agent model natively extends actors reactivity with a form of *pro-activity*, which allows us to describe and more easily implement goal/task-driven behaviours.

2. Agents and Objects in ALOO

Differently from threads and analogously to actors, agents in ALOO are logical concurrent entities, so you can have thousands of agents running on top of a few number of physical threads/processes. Like actors, agents encapsulate a state, a behaviour and the *logical thread of control* of such a behavior. Differently from actors, agents are not only reactive but also *pro-active*, in the sense that they are spawned with some explicit *task* to-do (e.g. a Counting-Task in the example) – that could be shared/cooperative, not only individual. As soon as they complete their task, they terminate—so no garbage collection is needed. The type of an agent is called *role* (e.g. Worker in the example), and allows to specify the list of tasks that agents that declare to play that role must be capable to accomplish.

The behaviour of an agent is governed by a control loop [4], repeatedly selecting and executing actions to accomplish its task(s), possibly reacting to relevant events perceived from the environment (the objects). The programmer encodes the practical knowledge to accomplish tasks into *plans*, collected in *scripts*—that are interpreted and executed by the agent. Plans are similar to procedures, with the important difference that they are not a simple sequence of statements but a collection of *action rules*, each one specifying when (condition, event) execute some action—that can be a further block of action rules. Inside a plan the this-task variable refers to the actual task (object) to accomplish, while this-env refers to the object storing information about the system environment (including e.g. standard output, referred by the stdout observable property).

```
interface Count {
  count: int
  inc() }

interface CountingTask { tool: Count }

role Worker { tasks: CountingTask }

agent-script WorkerScript plays Worker {
  plan-for CountingTask {
    jobDone: boolean = false
    observing: this-task.tool as: t {
      #completed-when: jobDone
      /* a block repeating a sequence of actions */
      { #to-be-repeated
        this-env.stdout.println(msg: "..working.."); t.inc()}
      /* reactions */
      every-time changed: t.count as: v => {
        this-env.stdout.println(msg: "new value: "+v);
        if (v > 1000){ jobDone = true }}
    };
    this-env.stdout.println(msg: "job done.") }}

org-script SimpleExample {
  workspace main {
    c: Count <= new-obj CountImpl(count: 0)
    t: CountingTask <= new-obj CountingTaskImpl(tool: c)
    a1: Worker <= new-agent WorkerScript task: t
    a2: Worker <= new-agent WorkerScript task: t }}
```

Figure 1. A program example in ALOO.

Such a model has been devised so as to allow for effectively implementing behaviours composed by structured workflows mixing actions (sequence, parallel,..) and reactions to events [4], without incurring problems like inversion of control or asynchronous spaghetti. In the example, the plan for the CountingTask in WorkerScript accounts for repeatedly incrementing the counter, logging some msg on standard output (pro-active part); besides, every time a new value of the count observable property of the counter is perceived, the agent reacts by *suspending* what is doing (interrupt-like behaviour), in order to print a message and do some checks for eventually terminating the job. We believe that the capability of easily expressing behavior integrating pro-activity and re-activity is a key distinguishing feature of agents with respect to actors, active objects and related abstractions existing in literature.

Objects in ALOO are passive entities, analogously to plain old objects, with their own identity and independent existence from agents. They encapsulate set of actions (analogous to methods) that agents may invoke (e.g. inc() in the example) and a set of variables called *observable properties* (e.g. count, tool), both part of the object interface (i.e. type), representing object observable state that agents can perceive in an event-driven fashion. Besides, objects can have an inner, not observable state. Also tasks at runtime are uniformly represented by objects with a proper interface.

3. Use, Observation and Safe Sharing

Conceptually, agent-object interaction is *not* based on message passing (like in actors), neither on procedure call – but on action invocation (by agents on objects) and perception of asynchronous events generated by changes to objects' observable state (see Figure 2). Agents interaction is always mediated by objects—used and observed: direct communication among agents can be modeled on top, using suitably designed communication objects like message boxes, channels, blackboards and so on.

Actions executed inside an object can change its (observable or not) state and possibly invoke other actions over other objects. To make this interaction model effective, the object model has been devised so as to enforce safe sharing, so that multiple agents can work concurrently on the same shared objects without incurring

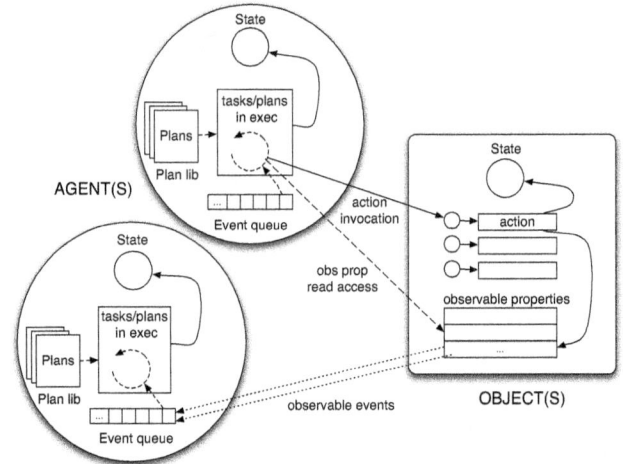

Figure 2. Agents and objects in ALOO

races. Similarly to monitors, inside an object, only one action can be in execution at a time and the effect of action execution on the object is made observable only when the action has completed. Differently from processes with monitors, the interaction model does not imply any (logical/physical) control coupling between agents and objects. Action completion/failure can be perceived by the agent as an asynchronous event, fetched by the agent control loop.

Besides actions, a main part of the interaction model is given by *observation*, which is natively supported by the model: an agent can dynamically decide to observe some group of objects (observing: construct) and, consequently, it automatically perceives an asynchronous event for every atomic change of the observable state of those objects, with guarantees about the ordering of events.

4. The Task Framework

Tasks are a key concept of the approach, founding agents' pro-activity and representing an important conceptual bridge to the design level. Besides the enabling mechanisms for task handling and management provided directly by the language, a Task Framework (TF) is provided on top of it, including a domain specific language to ease the description of complex tasks. The objective of the framework is to ease the definition of complex cooperative tasks, implementing a direct support for patterns of task organization and coordination which are recurrent in concurrent programming.

References

[1] G. Agha. Concurrent object-oriented programming. *Commun. ACM*, 33(9):125–141, Sept. 1990.

[2] J.-P. Briot, R. Guerraoui, and K.-P. Lohr. Concurrency and distribution in object-oriented programming. *ACM Comput. Surv.*, 30(3):291–329, 1998.

[3] A. Ricci and A. Santi. From actors to agent-oriented programming abstractions in simpAL. In *Proc. of SPLASH '12*, pages 73–74, New York, NY, USA, 2012. ACM.

[4] A. Ricci and A. Santi. Programming abstractions for integrating autonomous and reactive behaviors: an agent-oriented approach. In *Proc. of AGERE!'12*, pages 83–94, New York, NY, USA, 2012. ACM.

[5] S. Tasharofi, P. Dinges, and R. Johnson. Why do scala developers mix the actor model with other concurrency models? In *ECOOP'13, Montpellier, France, July 1–6, 2013*, 2013.

[6] A. Yonezawa, J.-P. Briot, and E. Shibayama. Object-oriented concurrent programming in ABCL/1. In N. K. Meyrowitz, editor, *OOPSLA*, pages 258–268. ACM, 1986.

PyLOM: A Language and Run-Time System for Planning Applications

Scotty Smith

The George Washington University
cssmith@gwmail.gwu.edu

Gedare Bloom

The George Washington University
gedare@gwmail.gwu.edu

Rahul Simha

The George Washington University
simha@gwmail.gwu.edu

Abstract

Controlling software systems autonomously has been a challenging research area. Modern autonomous systems are guided by a plan, which is a sequence of actions to take to achieve a goal. Many planning algorithms exist today to produce plans given a problem definition and goal. To ease programmability of autonomous systems, many languages have been developed for defining problems and goals. However, planning algorithms tend to need to be customized not only for the problem definition language, but also for the problem definition itself. This work presents a new problem definition language called *PyLOM*, an interpreted, object-oriented language. The PyLOM run-time system uses generic algorithms, which do not need to be customized for each problem definition. Thus, PyLOM separates problem definitions from planning algorithms to ease programmability and software reuse. The choice of an object-oriented language also is intended to aid programmability, since prior problem definition languages adopt a functional programming style.

Categories and Subject Descriptors D.3.2 [*Programming Languages*]: Language Classifications—Object-oriented languages; D.3.0 [*Programming Languages*]: General

Keywords Planning, PyLOM

1. Introduction

Creating software to autonomously control other software systems has been the focus of research since the 1960's. *Planning* is the act of computing a sequence of actions that accomplish some defined goal. Many general planning algorithms have been developed, such as A*[5], GraphPlan[2], and SATPlan[7]. These algorithms take a specially format-

ted problem definition and goal as inputs, and produce a sequence of actions, or plan, as outputs.

Planning algorithms do not specify how to formulate problem definitions. Programmers can use any mechanism for defining the problem, as long as the algorithm implementation is expecting that formulation. Research has worked towards developing generic problem definition languages, such as PDDL [8], NDDL [1], and MDLe [6]. These languages help to define planning problems.

Usually, planning algorithms are embedded in the applications that use the plan. While object-oriented abstractions such as classes and components have reduced this complexity slightly, many high-profile, successful autonomous systems still customize the planning algorithm for each problem definitions.

This research proposes a new problem definition language known as *PyLOM*[1]. PyLOM is a Python-based object oriented language that supports defining planning problems. PyLOM is an interpreted language with a run-time environment that interprets and executes problem definitions in generic planning algorithms.

2. Prior Work

Heavily influenced by STRIPS [4], PDDL is the de facto standard planning problem definition language. PDDL is a functional language that allows definition of objects and Boolean predicates involving those objects. Planners can be written to interpret these definitions, to produce a plan. However, planners often have to be configured to interpret PDDL, and may need to be configured specifically for the problem definition.

The Spirit and Opportunity Martian Exploration Rovers were planned using a system known as Europa [1]. Europa is a Java-based framework for planning robotic missions that is partially based on the Remote Agent [9]. Europa uses NDDL as the problem and robot definition languages. NDDL is a declarative language that borrows syntax from C++ and Java. The programmer must write not only the NDDL definitions, but also write planners specific to the problem def-

SPLASH '13, October 26–31, 2013, Indianapolis, Indiana, USA.
Copyright is held by the owner/author(s).
ACM 978-1-4503-1995-9/13/10.
http://dx.doi.org/10.1145/2508075.2522608

***

[1] PyLOM stands for Python-based Language for Object Modeling

initions. The Mars Exploration Rovers use custom planning algorithms.

3. PyLOM

At its core, PyLOM is heavily based on the Python 2.5 syntax. One of the core added features to PyLOM is a rudimentary typing system, which allows for the reduction of the state space. The PyLOM interpreter takes the problem as defined, and produces two separate Python files: one for the planners, and one for the plannable object that executes the plans produced by the PyLOM system.

Class definitions work much the same way as normal class definitions in Python, with two major differences. The first difference is that class attributes that are used in planning must be defined outside of the `__init__` method, with associated type information. The typing system extends to the method parameter lists as well.

The second difference pertains to how methods are defined for the classes. In addition to the traditional `def` keyword, three new keywords are used to distinguish between the methods that are defined for the planning algorithms, and the methods that are used for controlling of the planned system. Operators are used by the planning algorithms as actions that update the planner's state. Functions define how the system executes a planned action. Predicates are boolean functions that simplify specification of operators and functions.

The PyLOM run-time environment facilitates the planning and execution of plans. The PyLOM run-time is influenced by the work on the Titan Executive system, co-developed by MIT and the Applied Physics Laboratory at Johns Hopkins University [3]. The PyLOM compiler is responsible for reading a specification file, and producing the two separate files that go to the planning and execution engines. The execution file can be run within the PyLOM engine as a simulation, or executed directly on an external system.

PyLOM delegates control between the planners, and the plannable objects. Plannable objects communicate to the PyLOM run-time via sockets, which allows for the plannable object to either execute as part of the PyLOM run-time, or externally on the system that is being planned for, such as a robotic system.

4. Simulators and Evaluation

We have created a couple of simulated environments for full evaluation of the PyLOM system. The first simulated environment is known as GridWorld. GridWorld is a 32×27 grid based 2-d environment. Each grid location can be set as occupied, or unoccupied. GridWorld provides one class, called "robots", which are the "actionable" entities. The robots in GridWorld are two-wheeled, with an eight-way sensor array that uses simulated laser range sensors that originate from the center of the robot. GridWorld has targets that can be placed in any unoccupied grid location. These targets can be picked up by robots, and placed in any unoccuped grid location orthogonally adjacent to the current location of the robot. Typical scenarios in GridWorld include target acquisition and target fetch and return.

Another simulator we have developed is a for a multi-link arm problem. The environment is a 2-d continuous environment that allows for the manipulation of an arm, which is represented by a series of nodes joined by rigid links. Each node, with the exception of the nodes at the two ends of the arm, can be unfolded to extend the reach of the arm. In this scenario, a target is placed in the environment, and several rectangular shaped objects can be specified to occupy the environment. The goal of the simulation is to unfold the arm into a configuration where the final node intersects the target.

For evaluation, we plan on comparing PDDL and a custom planner against PyLOM for several working scenarios in both simulators. Using these setups, we will compare the LOC and run-time performance of a full PDDL plan and execute system against PyLOM using the same planning algorithm.

References

[1] T. Bedrax-Weiss, J. Frank, A. Jónsson, and C. McGann. Europa2: Plan database services for planning and scheduling applications. 2004.

[2] A. L. Blum and M. L. Furst. Fast planning through planning graph analysis. *ARTIFICIAL INTELLIGENCE*, 90(1):1636–1642, 1995.

[3] L. Fesq, M. Ingham, M. Pekala, J. V. Eepoel, D. Watson, and B. Williams. Model-based autonomy for the next generation of robotic spacecraft, 2002.

[4] R. E. Fikes and N. J. Nilsson. Strips: A new approach to the application of theorem proving to problem solving. *Artificial Intelligence*, 2(34):189 – 208, 1971. ISSN 0004-3702.

[5] P. Hart, N. Nilsson, and B. Raphael. A formal basis for the heuristic determination of minimum cost paths. *Systems Science and Cybernetics, IEEE Transactions on*, 4(2):100–107, 1968. ISSN 0536-1567. .

[6] D. Hristu-Varsakelis, M. Egerstedt, and P. S. Krishnaprasad. On the structural complexity of the motion description language mdle. In *Decision and Control, 2003. Proceedings. 42nd IEEE Conference on*, volume 4, pages 3360–3365 vol.4, 2003. .

[7] H. Kautz and B. Selman. Planning as satisfiability. In *Tenth European Conference on Artificial Intelligence*, 1992. Vienna, Austria.

[8] D. McDermott, M. Ghallab, A. Howe, C. Knoblock, A. Ram, M. Veloso, D. Weld, and D. Wilkins. Pddl-the planning domain definition language. 1998.

[9] M. D. Rayman, P. Varghese, D. H. Lehman, and L. L. Livesay. Results from the deep space 1 technology validation mission. *Acta Astronautica*, 47(2):475–487, 2000.

Model-driven Generative Framework for Automated OMG DDS Performance Testing in the Cloud *

Kyoungho An, Takayuki Kuroda
Aniruddha Gokhale

ISIS, Vanderbilt University, Nashville, TN 37235, USA
{kyoungho, kuroda, gokhale}@isis.vanderbilt.edu

Sumant Tambe and Andrea Sorbini

RTI, Sunnyvale, CA, USA
{sumant, asorbini}@rti.com

Abstract

The Object Management Group's (OMG) Data Distribution Service (DDS) provides many configurable policies which determine end-to-end quality of service (QoS) delivered to the applications. It is challenging, however, to predict the application's performance in terms of latencies, throughput, and resource usage because diverse combinations of QoS configurations influence QoS of applications in different ways. To overcome this problem, design-time formal methods have been applied with mixed success, but a lack of sufficient accuracy in prediction, tool support, and understanding of formalism has prevented wider adoption of the formal techniques. A promising approach to address this challenge is to emulate application behavior and gather data on the QoS parameters of interest by experimentation. To realize this approach, we have developed a middleware framework that uses model-driven generative mechanisms to automate performance testing of a large number of DDS QoS configuration combinations that can be deployed and tested on a cloud platform.

Categories and Subject Descriptors D.2.5 [*Testing and Debugging*]: Testing tools

Keywords Model-driven Engineering, Generative Programming, Publish/Subscribe, Performance Testing

1. Introduction

The OMG Data Distribution Service (DDS) [2] is a general-purpose middleware supporting real-time publish/subscribe semantics [1] for mission-critical applications. Specifically, the OMG DDS supports real-time, topic-based, data-centric, scalable, deterministic and anonymous pub/sub interaction semantics for large-scale distributed applications. To support the quality of service (QoS) requirements of a broad spectrum of application domains,

OMG DDS supports many QoS configuration policies (in the form of configuration parameters) that when used in different combinations determine the delivered end-to-end QoS properties.

The OMG DDS specification supports a total of 22 individual QoS policies that can be combined in a variety of ways that influences the delivered QoS in different ways. Each QoS policy may have multiple attributes associated with it, such as the data topic of interest, data filter criteria, and the maximum number of data messages to store when transmitting data. Moreover, each attribute can be assigned one of a range of values, such as the legal set of topics, a range of integers for the maximum number of data messages stored for transmission, or the set of criteria used for filtering.

Every individual QoS policy tends to impact the end-to-end performance and behavior of the application in certain specific ways. When these QoS policies are combined in various combinations, it is hard to predict the resulting QoS delivered to applications. This challenge is faced not just by application developers but also by the OMG DDS vendors themselves, who must have an in-depth knowledge of how various combinations of configuration parameters interact, which help them to address issues raised by their customers.

It is not feasible for an application developer or a vendor to manually write test cases that can test every QoS policy and all possible combinations of these QoS policies (along with their values), not to mention that they must also ensure that these combinations are valid. Even if one were to develop these large number of tests, executing them sequentially is time consuming, which impacts both the application developers who aim at getting their applications to market rapidly and vendors who must address customer problems in a timely manner.

To address the combinatorial testing problem and limitations of sequential testing, this poster presents a middleware framework called AUTOMATIC (AUTOmated Middleware Analysis and Testing In the Cloud), which combines model-driven engineering techniques with multiple stages of generative capabilities to automate performance testing of DDS-based applications. Specifically, AUTOMATIC provides a domain-specific modeling language (DSML) that developers use to model their applications and QoS policies of interest. Generative tools synthesize essentially a product line of test cases, each testing different QoS policies for the same publish/subscribe business logic which is encoded by a user in a modeling environment. A second set of generators synthesize cloud-based deployment logic. Finally, testing mechanisms in AUTOMATIC automate the testing of the generated test cases in parallel in the cloud.

2. Design and Implementation of AUTOMATIC

Figure 1 describes the overall architecture and workflow of our automated performance testing framework called AUTOMATIC. AU-

* This work was supported in part by NSF CAREER Award CNS 0845789. Any opinions, findings, and conclusions or recommendations expressed in this material are those of the author(s) and do not necessarily reflect the views of the National Science Foundation.

TOMATIC comprises three activity domains: User, Test Automation System, and Cloud Infrastructure. The Modeling and Monitoring functions included in the User domain should be conducted by a user who prototypes DDS applications and performs performance testing of the applications. In the Test Automation System domain, Test Planning and Test Deployment functions are carried out by predefined tools in our framework. When the Test Planning is completed and ready to be deployed in a testing infrastructure, a test environment is generated for our cloud infrastructure to emulate application testing. In the following we briefly describe the key architectural blocks in AUTOMATIC.

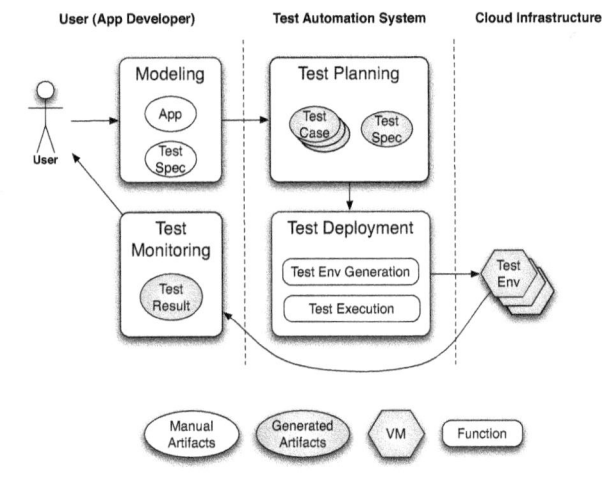

Figure 1. Framework Architecture

First, our framework provides a domain-specific modeling language – in this case for the DDS pub/sub domain – for users to define DDS entities and test specifications as inputs in the Modeling function. Users can develop and define their testing DDS applications easily by means of intuitive interfaces provided by modeling environment. Moreover, the defined DDS modeling language can be reused and extended for purposes other than testing through different interpreter implementations. Our modeling language is categorized into 2 parts: DDS entities, and testing specifications. The part for DDS entities contains modeling elements, such as Domain, Participant, Topic, and QoS that are used to prototype a DDS application. The test specification part incorporates required information for testing, such as duration of test execution, and hardware specification. As our framework is focused on experimenting performance of different DDS QoS, the desired ranges for testing of QoS configurations need to be set in the modeling language. Otherwise, the number of test cases cannot be bounded and it is not feasible to test them.

Generative techniques are most appropriate for software product lines which are characterized by commonalities and variabilities. For our work, the test cases represent a product line. Thus, in our case, a model interpreter traverses a given model instance that is designed using our DSML and generates DDS applications for each test case and specifications for testing and deployment. The generated applications are forms of executable artifacts for the testing environment, and the specifications are in a form, such as XML, that can be interpreted by an external deployment tool. In our testing framework, the common artifacts for each test case include the application's business logic and its topology while the variable artifacts are QoS configurations, which are automatically generated according to the assigned scopes defined by a user. Our interpreter automatically generates common and variable artifacts, and then merges them to create complete executable artifacts. The interpreter

also generates the test specifications by traversing relevant modeling elements. The test specifications contain application-related information such as executing command, and topology and test environment related information such as virtual machine specification and test running duration.

The generated artifacts are fed into a deployment tool in the next stage called Test Deployment. The Test Deployment is comprised of sub-functions: Test Environment Generation and Test Execution. The sub-functions run sequentially. First, the Test Env Generation function generates test environment according to test env specification obtained from Test Planning function. This function provides the environment as a set of virtual machines by utilizing a cloud platform so that the specified environment with various conditions can be generated in a flexible way. Test Execution function executes several test cases on the generated environment repeatedly. If users like to run test cases concurrently, the Test Deployment function generates more than one test environment and schedules test cases in parallel.

Lastly, monitoring information is collected by executing applications in our cloud testing infrastructure. To collect the monitoring information, in our framework, DDS monitoring modules are added into testing applications and processes of the monitoring modules are run together. Then, the users can monitor performance of applications with different QoS by subscribing the monitoring information from the modules.

3. Concluding Remarks

To address the challenges pertaining to combinatorial performance testing of OMG DDS middleware, this paper combines model-driven engineering and generative programming techniques within a middleware framework called AUTOMATIC (AUTOmated Middleware Analysis and Testing In the Cloud). MDE helps application developers with intuitive abstractions to rapidly describe their scenarios. Generative programming is needed since the test cases that combine configuration options can be considered a product line where the DDS application business logic remains common while the configurations can vary. Deployment and testing in the cloud is chosen as an approach because of its elastic nature where we can automate the parallel execution and collection of test statistics for a large number of generated tests from our tooling. Although the presented technology is showcased for the OMG DDS middleware, the principles behind AUTOMATIC are applicable to other middleware. Moreover, our technology has significant practical utility to both application developers and middleware vendors.

The presented work illustrates the feasibility of such an idea. Our ongoing work is focusing on making AUTOMATIC complete and robust for OMG DDS, and test it on a large number of deployment scenarios. Future work is also looking into generating application business logic. Current artifacts in AUTOMATIC are available for download from `www.dre.vanderbilt.edu/~kyoungho/AUTOMATIC/`.

References

[1] Patrick Th. Eugster, Pascal A. Felber, Rachid Guerraoui, and Anne-Marie Kermarrec. The many faces of publish/subscribe. *ACM Computer Survey*, 35:114–131, June 2003.

[2] Object Management Group. *Data Distribution Service for Real-time Systems Specification*, 1.2 edition, January 2007.

On The Implications of Language Constructs for Concurrent Execution in the Energy Efficiency of Multicore Applications

Gustavo Pinto

Informatics Center, Federal University of Pernambuco
Recife, PE, Brazil
ghlp@cin.ufpe.br

Fernando Castor

Informatics Center, Federal University of Pernambuco
Recife, PE, Brazil
castor@cin.ufpe.br

Abstract

Our study analyzed the performance and energy consumption of multicore applications, using a number of techniques to manage concurrent execution. We concluded that language constructs for concurrent execution can impact energy consumption. Nonetheless, the tradeoff between performance and energy consumption in multicore applications is not as obvious as it seems.

Categories and Subject Descriptors D.1.3 [*Programming Techniques*]: Concurrent Programming, Parallel programming

Keywords Energy-Efficiency, Language Constructs, Concurrent Execution

1. Introduction

Measuring the energy consumption of an application and understanding where the energy usage lies provides new opportunities for energy savings. In order to understand the complexities of this approach, we specifically look at multithreaded applications. The performance of the existing constructs for concurrent execution is reasonably well-understood [3, 5]. Furthermore, since parallel programming enables programmers to run their applications faster, a common belief is that this application will also consume less energy [2]. We call this as the "Race to idle" philosophy. In summary: faster programs will theoretically consume less energy because they will have the machine idle fast.

This paper presents an empirical study consisting of the evaluation of the performance and energy consumption of four applications that use three concurrent constructs plus a sequential implementation with the goal of demonstrating that is hard to trace tradeoffs between energy-efficiency and performance. By an evaluation of these applications in multiple environments, we show how basic parameters, such as clock frequency, threading options, and different VMs can impact energy consumption. Our study highlights the non-obvious and context-dependent nature of tradeoffs between performance and energy consumption.

SPLASH '13,   October 26–31, 2013, Indianapolis, Indiana, USA.
Copyright is held by the owner/author(s).
ACM 978-1-4503-1995-9/13/10.
http://dx.doi.org/10.1145/2508075.2514880

2. Study Setting

To achieve the goal of this study, we ran a set of benchmark applications from different domains in a number of different configurations while varying a group of attributes. We can divide these attributes in two groups: internal (programming language construct, number of threads in use and resource usage - CPU and/or IO) and external (the clock frequency and the JVM implementation). We then provide a set of variant implementations for each benchmark using four concurrent constructs, plus a sequential implementation[1].

In this experiment, we used commodity hardware: an Intel(R) Xeon(R), 2.13 GHz, 4 cores/8 threads and with 16Gb of memory, running Linux 64-bit, kernel 3.0.0.-31-server. These experiments were run using three JVM: i) OpenJDK version 1.7.0_09, ii) HotSpot JDK version 1.7, and iii) JRockit version 1.6. When the experiments were performed using JRockit, we provided an external jar file containing the ForkJoin implementation.

Our experiments consisted of running these four applications in each of the three JVM implementations, scaling the CPU frequency, and limiting the number of threads in use. We ran each experiment twelve times for each workload, while measuring the system using the *powertop* utility[2]. We discarded the executions with the lowest and the highest to reduce bias caused by outliers. Therefore, we have two main metrics that evaluate the experiments: the energy consumed (in Joules) and the execution time (in seconds).

3. Study Results

Table 1 shows the overall view of our experimental results. The column named "Energy Consumption (J)" organizes the results of the 10 executions. The value contained in each cell represents the median of the 10 executions, where each sample represents the total of energy consumed in this given execution. We use **boldface** to highlight the best result for the given benchmark application. The column "Time (s)" works similarly.

As Table 1 shows, we can notice that the results of the concurrent constructs can have significant differences. For instance, the Thread results are always more inefficient in terms of both consumption and performance, when compared to Executors. Thus, since the usage of Thread and the Executors is very similar, with a little effort, a programmer could use Executors. Table 1 also shows that the same technique can have different impact on the energy consumed. If we take into consideration the ForkJoin variant, we have, for the N-Queens and Knucleotide benchmark applications, a highly efficient trend for both performance and energy. On the other hand, considering the LargestImage application, we notice that the same ForkJoin variant consumed more energy than

---

[1] The implementation details are available at http://bit.ly/parallel-construct

[2] https://01.org/powertop/

	Energy Consumption (J)			
	N-Queens	LargestImage	Mandelbrot	Knucleotide
Sequential	**732.8**	679.8	1978.1	5395.5
Thread	1023.7	766	1290.8	4808.2
Executors	984.2	**633.5**	**1287.5**	3281.2
Fork/Join	753.1	749.3	1292.4	**2993.4**

	Time (s)			
	N-Queens	LargestImage	Mandelbrot	Knucleotide
Sequential	85	78	71	106
Thread	44	42	41	68
Executors	38	**31**	41	62
Fork/Join	**27**	54	**35**	**55**

Table 1. The comparision between the language constructs in terms of energy consumption and time. The obtained values for Energy consumption and time are the medians of 10 executions.

every other variant except for the one using threads. Nonetheless, LargestImage is a benchmark application that made heavy use of IO operations, and it is well know that `ForkJoin` is not adequate for this kind of computation. This fact is a possible reason for the poor energy consumption.

Moreover, it is interesting to discuss about the `Sequential` variant of the N-Queens benchmark application, which presented the best energy consumption result, in spite of presenting the worst performance. This benchmark's result can vary according to the input data (in case, the NxN size of the matrix). In this experiments, we realised that, for a small matrix, the overhead caused by the thread creation led to an increase in energy consumption. But, for example, if we doubled the matrix size, the `ForkJoin` variant becomes the most energy efficient as well.

Furthermore, we analyzed how the benchmark applications scale with respect to the number of threads. Both the Mandelbrot and Knucleotide benchmark applications scale well. This means that: the more cores available, the faster the applications run, and more energy is saved. Nonetheless, for the other ones, it is not true. For instance, in the LargestImage benchmark, the more cores we have, more inefficient the `ForkJoin` variant is, in terms of both performance and energy. In summary, we collected a total of 128 samples (4 benchmarks x 4 variants x 4 nr. of threads x 2 clock frequencies), and for 36 of those, the variation which achieve the best performance were not the same that consumes less energy.

We then repeated the experiments varying the CPU frequency from 1.2 GHz to 2.13 GHz. We notice that even after reducing the clock frequencies, the results seems to be fairly similar to the latter one, in terms of the better technique remains the better. However, for the LargestImage benchmark, we found out that the lowest frequency consumes the same amount of energy as a middle clock frequency. It is interesting and acceptable, since it is an application that does not use a huge amount of CPU. Thus, for IO-bound applications, a low cpu frequency could reduce energy usage, without sacrificing performance.

Finally, we have also analyzed whether different JVM had different impacts on performance and energy consumption. We observed that, in general, results are very similar, specially for OpenJDK and HotSpot. It does not surprise us, since the HotSpot is the primary reference implementation of JVM, and OpenJDK is heavily inspired by them. On the other side, the JRockit JVM presents the worst case scenario, for all variants. For example, taking into consideration the `Thread` variant, the results increased in more than 10%. For the other benchmark applications, the JRockit also exhibited the worst results among the JVMs. Although the different JVMs did affect execution time and energy consumption, similarly to different clock frequencies, they did not significantly change the behavior of the variants, e.g. the fastest and slowest variants in one JVM were the fastest and lowest variants for all of them.

4. Related Work

To the best of our knowledge, only two studies have dealt with the topic of understanding the impact of concurrent constructs on the energy efficiency of applications [1, 4]. Gautham et al. [1] explore the following synchronization techniques to find an ideal solution for synchronization intensive workloads: i) spin lock ii) mutexes iii) software transactional memory. They show that Software Transactional Memory (STM) systems can perform better than locks for workloads where a significant portion of the execution time is spent in the critical sections. Trefethen [4] studies the behaviour of the NAS Benchmark suite for its energy and runtime performance. The benchmark suite considered includes I/O and compute-intensive applications. The authors concluded that there is a clear interaction between execution time and energy but this is not a simple relationship and can be affected by the computer environment and algorithmic approach used in the application. Nonetheless, none of these papers compare the energy-efficiency between techniques to manage concurrent execution.

5. Conclusion

This paper presented an empirical study targeting four benchmark applications using a number of concurrent programming constructs with the goal of finding interesting tradeoffs between energy-efficiency and performance. Our approach indicates that it is possible to switch from one technique to another in order to consume less energy. Nonetheless, we also conclude that it is very hard to identify which technique is the better for a given scenario. Moreover, our experiments show that factors such as the nature of the problem to be solved, the technique used to manage concurrent execution, the CPU clock frequency, and the JVM implementation can create variations. These results lead us to conclude that it is very difficult to generalize a relationship between performance and energy consumption for concurrent systems. For these systems, winning the race to idle does not imply more energy efficiency. In the future, we intent to address this problem by conducting a broader-scoped study. The results of this new study will provide input for us to derive a catalog of energy code smell for concurrent software. Then we plan to proceed with the design of refactoring catalog that will enable application programmer to safely restructure their applications to use less energy.

6. Acknowledgments

Gustavo is supported by CAPES and Fernando is supported by CNPq (306619/2011- 3), FACEPE (APQ-1367-1.03/12), and by INES (CNPq 573964/2008-4 and FACEPE APQ-1037- 1.03/08).

References

[1] A. Gautham, K. Korgaonkar, P. Slpsk, S. Balachandran, and K. Veezhinathan. The implications of shared data synchronization techniques on multi-core energy efficiency. In *Proceedings of the*, HotPower'12, Berkeley, CA, USA, 2012.

[2] J. Jelschen, M. Gottschalk, M. Josefiok, C. Pitu, and A. Winter. Towards applying reengineering services to energy-efficient applications. In *CSMR*, pages 353–358, 2012.

[3] L. A. Smith, J. M. Bull, and J. Obdrzálek. A parallel java grande benchmark suite. In *Proceedings of the 2001 ACM/IEEE conference on Supercomputing*, Supercomputing '01, pages 8–8, New York, NY, USA, 2001. ACM.

[4] A. Trefethen and J. Thiyagalingam. Energy-aware software: Challenges, opportunities and strategies. *Journal of Computational Science*, 1(0):–, 2013. ISSN 1877-7503. .

[5] W. Zhu, J. del Cuvillo, and G. R. Gao. Performance characteristics of openmp language constructs on a many-core-on-a-chip architecture. In *IWOMP*, pages 230–241, 2006.

Open Pattern Matching for C++

Yuriy Solodkyy   Gabriel Dos Reis   Bjarne Stroustrup

Texas A&M University
Texas, USA
{yuriys,gdr,bs}@cse.tamu.edu

Abstract

Pattern matching is an abstraction mechanism that can greatly simplify source code. We present functional-style pattern matching for C++ implemented as a library, called *Mach7*[1]. All the patterns are user-definable, can be stored in variables, passed among functions, and allow the use of open class hierarchies. As an example, we implement common patterns used in functional languages.

Categories and Subject Descriptors   D.3.3 [*Programming Languages*]: Language Constructs and Features; D.1.5 [*Programming techniques*]: Object-oriented Programming

Keywords   Pattern Matching, C++, Expression Problem

1. Introduction

Pattern matching is an abstraction mechanism popularized by the functional programming community, such as ML, OCaml and Haskell, and recently adopted by object-oriented programming languages such as Scala, F#, and dialects of C++ and Java. It provides syntax very close to mathematical notation and allows the user to describe tersely a (possibly infinite) set of values accepted by the *pattern*.

We present functional-style pattern matching for C++ built as an ISO C++11 library. Our solution:

- Is *open* to introduction of new patterns into the library, while not making any assumptions about existing ones.
- Is *type safe*: inappropriate applications of patterns to subjects are compile-time errors.
- Makes patterns *first-class* citizens in the language.
- Is *non-intrusive* and can be retroactively applied to existing types, both built-in and user-defined.

- Provides a *unified syntax* for dealing with various encodings of extensible hierarchical datatypes in C++.
- Provides an alternative interpretation of the controversial *n+k patterns* (in line with that of constructor patterns), leaving the choice of exact semantics to the user.
- Supports a limited form of *views*.
- Generalizes open type switch to *multiple scrutinees* and enables patterns in case clauses.
- Demonstrates that *compile-time composition* of patterns through concepts is superior to run-time composition of patterns through polymorphic interfaces in terms of performance, expressiveness and static type checking.

The library sets a standard for performance, extensibility, brevity, clarity and usefulness of any language solution for pattern matching. It provides full functionality, so we can experiment with pattern matching in C++ and compare it to existing alternatives. Our solution requires only current support of C++11 without any additional tool support.

2. Pattern Matching in C++

As an example of syntax, enabled by *Mach7*, we present here a complete implementation of an evaluator in λ-calculus:

```
struct Term      { virtual ~Term() {} };
struct Var : Term { std::string name; };
struct Abs : Term { Var& var;  Term& body; };
struct App : Term { Term& func; Term& arg; };
Term* eval(Term* t) {
  var⟨const Var&⟩ v; var⟨const Term&⟩ b,a;
  Match(*t) {
    Case(C⟨Var⟩())            return &match0;
    Case(C⟨Abs⟩())            return &match0;
    Case(C⟨App⟩(C⟨Abs⟩(v,b),a)) return eval(subs(b,v, a));
    Otherwise() std::cerr ≪ "error"; return nullptr;
  } EndMatch
}
```

This corresponds directly to a functional language solution involving algebraic data types, which are encoded here with polymorphic classes. The solution is open to class extensions, including those due to dynamic linking, as well as fully supports generic multiple inheritance of C++. The statement also accepts multiple *scrutinees* to allow for re-

[1] The library is available at http://parasol.tamu.edu/mach7/

Permission to make digital or hard copies of part or all of this work for personal or classroom use is granted without fee provided that copies are not made or distributed for profit or commercial advantage and that copies bear this notice and the full citation on the first page. Copyrights for third-party components of this work must be honored. For all other uses, contact the owner/author(s). Copyright is held by the owner/author(s).
SPLASH '13,   October 26–31, 2013, Indianapolis, Indiana, USA.
ACM 978-1-4503-1995-9/13/10.
http://dx.doi.org/10.1145/2508075.2508098

lational checks as demonstrated by the following functional solution to balancing red-black trees:

```
class T {enum Color {blk,red} col; T* lt; K key; T* rt;};

T* balance(T::Color color, T* l, const K& key, T* r) {
  const T::Color B = T::Color::blk, R = T::Color::red;
  var⟨T*⟩ a, b, c, d; var⟨K&⟩ x, y, z; T::Color col;
  Match(color, l, key, r) {
    Case(B, C⟨T⟩(R, C⟨T⟩(R, a, x, b), y, c), z, d) ...
    Case(B, C⟨T⟩(R, a, x, C⟨T⟩(R, b, y, c)), z, d) ...
    Case(B, a, x, C⟨T⟩(R, C⟨T⟩(R, b, y, c), z, d)) ...
    Case(B, a, x, C⟨T⟩(R, b, y, C⟨T⟩(R, c, z, d))) ...
    Case(col, a, x, b) return new T{col, a, x, b};
  } EndMatch
}
```

The ... in the first four case clauses above stands for:
return new T{R, **new** T{B,a,x,b}, y, **new** T{B,c,z,d}};.

Built-in types can be analyzed and decomposed through pattern matching too. The following example defines a function for fast computation of Fibonacci numbers with so called "n+k patterns" given here an *equational interpretation* of *application patterns*:

```
int fib(int n) {
  var⟨int⟩ m;
  Match(n) {
    Case(1)       return 1;
    Case(2)       return 1;
    Case(2*m)     return sqr(fib(m+1)) − sqr(fib(m−1));
    Case(2*m+1)   return sqr(fib(m+1)) + sqr(fib(m));
  } EndMatch
}
```

The solution is not bound to such equational interpretation. Instead, we offer to look at n+k patterns as mathematical notation that can be used to decompose various mathematical objects into subcomponents in much the same way as constructor patterns decompose algebraic data types.

3. Implementation

Our *Match*-statement extends the efficient type switch for C++ [3]. The core of this extension amounts to handling of multiple subjects (both polymorphic and non-polymorphic) as well as the ability to accept patterns in case clauses.

Our approach to open patterns is based on compile-time composition of pattern objects through *concepts*, using a common C++ technique – *expression templates* [5]. We demonstrate in [2] that it is superior (in terms of performance and expressiveness) to previous approaches based on run-time composition of pattern objects through *interfaces*. In particular, the average overhead of our approach in comparison to a handcrafted solution is 25%, occasionally becoming even faster by about 10%. The average overhead of the approaches based on run-time composition (timed on the same examples) is 934%. Neither of the approaches introduces a noticeable compile-time overhead.

4. Evaluation Methodology

We performed several independent studies of our approach to demonstrate its effectiveness. The results of most of these studies are shown on the accompanying poster.

The first study compares our approach to the visitor design pattern, while the second does a similar comparison to built-in facilities of Haskell and OCaml. In the third study, we looked at the efficiency of hashing used in type switching on up to four scrutinees on some large real-world class hierarchies. In the fourth study, we compare the performance of matching N polymorphic arguments against double, triple and quadruple dispatch via visitor design pattern as well as open multi-methods extension to C++ [1]. In the fifth study we estimate the overhead of our and existing solutions to open patterns in comparison to a handcrafted code, while in the sixth study we compare their impact on the compilation times. In the last study, we rewrote two existing applications in order to compare performance, memory footprint, the ease of use, readability, maintainability etc. of each solution in a real application. The first application was a visitor-based C++ pretty-printer, while the second was a peephole optimizer written in Haskell.

5. Conclusions and Future Work

The *Mach7* library provides functional-style pattern-matching facilities for C++. The solution is open to new patterns, with the traditional patterns implemented as examples. It is non-intrusive and can be applied retroactively. The library provides efficient and expressive matching on multiple scrutinees and compares well to multiple dispatch alternatives in terms of both time and space. We also offer an alternative interpretation of the n+k patterns and show how some traditional generalizations of these patterns can be implemented in our library.

In the future, we would like to implement an actual language extension capable of working with open patterns and look into how code can be optimized without hardcoding the knowledge of pattern's semantics into the compiler.

We refer the reader to the first author's PhD thesis [2] as well as an accompanying paper [4] for a detailed discussion of our solution to open and efficient pattern matching in C++.

References

[1] P. Pirkelbauer, Y. Solodkyy, and B. Stroustrup. Open multi-methods for C++. In *Proc. GPCE'07*, pp 123–134. ACM.

[2] Y. Solodkyy. *Simplifying the Analysis of C++ Programs*. PhD thesis, Texas A&M University, August 2013.

[3] Y. Solodkyy, G. Dos Reis, and B. Stroustrup. Open and efficient type switch for C++. In *Proc. OOPSLA'12*, pp 963–982. ACM.

[4] Y. Solodkyy, G. Dos Reis, and B. Stroustrup. Open pattern matching for C++. In *Proc. GPCE'13*. ACM, October 2013.

[5] T. Veldhuizen. Expression templates. *C++ Report*, 7:26–31, 1995.

SPLASH INDIANAPOLIS 2013 OCTOBER 26-31

Welcome Message from the SRC Chairs

It is our great pleasure to welcome you to Indianapolis and the 2013 OOPSLA Student Research Competition! This year's SRC continues the tradition of allowing both graduate and undergraduate students to present their ongoing work and get productive feedback on their latest results.

We were very pleased with the overall quality of this year's SRC entries. The SRC judging committee accepted 15 abstracts whose topics comprise type systems, program analysis, software engineering, theorem proving, debugging, and security. As in previous years, the SRC participants will get a chance to give both poster and oral presentations about their work during the main SPLASH conference, and selected students will receive prizes and get a chance to compete at the ACM Student Research Competition Grand Finals!

We are very happy that you are able to join us for this exciting event, and we sincerely hope that you get constructive feedback on your ongoing work at this year's student research competition.

Isil Dillig
Microsoft Research

Sam Guyer
Tufts University

The Poor Man's Proof Assistant

Using Prolog to Develop Formal Language Theoretic Proofs

Joey Eremondi

University of Saskatchewan
joey.eremondi@usask.ca

Abstract

While proving a theorem from a set of axioms is undecidable in
first order logic, recent development has produced several tools
which serve as automated theorem provers. However, often these
systems are too complex for a given problem. Their usefulness is
outweighed by the difficulty of learning a new tool or translating
results into computer-readable form.

I describe tools developed in Prolog to partially characterize
the shuffle-inclusion problem. These tools allowed for rapid development of proofs with little intellectual overhead. While focused
around a specific problem, the techniques described are general,
and well suited to many problems on discrete structures.

Categories and Subject Descriptors   D.1.6 [*PROGRAMMING
TECHNIQUES*]: Logic programming

Keywords   Prolog; shuffle; proof assistant

1. Problem and Motivation

This paper shows how logic languages such as Prolog provide a
fast and easy way to develop assistive tools in theorem proving.
As a case study, I use the characterization of the shuffle inclusion
problem.

The shuffle operator, which represents the set of all ways of
"merging" two strings, has received much attention in recent research. Its main application is in modelling parallelism [10]. Moreover, it represents a fundamental operation on strings, so researching it contributes to a greater understanding of the theory underlying computation.

I examined shuffle inclusion, the question of whether one shuffle set was a subset of another. The search tools I developed for this
problem serve as an example of how logic languages can be used
to facilitate the development of proofs in formal languages and discrete mathematics.

2. Background and Related Work

2.1 The Prolog Language

A detailed introduction to Prolog can be found in [6]. There are
three features which are particularly relevant here. *Unification* allows logical predicates to generate answers, rather than simply test
conditions, by leaving some variables *unbound*. Roughly, Prolog
searches for a value causing a goal to succeed. *Nondeterminism* allows for multiple definitions of a predicate. These are each tried in
sequence when proving a goal, allowing queries to return multiple
answers. The *Definite Clause Grammar* (DCG) feature provides
tools for string parsing and generation. While based on context-
free grammars, they can be mixed with arbitrary Prolog code for
context-sensitve testing.

2.2 Shuffle Inclusion

I use Σ^* to denote the set of all (possibly empty) words over the
alphabet Σ, and $|w|$ to denote the length of a word w. The shuffle
operator $\sqcup\!\sqcup$ denotes all ways of interleaving the letters from two
words while preserving their order relative to the original words. It
maps two strings to a finite set of strings, and is formally defined in
[3] as follows:

$$u \sqcup\!\sqcup v = \{u_1 v_1 \cdots u_n v_n \mid u = u_1 \cdots u_n, v = v_1 \cdots v_n,$$
$$u_i \in \Sigma^*, v_i \in \Sigma^*, 1 \le i \le n\}$$

In [3] and [2] it was shown that $u \sqcup\!\sqcup v = x \sqcup\!\sqcup y \iff \{u, v\} =
\{x, y\}$ when u and v contain at least two distinct letters. When
equality is so easily described, it is natural to ask a similar question
about the inclusion problem, and to examine when $u \sqcup\!\sqcup v \subseteq x \sqcup\!\sqcup y$.

2.3 Proof Assistants

Despite the undecidability of first-order logic [5], many successful
proof-assistants exist. HOL [9] is based on higher-order logic. Coq
uses dependent types, and was used to verify proof of the four
color theorem [8]. Several of these languages have counter-example
search packages, such as Nitpick [4] and Kodkod [11]. The Alloy
Analyzer provides counter-example search with SAT-solvers, with
a focus on specifying Object-Oriented systems [1]. However, these
languages can be challenging to learn, and translating statements
into computer-readable code is difficult and tedious. Some Prolog
tools, such as PFLAT [12] have been developed for formal language
work, but these are geared more towards education rather than real
theorem proving.

3. Approach and Uniqueness

My approach to the inclusion problem was to find a complete characterization of cases when the subset relation holds. For example,
$xwy \sqcup\!\sqcup w \subseteq xw \sqcup\!\sqcup wy$ for all $w, x, y \in \Sigma^*$. My research followed a cyclic approach. Initially, a list of all u, v, x, y fulfilling
$u \sqcup\!\sqcup v \subseteq x \sqcup\!\sqcup y$ and $|uv| \le k$ was generated. I examined this list
to find patterns and develop hypotheses about the subset relation.
Once a conjecture was formulated, I would use a search framework
to search for counter-examples of length k. If no counter-example
was found, I attempted a pen-and-paper formal proof, then wrote a

predicate to test which strings matched its pattern. The process was repeated, but strings matching previously proved theorems were filtered out. Thus I could gauge the completeness of my characterization, continually narrowing the list of strings I examined.

3.1 Enumeration

Since strings are discrete objects, it is possible to enumerate all cases where $u \sqcup v \subseteq x \sqcup y$ with bounds on $|uv|$. In order to help find patterns, my program printed all such u, v, x, y of a given length. With Prolog's nondeterminism and unification, the predicate specifying such u, v, x, y also served to enumerate them. This predicate declared a list with unbound members, then declared u, v as a partition of that list. Another predicate, `hasSameParikh`, selected a number of a's and b's for uv to have, then unified x, y with words having the same number of each letter. Finally, x, y were unified with words fulfilling the subset relation. Once a theorem was proved and added to the characterization, any u, v, x, y which fulfilled the conditions of the theorem were filtered out. This enumeration allowed me to experimentally prove that my characterization was complete up to length 8.

3.2 Counter-example Search and Hypothesis Testing

The hypothesis-testing tool generated strings u, v, x, y matching a hypothesis' conditions with $|uv| = k$, then tested if $u \sqcup v \subseteq x \sqcup y$. Two k-element lists were declared with unbound contents. Then u, v and x, y were declared as a partitioning of these lists.

The search called a rule `counterCond` which unified a query u, v, x, y with strings matching my hypothesis. The rule was rewritten for each conjecture being tested, usually using DCG clauses.

By passing an unbound list to `counterCond`, the predicate generated strings that matched the hypothesis condition. This was more efficient than generating every pair of strings of a given length and testing if they matched the hypothesis condition. The logic-programming approach meant that no additional code was written to perform this optimization.

Restricting search to a given length was necessary, since recursion on unbound-length strings caused infinite loops. Continually increasing k led to an iterative-deepening search, ensuring that the search would halt and find a counter-example of length k if it existed.

3.3 Definite clause grammars

The task of matching a set of strings against a given "pattern" arose frequently. DCG's provided a useful tool for expressing such patterns. Regularly used clauses were written, such as `aToMbToN` to match $a^m b^n$, $m, n \in \mathbb{N}_0$. These could be combined and composed. For example, `concatStr` concatenated strings matching different DCG clauses. Likewise, calling `concatStr` on two different words could then be used to test for a common infix between them. By using Prolog's DCG tool, patterns and conditions could be coded in an easily readable form without requiring a parser or generator to be written.

3.4 Inductive queries

Prolog is designed to have programs run interactively from a console, rather than compiled to an executable. This allowed my framework to answer queries without having to write any sort of user interface. A common usage of this feature was querying which discovered patterns, if any, proved $u \sqcup v \subseteq x \sqcup y$ for a given u, v, x, y. Many of the proofs that patterns held were based on induction, constructing new relations from ones I had already proved. While these proofs were completed manually, the process was made much easier with the ability to query previously-proved theorems.

4. Results and Contribution

Using the techniques described above, I found a list of over 40 patterns which completely characterize when $u \sqcup v \subseteq x \sqcup y$, with $uv \in \{a, b\}^*$, $|uv| \le 8$. For example, $w \sqcup xwy \subseteq xw \sqcup wy$, and $a^p w b^k \sqcup a^q w b^l \subseteq a^{p+q} w \sqcup w b^{k+l}$.

While human-developed proofs verified the correctness of each subset relation, their completeness for length 8 was verified using my search tools. The development of pen-and-paper proofs was made easier with the use of my assistive tools. The full list of patterns, as well as proof of each pattern's correctness, can be found in [7]. The techniques used here can be generalized to other problems. In particular, the counter-example search could be used to test any hypothesis involving a finite number of discrete structures.

5. Conclusion

I presented Prolog tools for assisting with proofs and formal language-theoretic research. These demonstrate how software can help automate the proof developing process, and how Prolog's unique feature-set allows for rapid development and interactive use of such software. While more complete tools exist, my framework provided a shallower learning curve better suited to the day-to-day challenges of formal language research. My success in partially characterizing the shuffle inclusion problem provides a strong example of both the ease and effectiveness of these tools.

Acknowledgments

The author was supervised by Dr. Ian McQuillan and supported by the Natural Sciences and Engineering Research Council of Canada.

References

[1] K. Anastasakis, B. Bordbar, G. Georg, and I. Ray. On challenges of model transformation from uml to alloy. *Software & Systems Modeling*, 9(1):69–86, 2010. ISSN 1619-1366. .

[2] J. Berstel and L. Boasson. Shuffle factorization is unique. *Theoretical Computer Science*, 273:47–67, 2002.

[3] F. Biegler, M. Daley, M. Holzer, and I. McQuillan. On the uniqueness of shuffle on words and finite languages. *Theoretical Computer Science*, 410:3711–3724, 2009.

[4] J. Blanchette and T. Nipkow. Nitpick: A counterexample generator for higher-order logic based on a relational model finder. In M. Kaufmann and L. Paulson, editors, *Interactive Theorem Proving*, volume 6172 of *Lecture Notes in Computer Science*, pages 131–146. Springer Berlin Heidelberg, 2010. ISBN 978-3-642-14051-8. .

[5] A. Church. A note on the entscheidungsproblem. *J. Symb. Log.*, 1(1): 40–41, 1936.

[6] W. F. Clocksin and C. S. Mellish. *Programming in Prolog: Using the ISO Standard*. Springer, 5th edition, 9 2003. ISBN 9783540006787.

[7] J. Eremondi and I. McQuillan. A Partial Characterization of the Shuffle Inclusion Problem on Words. Manuscript in preparation, 2013.

[8] G. Gonthier. Formal proof the four-color theorem. *Notices of the AMS*, 55(11):1382–1393, 2008.

[9] M. J. C. Gordon and T. F. Melham, editors. *Introduction to HOL: a theorem proving environment for higher order logic*. Cambridge University Press, New York, NY, USA, 1993. ISBN 0-521-44189-7.

[10] A. Mateescu, G. Rozenberg, and A. Salomaa. Shuffle on trajectories: Syntactic constraints. *Theoretical Computer Science*, 197(1–2):1–56, 1998.

[11] E. Torlak and D. Jackson. Kodkod: A relational model finder. *Tools and Algorithms for the Construction and ...*, pages 632–647, 2007.

[12] M. Wermelinger and A. M. Dias. A prolog toolkit for formal languages and automata. *SIGCSE Bull.*, 37(3):330–334, June 2005. ISSN 0097-8418. .

Dictionary-Based Query Recommendation
for Local Code Search *

Xi Ge

NC State University, Raleigh, NC, USA
xge@ncsu.edu

Abstract

Local code search tools help developers efficiently find code snippets in the code base under development. The quality of the retrieved code largely depends on the quality of queries provided by developers. Manually synthesizing high-quality queries is a non-trivial task, partially because it places a cognitive burden on developers by requiring them memorize words used in the code base under search. To help developers synthesize better queries, this paper proposes a recommendation technique called MultiD that uses multiple dictionaries. We also report an ongoing study to evaluate the effectiveness of MultiD.

Categories and Subject Descriptors D.2.3 [*Software Engineering*]: Coding Tools and Techniques

General Terms Design, Languages

Keywords search, navigation, tool, recommender, IDE

1. Introduction

Software is probably the most complex system that human beings have ever made. Due to the complexity of software systems, developers' working on them are never easy. One cause of this hardness is that a developer needs to collect enough information before she can work properly; while collecting the information is both arduous and labor-intensive. Existing study shows that collecting information is an unavoidable step for software maintenance tasks [3]. To help developers meet with their information need, researchers proposed local code search (LCS) tools that assist developers efficiently locate the intended code snippets in the code base under development [7].

The effectiveness of using LCS tools largely depends on the quality of queries. A high-quality query should contain terms that are both informative and relevant. Being informative means that a term does not happen too often in the code base under search ("a" is not informative, for instance); being relevant suggests that the term exists at least somewhere in the code base under search. Synthesizing highly relevant queries is especially hard, partially because

---

* Work during the author's internship at ABB Inc.

SPLASH '13,   October 26–31, 2013, Indianapolis, Indiana, USA.
Copyright is held by the owner/author(s).
ACM 978-1-4503-1995-9/13/10.
http://dx.doi.org/10.1145/2508075.2522609

it places a cognitive burden on developers. For instance, to synthesize a relevant query, a developer needs to remember the exact words that are used in the code base under search, even though those words used are sub-optimal. For instance, if the code base under search uses "instantiate" to describe the action of creating an object, the developer's searching of "create" may lead to no useful results.

Conventional techniques to find synonyms, such as by using WordNet [5], may solve this problem. However, these techniques fail to consider the context of the code base under search; hence they may lead to the synonyms that generally make sense in the English language, but are not relevant to the code base under search. For example, WordNet can suggest multiple synonyms of "create", but most of these synonyms may not exist in the code base under search. To make things even worse, WordNet, as a general English dictionary, does not consider that "instantiate" is a synonym of "create", in spite of the fact that developers typically do. To solve this problem, we propose a query recommendation technique that uses multiple dictionaries. In summary, we make the following contributions:

- A query recommendation technique called MultiD that uses multiple dictionaries to help developers correct and improve queries on LCS tools. MultiD takes an original query from the developer as input, outputs a set of recommended queries.

- An implementation of the technique as an extension to a state-of-the-practice LCS tool called Sando [7].

2. Approach

In this section, we detail the MultiD implementation. We first present the different dictionaries used by MultiD, next explain the query improvement algorithm by using these dictionaries.

2.1 Dictionaries

Currently, MultiD uses three different dictionaries that vary in terms of the amount of the information contained and their relevance to the code base under search. Although we start at these three dictionaries, we may later add more to the technique.

Level I: project-specific dictionary. Level I dictionary is the lowest level of dictionaries in MultiD. This dictionary contains terms that appear in the project under search. To collect these terms, MultiD needs to traverse the project under search. Fortunately, LCS tools such as Sando usually index source code documents before developers can use them. Taking advantage of this process, MultiD builds the level I dictionary by reusing the terms collected during the indexing.

After collecting the terms, the level I dictionary represents these terms through two ways. The first way is a binary search tree of these terms to facilitate looking for a specific term. The second way is a co-occurrence matrix that records the counts of every two terms occur together. Building the term co-occurrence matrix is equally easy. Initialized as every cell being 0, for each pair of terms $[t_1, t_2]$ that occurs together in a source document, the dictionary builder increments the current value of the cell at $[t_1, t_2]$ by one. MultiD uses the co-occurrence matrix to sort recommended queries, as illustrated in Section 2.2.

Level II: software-engineering-specific thesaurus. Level II dictionary is a thesaurus of terms that are frequently used in software development. As a field with fast growth, software development has evolved its own set of terms, synonyms and abbreviations that do not exist in the conventional English. Simply reusing a general dictionary cannot get the field-specific information, or even be detrimental to client software tools [2]. To build a field-specific thesaurus, we reuse Gupta and colleagues' work that mines the relationship between different words in source code, generating 1724 pairs of semantically related terms, among which 91% are synonyms specific to the field of software development [2]. Several examples of these field-specific synonyms are "execute"–"invoke", "load"–"initialize" and "instantiate"–"create".

level III: General English thesaurus. The highest level of dictionaries used in our technique is a general English thesaurus. To build this thesaurus, we reused Miller's lexical database called WordNet [5]. WordNet groups English words by their meanings, therefore finding synonyms by using WordNet is trivial. Although WordNet obtains a complete set of English words, using it directly is costly in memory. Hence, we reduced the size of WordNet by only including the $50k$ most frequently used words in English [1], partially because $50k$ is the upper bound of the vocabulary size for an average individual [6]. We queried WordNet to collect the synonyms of these frequent words and saved them to a file. MultiD uses this file as a general English thesaurus.

2.2 Recommendation Algorithms

We next present the algorithm to generate recommended queries by using these dictionaries. The goal of this algorithm is to transform the original query to a set of queries that consist of terms in the Level I dictionary. Supposing the original query having several space-separated words, MultiD first queries the level I dictionary to decide whether each word exists in the code base. If a word does, MultiD does not transform the word; otherwise our technique tries to use the following three steps to transform the word.

Word splitting. Firstly, MultiD greedily extracts the parts of the word that exist in the Level I dictionary. More specifically, for a given word, MultiD tries to find its longest prefix and suffix that exist the level I dictionary; next, the technique recursively splits the middle part of the word until no in-dictionary prefix or suffix can be found. For instance, supposing the level I dictionary only contains the terms of "get" and "name", splitting the word of "getelementname" leads to three new words which are "get", "element", and "name".

Word recommendation. After splitting, if the query still contains words that are not in the level I dictionary, MultiD tries to find their synonyms in the dictionaries of higher levels as recommendations. Our technique starts with the level II dictionary due to its higher relevance. If no synonyms in the level II dictionary are found, MultiD tries to find synonyms in the level III dictionary. After retrieving the synonyms, the technique next excludes those synonyms that are not in the level I dictionary. The remaining synonyms are recommended to the developer as the replacements to the original word. If finding multiple synonyms to recommend, MultiD uses the co-occurrence matrix stated in Section 2.1 to rank them. The synonyms that occur more frequently with the rest part of the input query rank higher.

Word correction. For those words that neither exist in the level I dictionary by themselves nor have synonyms in the dictionaries of higher levels, our technique considers them as the typos of the terms in the level I dictionary. Therefore, MultiD uses the terms in the level I dictionary to correct them. The algorithm for correction adopts 2-gram indexing to quickly find the terms that spell similarly with a given typo [4].

3. Evaluation

Although we have implemented MultiD as an extension to Sando [7], the evaluation of MultiD is an ongoing work. While a developers is using Sando, a data collector running in the background of Sando logs usage information of the search tool, including the queries the developer provided, the recommendations she reviewed and the search results she examined. By investigating the collected data, we can measure whether MultiD can help developers synthesize high-quality queries. In addition, we also plan to distribute a survey among Sando users to collect their subjective opinions towards MultiD recommendations. In summary, we plan to answer the following three research questions: (1) what is the percentage of queries recommended by MultiD that are actually adopted by developers? (2) How much can the MultiD-recommended queries improve search results in terms of recall and precision? (3) According to Sando users' subjective opinions, how can we improve MultiD?

4. Conclusion

In this extended abstract, we introduce a dictionary-based technique to assist developers improve the queries they put in LCS tools. Our technique uses multiple levels of dictionaries that vary in terms of the amount of information contained and their relevance to the code base under search. By using these dictionaries, our technique recommends developers queries that are potentially more promising in retrieving useful results.

Acknowledgment

This work is under mentoring of Dr. David Shepherd from ABB Inc. I thank the comments from Dr. Emerson Murphy-Hill.

References

[1] Frequent Word Lists. http://invokeit.wordpress.com/frequency-word-lists/, 2013.

[2] S. Gupta, S. Malik, L. Pollock, and K. Vijay-Shanker. Part-of-speech tagging of program identifiers for improved text-based software engineering tool. In *Proc. ICPC*. IEEE, 2013.

[3] A. J. Ko, B. A. Myers, M. J. Coblenz, and H. H. Aung. An exploratory study of how developers seek, relate, and collect relevant information during software maintenance tasks. *TSE*, 32(12):971–987, 2006.

[4] K. Kukich. Techniques for automatically correcting words in text. *ACM Computing Surveys*, 24(4):377–439, 1992.

[5] George A. M. Wordnet: A lexical database for english. *Communications of the ACM*, 38:39–41, 1995.

[6] S. Pinker. *The language instinct*. New York: W. Morrow, 1994.

[7] D. Shepherd, K. Damevski, B. Ropski, and T. Fritz. Sando: an extensible local code search framework. In *Proc. FSE*, pages 15:1–15:2, 2012.

Secure Development Tool Adoption in Open-Source

Jim Witschey

North Carolina State University
jwshephe@ncsu.edu

Abstract

Although the use of secure software development tools can help developers build more secure software, many developers do not use these tools. In previous work, a colleague conducted interviews with professional developers to develop a qualitative model of factors that influence developers' decisions to use or not use security tools. In the work described in this abstract, I conducted interviews with open-source software developers to evaluate how our findings generalize outside of corporate software development populations. With the data from these interviews, I aim to gain insight into open-source software developers' behavior and values. I aim to refine, expand, and generalize our security tool adoption model so it may be used to foster wider adoption of security tools.

Categories and Subject Descriptors D.2.0 [*SOFTWARE ENGINEERING*]: Tools

General Terms Human Factors, Security

Keywords adoption, security tools, social factors

1. Introduction

Secure software is software that functions correctly even when under attack by malicious parties [1]. Security is a complex, emergent property of software. As such, there is no generally effective way to deploy secure software without considering security through the entire software development lifecycle [2]. Attempting to fix security errors in insecurely-built software is both less effective and more costly than using secure development practices from design to deployment [3]. One important secure development practice is the use of *secure development tools*, or "security tools" for short, which help developers write more secure code.

Broadly, security tools include static and dynamic analysis tools. Static analysis security tools (e.g. Fortify SCA [4], Armorize CodeSecure [5], and FindBugs [6]) analyze programs at compile time to find security defects, such as unsanitized inputs and potential array-out-of-bounds errors [7]. Dynamic analysis security tools (e.g. HP WebInspect [8] and IBM AppScan [9]) analyze program behavior at run time to find security faults, such as memory leaks, buffer overflows, and SQL injections. Developers can use these security tools to locate and repair vulnerabilities that could otherwise lead to costly failures. Unfortunately, many developers do not use

security tools during the development process [10], leading to the deployment of needlessly vulnerable software.

We have used data from interviews with 42 professional developers to develop a qualitative model of influences on security tool adoption. This model is based on a sociological approach to studying adoption of new technologies and ideas. However, since these interviews only concerned development in corporate settings, this model may not generalize to other development populations, such as the open-source software (OSS) community. I aim to refine and generalize this model to account for and predict the adoption or rejection of security tools within a software development community, corporate or otherwise. I have conducted interviews with 10 OSS developers to augment my colleague's interviews. I will analyze these interviews to seek new insights on the differences between corporate and OSS development communities with respect to security tool adoption.

2. Related Work

2.1 Secure Development Practice Adoption

Other researchers have also investigated how developers think about security and the use of security tools. In an online survey of 46 developers, Geer found that many developers do not adopt formal secure development lifecycles because they do not know of any methodologies or think adopting one would be too expensive in time and resources [11]. Xie and colleagues found that many professional developers do not consider security when developing software because they feel that others are responsible for security or because adopting secure development processes would require greater expertise than they have [10]. My work is broader in that I consider more factors than individual developers' attitudes. It also accounts for both corporate and OSS development communities and investigates differences between them.

2.2 Diffusion of Innovations in Software Development

Others have also applied o software development problems. It has been used in discussions of adoption of software engineering methods [12] and of programming languages and language features [13]. Hardgrave and colleagues developed a quantitative model of developers' intentions to adopt methodologies based on nd other adoption theories using a survey study, and Singer [14] used n developing a means to increase adoption of testing methodologies. The work described here is novel in using a qualitative empirical study to develop a quantitative account of developers' reasons for adopting tools. This work also focuses on developers' attitudes toward security, and may show interesting contrasts between developers in open-source and commercial software development.

3. Background

In previous work, a colleague conducted interviews with 42 professional developers to investigate why they adopt or reject new secu-

SPLASH '13,   October 26–31, 2013, Indianapolis, Indiana, USA.
Copyright is held by the owner/author(s).
ACM 978-1-4503-1995-9/13/10.
http://dx.doi.org/10.1145/2508075.2514872

rity tools. We developed a model of security tool adoption through quantitative analysis of these interviews. This domain-specific application of dentifies factors that influence developers' adoption or rejection of new security tools. We divide factors into four broad categories:

- characteristics of the *communication channels* by which they learn about security tools,

- characteristics of the security tools, or the *innovations*,

- characteristics of the *social system* whose members are exposed to a security tool, and

- characteristics of the developers who are exposed to security tools and must choose to adopt or reject them.

This analysis uncovered a some interesting patterns in the ways developers discover, perceive, and adopt security tools. For instance, like Xie and colleagues [10], we found that some developers feel that the presence of a dedicated security team makes them less personally responsible for the security of their code. In contrast, we found that developers who work closely with that security team tend to see security as a responsibility that they share.

However, since most open-source development projects do not have a dedicated security team, we cannot predict how open-source developers will feel about their responsibility for security. In this and other instances, we cannot generalize the results of our previous study until we better understand perceptions of security and security tools among open-source developers.

4. Research Plan

I used the security tool adoption model to design an interview script, modifying the previous interview script to accommodate OSS development. I then interviewed 10 developers who actively develop OSS to explore their reasons for using or not using security tools. I conducted semi-structured interviews [15]; I used the script as a guide, but was free to ask further exploratory questions. In these interviews, I focused my questions on three broad areas:

1) Software Security: I asked OSS developers about their relationship to software security. For instance, I asked what developers know about software security, how important they feel it is and why, and what they believe is necessary to ensure it. This will help me discover how the characteristics of individual developers affect their adoption of security tools.

2) Open-source software: I asked developers about their relationship to OSS and to OSS communities. For instance, I asked developers about the roles that they fulfill in OSS projects. This will help me discover how characteristics of the OSS social system and the communication channels used in that system affect developers' adoption patterns.

3) Coding Practices: I asked developers how they actually write code. In particular, I asked what, if any, security tools they use to improve the security of the software they write. This will allow me to find correlations between developers' attitudes and behavior. It will also help me discover how characteristics of particular security tools affect OSS developers' adoption of those tools.

I will code and analyze the data gathered in these interviews to find patterns in developers' responses. I will compare the results of these analyses with the results of our previous interview study. I will consider factors that influence developers in both corporate and OSS development to work towards a generalized model of security tool adoption.

The differences I find between professional and OSS developers will likely show interesting contrasts between the two communities. For instance: of the 42 professional developers interviewed previously, only 13 used security tools on a regular basis. Of those 13, seven reported that their employers had formal policies in place that required the use of security tools. These results suggest that as many as half of the regular users of security tools who we interviewed may do so only because they are required to.

However, I have not interviewed any OSS developers whose projects follow formal secure development practices or have explicit security standards. As this includes developers who develop OSS professionally, OSS developers who use security tools have different motivations than those developing closed-source software.

Taken as a whole, this project will help us better understand, predict, and encourage adoption of secure development practices. It is my hope that educators, toolsmiths, researchers, and software development communities at large can use this understanding to cultivate a widespread culture of secure software development. I have conducted interviews for the OSS interview portion of this project, and I hope that my analysis will create new insights into the characteristics of OSS developers and OSS development communities.

Acknowledgments

I thank the National Security Agency for funding this work. I also thank Shundan Xiao and Dr. Emerson Murphy-Hill for the opportunity to expand their work on security tool adoption.

References

[1] G. McGraw, "Software security," *IEEE Security & Privacy*, vol. 2, no. 2, pp. 80 – 83, Mar-Apr 2004.

[2] ——, "Building secure software: better than protecting bad software," *IEEE Software*, vol. 19, no. 6, pp. 57 – 58, Nov/Dec 2002.

[3] M. Howard and S. Lipner, *The Security Development Lifecycle*. Microsoft Press, 2006, vol. 34, no. 3.

[4] Hewlett-Packard Development Company, "HP Fortify static code analyzer," http://www.hpenterprisesecurity.com/products/hp-fortify-software-security-center/hp-fortify-static-code-analyzer, Dec. 2012.

[5] Armorize Technologies Incorporated, "Codesecure download," http://www.armorize.com/codesecure/, Dec. 2012.

[6] D. Hovemeyer and W. Pugh, "Finding bugs is easy," *SIGPLAN Not.*, vol. 39, no. 12, pp. 92–106, Dec. 2004.

[7] B. Chess and G. McGraw, "Static analysis for security," *Security Privacy, IEEE*, vol. 2, no. 6, pp. 76 – 79, Nov.-Dec. 2004.

[8] Hewlett-Packard Development Company, "HP WebInspect," http://www.hpenterprisesecurity.com/products/hp-fortify-software-security-center/hp-webinspect, Dec. 2012.

[9] International Business Machines Corp., "IBM security AppScan family," http://www-01.ibm.com/software/awdtools/appscan/, Dec. 2012.

[10] J. Xie, H. Lipford, and B. Chu, "Why do programmers make security errors?" in *VL/HCC, 2011*, Sept. 2011, pp. 161 –164.

[11] D. Geer, "Are companies actually using secure development life cycles?" *Computer*, vol. 43, no. 6, pp. 12 –16, June 2010.

[12] S. Raghavan and D. Chand, "Diffusing software-engineering methods," *IEEE Software*, vol. 6, no. 4, pp. 81 –90, July 1989.

[13] L. A. Meyerovich and A. S. Rabkin, "Socio-plt: principles for programming language adoption," in *Onward!* ACM, 2012, pp. 39–54.

[14] L. Singer, "Improving the adoption of software engineering practices through persuasive interventions," Ph.D. dissertation, Leibniz Universität Hannover, 2013.

[15] C. Seaman, "Qualitative methods in empirical studies of software engineering," *IEEE TSE*, vol. 25, no. 4, pp. 557–572, 1999.

Documenting Software Using Adaptive Software Artifacts

Filipe Figueiredo Correia

Faculdade de Engenharia, Universidade do Porto, Portugal
filipe.correia@fe.up.pt

Abstract

Creating and using software documentation presents numerous challenges, namely in what concerns the expression of knowledge structures, consistency maintenance and classification. *Adaptive Software Artifacts* is a flexible approach to expressing structured contents that tackles these concerns, and that is being realized in the context of a Software Forge.

Categories and Subject Descriptors D.2 Software Engineering [*D.2.7 Distribution, Maintenance, and Enhancement*]: Documentation

Keywords documentation, wikis, modeling, knowledge

1. Research Problem and Motivation

Software developers capture knowledge as software artifacts of different kinds, from source-code, to models, to textual documents. Not only are some of them an integral part of the software being built, they are vital for team communication and to preserve knowledge for future use.

These artifacts are not created at the same time and evolve throughout the project's lifetime. They take part of the sense-making process in which the team identifies the information *patterns* (i.e., structure) that underly a given body of knowledge. The team may need to capture, share and reason about those ideas to discover how they can be structured, therefore they may first capture them as free-form contents and, only afterwards, capture them as increasingly more specialized artifacts, such as tasks, models and source-code.

On the one hand, capturing information's structure *explicitly* makes it more concrete, unambiguous and terse. On the other hand, free-form contents have the benefit of not being subject to structural constraints, which is important during exploratory work. One of the downsides of free-form contents, however, is that they don't directly support sharing information patterns between team members. Information is also not easily automatable — e.g., the cost of maintaining free-form contents is high, as keeping their consistency requires continuous review. Moreover, organizing and classifying information for efficient access is often difficult and classification schemes may also need to be constantly updated to reflect the evolving body of information.

Adaptive Software Artifacts combine the benefits of free-form and structured contents. It is an approach to make information within software development teams easier to use and evolve, especially in the context of medium-to-large projects where the amount of knowledge involved easily heightens all of these challenges.

2. Background and Related Work

A number of different approaches have addressed the capture of knowledge of a software project as *documentation*.

Their goals range from lowering the barrier to entry and collaboration (e.g. wikis), integration with other artifacts for added expressiveness, readability and maintainability (e.g. literate programming, code annotations, IDEs, software forges), or making it more unambiguous and concrete (e.g. modeling, semantic wikis).

Integrated Development Environments (IDEs) focus mainly on source code but try to provide a *whole* view of software artifacts and the processes that use them. **Software Forges** [7] differ from IDEs in that they are web-based and don't focus mainly on the source code. They allow to capture and integrate artifacts as diverse as wiki pages, version-controlled files, issue-tracking tickets, and milestones, among others. Their primary goal is to support open collaboration.

Modeling techniques are used by software developers to represent complex topics in simpler terms, focusing on capturing only their relevant aspects. Models allow to represent information with a degree of rigor and objectivity that free-form contents cannot, but modeling tools impose constraints that don't always play in the user's favor. For this reason developers often resource to *lighter* approaches, like textual documents or drawings. These approaches are especially popular for tasks of an exploratory or creative nature, when the importance of being able to record incomplete and/or non-structured information is higher that rigor. The research on **Flexible Modeling Tools** tries to fill this gap [6], by combining the benefits of free-form and model-based contents, allowing users to trade precision for flexibility whenever the occasion calls for it.

3. Approach

This approach is based on the notion of *Adaptive Software Artifacts*. A plugin was developed for the Trac Software Forge — instead of having at their disposal a finite set of software artifact types (wiki pages, tickets and milestones, to name a few), Trac users are able to create their own *types* of artifact, with a completely custom-tailored structure that fits their specific project's needs. These artifacts are *adaptive* in the sense that their attributes and relations with other artifacts are not established *a priori* and can be freely evolved by the users.

Permission to make digital or hard copies of part or all of this work for personal or classroom use is granted without fee provided that copies are not made or distributed for profit or commercial advantage and that copies bear this notice and the full citation on the first page. Copyrights for third-party components of this work must be honored. For all other uses, contact the owner/author(s).

SPLASH '13, October 26–31, 2013, Indianapolis, Indiana, USA.
Copyright is held by the owner/author(s).
ACM 978-1-4503-1995-9/13/10.
http://dx.doi.org/10.1145/2508075.2514873

They are not bound to strict constraints like other structured artifacts usually are.

The benefits of this approach over the traditional dichotomy between *structured* and *free-form* contents extend beyond the support to expressing *ad hoc* knowledge structures explicitly. It allows the consistency of the contents towards their expected structure to be automatically assessed, and access to the wiki contents can be supported by a classification scheme that is dynamically built from the tight integration between the wiki and the *adaptive artifacts*.

The *Adaptive Software Artifacts* plugin uses several *flexible modeling* principles to combine the benefits of free-form and structured contents. However, the end-result of using this approach is not necessarily a model. This approach focuses on structuring information of text documents (i.e., of wiki pages) into smaller and meaningful *elements*, on an as-needed basis. The result is the creation of instances (artifacts) and model elements (artifact types), which sets this solution apart from other *flexible modeling* approaches, that focus on the model and meta-model levels. Moreover, the main goal is not to represent this information as diagrams, or to directly play a part in the creation of executable artifacts, but to support structuring and organizing textual contents.

Literate Programming and it's derivatives (e.g., code annotations) also allow to combine source-code with textual descriptions, but they don't delve into structuring and organizing these textual contents. Comparatively, *Adaptive Software Artifacts* encourage and leverage the creation of semantically richer documentation.

4. Contributions and Results

The Adaptive Software Artifacts plugin is possibly the most tangible part of this research from an engineering standpoint, but it is not the only one. This work comprises:

- A *software-forge* supporting *adaptive software artifacts*;
- A design patterns catalog of best practices for building a system that supports this approach.
- An experiment, conducted in an academic setting, and a case study conducted in an industrial setting, both with the goal of validating the approach.

Weaki is a wiki engine developed in the context of this work, supporting the incremental capture and evolution of structured wiki pages [2]. The lessons learned from *Weaki* are being used to extend the Trac software forge to support the notion of *adaptive software artifacts*[1].

The implementation of the plugin can be regarded as a reference architecture but, more than specific implementations, the goal of this work is to address the key principles that underlie the approach. Such is the purpose of the design patterns catalog mentioned above. These patterns were mined from existing literature and tools, and sometimes driven by the development of the plugin itself. The catalog already includes patterns of maintaining the consistency of documentation ar-

tifacts [3], the classification and indexing of contents [1], the evolution of data and meta-data in systems using the Adaptive Object-Model architectural pattern [4], and of object-oriented meta-architectures [5].

Furthermore, two user studies are being conducted to validate the approach. An experiment was performed with the participation of a sample of 43 students divided in two groups — *control* and *experimental*, and is expected to provide preliminary evidence of the approach's benefits and liabilities. It consisted of a programming exercise, comprised by a series of simple tasks that required the use of a project's documentation, built using *adaptive software artifacts*. The plugin was instrumented to collect usage data, and the participants were asked to answer a questionnaire about their use of the tool. While some conclusions can be directly derived from the usage data, others are intrinsically subjective and will be based entirely on the results of the questionnaires. At the time of writing of this paper the data is still being subject of analysis, but it is expected to help answering (among other specific issues) if contents are regarded as more *precise, concise, easier to understand, easier to find* and more *consistent*, when using this approach.

If the results from this experiment are encouraging, they may help to motivate the use of the plugin in the industry. Two software companies have shown interest in providing feedback on the plugin, and one in particular has shown the will to take part of a case study. This case study is expected to provide some evidence regarding the authoring of contents and may reinforce the results of the experiment.

References

[1] F. F. Correia and A. Aguiar. Patterns of information classification. In *Proceedings of the 18th Conference on Pattern Languages of Programs*, Portland, OR, USA, Oct. 2011.

[2] F. F. Correia, H. S. Ferreira, N. Flores, and A. Aguiar. Incremental knowledge acquisition in software development using a Weakly-Typed wiki. In *Proceedings of the 5th International Symposium on Wikis and Open Collaboration*, Orlando, FL, USA, Oct. 2009.

[3] F. F. Correia, H. S. Ferreira, N. Flores, and A. Aguiar. Patterns for consistent software documentation. In *Proceedings of the Pattern Languages of Programs*, Chicago, IL, USA, Aug. 2009.

[4] H. S. Ferreira, F. F. Correia, and L. Welicki. Patterns for data and metadata evolution in adaptive Object-Models. In *Proceedings of the 15th Conference on Pattern Languages of Programs*, Nashville, TN, USA, Oct. 2008. ACM.

[5] H. S. Ferreira, F. F. Correia, J. Yoder, and A. Aguiar. Core patterns of object-oriented meta-architectures. In *Proceedings of the 17th Conference on Pattern Languages of Programs*, Reno, NV, USA, Oct. 2010.

[6] H. Ossher, A. van der Hoek, M. Storey, J. Grundy, R. Bellamy, and M. Petre. Workshop on flexible modeling tools: FlexiTools 2011. In *2011 33rd International Conference on Software Engineering (ICSE)*, pages 1192—1193. IEEE, May 2011.

[7] D. Riehle, J. Ellenberger, T. Menahem, B. Mikhailovski, Y. Natchetoi, B. Naveh, and T. Odenwald. Open collaboration within corporations using software forges. *IEEE Softw.*, 26(2): 52–58, 2009.

---

[1] The current implementation is a plugin for Trac, and can be found in the address *https://github.com/filipefigcorreia/TracAdaptiveSoftwareArtifacts*

Development of Automatically Verifiable Systems using Data Representation Synthesis

Bryce Cronkite-Ratcliff

Department of Computer Science, Stanford University
brycecr@stanford.edu

Categories and Subject Descriptors   D.2.4 [*Software Engineering*]: Software/Program Verification- Formal Methods, Reliability

Keywords   automatic verification; data representation synthesis; container reasoning

1.   Problem and Motivation

One of the greatest challenges in formal verification has been automatically reasoning about pointer data structures, where issues of aliasing - that multiple symbolic names may refer to the same memory location - and indirection greatly complicate automated reasoning [9]. This problem has impeded the development of more effective automatic formal analysis tools for general code, and an approach for automatically reasoning about such structures has proved elusive.

While the analysis of general pointer data structures remains difficult, more progress has been made on the related problem of analyzing containers, a restricted class of data structures that permit insertion, query, removal, and iteration operations. These structures are encountered in numerous heavily used libraries, including the C++ STL and Java Collections Framework. In particular, work by Dillig et al. has provided a general theory for automatic reasoning about containers, and the authors have implemented this work into a functional cross-platform automatic verifier called Compass [2]. Thus, if we can change the way software is written such that containers are used instead of pointer data structures, we can take advantage of Compass precise reasoning about containers to automatically verify the resulting code.

One approach to building code without pointer data structures is Data Representation Synthesis (DRS) [4]. In DRS, the programmer provides a high-level description of the data as mathematical relations, where this specification does not commit to any particular implementation. Then, a compiler selects a particular data structure implementation for the specified relation. The choice of data structure implementation is now under compiler control. As a result, the correctness of data structure operations is now by construction.

In this work, we show that DRS encapsulates arbitrary data handling in an interface that supports operations that can be expressed in terms of operations on containers. Thus, we can use the precise reasoning techniques for containers already mentioned to perform automatic verification of systems built on structures generated by Data Representation Synthesis.

Thus, the use of Data Representation Synthesis and techniques for precise automatic reasoning about containers can provide automatically verifiable complete systems that are performant and relatively simple to build and maintain.

SPLASH '13,   October 26–31, 2013, Indianapolis, Indiana, USA.
Copyright is held by the owner/author(s).
ACM 978-1-4503-1995-9/13/10.
http://dx.doi.org/10.1145/2508075.2514874

2.   Background and Related Work

This work is based on the union of Precise Container Reasoning and Data Representation Synthesis techniques already mentioned, so some further elaboration of these techniques is warranted.

2.1   Precise Container Reasoning

Containers are a class of abstract data structures that allow elements to be inserted, retrieved, removed, or iterated over. A wide range of familiar data structures including maps, vectors, lists, sets, stacks, and deques are containers. Because container interfaces are widely used in standard libraries such as the C++ STL, automatic analysis of container client programs can be decoupled from the potentially more tedious task of verifying the particular container implementation; one implementation analysis can serve for all the clients of the container [2].

Recent work by Dillig, Dillig, & Aiken developed a technique for precise automatic static analysis of container-manipulating programs, which we will refer to as Precise Container Reasoning (PCR) [2]. PCR differs from previous approaches to container analysis in that it separates containers into position-dependent containers (such as stacks, vectors, and lists) and value-dependent containers (such as maps and sets), and provides a constraint-based means to reason about key-value and position-value relationships for value-dependent and position-dependent containers, respectively. In tests conducted by the authors, PCR found all container usage errors detected by a technique that did not consider these key-value and position-value relationships and produced many fewer false positives, to the point where false positives never outnumbered actual errors and usually accounted for far fewer warnings.

Compass is an analysis application that implements PCR to allow for automatic analysis of container-manipulating programs [2]. Compass currently supports analysis of C++.

2.2   Data Representation Synthesis

Data Representation Synthesis (DRS) is a technique developed recently by Hawkins and colleagues to provide a means of decoupling the data structure interface from the data structure implementation [4]. In DRS, the programmer provides a relational specification and decomposition. The relational specification is a description of the data to represent, how each piece of data relates to others (for example, which attributes act as relational keys), and which relational operations should be supported. The decomposition provides a description of how the data structure should be implemented as a combination of existing data structure primitives. Thus, the programmer defines the interface to their data structure via a relational specification, and this definition is entirely separate from the definition of the backing decomposition.

DRS has been implemented by Hawkins in the form of RelC. RelC takes as input relational specifications and decompositions written in a simple ML-like language and generates data structures in C++ or Java that implement the requested relational specification using the supplied decomposition.

DRS has an advantage in the development of verifiable programs: because DRS is capable of generating high-performance encapsulated data structures that can represent arbitrary relations, the need use hand-coded pointer data structures is reduced or eliminated. In particular we can use existing techniques for precise reasoning about containers to reason about DRS-generated relations.

2.3 Related Work

Several other projects have sought to verify microkernel code. In particular, NICTAs seL4 was the first operating system kernel to be completely formally verified [8]. seL4 was custom-built for the verification project and verification was performed by automatically verifying that the kernel code faithfully implemented a manually written formal specification for the kernel behavior. seL4 built on work on the EROS kernel, and a small number of other verified operating systems exist in both academic and industrial sectors. The VFiasco project is perhaps most similar to the work presented here in that it attempts to verify Fiasco [5]. However, VFiasco focuses in particular on proving properties such as whether the internal page-fault handler terminates for all page faults or whether the memory allocator works correctly (in our work we focus on demonstrating memory safety).

Our work differs from the approaches in these systems in that we focus on demonstrating the feasibility of building a system suitable for automatic verification of memory safety instead of building an operating system with verified higher-order properties for use in critical embedded applications.

Automatic software verification is an active field of research in programming systems and many promising approaches are under study. Type Qualifiers present one approach, where qualifiers inferred or programmer-supplied carry information about expected program behavior and potential security risks [3]. Type Qualifiers have been applied to verify pointer safety in operating system code; one study by Johnson and Wagner used Type Qualifiers to find pointer bugs in Linux kernel code [6].

Recent research in path-sensitive data-flow analysis has extended the scope of programs that can be analyzed with data-flow techniques greatly, and has promising applications in automatic compiler optimizations and formal verification [1].

Work by Kim and colleagues has focused on verification of specific pointer-based data structures, particularly linked data structures [7]. This work indicates the possibility of reasoning about pointer data structures without porting code, but it is not fully automatic and does not come with the advantages besides verifiability - in modularty, implementation independence, and potentially performance - of developing with relations.

These and similar automatic verification techniques vary from our approach in that they do not reason about containers and thus are not able to separate interface from implementation in analysis. It should be mentioned that we see our approach as complementary to those mentioned above to verify code that is not container-manipulating or to verify container implementations.

3. Approach

Our primary motivation for this work is to demonstrate the automatic verifiability of code using DRS-generated structures. To a first approximation, a relation can be seen as a container of the tuples in the relation, where queries on the attributes serve as the indices into the relation. Thus, if we can express the relational operations as operations on containers, we can use the automatic approach to verifying code that manipulates containers implemented in Compass.

Briefly, we model a relation R as a trie where each non-leaf node at level l is a container mapping an particular value of an attribute a_l in the relation to a set of partial tuples that correspond to the attributes a_i, $l \leq i \leq S_R$ where S_R is the size of the attribute schema of R. Each leaf node is simply a terminal node that indicates the presence of a particular tuple formed by traversing edges from the root of the trie.

With a mechanism for reasoning about relations as containers, we developed a system to demonstrate the efficacy of this approach.

In particular, we removed all the core pointer data structures from the Fiasco.OC microkernel and replaced them with RelC-generated relations. We then benchmarked the result to demonstrate good performance – we see an average performance loss relative to the original kernel of about 4%. Finally, we are currently working with Compass to determine if we can automatically verify security properties of the resulting code.

This work, to our knowledge, represents the first attempt at a validated approach for automatically verifying non-trivial safety properties of complex computer systems that use arbitrary data relationships.

4. Results

We set out to develop a significant proof of concept for the verification of software systems developed using Data Representation Synthesis. We were able to port core structures of the Fiasco microkernel to structures compiled by Data Representation Synthesis, verify performance, and are currently applying precise container reasoning techniques to determine the verifiabiliy of the code.

We hope this work will be evidence of the effectiveness of developing arbitrary systems with Data Representation Synthesis. Without increasing code complexity or decreasing performance, the use of relations could create automatically verifiable container-manipulating code where analysis-confounding pointer data structure code once stood.

Acknowledgments

Thank you to Alex Aiken, Peter Hawkins, Tom & Isil Dillig, and Mooly Sagiv for guidance and support.

References

[1] I. Dillig, T. Dillig, and A. Aiken. Sound, Complete and Scalable Path-sensitive Analysis. *PLDI*, 43(6):270–280, 2008.

[2] I. Dillig, T. Dillig, and A. Aiken. Precise Reasoning for Programs Using Containers. *PLDI*, 46(1):187–200, 2011.

[3] J. S. Foster, M. Fähndrich, and A. Aiken. A Theory of Type Qualifiers. *PLDI*, 34(5):192–203, 1999.

[4] P. Hawkins, A. Aiken, K. Fisher, and M. Rinard. Data Representation Synthesis. *PLDI*, 47(6):38–49, 2011. ISSN 03621340.

[5] M. Hohmuth, H. Tews, and S. G. Stephens. Applying Source-code Verification to a Microkernel The VFiasco Project. *ACM SIGOPS European Workshop: Beyond the PC*, 2002.

[6] R. Johnson and D. Wagner. Finding User/Kernel Pointer Bugs with Type Inference. *USENIX Security Symposium*, pages 119–134, 2004.

[7] D. Kim and M. C. Rinard. Verification of Semantic Commutativity Conditions and Inverse Operations on Linked Data Structures. *PLDI*, pages 528–541, 2011.

[8] G. Klein, K. Elphinstone, G. Heiser, and K. Engelhardt. seL4 : Formal Verification of an OS Kernel. *ACM SIGOPS Symposium on Operating Systems Principles*, 97(1):207–220, 2009.

[9] K. Zee, V. Kuncak, and M. Rinard. Full Functional Verification of Linked Data Structures. *PLDI*, 43(6):349, May 2008.

HJ-Hadoop: An Optimized MapReduce Runtime for Multi-core Systems

Yunming Zhang

Rice University

yz17@rice.edu

Categories and Subject Descriptors D.3.4 [*Processors*]: Runtime environments

Keywords Hadoop, Habanero Java

1. Introduction

This submission introduces HabaneroJava-Hadoop (HJ-Hadoop), an extension to the popular Hadoop MapReduce runtime system that is optimized for multi-core machines.

MapReduce allows programmers to write data parallel programs that can run on thousands of machines [1]. Going forward, it will become even more challenging for MapReduce to utilize memory and CPU resources efficiently, as the number of cores in future processors continues to increase, and the available memory per core starts to decrease. It is important to exploit massive parallelism without sacrificing the memory efficiency of the machines.

The current Hadoop MapReduce implementation uses multicore systems by decomposing a MapReduce job into multiple map/reduce tasks that can execute in parallel. Each map/reduce task is executed in a separate JVM instance. The number of JVMs created in a single node (machine) can have a significant impact on performance due to their aggregate effects on CPU and memory utilization.For *memory-intensive applications*, a significant drawback of the current design is that some data structures are duplicated across JVMs, including static data and in-memory data structures used by map/reduce tasks.

This submission proposes a solution to this memory bottleneck by exploiting multicore parallelism at the intra-JVM level, while limiting the number of JVMs created on each node. At the same time, we don't want to sacrifice the fault-tolerance and reliability of the system. Thus, in addition to parallelizing multiple map tasks, we also parallelize the execution of a single map task to exploit intra-task parallelism. *HJ-Hadoop* leverages the Habanero-Java (HJ) runtime model [2] for multicore parallelism.

Previous work in the Hadoop community to create multiple threads within a mapper JVM led to the Multithreaded Mapper.However, Multithreaded Mapper replicates in-memory data structures across threads, thereby leading to a larger memory footprint than the default sequential Mapper.

SPLASH '13, October 26–31, 2013, Indianapolis, Indiana, USA.
Copyright is held by the owner/author(s).
ACM 978-1-4503-1995-9/13/10.
http://dx.doi.org/10.1145/2508075.2514875

Our performance results for the memory-intensive KNN Join application (Figure 1) show that the performance of the Hadoop Multithreaded Mapper, standard Hadoop, and HJ-Hadoop peak at input sizes of approximately 50MB, 220MB and 400MB respectively, thereby demonstrating HJ-Hadoop's ability to improve memory utilization. At 250MB, HJ-Hadoop shows a $3\times$ performance improvement relative to standard Hadoop.For non-memory intensive clustering algorithms, the relative improvement is in the $8\% - 16\%$ range due to HJ-Hadoops ability to achieve better load balance across cores.

2. Motivating Examples

2.1 K Nearest Neighbor Join

K Nearest Neighbor (KNN) Join takes in two data sets R (Query Set)and S(Training Set). It compares every point in R against every point in S, and outputs results based on all pairwise comparisons. KNN Join is representative of many large scale data analytics applications such as Fragment Replicated Join in PIG. It is often true that S is much larger than R. In the map stage, the application loads the smaller data set R into the memory of each map task. The Hadoop MapReduce runtime splits up S into small pieces and uses them as input to each map task. The map function calculates the distance between two data points in R and S. The memory footprint of the mapper JVM is large because the data structure containing R takes up a lot of memory. In the reduce stage, the application goes through each data point in R and chooses the closest K data points in S. Because R has to be read into every mapper JVM, it will be duplicated across tasks, incurring significant memory inefficiency. Furthermore, the limited memory in each JVM makes it hard to process large R data sets efficiently.

2.2 FuzzyKMeans

FuzzyKMeans is representative of many popular machine learning algorithms. The application doesn't have a large memory footprint. I use it to show the performance benefit from the load balance optimizations. The results for KMeans and Dirchlet clustering algorithms are also included. In each map phase, the probability that the points belong to each cluster is calculated based on the distances to the centroids. In the reduce phase, the new means of the centroids are calculated. The algorithm chains together many MapReduce jobs to refine the coordinates of the centroids.

3. HJ-Hadoop Implementation

The computation in Hadoop MapReduce jobs is performed by user-defined mappers and reducers. Once the user submits a Hadoop MapReduce job, the runtime splits the input of the job based on the user specified split size. Each mapper then reads in its own input split. By default, mappers sequentially generate (key,val) pairs from their input split. Every time a (key,val) pair is generated, the Mapper JVM immediately processes it using the user defined map function to produce zero or more intermediate (key, value) pairs. This design is inherently sequential as the mapper JVM has to finish processing a (key,val) pair before moving on to process the next one.

Instead of reading in and processing one (key,val) pair at a time, HJ-Hadoop reads in a certain number of (key, val) pairs to create chunks of (key,val) pairs and process these different chunks in parallel. Automatic parallelization of map tasks must rely on an efficient parallel runtime to execute them. Habanero-Java parallel programming work sharing runtime was used to manage the creation, scheduling, execution, and termination of tasks. The runtime uses a single task queue and has worker threads pick work from the queue to achieve load balance across cores. To improve the performance, HJ-Hadoop overlaps I/O with computation by dedicating one worker thread to prefetch (key,val) pairs into a buffer while other worker threads are executing map tasks. To do this, the runtime allocates a new buffer for each async task. Once the buffer is full, the I/O thread starts an async task to process it.

Our experiments also show that chunk sizes have a non-trivial impact on the running time of the program and there isn't a fixed chunk size that is optimal for all applications. To find the right chunk size, I implemented a chunking of the (key, val) pairs that adapts to the execution time of the map function. The main thread reads in a small number of input (key, val) pairs as a sample chunk. It records the time it took to process the sample chunk. Based on an empirically chosen desired running time for each chunk, the runtime calculates the optimal chunk size knowing the running time of the sample chunk. Results show that dynamic chunking works better than fixed chunk sizes.

4. Experimental Results

4.1 Experimental Setup

Each worker node had two quad core 2.4 GHz Intel Xeon CPUs with an 8 MB last-level cache. 8 mappers were used on Hadoop with the standard sequential mapper to fully utilize the 8 cores in each node. The heap size limit was set to 1.5 GB for each JVM to simulate about 12 GB available RAM in a machine. I used 4 mappers for HJ-Hadoop and Hadoop with the multithreaded mapper, and I set the maximum heap size of each JVM to 2.5 GB.

4.2 KNN Join

For KNN Join, I benchmarked the performance on a single worker node, since I found that the performance is most strongly impacted by the number of times garbage collection is performed within each JVM. Increasing the number of worker nodes will have no impact on the execution time of individual map or reduce tasks.

The results are shown in Figure 1. The x axis represents the size of the Query Set for KNN Join. The Query Set is loaded into every map task. The input to the MapReduce job is 64 MB of Training Set. The block size is 128 MB and the split size is 8 MB. As we can see in Figure 1, as the Query Set size increases, the multithreaded mapper could only process up to 50 MB of Query Set data efficiently. The performance of standard Hadoop peaks at approximately 220 MB of Query Set data. I have logged a 3-fold increase in the number of garbage collection calls within each JVM between the two runs of Hadoop with 220 MB and 230 MB of Query Set data. The Hadoop JVMs with sequential mappers cannot process Query Sets larger than 250 MB. In contrast, HJ-Hadoop's running time increases linearly all the way to 400 MB due to the larger heap size available in a single HJ-Hadoop JVM. This allows each HJ-Hadoop KNN job to process almost twice as much Query Set data as a Hadoop KNN job.

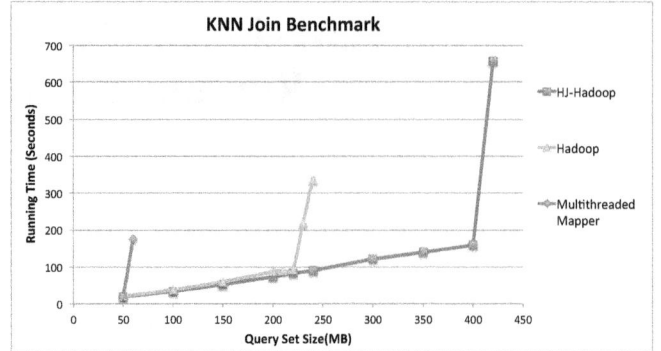

Figure 1: Running time of HJ-Hadoop, Hadoop and Hadoop with multi-threaded mapper using KNN Join benchmark on a single node with fixed 64MB Training Set and varying Query Set size.

Applications	FuzzyKMeans	KMeans	Dirichlet
Hadoop	560s	625s	466s
Multithreaded Mapper	614s(0.91)	625s(1.00)	511s(0.91)
HJ-Hadoop	483s(1.16)	559(1.11)	431s(1.08)

Table 1: Comparing the results of HJ-Hadoop, Hadoop and Hadoop with the multithreaded mapper to demonstrate the speedup from improved load balance across cores. The tests were conducted on 8 worker nodes with a 12 GB input.

4.3 Clustering Algorithms

For non-memory-intensive applications, I chose FuzzyKMeans, KMeans and Dirichlet clustering algorithms to demonstrate the performance benefit of HJ-Hadoop.

From row 2 in Table 1, we can see that Hadoop with the multi-threaded mapper using 4 JVMs per worker node actually results in a slowdown compared to Hadoop with the sequential mapper using 8 JVMs per worker node due to inefficient implementation. On the other hand, HJ-Hadoop achieved 8% – 16% speedup with 4 JVMs through improved load balance across cores.

5. Related Work

Phoenix is a shared memory MapReduce framework optimized for multi-core systems. It focuses on the performance of a single multi-core machine. The design was not concerned with duplicating static data structures across map tasks. No optimization for static data structures used in map tasks was mentioned. The paper discussed the optimization of a dynamic framework that discovers the best unit size for each program as future work but never implemented one. We have explored an approach to dynamically setting HJ async task sizes based on sampling the execution time for chunks.

Spark is a MapReduce system that is built using Resilient Distributed Datasets (RDDs). Spark keeps data structures in memory for successive MapReduce jobs to avoid redundant disk I/O operations. Our work, however, tries to improve memory efficiency by minimizing duplication of in-memory data structures within a single MapReduce job.

References

[1] Hadoop. http://hadoop.apache.org. URL http://hadoop.apache.org.

[2] V. Cavé, J. Zhao, J. Shirako, and V. Sarkar. Habanero-java: the new adventures of old x10. PPPJ '11.

Structured Statistical Syntax Tree Prediction

Cyrus Omar

Carnegie Mellon University

comar@cs.cmu.edu

Abstract

Statistical models of source code can be used to improve code completion systems, assistive interfaces, and code compression engines. We are developing a statistical model where programs are represented as syntax trees, rather than simply a stream of tokens. Our model, initially for the Java language, combines corpus data with information about syntax, types and the program context. We tested this model using open source code corpuses and find that our model is significantly more accurate than the current state of the art, providing initial evidence for our claim that combining structural and statistical information is a fruitful strategy.

Categories and Subject Descriptors D.3.m [*Programming Languages*]: Miscellaneous

Keywords statistical models; prediction

1. Introduction

Programming languages are both formal systems with rich syntactic and semantic structure and human systems, in that they are used by people in patterned ways to express their intent. Many tools are designed to help people write code more efficiently by predicting the source code that a developer intends. For example, code completion systems for editors like Eclipse for Java display pop-up menus containing relevant class members and other snippets.

These code completion systems make use of the semantic structure of the language and API information extracted from imported libraries, but do not incorporate data about how developers have written programs in the past. Several pieces of recent work have shown, however, that incorporating statistical information is useful in particular settings (e.g. [1]). Indeed, Hindle et al. [2] have demonstrated that the next token that a user will enter can be predicted with reason-

able accuracy using a purely statistical model that considers only a few previous tokens, neglecting all language, API and context-specific knowledge.

Our work aims to combine the structured and statistical approaches to source code prediction. Rather than using a tokenized representation of source code, we perform statistical prediction on a more natural representation of source code: the typed syntax tree. We can then condition our predictions on structural information, specifically:

- the *type*, denoted τ, of the expression being predicted (e.g. int or Color)

- the *syntactic context*, denoted σ, in which the expression occurs (e.g. whether the expression is an argument of a function call, the guard of an if statement, etc.)

- the *program context*, denoted Γ, in which the expression occurs (e.g. the set of variables paired with their types that are in scope at the location of the expression.)

For example, if a user enters the Java code Planet destination = where Planet is an enumeration type containing Mercury, Venus, Earth, etc. (but not Pluto, of course), then we have that the type of the expression being entered at the cursor is Planet, the syntactic context is *assignment*, and given a program context, our prediction space need only assign non-zero probabilities to:

1. literal members of the Planet enumeration

2. variables and fields of type Planet available from the program context

3. calls to methods available from the program context that have return type Planet[1].

The particular distribution of probability across expressions within these three categories is influenced in part by data derived from code corpus analyses.

In addition to the applications to code completion systems in code editors like Eclipse, more accurate source code prediction techniques could be useful for other programming tools. For example, programmers with severe physical impairments may benefit from predictive programming interfaces that allow them convey source code using devices more

SPLASH '13, October 26–31, 2013, Indianapolis, Indiana, USA.
Copyright is held by the owner/author(s).
ACM 978-1-4503-1995-9/13/10.
http://dx.doi.org/10.1145/2508075.2514876

---

[1] We can consider operators like + and [] as methods of the built-in types in Java.

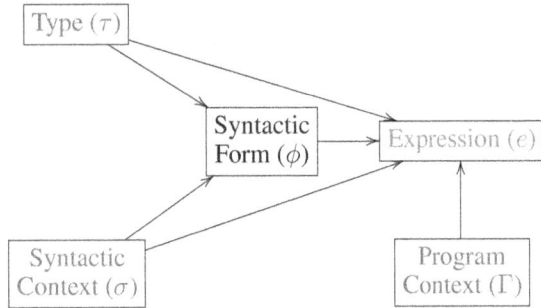

Figure 1. A graphical model representing our approach. Green variables are always observed (we do not assign marginal distributions to them). The syntactic form, ϕ, is a latent variable, and the expression, e, is unknown. The form is a function of the expression.

limited than a keyboard [3]. In addition, source code compression algorithms may benefit from more accurate probability models, which is an important consideration as applications are increasingly being sent over the network each time they are executed.

2. Methodology

To assign a probability to an expression, denoted e, we first determine how likely it is that the expression is of each of the three syntactic forms mentioned before, where syntactic forms are denoted ϕ. For each form, we can then assign probabilities to particular expressions of that form according to some form-specific conditional distribution. The conditional distributions for both the syntactic form and expression are learned using data gathered from analyses of prior code corpuses (smoothed using some suitable method in cases where enough information is not available).

Put more formally, our goal is to learn a model that allows us to produce $\mathbf{P}(e|\tau,\sigma,\Gamma)$. We determine this probability by marginalizing over a latent variable that represents the *syntactic form* of the expression, denoted ϕ:

$$P(e|\tau,\sigma,\Gamma) = \sum_{\phi\in\Phi} P(e|\phi,\tau,\sigma,\Gamma)P(\phi|\tau,\sigma)$$

As diagrammed in Figure 1, τ is the type of the expression, $\sigma \in \Sigma$ is the syntactic context, Γ is the program context, and $\phi \in \Phi$ is the syntactic form. We consider syntactic contexts $\Sigma = \{$**statement**, **assignment**, **arg**, **other**$\}$ representing plain statements, assignments to variables, method arguments and a catch-all for other syntactic contexts (e.g. conditional and loop guards, return statements, etc.). We consider syntactic forms $\Phi = \{$**lit**, **var**, **meth**$\}$, representing literals (of built-in and enumeration types), variables and method calls, respectively.

In the equations below, $\#\{e,\tau,\phi,\sigma\}$ represents the number of expressions in the training set constrained by the provided expression, type, syntactic form and program context (summing over any omitted categories.)

The conditional distribution for the syntactic forms is simply categorical, with the probability for each $\phi \in \Phi$ learned as:

$$P(\phi|\tau,\sigma) = \begin{cases} \frac{\#\{\phi,\tau,\sigma\}}{\#\{\tau,\sigma\}} & \#\{\tau,\sigma\} \neq 0 \\ \frac{\#\{\phi,\sigma\}}{\#\{\sigma\}} & \text{o/w} \end{cases}$$

That is, we use the empirical probability that that the expression has syntactic form ϕ given that the expression has type τ and is in syntactic context σ. If we have no data for type τ in that syntactic context, we marginalize over τ.

The conditional distribution for an expression e given the syntactic form, if the actual syntactic form of e is ϕ_e, is broken down according to the syntactic form as follows:

$$P(e|\phi,\tau,\sigma,\Gamma) = \begin{cases} P_{\text{lit}}(e|\tau,\sigma,\Gamma) & \text{if } \phi = \phi_e = \textbf{lit} \\ P_{\text{var}}(e|\tau,\sigma,\Gamma) & \text{if } \phi = \phi_e = \textbf{var} \\ P_{\text{meth}}(e|\tau,\sigma,\Gamma) & \text{if } \phi = \phi_e = \textbf{meth} \\ 0 & \text{if } \phi \neq \phi_e \end{cases}$$

The distributions for literals are determined by corpus data counting their frequencies. For variables, there is generally no relevant corpus data (because the lifespan of a variable is scoped), so we assign uniform probability to all variables in scope of the correct type. The distribution for methods benefits considerably from corpus data, however. To calculate the probability of a method itself, we consider two cases. It may be a method that we have seen in the training set, in which case we use the empirical probability of that method in the provided syntactic context. It may also be a method that hasn't been seen in the training set. In this case, we give a uniform distribution over all such methods callable via a variable or type in the program context.

2.1 Implementation

We used the Java language to implement our model and perform experiments to analyze the effectiveness of our methodology. Our prediction library is named **Syzygy** and is available at `http://github.com/cyrus-/syzygy`.

2.2 Results

We compared the probabilities generated in a cross-validated scenario to show that our method (SSCP) performed significantly better than the n-gram model of Hindle et al. across all six open source projects that we considered.

References

[1] M. Bruch, M. Monperrus, and M. Mezini. In *ESEC/FSE '09*, pages 213–222, New York, NY, USA. ACM.

[2] A. Hindle, E. T. Barr, Z. Su, M. Gabel, and P. Devanbu. On the naturalness of software. In *Software Engineering (ICSE), 2012 34th International Conference on*, pages 837–847. IEEE, 2012.

[3] C. Omar, A. Akce, M. Johnson, T. Bretl, R. Ma, E. Maclin, M. McCormick, and T. P. Coleman. A feedback information-theoretic approach to the design of brain–computer interfaces. *Intl. Journal of Human–Computer Interaction*, 27(1):5–23, 2010.

Identifying and Specifying Crosscutting Contracts with AspectJML

Henrique Rebêlo

Universidade Federal de Pernambuco, PE, Brazil
hemr@cin.ufpe.br

Abstract

I propose AspectJML, a simple and practical aspect-oriented extension to JML. It supports the specification of crosscutting contracts for Java code in a modular way while keeping the benefits of a design by contract language, like documentation and modular reasoning.

Categories and Subject Descriptors D.2.4 [*Software*]: Program Verification—Programming by contract; F.3.1 [*Specifying and Verifying and Reasoning about Programs*]: Assertions, Invariant, Pre- and postconditions, Specification techniques

General Terms Languages, Verification

Keywords Design by contract, crosscutting contracts, JML, AspectJ, AspectJML

1. Introduction

Design by Contract (DbC) is a useful technique for developing and checking program's correctness against its specification [7]. The key mechanism in DbC is the use of the so-called "contracts". Writing out these contracts in the form of specifications and verifying them against the actual code either at runtime or compile time has a long tradition in the research community. The idea of checking contracts at runtime was popularized by Eiffel [8] in the late 80's.

It is claimed in the literature [2, 3, 6, 10] that the contracts of a system are de-facto a crosscutting concern and fare better when modularized with AOP mechanisms such as pointcuts and advice [3]. The idea has also been patented [6]. However, Balzer, Eugster, and Meyer's study [1] contradicts this intuition by concluding that the use of aspects hinders design by contract specification and fails to achieve the main DbC principles such as contract inheritance, documentation and modular reasoning. Also, they go further and say that *"no module in a system (e.g., class or aspect) can be oblivious of the presence of contracts"* [1, Section 6.3]. Indeed, as AOP is a form of implicit invocation with implicit announcement (IIA), it also compromises modular reasoning [12] for other kinds of crosscutting concerns, like distribution and persistence [11].

SPLASH '13, October 26–31, 2013, Indianapolis, Indiana, USA.
Copyright is held by the owner/author(s).
ACM 978-1-4503-1995-9/13/10.
http://dx.doi.org/10.1145/2508075.2514877

1.1 Problem and Motivation

Balzer, Eugster, and Meyer's study [1] helped crystallize my thinking about the goals of a design by contract language, in particular about the portion of such languages that provides good documentation, modular reasoning, and non contract-obliviousness.

However, there are situations that the quantification property of AOP can be beneficial to a contracted module. For example, recall the class `Point`, of the classical figure editor [3], and let us specify some contracts expressed in JML [5]. The result is illustrated in Figure 1. Both methods `setX` and `setY` of class `Point` have a precondition (denoted by the **requires** clause) that states the input parameter must be at least zero; both also have an exceptional postcondition (represented by the **signals_only** clause) that forbids the methods by throwing exceptions (which includes runtime exception). Finally, the invariant defined in this example restricts points to the upper right quadrant.

```
class Point {
  int x, y;
  //@ invariant x >= 0 && y >=0;

  //@ requires x >= 0;
  //@ signals_only \nothing;
  void setX(int x) {this.x = x;}

  //@ requires y >= 0;
  //@ signals_only \nothing;
  void setY(int y) {this.y = y;}
  ... // other methods
}
```

Figure 1. The contract specifications of the class `Point` with JML.

In relation to modular reasoning and documentation [4], one can reason about `Point` objects using just that type's and method's specifications, contained in Figure 1. So, with those documented contracts, there is no need to look at unrelated, separated, and non-documented modules [1] as we do when using, for example, AspectJ aspects [3].

At this point, let me make two viewpoints of the specifications in Figure 1. The first one is that a design by contract language like JML can be used to modularize some contracts. Hence, the single invariant clause can be viewed as a form of modularization provided by these languages. Instead of writing the same pre- and postconditions for all methods in a class, we just write a single invariant statement that "modularizes" those pre- and postconditions.

On the other hand, these design by contract languages (e.g., JML) do not capture other forms of crosscutting contracts that can arise in the specifications. For instance, the precondition that constrains the input parameter, of the both set methods, to be at least zero, cannot be written only once and applied to these and other methods that can have the same design constraint. In the same sense, if we also assume that other methods are forbidden to throw exceptions, we need to explicitly write the same `signals_only` clause to these other methods as well. There is no way to express that which crosscuts like an invariant.

As observed, the main problem here is a trade-off. If we decide to use AspectJ to modularize such crosscutting contracts, the result would be a poor contract documentation or a compromised modular reasoning of a particular method under certain design constraints. If we decide to go back to a design by contract language, such as JML, we would face the scattered nature of common contracts that we explain above. This dilemma leads us to the following research question: Is it possible to have the best of both worlds? So, how can we achieve good documentation, modular reasoning and specify such crosscutting contracts in a modular way?

2. AspectJML

I propose AspectJML, a simple and practical aspect-oriented extension to JML. With just a few aspect-based constructs, AspectJML provides support for specifying crosscutting contracts in a modular and convenient way. The key concept behind AspectJML is what we call *crosscutting contract specifications*, or XCS.

Crosscutting Contract Specifications. Figure 2 illustrates the crosscutting contracts specifications for the `Point` class. As observed, I define a pointcut with all the crosscutting contract specifications. To be fully compatible to Java, the AspectJ constructs, I rely on, are based on the @AspectJ syntax, which are based on metadata annotations. So, in the example, I define a pointcut using the `@Pointcut` annotation. The method `setXY` represents a pointcut declaration since it is annotated with a `@Pointcut` annotation. This pointcut intercepts all the executions of set-like method declarations in the `Point` class. In Contrast to AspectJ, this is the simplest way to modularize crosscutting contracts at source code level. The major difference is that a specified pointcut is always processed when using the AspectJML compiler (ajmlc). In standard AspectJ, a single pointcut declaration, without an associated advice, does not contribute to the execution flow of a program. In AspectJML, we do not need to define an advice to check a specification in a crosscutting fashion. Hence, we have the specified crosscutting precondition and exceptional postcondition checked in a modular way.

One benefit to use AspectJ syntax is that we can see when a pointcut declaration is well-formed. In other words, we can see the arrows indicating where the specifications will be checked during runtime. In plain AspectJ/AJDT this example show no crosscutting structure information, because it has only pointcut declarations without advice. In AspectJ, we need to associate the declared pointcuts to advice in order to be able to browse the crosscutting structure of a system. Hence, I have implemented an option in AspectJML that generates the cross-references information for crosscutting contracts when we have only pointcut declarations.

Finally, with AspectJML, all the crosscutting contracts are well documented in the class it applies to. In the conventional approach, the aspects are separated from the type declarations and they do not provide a documented approach.

3. Related Work

As discussed throughout the paper, there are several works in the literature that argue in favor of implementing DbC with AOP [2, 3, 6, 10]. Kiczales opened this research avenue by showing a simple precondition constraint implementation in one of his first papers on AOP [3]. After that, other authors explored how to implement and separate the DbC concern with AOP [2, 3, 6, 9, 10]. All these works offer common templates and guidelines for DbC aspectization.

```
class Point {
    int x, y;
    //@ invariant x >= 0 && y >= 0;

    //@ requires xy >= 0;
    //@ signals_only \nothing;
    @Pointcut("execution(void Point.set*(int)) && args(xy)")
    void setXY(int xy){}

    void setX(int x) {this.x = x;}

    void setY(int y) {this.y = y;}
}
```

Figure 2. The AspectJML specifications of `Point` class.

However, as also discussed, DbC aspectization is more harmful than good [1]. I go beyond these works by showing how to combine the best design features of a design by contract language like JML and the quantification benefits of AOP such as AspectJ. As a result I conceive the AspectJML specification language that is suitable for specifying crosscutting contracts.

4. Acknowledgments

I would like to thank Professors Gary T. Leavens and Ricardo Lima (my supervisors) for the discussions about the ideas of this work.

References

[1] S. Balzer, P. T. Eugster, and B. Meyer. Can aspects implement contracts. In *In: Proceedings of RISE 2005 (Rapid Implementation of Engineering Techniques*, pages 13–15, September 2005.

[2] Y. A. Feldman, O. Barzilay, and S. Tyszberowicz. Jose: Aspects for Design by Contract80-89. *sefm*, 0:80–89, 2006.

[3] G. Kiczales, E. Hilsdale, J. Hugunin, M. Kersten, J. Palm, and W. Griswold. Getting started with aspectj. *Commun. ACM*, 44:59–65, October 2001.

[4] G. T. Leavens. JML's rich, inherited specifications for behavioral subtypes. In Z. Liu and H. Jifeng, editors, *Formal Methods and Software Engineering: 8th International Conference on Formal Engineering Methods (ICFEM)*, volume 4260 of *Lecture Notes in Computer Science*, pages 2–34, New York, NY, Nov. 2006. Springer-Verlag.

[5] G. T. Leavens, A. L. Baker, and C. Ruby. Preliminary design of JML: A behavioral interface specification language for Java. *ACM SIGSOFT Software Engineering Notes*, 2006.

[6] C. V. Lopes, M. Lippert, and E. A. Hilsdale. Design by contract with aspect-oriented programming. In *U.S. Patent No. 06,442,750*, issued August 27, 2002.

[7] B. Meyer. Applying "design by contract". *Computer*, 25(10):40–51, 1992.

[8] B. Meyer. *Eiffel: the language*. Prentice-Hall, Inc., Upper Saddle River, NJ, USA, 1992.

[9] H. Rebêlo, R. Lima, U. Kulesza, C. Sant'Anna, Y. Cai, R. Coelho, and M. Ribeiro. Quantifying the effects of aspectual decompositions on design by contract modularization: A maintenance study. *International Journal of Software Engineering and Knowledge Engineering*, 2013.

[10] H. Rebêlo, R. Lima, and G. T. Leavens. Modular contracts with procedures, annotations, pointcuts and advice. In *SBLP '11: Proceedings of the 2011 Brazilian Symposium on Programming Languages*, 2011.

[11] S. Soares, E. Laureano, and P. Borba. Implementing distribution and persistence aspects with aspectj. In *Proceedings of the 17th conference on Object-oriented programming (OOPSLA), systems, languages, and applications*, 2002.

[12] F. Steimann. The paradoxical success of aspect-oriented programming. In *Proceedings of OOPSLA 2006, ACM SIGPLAN Notices*, pages 481–497, New York, NY, Oct. 2006. ACM.

Task Fusion: Improving Utilization of Multi-user Clusters

Robert Dyer

Iowa State University
rdyer@iastate.edu

Abstract

Researchers use shared computing clusters to ask interesting questions and wish to maximize their utilization. Currently, optimizations focus on individual programs. We present *task fusion* to automatically merge multiple tasks into a single task. An example implementation shows fused tasks take 14–90% less time than running the tasks individually.

Categories and Subject Descriptors D.1.3 [*PROGRAMMING TECHNIQUES*]: Concurrent Programming

Keywords MapReduce; optimization; task fusion

1. Introduction

Big data techniques allow researchers to propose and answer many interesting hypotheses on very large sets of data. Analyzing big data is accomplished using a distributed cluster, which is typically shared by several users. Increasing the utilization of such shared resources is important in order to keep costs low and allow for more users.

Many techniques have previously been proposed to optimize programs that run on such clusters, however these optimizations typically focus on single programs. Assuming we have already used existing single-program optimization techniques to increase utilization of shared clusters, important research questions we wish to answer are: Can we further increase utilization by automatically optimizing groups of programs? If so, what pre-conditions must hold to apply such cross-program optimizations?

In this research we answer these questions and propose a new optimization technique called *task fusion*, which is inspired by a compiler optimization called loop fusion that increases data locality by fusing multiple loops together. Task fusion takes multiple, individual tasks and fuses them into a single task. This process creates a single program

SPLASH '13, October 26–31, 2013, Indianapolis, Indiana, USA.
Copyright is held by the owner/author(s).
ACM 978-1-4503-1995-9/13/10.
http://dx.doi.org/10.1145/2508075.2514878

that reads the input data only once and performs multiple computations on it, thus avoiding the overhead of reading the data multiple times.

We prove the feasibility of our optimization by implementing it in the Boa framework for software repository mining [4, 6]. Our early evaluation shows that task fusion in Boa provides performance benefits of up to ten times faster execution when compared to running tasks individually.

2. Background and Related Works

Dean and Ghemawat described a MapReduce framework [3] for distributed computations. In this framework, data is represented as key/value pairs. Each pair is given to a map (or *mapper*) function, which transforms it into zero or more output key/value pairs. This output is then fed into a second user-defined function called a *reducer*, which aggregates all values for a given key and produces a final result. The framework automatically sorts the data between the map and reduce phases. Hadoop [1] is an open-source implementation of MapReduce written in Java.

Chain folding and job merging [5] are two optimizations for MapReduce programs. *Chain folding* aims to take multiple map or reduce steps in a single program and fold them together into fewer steps. *Job merging* is when two un-related programs that operate over the same input are manually merged into a single program by merging the mappers and reducers together.

FlumeJava [2] is a library for Java that abstracts the details of MapReduce from the user, instead providing a set of high-level features such as parallel collections and functions. The library generates a query plan which may include multiple MapReduce phases. The query plan is optimized using *sibling fusion* and *MSCR fusion*, which are similar to chain folding and job merging, to reduce the total number of MapReduce tasks executed. This optimization is for a single FlumeJava program.

3. Task Fusion

The previously mentioned optimizations typically focus on individual programs. The only optimization that looks at multiple programs, job merging, assumes the programs are all by the same author and requires manually merging them together. In this section we propose a fully automated solu-

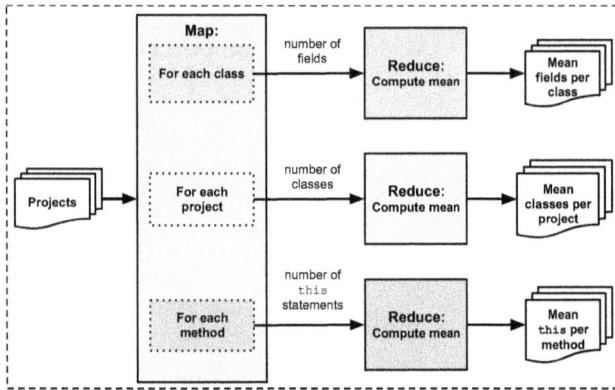

Figure 1. Three example tasks fused into a single MapReduce program, with 1 mapper and 3 reducers.

tion called *task fusion* that takes unrelated programs, possibly from different users in a shared cluster, and fuses them into a single task.

As an example, consider three MapReduce tasks to mine the mean number of fields per class, mean number of classes per project, and mean number of `this` statements per method. For these tasks, the mappers iterate over components and output values for each component. The reducers then compute the mean value across components.

With task fusion, the three separate MapReduce tasks are fused into a single MapReduce task (Figure 1). The map function is a composition of the three individual task's map functions. There are also multiple reducers, one per original task. One problem is ensuring the values output from the map task are routed to the correct reducer, thus giving the same (separate) output files as when running the tasks individually.

To solve this problem, we rewrite the map task's output calls to use a composite key and provide a custom partitioner. Partitioners take map output and routes it (based on the key) to reducers. Our partitioner uses the composite key to ensure the output from a map task goes to the correct reducer, ensuring the same final three outputs.

Currently task fusion only works if all tasks share the same input data, have no dependency conflicts, use no shared state, and do not have side effects (such as writing to files). Relaxing these assumptions to allow application to a wider range of systems is currently future work.

4. Evaluation

We evaluate the effectiveness of task fusion by implementing it in the Boa infrastructure [4, 6] for software repository mining. Boa programs compile to Hadoop MapReduce programs and we modified the compiler to use task fusion when more than one program is given as input.

We executed over 60 Boa tasks from several previous studies. These tasks have varying complexity and their execution takes anywhere from 25 seconds up to 24 minutes

each. We created workloads containing 21 fast tasks, 22 medium sized tasks, 18 slow tasks, and a mixed workload of 9 tasks containing an equal number of fast, medium, and slow tasks. The results of running these workloads are shown in Table 1.

	Sequential	Task Fusion	Speedup
Fast	486	45	10.80X
Medium	8,377	6,601	1.27X
Slow	16,642	14,211	1.17X
Mixed	4,687	3,255	1.44X

Table 1. Execution times (in seconds) for workloads.

The first column shows the time (in seconds) to run the tasks in a given workload individually. The next column shows the execution time when the tasks are fused together. The last column shows the speedup achieved by task fusion.

In the best case, task fusion is over ten times faster than running the tasks individually. Even in the worst case, task fusion runs in 14% less time than individually. These early results clearly demonstrate the potential benefit of using task fusion in shared clusters.

5. Conclusions and Future Work

Maximizing the utilization of shared clusters is important for researchers interested in answering questions with big data techniques. Task fusion is an optimization that allows multiple programs from different users to be fused and executed together, requiring 14%–90% less time than executing the tasks individually.

In the future we plan to investigate ways to relax some of the assumptions currently required for task fusion, allowing application of the technique to more infrastructures.

Acknowledgments

This work funded in part by NSF grants CCF-10-17334 and CCF-11-17937.

References

[1] Apache Software Foundation. Hadoop: Open source MapReduce. http://hadoop.apache.org/.

[2] C. Chambers, A. Raniwala, F. Perry, S. Adams, R. R. Henry, R. Bradshaw, and N. Weizenbaum. FlumeJava: easy, efficient data-parallel pipelines. In *PLDI'10*, pages 363–375, 2010.

[3] J. Dean and S. Ghemawat. MapReduce: simplified data processing on large clusters. In *OSDI'04*, 2004.

[4] R. Dyer, H. A. Nguyen, H. Rajan, and T. N. Nguyen. Boa: A language and infrastructure for analyzing ultra-large-scale software repositories. In *ICSE'13*, pages 422–431, 2013.

[5] D. Miner and A. Shook. *MapReduce Design Patterns: Building Effective Algorithms and Analytics for Hadoop and Other Systems*. O'Reilly Media, 2012.

[6] H. Rajan, T. N. Nguyen, R. Dyer, and H. A. Nguyen. Boa website. http://boa.cs.iastate.edu/, 2012.

Cloud Twin: Interactive Cross-Platform Replay for Mobile Applications

Ethan Holder

Software Innovations Lab, Virginia Tech
eholder0@vt.edu

Categories and Subject Descriptors D.2.2 [*Software Engineering*]: Design Tools and Techniques—Evolutionary prototyping Computer-aided software engineering (CASE)

Keywords Android; Automated; Cloud; Emulate; Mobile; Multi-Platform; Replay; Windows Phone

1. Research Problem and Motivation

To successfully compete in the software marketplace, modern mobile applications must run on multiple competing platforms, such as Android, iOS, and Windows Phone. Producers of mobile applications spend substantial amounts of time, effort, and money to port applications across platforms, so as to maximize the potential customer base. Creating individual program versions for different platforms further exacerbates the maintenance burden, as each bug fix and feature enhancement must be applied to all platforms.

Presented in this paper is a solution to the heterogeneity problem of the mobile application market that does not require manual porting of applications nor shifting development into cross-platform frameworks. The solution, called *Cloud Twin*, makes it possible to execute mobile applications written for one platform natively on another platform. The basic idea behind Cloud Twin is that a mobile application has two isomorphic versions: *the source*, executed on a cloud-based edge server, and *the target*, executed on a local mobile device. Initial case studies with third-party applications indicate that Cloud Twin can become a viable solution to the heterogeneity of the mobile application market.

2. Background and Related Work

Recognizing the need for heterogeneity, mobile application designers have created frameworks for cross-platform mobile development, such as PhoneGap [1]. These platforms typically leverage the mobile web browser that executes applications written in JavaScript and CSS. Despite the widespread use of cross-platform mobile frameworks, developing native applications remains the preferred practice in the mobile software market. Native applications (i.e., written for a specific platform using the platform's API) have a unique look-and-feel expected by the customers; they also take advantage of platform-specific features such as the platform's native maps (Google Maps for Android [2], Apple Maps for iOS [3], and Bing Maps for Windows Phone [4]).

Cloud Twin builds on prior work utilizing aspect-oriented programming and reflection to reverse-engineer UIs at runtime with the purpose of subsequently translating them to other platforms [7]. Cloud Twin employs the same strategy for extracting UI elements. Specifically, this mechanism is used to produce the initial UI screen of the target application. While in prior work, focus was placed on extracting UIs and statically translating them to multiple additional platforms, Cloud Twin translates and updates UIs across platforms continuously at runtime.

Cloud Twin conceptually relates to the work performed to map various platform APIs to one another. Mobile platform vendors commonly provide publicly accessible mappings that show which APIs of the target platform can be used to emulate the functionality of the source platform. For example, Microsoft provides such mappings between Android and the Windows Phone [8]. These mappings specifically relate API calls from one language to equivalent API calls in the other language in a dictionary-like fashion. Cloud Twin differs by using an intermediate form that abstracts away the logic of either language. Thus, Cloud Twin differs by lending itself to being easily extended to other platforms and languages. As long as the source language can be captured and output in the form of the Cloud Twin intermediate language, the source platform application can be supported on other target platforms.

The intermediate UI form of Cloud Twin resembles the universal UI representations of independent UI models, such as those used in UIML [9] and the aforementioned PhoneGap [1]. UIML and PhoneGap enable platform independent

SPLASH '13, October 26–31, 2013, Indianapolis, Indiana, USA.
Copyright is held by the owner/author(s).
ACM 978-1-4503-1995-9/13/10.
http://dx.doi.org/10.1145/2508075.2514879

design and development of user interfaces. UIML employs an XML base language to subsequently generate user interfaces in a desired language. However, these and other platform independent approaches require that mobile applications be constructed using a particular language and the accompanying framework. By contrast, Cloud Twin supports mobile applications that have been constructed using their native platform APIs. Thus, Cloud Twin enables the execution of such applications natively on other mobile platforms.

3. Approach and Uniqueness

Cloud Twin presents an approach to natively executing the functionality of a mobile application written for another platform. The functionality is accessed by means of interactive cross-platform replay, in which the source application's execution in the cloud is mimicked natively on the target platform. The reference implementation of Cloud Twin natively emulates the behavior of Android applications on a Windows Phone. Specifically, Cloud Twin transmits, via web sockets, the UI actions performed on the Windows Phone to the cloud server, which then mimics the received actions on the Android emulator. The UI updates on the emulator are efficiently captured by means of Aspect Oriented Programming and sent back to be replayed on the Windows Phone. In addition to its basic services, Cloud Twin also specially handles sensor input as well as time and location services. In other words, it ensures the target's environment is used by both versions of the application.

4. Results and Contributions

The central insight derived from experimenting with the prototype implementation is that the mimicking functionality of Cloud Twin is quite efficient, with the resulting latencies not adversely affecting the user experience. With the edge server running within the same administrative domain and connected to by a Wi-Fi network, the latencies of executing common UI actions in a typical application never surpassed the one second threshold [5] [6], thus making the Cloud Twin approach feasible and useful. In particular, Cloud Twin is able to natively execute several small but real Android applications natively on the Windows Phone, with the users not suspecting that they were natively interacting with applications written for a different platform. These initial experiences indicate that Cloud Twin has the potential to become a practical solution to the problem of making a mobile application available on a variety of platforms.

The best measurement to present such results thus far is the latency of a complete UI update. This was determined by measuring the total time it took between pressing a button on the target application and updating a text label in response. This measurement encompasses the following sequence of events: (1) the button pressed, (2) the resulting event is captured and transmitted to the source application, (3) the press is replayed on the source, (4) the text label update is in-

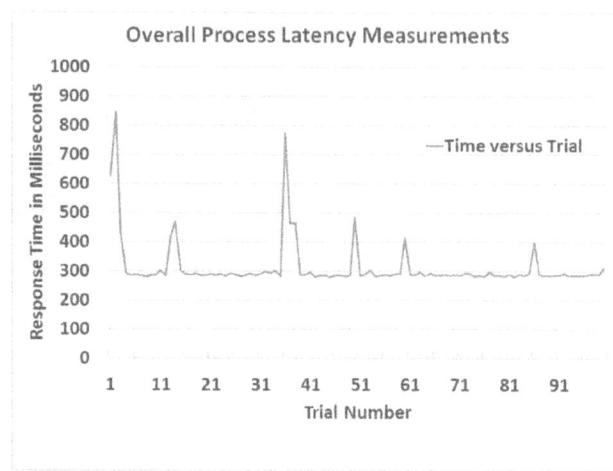

Figure 1. Measurements of the latency of the overall UI update process.

tercepted, (5) the update is sent back to the target, (6) the target's label is updated with the received data. Typical for modern user interfaces, the measured UI scenario demonstrates a realistic response time a user would encounter when interacting with Cloud Twin.

Figure 1 shows the results from repeating the measured operation 100 times. The overall average latency was 314 milliseconds, with a maximum of 846 milliseconds and minimum of 281 milliseconds. The important insight is that the response time never exceeded the one second threshold, thus not compromising the user experience [5] [6]. Future work will assess whether Cloud Twin can achieve comparable efficiency when processing more complex UI scenarios.

References

[1] R. Ghatol and Y. Patel. Beginning PhoneGap: Mobile Web Framework for JavaScript and HTML5. Apress, 2012.

[2] Google. Google Maps Android API. https://developers.google.com/maps/documentation/android/.

[3] Apple. Map Kit Framework Reference. http://developer.apple.com/library/ios/documentation/MapKit/Reference/MapKit_Framework_Reference/.

[4] Microsoft. Bing Maps APIs. http://msdn.microsoft.com/en-us/library/dd877180.aspx.

[5] R. B. Miller. Response Time in Man-Computer Conversational Transactions. In *AFIPS*, 1968.

[6] J. Nielson. Usability Engineering. Morgan Kaufmann, 1968.

[7] E. Shah and E. Tilevich. Reverse-engineering user interfaces to facilitate porting to and across mobile devices and platforms. In *Workshop on Next-generation Applications of Smartphones*, 2011.

[8] Microsoft Technologies. Windows Phone Interoperability. http://windowsphone.interoperabilitybridges.com.

[9] M. F. Ali and M. Abrams. Simplifying construction of multi-platform user interfaces using UIML. In *UIML Europe 2001 Conference*, 2001.

Do Language Constructs for Concurrent Execution Have Impact on Energy Efficiency?

Gustavo Pinto

Informatics Center, Federal University of Pernambuco
Recife, PE, Brazil
ghlp@cin.ufpe.br

Abstract

This study analyzed the performance and energy consumption of multicore applications, using three techniques to manage concurrent execution in a set of benchmarks. We conclude that these constructs can heavily impact on energy consumption. Nonetheless, the trade-off between performance and energy consumption in multicore applications is not so obvious.

Categories and Subject Descriptors D.1.3 [*Programming Techniques*]: Concurrent Programming, Parallel Programming

Keywords Refactoring, Concurrent/Parallel Programming, Energy Consumption

1. The research problem and motivation

Measuring the energy consumption of an application and understanding where the energy usage lies provides new opportunities for energy savings. In order to understand the complexities of this approach, we specifically look at multi-threaded applications. The performance of the existing constructs for concurrent execution is reasonably well-understood [4, 7]. Furthermore, since parallel programming enables programmers to run their applications faster, it makes sense to assume that an application that finish earlier will also consume less energy [3]. This idea is known as the "Race to idle" principle [1]. In summary: faster programs will theoretically consume less energy because they will have the machine idle fast, and modern processors consume very little energy when idle. Nevertheless, parallelism and the overheads inherent to concurrent and parallel programming constructs might impact energy consumption in ways that are hard to predict.

This paper presents an empirical study consisting of the evaluation of the performance and energy consumption of four applications that use three programming concurrent constructs plus a sequential implementation with the goal of demonstrating that it is hard to establish a trade-offs between energy-efficiency and performance. This study is relevant because it is known that concurrent construct is often used in high-level applications [5]. Moreover, the performance of the existing constructs for concurrent execution is reasonably well-understood [7], but little is know about its energy efficiency.

2. Related work

To the best of our knowledge, only two studies have dealt with the topic of understanding the impact of concurrent constructs on the energy efficiency of applications [2, 6]. Gautham et al. [2] analyzed synchronization primitives and explore the following synchronization techniques to find an ideal solution for synchronization-intensive workloads: i) spin lock ii) mutexes iii) software transactional memory. They show that Software Transactional Memory (STM) systems can perform better than locks for workloads where a significant portion of the execution time is spent in the critical sections. Trefethen [6] studies the behavior of the NAS Benchmark suite for its energy and runtime performance. The benchmark suite considered includes I/O and compute-intensive applications. The authors concluded that there is a clear interaction between execution time and energy but this is not a simple relationship and can be affected by the computer environment and algorithmic approach used in the application. Nonetheless, none of these papers compare the energy-efficiency between techniques to manage concurrent execution.

3. Approach and uniqueness

To achieve this study's goal, we ran a set of benchmark applications from different domains in a number of different configurations while varying a group of attributes. We can divide these attributes in two groups: internal (programming language construct, number of threads in use and resource usage - CPU and/or IO) and external (the clock frequency and the JVM implementation). We then provided a set of variant implementations for each benchmark using three concurrent programming constructs, plus a sequential implementation[1].

In this experiment, we used commodity hardware: an Intel(R) Xeon(R), 2.13 GHz, 4 cores/8 threads and with 16Gb of memory, running Linux 64-bit, kernel 3.0.0.-31-server. These experiments were run using three JVMs: i) OpenJDK version 1.7.0_09, ii) HotSpot JDK version 1.7, and iii) JRockit version 1.6. When the experiments were performed using JRockit, we provided an external jar file containing the ForkJoin implementation.

Our experiments consisted of running these four applications in each of the three JVM implementations, scaling the CPU frequency, and limiting the number of threads in use. We ran each experiment twelve times for each workload, while measuring the system using the *powertop* utility[2]. We discarded the executions

SPLASH '13, October 26–31, 2013, Indianapolis, Indiana, USA.
Copyright is held by the owner/author(s).
ACM 978-1-4503-1995-9/13/10.
http://dx.doi.org/10.1145/2508075.2514880

---

[1] The implementation details are available at http://bit.ly/parallel-construct

[2] https://01.org/powertop/

	Energy Consumption (J)							
	N-Queens		LargestImage		Mandelbrot		Knucleotide	
	Median	SD	Median	SD	Median	SD	Median	SD
S	**732**	1.3	679	1.2	1978	1.2	5395	3.3
T	1023	2.2	766	3.8	1290	3.9	4808	4.7
E	984	2.1	**633**	3.7	**1287**	3.4	3281	3.6
FJ	753	1.8	749	4.5	1292	3.6	**2993**	3.9

	Time (s)							
	N-Queens		LargestImage		Mandelbrot		Knucleotide	
	Median	SD	Median	SD	Median	SD	Median	SD
S	85	0.7	78	1.2	71	1.2	106	0.6
T	44	1.2	42	1.9	41	2.1	68	1.3
E	38	1.1	**31**	1.8	41	1.9	62	1.1
FJ	**27**	1.1	54	3.8	**35**	1.3	**55**	1.4

Table 1. The comparison between the language constructs in terms of energy consumption and time. The obtained values for energy consumption and time are the medians of 10 executions.

with the lowest and the highest to reduce bias caused by outliers. We have two main metrics that evaluate the experiments: the energy consumed (in Joules) and the execution time (in seconds).

4. Results

Table 1 shows the overall view of our experimental results. The column named "Energy Consumption (J)" organizes the results of the 10 executions. The value contained in each cell represents the median of the 10 executions, where each sample represents the total of energy consumed in this given execution. We use **boldface** to highlight the best result for the given benchmark application. The column "Time (s)" works similarly.

As Table 1 shows, we can notice that the results of the concurrent constructs can have significant differences. For instance, the `Thread` results are almost always more inefficient in terms of both consumption and performance, when compared to `Executors`. Thus, since the usage of `Thread` and the `Executors` is very similar, with a little effort, a programmer could use `Executors`. Table 1 also shows that the same technique can have different impact on the energy consumed. The `ForkJoin` variant exhibited the best performance for all the benchmarks with the exception of LargestImage, which is strongly IO-bound. It also exhibits the lowest consumption for Knucleotide and reasonably low consumption for N-Queens and Mandelbrot. On the other hand, considering the LargestImage application, we notice that the `ForkJoin` variant consumed more energy than every other variant except for the one using threads. Nonetheless, LargestImage is a benchmark application that makes heavy use of IO operations, and it is well know that `ForkJoin` is not adequate for this kind of computation. This fact is the probable reason for the poor energy consumption.

Moreover, it is interesting to note that the `Sequential` variant of the N-Queens benchmark application presented the best energy consumption result, in spite of presenting the worst performance. This benchmark's result can vary according to the input data (in case, the NxN size of the matrix). In this experiments, we realized that, for a small matrix, the overhead caused by the thread creation led to an increase in energy consumption. But, for example, if we doubled the matrix size, the `ForkJoin` variant becomes the most energy efficient as well.

Furthermore, we analyzed how the benchmark applications scale with respect to the number of threads. Both the Mandelbrot and Knucleotide benchmark applications scale well. This means that the more cores available, the faster the applications run, and more energy is saved. Nonetheless, for the other ones, it is not true. For instance, in the LargestImage benchmark, the more cores we have, more inefficient the `ForkJoin` variant is, in terms of both performance and energy. In summary, we collected a total of 128

samples (4 benchmarks x 4 variants x 4 nr. of threads x 2 clock frequencies), and for 36 of those, the variation which achieve the best performance were not the same that consume less energy.

We then repeated the experiments varying the CPU frequency from 1.2 GHz to 2.13 GHz. We notice that even after reducing the clock frequencies, the results seems to be very similar to the ones with the higher frequency, in terms of the better technique remaining the better. However, for the LargestImage benchmark, we found out that the lowest frequency consumes the same amount of energy as a middle clock frequency. It is interesting and acceptable, since it is an application that does not use a huge amount of CPU. This is something that requires further investigation.

Finally, we have also analyzed whether different JVMs had different impacts on performance and energy consumption. We observed that, in general, results are very similar, specially for OpenJDK and HotSpot. It does not surprise us, since the HotSpot is the primary reference implementation of JVM, and OpenJDK is heavily inspired by them. On the other side, the JRockit JVM presents the worst case scenario, for all variants. For example, taking into consideration the `Thread` variant, the results increased in more than 10%. For the other benchmark applications, JRockit also exhibited the worst results among the JVMs. Although the different JVMs did affect execution time and energy consumption, similarly to different clock frequencies, they did not significantly change the behavior of the variants, e.g. the fastest and slowest variants in one JVM were the fastest and lowest variants for all of them.

4.1 Contributions

This paper presented the following contributions:

- Different techniques for concurrent/parallel programming within the same language (Java, in this case) can impact both performance and energy consumption in very different ways for applications with different characteristics.

- For concurrent software, the Race to Idle principle is often not true. In fact, we found at least a few examples that go in the opposite direction.

- Some factors, such as clock frequency and different VMs, do not significantly affect the relationship between performance and energy consumption.

References

[1] S. Albers and A. Antoniadis. Race to idle: new algorithms for speed scaling with a sleep state. In *Proceedings of the Twenty-Third Annual ACM-SIAM Symposium on Discrete Algorithms*, SODA '12, pages 1266–1285. SIAM, 2012.

[2] A. Gautham et al. The implications of shared data synchronization techniques on multi-core energy efficiency. HotPower'12, Berkeley, CA, USA, 2012.

[3] J. Jelschen et al. Towards applying reengineering services to energy-efficient applications. In *CSMR*, pages 353–358, 2012.

[4] L. A. Smith, J. M. Bull, and J. Obdržálek. A parallel java grande benchmark suite. In *Proceedings of the 2001 ACM/IEEE conference on Supercomputing (CDROM)*, Supercomputing '01, pages 8–8, New York, NY, USA, 2001. ACM. ISBN 1-58113-293-X.

[5] W. Torres et al. Are java programmers transitioning to multicore?: a large scale study of java floss. SPLASH '11 Workshops, pages 123–128, New York, NY, USA, 2011. ACM. ISBN 978-1-4503-1183-0.

[6] A. Trefethen and J. Thiyagalingam. Energy-aware software: Challenges, opportunities and strategies. *Journal of Computational Science*, 1(0):–, 2013. ISSN 1877-7503. .

[7] W. Zhu, J. del Cuvillo, and G. R. Gao. Performance characteristics of openmp language constructs on a many-core-on-a-chip architecture. In *IWOMP*, pages 230–241, 2006.

CSI: Crash Scene Investigation

Peter Ohmann

University of Wisconsin–Madison
ohmann@cs.wisc.edu

Abstract

Prior work proposes inexpensive, tunable tracing of acyclic
paths and callsite coverage to enhance post-failure memory
dumps. To better understand this data, current work investigates the benefit of each piece of traced data independently,
their interplay, future low-cost data to collect, and further
analysis uses of the post-mortem data.

Categories and Subject Descriptors   D.2.5 [*Software Engineering*]: Testing and Debugging—Debugging aids, Tracing

Keywords   failure analysis; core dumps; program slicing

1. Background and Prior Work

Post-deployment failures are inevitable in complex software.
Comprehensive failure reports are invaluable but difficult to
obtain. Full execution traces and detailed failure analyses are
ideal, but, sadly, also usually impractical. The high-level goal
of this work is to support debugging using latent information
in postmortem core dumps, augmented by lightweight, tunable instrumentation. Prior work [4] uses two pieces of data:
path traces and call coverage.

Path profiling is traditionally used to compute path coverage during program testing. The approach we adopt from Ball
and Larus [2] efficiently profiles all acyclic, intraprocedural
paths. However, rather than a profile (which counts the occurrences of each path), we are interested in a trace (which
keeps a suffix of the execution–here, the last few paths).

Call-site coverage addresses two blind spots in path traces:
paths prior to the execution suffix, and interprocedural paths
through calls that have already returned. We keep one global
bit for each call site indicating whether that call ever executed
during a run. We also track local call-site coverage for each
active frame in the program stack. Both path traces and local
call coverage use stack-allocated storage.

SPLASH '13,   October 26–31, 2013, Indianapolis, Indiana, USA.
ACM 978-1-4503-1995-9/13/10.
http://dx.doi.org/10.1145/2508075.2514881

Prior work investigates the runtime cost of tracing and
the value of the data obtained with respect to two analyses.
The first analysis determines the set of Control Flow Graph
(CFG) nodes and edges which could not have executed given
the crashing program stack and tracing data collected, which
we refer to as Active Nodes and Edges. The path traces plus
CFG-backward-reachable nodes and edges (given the call
coverage data) were potentially active in the crashing run.

Given a program point, program slicing determines all
other points that may have affected variables of interest at
that point. Ottenstein and Ottenstein [5] first proposed the
program dependence graph (PDG), a useful program representation for slicing. The nodes of a PDG are the same as
those in the CFG, and edges represent possible transfer of
control (conditionals or jumps) or data (variable assignment).
Program slices can be *static* (valid for all program inputs) or
dynamic (restricted to a particular execution). Obviously, the
latter is preferable for debugging, but dynamic slicing can incur enormous cost, including tracing all executed statements
and memory accesses. Our second analysis computes a reduction of the PDG using our feedback data based on an early
dynamic program slicing algorithm proposed by Agrawal
and Horgan [1] and an interprocedural PDG slicing approach
proposed by Horwitz et al. [3]. This *dynamically-reduced*
graph can then be used for future *static* slicing queries.

Our results show great promise for this technique. Tracing
in instrumented code is easily customizable post-deployment.
A realistic scheme, enabling tracing for all call sites and path
tracing for any function appearing in any crash stack in our
test suite, incurs average overheads below 1.4% (with a maximum of 5.1%). Our analysis results on larger applications
show intraprocedural active node and edge reductions from
24–54%, and interprocedural reductions from 45–71%, relative to context-sensitive, stack-constrained, backward CFG-
reachability. Computing static slices from the crash point, our
PDG reduction reduces intraprocedural slice sizes 21–52%,
and interprocedural slices 49–78%, relative to stack-sensitive
static slicing. This is further detailed in our ongoing work.

2. Ongoing Work

To provide a compass for future work, we are investigating the
performance of each piece of tracing data separately. Slicing
results thus far are shown in fig. 1. We omit Active Nodes and

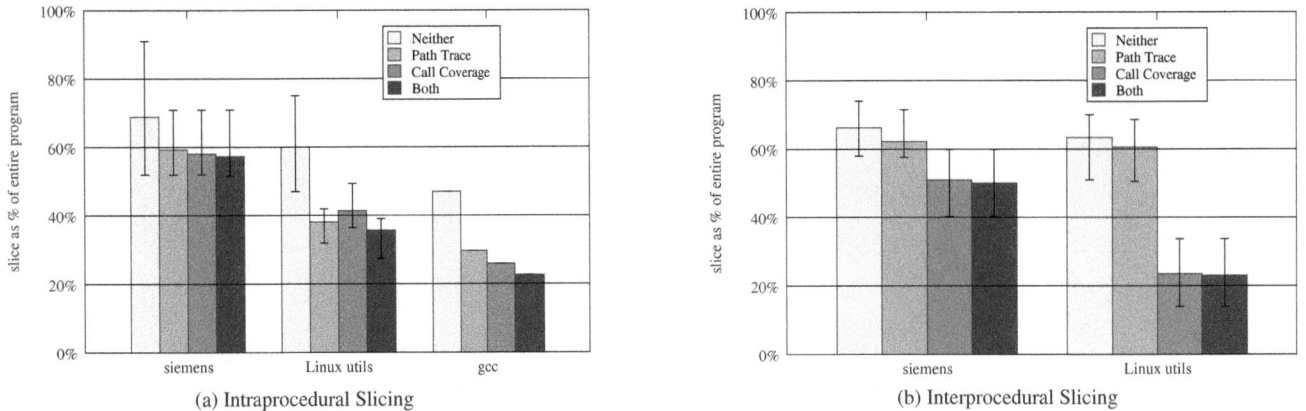

Figure 1. Slice Reduction due to feedback analysis

Edges results, which display similar patterns. All crashing runs analyzed are summarized by bug, application version, and finally by application. Our application suite is further summarized into categories: smaller applications from the Siemens benchmark suite; a diverse set of Linux utilities; and a larger C compiler, gcc. The graphs display slice size as a percentage of the entire program. Interprocedural results for gcc are currently unavailable due to our memory-bound analysis. Bars denote the average numbers for the category specified, and error bars indicate the minimum and maximum for any application in that summary group.

These results suggest that path tracing tends to be slightly more beneficial for intraprocedural analysis, and call coverage tends to be favored for interprocedural analysis. Neither, however, is completely sufficient on its own in either category, lending support to the use of multiple lightweight tracing methods. The results for gcc are somewhat misleading. While call coverage appears more beneficial, closer examination reveals otherwise. All functions excluding *main* see more benefit from path tracing, sometimes very significantly. However, call coverage enjoys a disproportionate advantage in *main*, which appears in every trace. Overhead results (not shown) indicate that path tracing alone averages 0.8% overhead (with a maximum of 3.5%), while call coverage averages 0.3% (with a maximum of 1.7%).

This suggests a number of possible future directions. We continue to investigate further useful tracing data such as interprocedural paths, call-return traces, and dataflow; and further tracing methods such as hardware debug counters. Currently, we are exploring methods to compactly record calling contexts and call traces.

Reducing the cost of tracing is always a priority. To this end, we are investigating statically categorizing functions to predict which piece of tracing data would be most useful. This involves considerations such as the call-site density of the function and its looping structure. At a finer granularity, we believe it may be beneficial to trace some subset of

a function's acyclic paths or call sites, thereby increasing ambiguity but reducing instrumentation overhead.

We are also interested in exploring feedback-directed tracing strategies. Data from previous failures could be used to focus tracing schemes, making future failures more useful. This prospect has the potential to eliminate any developer burden in improving failure traces. Our feedback data could be useful for reproducing failures via symbolic execution. Previous work (e.g. [6]) has shown great strides in this area, and our trace data holds promise to improve both the runtime and accuracy of symbolic execution engines.

References

[1] H. Agrawal and J. R. Horgan. Dynamic program slicing. In *Proceedings of the ACM SIGPLAN 1990 conference on Programming language design and implementation*, PLDI '90, pages 246–256, New York, NY, USA, 1990. ACM.

[2] T. Ball and J. R. Larus. Efficient path profiling. In *Proceedings of the 29th annual ACM/IEEE international symposium on Microarchitecture*, MICRO 29, pages 46–57, Washington, DC, USA, 1996. IEEE Computer Society.

[3] S. Horwitz, T. Reps, and D. Binkley. Interprocedural slicing using dependence graphs. *ACM Trans. Program. Lang. Syst.*, 12 (1):26–60, Jan. 1990.

[4] P. Ohmann and B. Liblit. Lightweight control-flow instrumentation and postmortem analysis in support of debugging. In *28th International Conference on Automated Software Engineering (ASE 2013)*, Palo Alto, California, Nov. 2013. IEEE and ACM.

[5] K. J. Ottenstein and L. M. Ottenstein. The program dependence graph in a software development environment. In *Proceedings of the first ACM SIGSOFT/SIGPLAN software engineering symposium on Practical software development environments*, SDE 1, pages 177–184, New York, NY, USA, 1984. ACM.

[6] J. Rößler, A. Zeller, G. Fraser, C. Zamfir, and G. Candea. Reconstructing core dumps. In *ICST '13: Proceedings of the Sixth IEEE International Conference on Software Testing, Verification and Validation*, Mar. 2013.

Orchestrating Mobile Application Execution for Performance and Energy Efficiency

Young-Woo Kwon

Software Innovations Lab, Virginia Tech
ywkwon@cs.vt.edu

Abstract

This research reduces the energy consumption of mobile applications via cloud offloading, a technique for executing energy-intensive functionality in the cloud. The contributions of this research lie in addressing the inefficiencies of static offloading by exploiting dynamic offloading mechanisms (program transformation and middleware) configured through intuitive and expressive programming constructs.

Categories and Subject Descriptors   C.2.4 [*Distributed Systems*]: Distributed applications

General Terms   Language, Design, Experimentation

Keywords   Energy-efficiency; mobile computing; cloud offloading; middleware adaptation; domain-specific languages

1. Research Problem and Motivation

An important design consideration in the engineering of mobile applications is *energy efficiency*—fitting an energy budget and maximizing application utility under given battery constraints [5, 6]. *Cloud offloading* reduces the amount of energy consumed by mobile devices by executing the application's energy intensive functionality in the cloud. Due to the volatility in mobile execution environments and heterogeneity of mobile hardware, offloading the energy intensive functionality is non-trivial [1]. However, the current state of the art in cloud offloading is dominated by predetermined offloading strategies that statically assign each piece of application functionality to run either on the mobile device or in the cloud. By contrast, the goal of this research is to address the inefficiencies of static offloading by exploiting dynamic offloading mechanisms configured through intuitive and expressive programming constructs.

Our recent study of the impact of distributed programming mechanisms on energy efficiency [4] has shown that the network conditions in place affect the amount of energy spent on remote data transfer, and that tailoring the communication patterns for given network conditions and hardware reduces the energy consumed by network communication. By leveraging these insights,

cloud offloading can maximize the resulting energy savings. Because mobile applications commonly run on a variety of mobile devices over networks with divergent characteristics, the offloading decisions should be postponed until the runtime, as expressed by intuitive programming abstractions mapping the triggering of offloading operations to runtime conditions.

2. Background and Related Work

The technical concepts behind this research are concerned with cloud offloading [2, 3] and middleware mechanisms. In the last couple of years, we have conducted research on cloud offloading [2, 3], which provides a technical foundation of this work. In contrast to prior approaches to cloud offloading, which splits mobile applications into distinct client and server parts, our offloading approach does not destroy the ability of applications to run in their original form to handle possible network disconnections.

Middleware offers convenient building blocks for constructing distributed systems by eliminating the need for low-level network programming (i.e., at the level of protocol packets). Due to the highly volatile nature of mobile execution environments, however, static middleware mechanisms cannot properly support divergent execution demands. Therefore, the approach discussed here draws on our prior work for the required state-of-the-art program analysis and transformations, but innovates in the middleware space by providing a sophisticated runtime support capable of dynamically selecting the most advantages offloading plan, given a set of offload server connected by heterogeneous mobile networks.

3. Approach and Uniqueness

We introduce *adaptive, multi-target cloud offloading*, a two-fold approach: (1) *multi-target cloud offloading* transparently transforms a mobile application, so that its local/remote distribution can be determined at runtime based on the current execution environment; (2) *energy-aware adaptive middleware* determines an optimal offloading component and an offloading location from multiple alternate servers configured through a declarative domain-specific language. By combining the advantages of the prior state of the art both in program transformation and in dynamic offloading adaption, adaptive, multi-target cloud offloading has the potential to maximize energy savings.

3.1 Multi-Target Cloud Offloading

To use our approach, programmers only need to mark the components suspected of being energy hotspots by using a special Java annotation. Based on this input, a pre-analysis step collects all the components marked with the Java annotation and their subcomponents, and then the main analysis identifies the state to be transferred for each offloading scenario. One technical advantage of the main analysis is that it reduces the amount of transferred state,

SPLASH '13,   October 26–31, 2013, Indianapolis, Indiana, USA.
Copyright is held by the owner/author(s).
ACM 978-1-4503-1995-9/13/10.
http://dx.doi.org/10.1145/2508075.2514882

as transferring large data volumes across the network can quickly negate the energy savings afforded by offloading. To reduce the transferred state, our approach leverages forward dataflow and side-effect analyses, thus rendering state transfer practical for energy optimizations. The algorithm examines assignment and invocation statements to determine whether the current state has changed during the cloud offloading.

The bytecode enhancer transforms the identified offloading candidates to be able to run them on the device or the cloud to realize any given offloading scenario. The bytecode enhancer inserts the code that checkpoints and restores the necessary program state at the entry and exit of the potentially offloaded methods, respectively.

The cloud offloading engine synchronizes the checkpointed state using copy-restore, an advanced semantics introduced into RMI middleware to be able to pass linked data structures as parameters. Copy-restore copies all reachable state to the server and then overwrites the client's state with the server modified data in-place.

3.2 Energy-Aware Adaptive Middleware

As the energy efficiency of cloud offloading operations is affected by the mobile device's execution environment, we have created a new middleware architecture with dynamic adaptation capabilities to minimize the amount of energy consumed by mobile applications on offloading operations. The middleware features a declarative, domain-specific language that enables the programmer to express a set of offloading plans. An offloading plan consists of a marked energy hotspot (i.e., hotspot), available offloading locations (i.e., locations), and an offloading candidate selection criteria (i.e., criteria). The runtime adaptation module makes use of the selection criteria values to select an optimal offloading location. The criteria directive defines which notion of *effectiveness* should be used with a given plan.

At runtime, the middleware runtime system continuously monitors the current execution environment and predicts how much energy will be consumed in a given offloading operation by analyzing the collected runtime execution values and cached prior executions. To predict the amount of energy that is likely to be consumed during remote communications, the runtime system correlates the device- and execution-specific values that were previously measured and cached. Then, having obtained the current values of network delay, connectivity type, CPU frequency, and voltage, the runtime system computes the future energy consumption.

Based on the predicted future energy consumption, the runtime system selects the optimal offloading component and offloading location that would yield either the lowest expected energy consumption, or the shortest expected execution time, or the highest expected energy/performance, as specified by a given offloading plan. (i.e., the criteria options of energy, performance epr). While the first two parameters are self-explanatory, epr (the energy/performance ratio) is a parameter that we have formulated in our prior research [4]. This ratio correlates performance and energy consumption values so as to maximize the resulting correlation. Then, the runtime offloads the selected offloading components and synchronizes remote and local states in place.

4. Preliminary Results and Contributions

To evaluate our approach, we have separately applied our two major technical solutions to third-party mobile applications. First, we have shown how the multi-target cloud offloading can effectively reduce the overall amount of energy consumed by the applications [3]. In particular, the multi-target cloud offloading optimizes the application to consume between 25% and 50% less energy than a state-of-the-art static cloud offloading approach [2] [3]. Then, we evaluated how the energy-aware adaptive middleware can reduce the energy budget of a typical remote interaction by selecting optimal remote servers among multiple alternate remote servers. This experiment indicates that the new middleware mechanism can effectively reduce the energy consumption by as much as 30%.

Based on these experimental results, this research makes the following contributions:

- **Automated cloud offloading program transformation** rewrites a mobile application and efficiently synchronizes execution state between the mobile device and remote server.

- **Energy-aware middleware with dynamic adaptation capabilities** makes possible to postpone until the runtime the decisions about which parts of the application should be executed at which location.

- **A declarative domain-specific language for expressing offloading plans** enables programmers to concisely specify multiple offloading conditions and parameters.

5. Conclusion

In this paper, we introduced a novel approach, *adaptive, multi-target cloud offloading* to reduce the energy consumption of mobile applications and have shown the effectiveness of technical solutions through our prior research. By combining the advantages of the prior state of the art both in program transformation and in dynamic offloading adaption, the proposed approach will effectively reduce the amount of energy consumed by mobile applications.

Acknowledgments

This research is supported by the National Science Foundation through the Grant CCF-1116565.

References

[1] N. Fernando, S. W. Loke, and W. Rahayu. Mobile cloud computing: A survey. *Future Generation Computer Systems*, 29(1):84–106, 2013.

[2] Y.-W. Kwon and E. Tilevich. Energy-efficient and fault-tolerant distributed mobile execution. In 32nd *International Conference on Distributed Computing Systems*, 2012.

[3] Y.-W. Kwon and E. Tilevich. Reducing the energy consumption of mobile applications behind the scenes. In 29th *IEEE International Conference on Software Maintenance*, 2013.

[4] Y.-W. Kwon and E. Tilevich. The impact of distributed programming abstractions on application energy consumption. *Information and Software Technology*, 55(9):1602–1613, 2013.

[5] A. Pathak, Y. Hu, and M. Zhang. Where is the energy spent inside my app?: fine grained energy accounting on smartphones with eprof. In 7th *ACM European Conference on Computer Systems*, 2012.

[6] K. Pentikousis. In search of energy-efficient mobile networking. *Communications Magazine, IEEE*, 48(1):95–103, 2010.

Investigation of Error Notifications Through Categorization

Michael Bazik

North Carolina State University

mdbazik@ncsu.edu

Abstract

Program analysis tools often output error notifications that novice and industry programmers both have trouble understanding. The lack of expressive, scalable error notifications makes programming difficult to novice developers and hinders the progress of industry developers. Here, I propose a taxonomy of error notifications containing categories each with a model syntax for error notifications of similar type. By categorizing error notifications into 39 categories, and developing a questionnaire to aid in the categorization process, error notification creators can edit and refine existing error notifications as well as use the categories to create expressive, scalable error notifications that offer developers a better opportunity to resolve errors.

Categories and Subject Descriptors   D.2.0 [*SOFTWARE ENGINEERING*]: Tools

Keywords   taxonomy, questionnaire, notifications, analysis tools

1. Research Problem and Motivation

Developers encounter bugs and errors on a daily basis. They rely on the output of code analysis tools to provide information useful to resolving bugs and errors, yet these analysis tools often output messages that are unhelpful to resolving the problem. Here, I consider two static analysis tools: FindBugs [2] and the Eclipse JDT compiler [1]. Using error messages from these two tools, I populate my taxonomy of notifications and propose a questionnaire that strives to aid error message creators in creating the most unique, meaningful error messages possible. The qustionnaire's design highlights its purpose: to aid in the creation of error messages by consisting of specific, unique questions that clearly demostrate to error notification creators which categories in our taxonomy a specific error belongs.

Categorization and improvements to the questionnaire was made using a combination of two techniques: (1) I used the questionnaire to identify potential categories and (2) created code snippets that generated the errors so that they could be seen in context.

Through categorization, I suggest that error notifications fall in distinct subsets of categories within the taxanomy which implies that unique, more discriptive error messages can be generated. Utilizing the questionnaire, toolsmiths and compiler creators possess the ability to create and refine error messages consistant with the categories described by my taxonomy.

2. Background and Related Work

Error notifications and compiler messages have long been known to be hard to understand [6]. Traver supports this claim describing compiler messages as "more often than not, difficult to interpret, resolve, and prevent in the future." His research resulted in several suggestions for resolving error notifications in both compiler messages and in error notifications. Similarly, Scheiderman's research resulted in guidelines that desribed how systems notifications should and should not be [5].

Brown's work, "Error Messages: The Neglected Area of the Man/Machine Interface," stands as a fundamental peice of of related work because of his explaination on the decision to chose compiler messages as the primary tools to study [3]. Brown describes compilers' availability and text output as the ideal error notifications to study.

Johnson et al. described ideal error notifications using two critera: expressiveness and scalability [4]. These criteria are utilized in this paper as a means of judging the usefulness of a generated error notification.

3. Approach and Uniqueness

3.1 The Questionnaire

I devised the questionnaire as a means of lowering the overhead associated with becoming familiar with the large taxonomy. It seemed natural to consider a questionnaire because the categorization process involved asking myself a series of questions to narrow down potential categories for each notification. The questionnaire models the taxonomy in that it has major sections i.e. "reference notifications, runtime notifications, etc." and then a series of questions for each specific category housed in the major section. Each category's question or questions reflect the need for specificity and detail; since some of the categories share properties, the questionnaire requires immense effort to reduce/eliminate consistencies.

The first few iterations of the questionnaire became refined through constant use in the categorization process. Refinements included adding new questions to each category and editing existing questions for clarity.

3.2 Code Snippets

My initial source of information for interpreting a JDT or FindBugs error was the internet; this often yielded undesirable results and was untimly because of varying avaliablilty of valid error producing code. Here, valid means that the code does not exist as part of some larger system and that the code throws only one particular error in a demonstrative fashion.

To mitigate time loss, I eventually decided to code my own snippets that replicated the errors in a simple, easy to understand manner. I indexed each of the snippets and included the canonical number of the error, the reason the error was thrown in plain English, and the code itself, appropriately commented where the error notification occurs. The code snippets allowed me the opportunity to see the error notification in the context of code that generates it. This gave me several chances to reflect on the original notifications and their shortcomings, as well as, amend some of the current model notifications.

3.3 Sanitized Model Notifications

Another effort made to validate the novelty of my approach involved creating a small set of "sanitized model notifications" which represent potential error notifications that could be generated from the taxonomy. Error notifications became output in the form:

<line, program element, type, intersection information>

The first step involved identifying the most necessary parts of a general error notification that could be extrapolated to all errors. This includes the line number, the program element and its type in the language's type system. Following the general information, the intersection information section highlights the taxonomies worth; leveraging the specific subset of categories the notification lies, there exists an intersection of information which expresses the cause of the error in a scalable fashion. An example of an error containing intersection information could potentially be:

<reference 1, type 1, reference 2, type 2, "reference of the type (type) cannot reference (mismatched type). Consider referencing (likely referee)"

Here, a reference mismatch occured. The compiler, leveraging sanitized notifications, outputs the two references, their types, and recommends a likely referee that the user may have been attempting to reference. This new error notification is short, yet provides a lot of information and even a recommendation while phrasing everything in English to make it readable and give the programmer confidence.

4. Results and Contributions

The results of the study are still preliminary but encouraging; the large amount of error notifications being categorized coupled with the variety of tools being examined reinforces this confidence. Error notifications fall into categories suggesting that the categories, although not perfect, tend to provide more context to errors within code. The large amount of errors already categorized and the larger set to still be categorized ensures that there is still plenty of data to be gathered while providing preliminary results. The questionnaire also stands as a contribution as it is a tool meant to enable other researchers and error notification creators to apply my taxonomy and results.

The large code base of error producing code that I am developing in Java also stands to aid other researchers and toolsmiths. To my knowledge, there is not a complete set of code that produces Java JDT errors like mine, being developed. This library of code could be used in a variety of ways by researchers requiring a large code base of simple, clean error producing code.

4.1 Limitations

Inconsistancy in the categorization continues to be a huge potential problem in the categorization of error notifications. Human error, sloppiness and misinterpretation of the categories can cause notifications to be misplaced which could lead to an error notification potentially becoming less expressive and scalable. Sloppiness plays a huge role in limiting the taxonomy; categorizing an entire set of error notifications is a daunting task that requires careful, constant consideration.

Another concern is that only Java notifications are used, particularly notifications output by the Eclispe IDE. Although I believe the taxononmy will scale well to other programming languages and tools, this has not been tested.

4.2 Future Work

To verify the effectiveness of both the questionnaire and the taxonomy itself, I plan on conducting interviews with two sets of participants, the first being a general set of programmers, mostly students from NCSU and the second being industry developers that create error notifications. The students will be asked to categorize five notifications that I have already categorized. The accuracy of their categorizations, using the questionnaire will reflect the quality of both the categories and the questionnaire. The industry developers will be asked to do the same ensuring that the questionnaire is robust enough for both novices and expert developers.

In a similar effort, the sanatized error notifications will also be presented to expert and novice developers alike, in order to determine whether or not the new context generated by the taxnonmy increases the rate at which developers resolve bugs in their code.

5. Conclusion

Error notifications continue to confuse programmers everywhere – when will the madness end?! My approach is novel in that it is the first attempt to allow industry developers to categorize their error notifications and then to use my taxonomy to create better error notifications for both novices and expert programmers.

Acknowledgments

Thanks to Jim Witschey, Emerson Murphy-Hill, Brittany Johnson, Yoonki Song, and Xi Ge.

References

[1] Eclipse Java development tools (JDT). http://www.eclipse.org/jdt/, November 2012.

[2] FindBugs. http://findbugs.sourceforge.net/, November 2012.

[3] P. J. Brown. Error messages: the neglected area of the man/machine interface. *Commun. ACM*, 26(4):246–249, Apr. 1983. ISSN 0001-0782. . URL http://doi.acm.org/10.1145/2163.358083.

[4] B. Johnson, Y. Song, E. Murphy-Hill, and R. Bowdidge. Why don't software developers use static analysis tools to find bugs? In *Proceedings of the 2013 International Conference on Software Engineering*, ICSE '13, pages 672–681, Piscataway, NJ, USA, 2013. IEEE Press. ISBN 978-1-4673-3076-3. URL http://dl.acm.org/citation.cfm?id=2486788.2486877.

[5] B. Shneiderman. Designing computer system messages. *Commun. ACM*, 25(9):610–611, Sept. 1982. ISSN 0001-0782. . URL http://doi.acm.org/10.1145/358628.358639.

[6] V. J. Traver. On compiler error messages: what they say and what they mean. *Adv. in Hum.-Comp. Int.*, 2010:3:1–3:26, Jan. 2010. ISSN 1687-5893. . URL http://dx.doi.org/10.1155/2010/602570.

Tackling the Efficiency Problem of Gradual Typing

Esteban Allende *

PLEIAD Laboratory
Computer Science Department (DCC)
University of Chile
eallende@dcc.uchile.cl

Categories and Subject Descriptors   D.3.4 [*Programming Languages*]: Processors

General Terms   Languages, Performance

Keywords   gradual typing, casts, performance

1.   Extended abstract

The popularity of dynamic languages and their use in the construction of large and complex software systems makes the possibility to fortify grown prototypes or scripts using the guarantees of a static type system appealing. While research in combining static and dynamic typing started more than twenty years ago, recent years have seen a lot of proposals of either static type systems for dynamic languages, or partial type systems that allow a combination of both approaches [2–6, 8, 10, 14].

Gradual typing [11, 12] is a partial typing technique proposed by Siek and Taha that allows developers to define which sections of code are statically typed and which are dynamically typed, at a very fine level of granularity, by selectively placing type annotations where desired. The type system ensures that dynamic code does not violate the assumptions made in statically-typed code. This makes it possible to choose between the flexibility provided by a dynamic type system, and the robustness of a static type system.

The semantics of a gradually-typed language is typically given by translation to an intermediate language with casts, *i.e.* runtime type checks that control the boundaries between typed and untyped code. A major challenge in the adoption of gradually-typed languages is the cost of these casts, especially in a higher-order setting. Theoretical approaches have been developed to tackle the space dimension [7, 13], but execution time is also an issue. This has led certain languages to favor a coarse-grained integration of typed and untyped code [15] or to consider a weaker form of integration that avoids costly casts [16].

---

* Esteban Allende is funded by a CONICYT-Chile Ph.D. Scholarship.

SPLASH '13,   October 26–31, 2013, Indianapolis, Indiana, USA.
Copyright is held by the owner/author(s).
ACM 978-1-4503-1995-9/13/10.
http://dx.doi.org/10.1145/2508075.2514884

Other approaches include the work of Rastogi *et al.*. [10], using local type inference to significantly reduce the number of casts that are required; the work of Herman *et al.* [7], in which they propose to use coercions instead of proxies in a chain of higher-order cast, so as to be able to combine adjacent coercions in order to limit space consumption; the work of Siek *et al.* [13], in which they go a step further, developing threesomes as a data structure and algorithm to represent and normalize coercions. A threesome is a cast with three positions: source, target, and an intermediate lowest type. Combining a sequence of threesomes is done by taking the greatest lower bound of the intermediate types.

In developing Gradualtalk[1], a gradually-typed Smalltalk, our first concern was the design of the gradual type system, with its various features [1]. However, in the current stage of this work, we are concerned with the efficiency of casts. There are two concerns about casts insertions that we like to tackle.

The first concern is where to insert casts, especially those relate to method invocations. This is because method invocations are naturally very frequent in object-oriented programs, especially in pure object-oriented languages like Smalltalk. In the foundational paper on gradually-typed objects [12], Siek and Taha describe the semantics of cast insertion using a caller-side strategy—which we term the *call strategy*. Due to implementation issues, our first implementation of cast insertion was however based on a different approach, which we name the *execution strategy*. Here, casts are inserted on the callee side, at the beginning of each typed method. Studying the performance of both approaches revealed that they have complementary strengths, and that a third approach, which we call the *hybrid strategy*, could combine the best of both approaches.

We evaluated all three strategies with both microbenchmarks and macrobenchmarks. The microbenchmarks were designed to test the best and worst case of the execution strategy and call strategy and see how the hybrid strategy perform in those cases. The objective of the macrobenchmarks is to see how well these strategies translate to real world applications. Both benchmark confirm that the hybrid strategy performs as good as its best competitor in all cases.

The second concern is controlling when inserting casts. A gradual type system make the assumption that all the values can be implicitly casted from or to a dyn type, inserting the necessary cast to ensure type safety. However, this could not be the desire of the programmer. The programmer could have forgotten to type a variable or incorrectly pass the value to an untyped method without is knowledge. For normal methods or values, the additional cost of cast is negligible. However, for critical methods who are called multiple times, or blocks value where a cast insert a wrapper to the

---

[1] http://www.pleiad.cl/gradualtalk

block, the additional cost in performance can be significant. In that case, the programmer could desire to disable the automatic cast between the statically typed and dynamically typed world and be warned at compile time. However, the programmer does not have that choice in the gradual typing described by Siek and Taha.

Following the philosophy of gradual typing, disabling the insertion of implicit cast should be done in a fine grained way. The deactivation can be done from both ways: disallowing the automatic casting from the dynamically typed world to the statically typed world, which is annotated with !T, and viceversa, *i.e.* disallowing automatic casting from statically typed to dynamically typed, which is annotated with ~T.

Both of these operators, ! and ~, have practical uses. The operator ! can be used in the parameter type of a method to enforce that the method could be called only with statically typed variables, catching at compile time all clients who are trying to use the method with a dynamically typed variable. The operator ~ can be used in an instance or local variable type to catch at compile time if a value is being inserted incorrectly in the dynamically typed world.

To describe how these operators work formally, we need to introduce the relationships of consistency and consistency subtype. Gradual typing extends traditional subtyping to *consistent subtyping* [12]. Consistency, denoted ~, is a relation that accounts for the presence of Dyn: Dyn is consistent with any other type and any type is consistent with itself. The consistency relation is not transitive in order to avoid collapsing the type relation [11]. A type σ is a consistent subtype of τ, noted $\sigma \lesssim \tau$, iff either $\sigma <: \sigma'$ and $\sigma' \sim \tau$ for some σ', or $\sigma \sim \sigma''$ and $\sigma'' <: \tau$ for some σ''. A cast is inserted when an operation requires that a value of type τ is consistent subtype of a σ type, but is not strictly subtype.

In the case of the two operators ! and ~, the type !T is consistent with Dyn, but Dyn is not consistent with the type !T. For the operator ~ is in the inverse order: Dyn is consistent with ~T, but ~T is not consistent with Dyn. Looking at the description of consistency, these two operators make two important changes to the consistency relationship: there are types that that are not consistent with Dyn and the consistency relation is now asymmetrical. The consistency rules for the ! operator makes that Dyn is not a consistent subtype of !T, raising a type check error instead of inserting a cast when a Dyn typed value is assigned to a !T typed variable, but still allowing that a value of type !T can be assigned (and automatically casted) to a Dyn typed variable. For the ~ operator is the same principle, but in inverse order.

Both of these two concerns are complementary. The restricted automatic casts permits to choose when automatic cast insertion is not desired maintaining the flexibility of gradual typing, while the hybrid cast insertion strategy increase the performance of the application when automatic checks are used. We still need to fully formalize the two operators ! and ~, how they relate with the different kinds of types and what is the impact of making the consistency relationship asymmetrical. We believe that tacking these two concerns allows that gradual typing can be used in real world applications, where debugging a big application can be a daunting task, without the concern of significant sacrifice of the performance of those applications.

References

[1] E. Allende, O. Callaú, J. Fabry, É. Tanter, and M. Denker. Gradual typing for Smalltalk. *Science of Computer Programming*, 2013. To appear.

[2] B. Bloom, J. Field, N. Nystrom, J. Östlund, G. Richards, R. Strniša, J. Vitek, and T. Wrigstad. Thorn: robust, concurrent, extensible scripting on the JVM. In *Proceedings of the 24th ACM SIGPLAN Conference on Object-Oriented Programming Systems, Languages and Applications (OOPSLA 2009)*, pages 117–136, Orlando, Florida, USA, Oct. 2009. ACM Press.

[3] G. Bracha. Pluggable type systems. In *OOPSLA Workshop on Revival of Dynamic Languages*, pages 1–6, 2004.

[4] G. Bracha and D. Griswold. Strongtalk: Typechecking Smalltalk in a production environment. In *Proceedings of the 8th International Conference on Object-Oriented Programming Systems, Languages and Applications (OOPSLA 95)*, pages 215–230, Washington, D.C., USA, Oct. 1993. ACM Press. ACM SIGPLAN Notices, 28(10).

[5] R. Cartwright and M. Fagan. Soft typing. In *Proceedings of the ACM SIGPLAN International Conference on Programming Language Design and Implementation (PLDI)*, pages 278–292, Toronto, Ontario, Canada, 1991.

[6] M. Furr. *Combining Static and Dynamic Typing in Ruby*. PhD thesis, University of Maryland, 2009.

[7] D. Herman, A. Tomb, and C. Flanagan. Space-efficient gradual typing. *Higher-Order and Sympolic Computation*, 23(2):167–189, June 2010.

[8] K. Knowles and C. Flanagan. Hybrid type checking. *ACM Transactions on Programming Languages and Systems*, 32(2):Article n.6, Jan. 2010.

[9] POPL 2010. *Proceedings of the 37th annual ACM SIGPLAN-SIGACT symposium on Principles of programming languages (POPL 2010)*, Madrid, Spain, Jan. 2010. ACM Press.

[10] A. Rastogi, A. Chaudhuri, and B. Hosmer. The ins and outs of gradual type inference. In *Proceedings of the 39th annual ACM SIGPLAN-SIGACT symposium on Principles of programming languages (POPL 2012)*, pages 481–494, Philadelphia, USA, Jan. 2012. ACM Press.

[11] J. Siek and W. Taha. Gradual typing for functional languages. In *Proceedings of the Scheme and Functional Programming Workshop*, pages 81–92, Sept. 2006.

[12] J. Siek and W. Taha. Gradual typing for objects. In E. Ernst, editor, *Proceedings of the 21st European Conference on Object-oriented Programming (ECOOP 2007)*, number 4609 in Lecture Notes in Computer Science, pages 2–27, Berlin, Germany, july/august 2007. Springer-Verlag.

[13] J. Siek and P. Wadler. Threesomes, with and without blame. In POPL 2010 [9], pages 365–376.

[14] S. Tobin-Hochstadt. *Typed Scheme: From Scripts to Programs*. PhD thesis, Northeastern University, Jan. 2010.

[15] S. Tobin-Hochstadt and M. Felleisen. The design and implementation of Typed Scheme. In *Proceedings of the 35th ACM SIGPLAN-SIGACT Symposium on Principles of Programming Languages (POPL 2008)*, pages 395–406, San Francisco, CA, USA, Jan. 2008. ACM Press.

[16] T. Wrigstad, F. Zappa Nardelli, S. Lebresne, J. Östlund, and J. Vitek. Integrating typed and untyped code in a scripting language. In POPL 2010 [9], pages 377–388.

Welcome Message from the Wavefront Chairs

Welcome to the SPLASH 2013 Wavefront and Wavefront Experiences tracks. Wavefront is a forum for innovative work that connects academic computer science research and the software currently being developed in industry. Wavefront Experience is a "practical experience" track – a forum to talk about how software technology affects our daily lives. Both of the Wavefront tracks are about how industry applies the best lessons that software development is learning and deploying in today's software systems and products. Software technology advances fastest when the software community builds on this synergy.

Our Wavefront presenters are extending many innovative ideas from the world of objects, patterns, frameworks, and software tools: applying these ideas to new problems and expanding the effectiveness of a large community of software professionals. Their lessons should inspire you to explore using some new technology in your own work environment.

The Wavefront Experience papers may not be as "academic" as some conference papers, but there is a lot to learn from practical experiences. Experience reports are a blend of science and engineering: some innovative ideas used in a practical setting. Each experience report is filled useful ideas, insights, and lessons. The experiences are built on some great ideas from the research world, and many of the ideas have been the subject of research papers in the OOPSLA and Onward tracks in previous years. For all of these technologies, we can honestly say "the future is now."

In the future, we want you to be involved in SPLASH – especially if you have some innovative ideas to share. After you read these papers, think about how you could apply some of their lessons, share some of your own thoughts with us, and think about submitting a Wavefront paper or a Wavefront Experience paper at a future SPLASH conference!

Dennis Mancl
Wavefront Chair
Alcatel-Lucent, USA

Eduardo Guerra
Wavefront Experience Chair
Instituto Nacional de Pesquisas Espaciais - INPE, Brazil

Effective Use of Non-blocking Data Structures in a Deduplication Application

Steven Feldman

University of Central Florida
Feldman@knights.ucf.edu

Akshatha Bhat

University of Texas at San Antonio
akshathab@gmail.com

Pierre LaBorde

University of Central Florida
pierrelaborde@knights.ucf.edu

Qing Yi

University of Colorado at Colorado Springs
qyi@uccs.edu

Damian Dechev

University of Central Florida
dechev@eecs.ucf.edu

Abstract

Efficient multicore programming demands fundamental data structures that support a high degree of concurrency. Existing research on non-blocking data structures promises to satisfy such demands by providing progress guarantees that allow a significant increase in parallelism while avoiding the safety hazards of lock-based synchronizations. It is well-acknowledged that the use of non-blocking containers can bring significant performance benefits to applications where the shared data experience heavy contention. However, the practical implications of integrating these data structures in real-world applications are not well-understood. In this paper, we study the effective use of non-blocking data structures in a data deduplication application which performs a large number of concurrent compression operations on a data stream using the pipeline parallel processing model. We present our experience of manually refactoring the application from using conventional lock-based synchronization mechanisms to using a wait-free hash map and a set of lock-free queues to boost the degree of concurrency of the application. Our experimental study explores the performance trade-offs of parallelization mechanisms that rely on a) traditional blocking techniques, b) fine-grained mutual exclusion, and c) lock-free and wait-free synchronization.

Categories and Subject Descriptors D.1.3 [*Concurrent Programming*]: Parallel Programming

Keywords lock-free synchronization, parallel data structures, concurrent data deduplication, multiprocessor software design, C/C++ multithreading

1. Introduction

As modern architectures evolve to feature an increasingly large number of CPU cores, a key challenge in developing multi-threaded applications is correctly synchronizing shared data while avoiding excessive performance penalties. Unsafe low-level synchronization mechanisms can easily introduce errors, e.g. race conditions and deadlock, which are extremely difficult to debug. At the same time, application performance and scalability are frequently compromised due to inefficient implementations of synchronous operations on shared data.

Recent advances in the design of lock-free and wait-free data structures bring the promise of practical and highly scalable library containers for concurrent programming [1, 2]. Existing results indicate that these non-blocking data structures can avoid the safety hazards of blocking synchronization and outperform their lock-based counterparts in many scenarios [1–6], especially when the shared data experience high degrees of contention. As demonstrated by Tsigas et al. [7], large scale scientific applications using non-blocking synchronization generate fewer cache misses, exhibit better load balancing, and show better scalability when compared to their blocking counterparts.

In spite of the increasing demand for non-blocking data structures and the existing design of a variety of non-blocking containers, the practical implications of integrating these data structures into existing applications are not well-understood. In this paper we present a study on integrating non-blocking data structures within a data deduplication application from the PARSEC benchmark suite [8]. Data deduplication algorithms are highly concurrent and extremely important in new-generation backup storage systems to compress storage footprints, and in bandwidth-optimized networking applications to compress communication data transferred over the network.

The algorithm implementation applies a large number of concurrent operations to a data stream using the pipeline parallel processing model, in a scenario different from the typical use case scenarios explored in previous studies of non-blocking algorithms. By demonstrating the use of non-blocking synchronization within this implementation of data deduplication, we expect our results to be applicable to other applications of a similar behavior pattern and to potentially enable better implementations of such algorithms in terms of performance, scalability, and progress guarantees.

We have manually refactored the original *Dedup* application from PARSEC from using conventional lock-based synchronization mechanisms to using a wait-free hash map and several lock-free queues to enhance the degree of concurrency within the application. We seek a better understanding of two important issues: 1) the transformations required to modify an existing multi-threaded application from using lock-based synchronizations to using non-blocking synchronizations; 2) the use case scenarios where non-blocking data structures provide significant performance benefits. Our contributions include the following:

- We analyze the design of two non-blocking data structures, a hash map and a queue, present detailed steps necessary to incorporate them within an existing C/C++ multi-threaded application, and study their behavior when used in combination with blocking algorithms and data structures.

- We use a full-scale application and several micro benchmarks to study the performance trade-offs of traditional blocking mechanisms, fine-grained mutual exclusion, and the up-and-coming non-blocking techniques.

- We outline semantic differences between the use of traditional shared containers and their non-blocking counterparts and outline important tactics in the design and utilization of existing non-blocking data structures to enhance their usability in real-world applications.

The rest of the paper is organized as follows. Section 2 introduces some basic concepts of non-blocking synchronization. Section 3 describes the overall structure of Dedup. Section 4 outlines our methodology for refactoring the application and the alternative concurrent data structures that we have integrated with the refactored *Dedup* code. Section 5 presents experimental results to evaluate the performance and scalability of the various synchronization approaches. Finally, Section 10 discusses related work, and Section 11 summarizes our findings.

2. Background

In multi-threaded programming, shared data among multiple threads need to be protected to ensure thread safety. A commonly used protection mechanism is to use a global lock to enforce mutual exclusion, so that at most one thread can update a shared data item at any time. However, when many threads are contending for a single lock, the sequential ordering of updates becomes a serious performance bottleneck that limits the scalability of parallel applications.

Existing research has sought to ameliorate this problem by re-designing data structures to support fine-grained locking [9, 10], which uses different locks for disjoint components of the data structure, e.g. one lock per bucket in a hash map, allowing operations that modify disjoint items of a compound data structure to proceed concurrently. Besides potential performance scalability issues, lock-based synchronization requires meticulous attention to details when threads need to acquire and release multiple locks, to avoid unsafe situations such as deadlock, livelock, starvation, and priority inversion [2].

Using atomic primitives supported by hardware, a large collection of *non-blocking algorithms* has been developed to support lock-free and wait-free synchronizations over shared data, where in a finite number of steps, a subset of the participating threads is guaranteed to make progress [2, 11] (lock-free), or *all* participating threads are guaranteed to make progress [2, 11] (wait-free). These guarantees are typically based on constructing shared data structures that support *linearization* of concurrent operations as a main correctness invariant; that is, they support seemingly instantaneous execution of every operation on the shared data, so that an equivalent sequential ordering of the concurrent operations can always be constructed [2].

The practical design of non-blocking data structures is known to be difficult. In particular, non-blocking algorithms are known to vary widely, and there is no general recipe for their design. A typical non-blocking algorithm generally includes three phases: 1) determining the current state of the shared object, 2) deciding whether to assist a pending operation or proceed with own operation, 3) at-

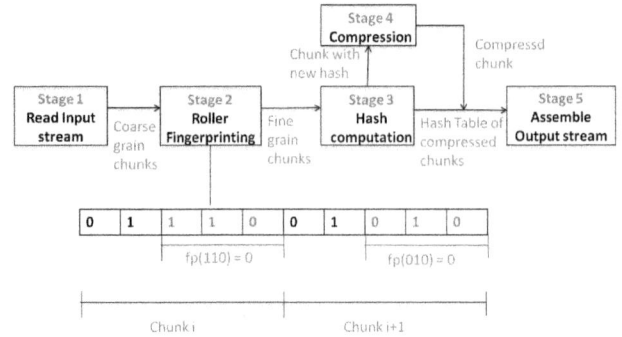

Figure 1: Pipeline stages of Dedup

tempting own operation, retrying (return to step 1) if necessary. While widely adopted, this approach is susceptible to the ABA[1] problem [12], which occurs when the value of a memory location changes from A, to B, and then back to A. An erroneous solution to the ABA problem occurs when a thread does not realize the intermediate nature of the update to B and proceeds to incorrectly change the final value of the entire update sequence from A to B.

3. The Dedup Application

To study the impact of using differently synchronized data structures on the performance and scalability of real-world applications, we selected *Dedup*, a data deduplication application which applies several global and local compressions to an input data stream, from the PARSEC benchmark suite [8]. The algorithm uses a pipelined programming model to parallelize the compression, where the input stream is first broken into coarse-grained chunks and then divided into fine grained segments, with each segment hashed and compressed before stored into a hash map. Finally, an output stream is assembled from the hash values and compressed data segments. The algorithm is widely used in new-generation backup storage systems, e.g., the IBM ProtecTIER Deduplication Gateway, to compress storage footprints, and in bandwidth-optimized networking applications, e.g., the CommVault Simpana 9, to compress communication data.

3.1 Computation Structure

Fig. 1 illustrates the overall computational structure of *Dedup*, which is comprised of five pipeline stages. The three stages in the middle (Roller Fingerprinting, Hash computation, and Compression) are parallelized using multiple threads, while the first (Read Input stream) and last (Assemble Output stream) stages are single-threaded and mostly serve to handle program I/O. The first stage reads the input stream and breaks it up into coarse-grained chunks as independent work units to be operated on by the threads of the second stage. The second stage further fragments the chunks into finer-grained segments via rolling fingerprinting, which uses the Rabin-Karp fingerprinting technique to break up coarse-grained chunks into finer-grained ones. A unique sequence number is associated with each chunk so that they can be ordered correctly when they are reassembled. The third stage computes a SHA-1 hash value for each fine-grained chunk and stores the chunks into a hash map; if any chunk already exists in the hash map, the chunk is considered a duplicate and omitted by the later stages. Next, the fourth stage compresses each remaining chunk before storing it back into the hash map. Finally, the last stage

---

[1] ABA is not an acronym; it refers to a value in shared memory changing from A to B and then to A again.

assembles the deduplicated output stream by combining the compressed data segments in the correct order based on their unique sequence numbers while replacing the duplicate chunks with their hash values (fingerprints) in the final result.

The algorithm uses two types of concurrent data structures, a global hash map and four shared queues, one per pipeline stage, to store the data generated from each pipeline stage before they are further processed. In the original implementation of the algorithm, both the hash map and the local queues are synchronized via global locks to support concurrent access of their data. Our study focuses on replacing the implementations of these lock-based concurrent data structures with alternative non-blocking data structure implementations, to observe the impact of non-blocking containers on the overall application performance.

3.2 Execution Configurations

The *Dedup* application supports a number of ways to reconfigure the concurrent execution of its pipeline stages. e.g. by using different numbers of threads or local queues within each pipeline stage. In particular, it maintains a separate thread pool for each of the middle three pipeline stages so that an arbitrary number of threads can be assigned to work on each stage. The default configuration uses a single queue to maintain the data stream between each pair of pipeline stages. However, to reduce contention among the threads, the application can be configured to automatically use multiple queues so that only a small group of threads are sharing each queue.

Overall, the *Dedup* application can be configured with two parameters: n, the number of threads to be allocated to each of the middle three pipeline stages; and Max_{th}, the maximum number of threads allowed to share a single local queue (by default, Max_{th} = 4). Based on these two parameters, the application adjusts the number of local queues per pipeline stage as $\lceil n/Max_{th} \rceil$. For example, if the user specifies that 32 threads should be used per pipeline stage and a maximum of 4 threads are allowed to share a single queue, then 8 local queues are created per stage.

The strategy within *Dedup* to dynamically adjust the number of local queues per pipeline stage serves as a scheduling mechanism within the application to ensure proper load-balancing among the threads and to reduce contention on the local queues. Section 5 presents our results when experimenting with different configurations of these two parameters to determine their impacts on the overall performance of the application.

4. Refactoring Dedup

To investigate the potential of automatically refactoring existing applications to use non-blocking concurrent data structures and the overall impact of such application transformations in terms of promoting stronger progress guarantees, better scalability, and improved overall performance, we have manually replaced the lock-protected data structures within *Dedup* with several alternative implementations and have modified the externally synchronized operations on the original shared data with new internally synchronized APIs. The following subsections detail our modifications to the application and their semantic implications.

4.1 Application Transformations

Modifying existing parallel codes to use non-blocking concurrent data structures requires a number of considerations, including semantic differences of the alternative data structures, the API's used to access them, modifications of synchronization schemes to protect shared data, and the implications of making them lock-free. We have taken the following three steps to systematically modify the *Dedup* application to address these issues.

1. Identify shared data structures protected by global locks. Through manual examination of the application source code and its profiling runs, we have identified two critical shared data structures within *Dedup*: the hash map used to track duplications of data items, and the local queues used to store the data stream between pipeline stages. The use of these data structures within the application is illustrated in Fig. 1.

2. Analyze the use of the shared data structures and identify equivalent concurrent containers that can be used as alternative implementations. Determine a common API, e.g., similar to that of the unordered maps and queues from the C++ Standard Template Library (STL), for the alternative concurrent containers.

3. Rewrite the application to organize their shared data using the alternative containers and to access the shared data using a designated common API for the containers. In particular, to substitute the original lock-protected hash map and queue operations in *Dedup*, we manually identified all instances of blocking synchronizations within the application and replaced them with equivalent alternative operations to the new concurrent data structures.

We have explored several alternative implementations of the hash maps and local queues. The following subsections summarize each of these implementations, the progress guarantees they provide, and their expected performance characteristics.

4.2 Substituting The Hash Map

The original hash map used within *Dedup* has a similar interface as that of the *unordered_map* in the C++ Standard Template Library (STL) except that it allows the insertion of duplicate keys. Additionally, a special function, *hashtable_getlock(key)*, is provided that returns a lock to support mutual exclusion for all operations related to the designated hash key. While a thread holds this lock, no other thread can make progress on the hash map with a key that hashes to the same position.

Fig. 2a shows an example code fragment that operates on the *Dedup* hash map. Here the first instruction at line 1 acquires the lock for some hash key, line 2 calls the search function, lines 3-6 insert a new entry to the map if the key is not found, lines 7-10 process the returned result, and finally line 11 releases the lock. This fine-grained locking approach supports the parallelism of operations that operate on disjoint positions in the map. However, if two or more threads are operating on the hash map with keys that hash to the same position, these operations will be serialized. A linked list is used to store an arbitrary number of keys at each location to accommodate hash collisions. As a result, while a typical search operation is expected to take constant-time, it could take O(n) time, where n is the number of entries already in the hash map, in the worst case. The size of the hash map is a hard-coded constant that must be chosen wisely to avoid lengthy linked lists.

To explore the performance trade-offs of varying concurrent hash maps, we substituted the original *Dedup* hash map with the following alternative implementations.

- The Concurrent Hash Map from Intel's Thread Building Blocks (TBB) library. The TBB hash map incorporates both lock-free and fine-grained synchronization techniques to provide a high degree of concurrency and scalability [9]. All operations on this hash map, except for the resize, are performed in O(1) time. It utilizes internal locks to maintain correctness and provides the user the option of holding read or write locks on each specific key value [9]. It differs from the *Dedup* hash map in that a thread needs to acquire a lock only if it needs to update the value associated with a key. If a thread is simply inserting a new key or reading the value of a key, no explicit locking is required.

```
1   lock=hashtable_getlock(key);
2   hash_entry *res= hashtable_search(hashtable,key);
3   if(!res){
4       ....
5       hashtable_insert(hashtable,key, value);
6   }
7   else{
8       ....
9       res.value=...
10  }
11  lock.unlock();
```

(a) Blocking Hash Map

```
1
2   void *res= hash_get(hashtable,key,thread_id);
3   if(!res){
4       ...
5       bool res2=hash_insert(hashtable,key,value,thread_id)
6       if(!res2)
7           goto found;
8   }
9   else{
10  found:
11      ...
12      atomic_update(res,value)
13  }
```

(b) Wait-free Hash Map

Figure 2: Hash Map Code Transformation Example

- The Wait-Free Hash Map implemented by [13, 14]. This implementation provides a high degree of concurrency and scalability in addition to guaranteeing that all operations complete in a constant number of steps. In particular, it uses a bounded number of linked arrays to store the inserted key-value pairs. Each entry of an array may hold nothing, a reference to a key-value pair, or a reference to another array. Each hash key is interpreted as a sequence of bits, where pre-determined sub-sequences of these bits are used to determine the path to follow to find a key-value pair in the linked arrays. The first sub-sequence of bits determines the entry on the root array where the key-value pair would be placed. If the desired entry already holds a reference to another array, the next sub-sequence of bits is used to determine the entry on the next array to place the key-value pair. The process repeats until the key-value pair has been placed successfully, and the number of repetitions is bounded by a constant value (the maximum length of the key). New arrays are added incrementally when hash collisions occur, with the total number of referenced arrays limited by the number of bits in each hash key.

It is also important to consider Doug Leas java implementation of a concurrent hash map [15] which is similar in design to Dedups concurrent hash table, in that they both resolve hash collisions by using linked lists. However, Lea's concurrent hash map allows for get (search) operations to concurrently execute without the need to block or synchronize with other operations unless an inconsistent state is detected. Additionally, it supports the remove operation by cloning the portion of the linked list before the node to be removed and joining it to the portion of the linked list pointed to by that node. Allowing for the get function to "detect that its view of the list is inconsistent or stale. If it detects that its view is inconsistent or stale, or simply does not find the entry it is looking for." In the event that it does detect this "it then synchronizes on the appropriate bucket lock and searches the chain again." The design of Lea's concurrent hash map allows for non-conflicting operations to proceed independently, and serializes modification operations that operate on the same segment of data. Since his design is based on Java's garbage collection and synchronization functions it is not compatible with dedup and was not included in the implementations tested.

Fig. 2 illustrates the program transformations we made in order to substitute Dedup's hash map with the above alternative concurrent hash maps. The main difference in the transformed code is that by using a concurrent hash map, explicit locking is no longer required when performing an update operation, as the APIs are already thread-safe when working concurrently. In Fig. 2a, Dedup uses locks to ensure that its hash map only contains unique keys.

These locks are not necessary when using a thread-safe hash map. In the event that between the search and insert operations of the hash map at lines 2 and 5 of Fig. 2b, a different thread inserts the same key, the insert operation at line 5 would return false, and the execution would proceed as if the search function had found the key in the data structure.

4.3 Substituting The Queues

Fig. 3a outlines the original implementations of the three queue operations in *Dedup*, where a global lock is used to enforce mutual exclusion of operations on each queue container. In contrast to the typical API of queues in the C++ STL, a key difference in *Dedup's* queue implementation is that each enqueue and dequeue operation performs a batch operation of multiple elements to increase throughput every time a thread acquires the global lock of a queue. Additionally, multiple queues could be employed at each pipeline stage to reduce the number of threads operating on the same queues, further reducing contention among the threads and wait time induced by the locks.

A shared queue is a fundamentally sequential data structure where a high degree of contention can be experienced by its head and tail pointers, leading to increased contention and reduced parallelism even when using fine-grained synchronization on the few heavily-contended data of interest. As a result, using non-blocking methods may not deliver as large of a performance boost as that provided by fundamentally concurrent containers such as the hash maps. To investigate such contention issues, we have replaced the original local queue implementation within *Dedup* with the following non-blocking alternative implementations.

- The non-blocking concurrent queue from Intel's Thread Building Blocks library is implemented using a sequence of arrays called micro-queues [9]. Each queue operation is assigned to one of the micro-queues, with the Kth operation assigned to the $K\%N$th micro-queue, where N is the number of micro-queues (by default, N = 8). In essence, the micro-queues are used to remove the contention from a single head or tail at the cost of relaxing the FIFO property of a queue.

- The lock-free queue based on the popular Michael-Scott queue algorithm [16] from the Amino Concurrent Building Blocks library is fundamentally a linked list in which each value is stored in a distinct node. A back-off scheme was added to the queue to allow contending threads to sleep for a pre-defined amount of time in hopes that the scheduler will provide a more favorable ordering of the threads in the future, so that they no longer impede each other's progress. ABA-prevention [12] has

136

been added to the Amino implementation based on Michael's safe memory-reclamation algorithm [17].

To substitute the original queue implementation in Fig. 3a with the alternative lock-free implementations, we have modified each implementation of the three batch operations with alternative implementations that operate on a non-blocking concurrent queue data structure, outlined in Fig. 3b. In essence, the `decorator` design pattern is used to adapt a concurrent queue to the original batch operation interface of `Dedup`. Compared with the the original queue implementations, the new implementation in Fig. 3b has removed from Fig. 3a the locking and unlocking operations at lines 2, 9, 23, and 31; and the waiting-while-full block at lines 3–4, as the enqueue and dequeue functions of a lock-free queue are thread-safe and have unbounded capacities. Further, the locking around the variable that tracks the number of completed threads (lines 36–38) has been replaced with a single atomic increment of the *thCmpl* value. Finally, the enqueue and dequeue APIs of the lock-free queue are called a specified number of times to support the original batch enqueue and dequeue operations of *Dedup*.

4.4 Semantic Implications

As discussed in Section 4.1 and illustrated in Figs. 2 and 3, a key challenge in refactoring *Dedup* to use alternative hash map and queue implementations is to recognize the uses of these data structures and their respective programming interfaces within the application and to identify equivalent concurrent data structures to substitute the original APIs. In many cases, equivalent data structures provide slightly different APIs due to their different internal synchronization mechanisms. For example, using lock-based synchronization, an application can first examine the head of a queue before popping it off. However, such operations may not be possible using a non-blocking queue designed without support for a linearizable "check-and-pop" method. Similarly, the application may need to check whether an element is present in a hash map before insertion, which is not easily implemented in a non-blocking hash map. Fortunately both TBB's concurrent hashmap and the wait-free hash map we used support such combination of operations, as shown in Fig. 2.

To automate the process of refactoring *Dedup*, a full understanding of the semantics of the involved hash map and queue implementations is required. In particular, a data structure annotation language could be used to convey their APIs and expected use patterns, so that an automated source-to-source translation framework could be developed to identify the relevant code fragments and perform the necessary program transformations. However, due to the highly complex and dynamic nature of C/C++ applications, we expect that user interaction will be required to ensure correct and complete coverage of the necessary transformations.

5. Experimental Configurations

To understand the performance implications of integrating non-blocking data containers within existing well-tuned multi-threaded applications, we studied the performance variations of *Dedup* when using the alternative implementations for its two shared data structures, the hash map and local queues. To gain a deeper insight into the observed performance differences, we additionally designed a number of synthetic tests to evaluate the relative efficiencies of these data structures independently of the *Dedup* application.

Each synthetic test starts with a main thread that initializes a set of global variables, creates an instance of each data structure to be studied, and then spawns a predetermined number of threads to evaluate a mixture of different operations on the data structure of interest. The main thread records the elapsed time between signaling the threads to begin execution and after all threads have com-

pleted execution. Care has been taken to remove all unnecessary work between operations.

Input files (small to larger)	Simsmall (10.10mb), Simmedium (30.70mb), Simnative (671.58mb)
Threads per Pipeline Stage (TPPS)	1,2,**4**,8,16,32,48,64
Maximum Number of Threads per Queue (MTPQ)	1,2,**4**,8,16,32,48,64
Items per En/Dequeue (EDITEMS)	1,5,10,15,**20**,...60

Figure 4: Execution Configurations

Fig. 4 summarizes the different execution configurations (see Section 3.2) of *Dedup* that we have evaluated for each combination of hash map and queue implementation. All experimental evaluations were performed on a 64-core SuperMicro server, with four sixteen-core AMD Opteron (Model 6272) 2.1 Ghz processors and 64GBs of memory. The machine runs 64-bit Ubuntu Linux version 11.04. All programs were compiled with g++ version 4.7 with the -O3 optimization flag. The default configurations of these parameters are printed in bold in Fig. 4 and are used when comparing the hash map and queue implementations in Sections 6 and 7. Each evaluation has been repeated ten times, and the average of the ten runs are reported as the result of the evaluation. Since we have a dedicated machine for our evaluations, the average variation across different runs of the same evaluation is about 0.3%.

6. Comparing Hash Map Implementations

This section provides a study of the performance trade-offs of the original *Dedup* hash map, TBB's unordered map, and the wait-free hash map discussed in Section 4.2. Fig. 5 shows the performance comparison of *Dedup* when using the three different hash map implementations and when operating on a small (Simsmall), a medium (Simmedium), and a large (Simnative) size input data streams. The key differences between these implementations are the progress guarantees they provide and how they handle hash collisions and resizes. We expect the wait-free hash map to perform the best when the number of keys is relatively large and hash collisions occur often, and the original *Dedup* hash map to degrade in performance as the number of keys increases due to the unbounded linked lists that must be searched during every operation.

From Fig. 5a and 5b, we see that when using the small or medium-sized input, the performance differences from using different hash map implementations are minor, with the wait-free hash map performing slightly better than the other two implementations. Since only a limited amount of work is available at each pipeline stage, all versions reached their best performance when using 4 threads per stage, and adding more threads produces either no benefit or leads to performance degradation (e.g., when using more than 32 threads per stage to operate on the *Simsmall* input).

When operating on the much larger *Simnative* input, for all different thread configurations, the wait-free hash map consistently produces a 7-21% performance boost over the alternative hash map implementations. Here, since a much larger amount of work is available at each pipeline stage, the performance peak is not reached until at least 16 threads are used per stage. The increased work leads to the possibility for a higher degree of contention when multiple threads attempt to simultaneously update the same entries of the shared hash map. Further, since a large amount of data need to be stored in the global hash map, many of these data may incur hash collisions. To achieve scalable performance, an implementation with an efficient collision management methodology is needed. Intel TBB's unordered map performs similarly to the original *Dedup* map for the majority of cases, with about a 2-6% improvement over *Dedup's* hash map when a large number of threads are used per pipeline stage (e.g., 64 threads/stage in Fig. 5c).

```
1  function enqueue(queue q, int chunk_size, void *buf){
2      q.lock();//Enter Critical Region
3      while( q.isFull() ) //Block until queue is full
4          q.wait();
5
6      for( item=0; item<chunk_size; item++)//Enqueue items
7          q.data[queue.head++] = buf[item];
8      q.signal();//Signal enqueue
9      q.unlock();//Leave Critical Region }
10
11
12 function dequeue(queue q, int chunk_size, void *buf){
13     q.lock();//Enter Critical Region
14
15     //Block if queue is empty and if other threads
16     //are still working on the queue
17     while( (q.head==q.tail) && (q.thCmpl < q.threads) ){
18         q.wait();}
19
20     //Exit condition
21     if( (q.tail == q.head) && (q.thCmpl == q.threads) ) {
22         q.signal();
23         q.unlock();
24         return; }
25
26     for( item=0; item<chunk_size; item++){//Dequeue items
27         buf[item] = q.data[q.tail++];
28         if(q.tail == q.head) //Queue is Empty
29             break; }
30     q.signal();
31     q.unlock(); //Leave Critical Region
32 }
33
34
35 function terminate(queue q){
36     lock(); //Enter Critical Region
37     q.thCmpl++;
38     unlock(); } //Leave Critical Region
```

(a) Using blocking queues

```
1  function enqueue(queue q, int chunk_size, void *buf){
2      //No locking required
3
4
5
6      for( item=0; item<chunk_size; item++)//Enqueue items
7          q.concq.enqueue( buf[item] );
8
9  }
10
11
12 function dequeue(queue q, int chunk_size, void *buf){
13     //No locking required
14
15
16     //Conditional wait replaced with Busy Wait
17     while( q.concq.empty() && (q.thCmpl < q.threads) )
18     {  }
19
20     //Exit condition
21     if( q.concq.empty()&& (q.thCmpl == q.threads) ) {
22
23
24         return; }
25
26     for( item=0; item<chunk_size; item++){//Dequeue items
27         r = q.concq.dequeue( buf[item] );
28         if( !r ) //If Dequeue fails
29             break; }
30
31
32 }
33
34
35 function terminate(queue q){
36     //No locking required
37     //q.thCmpl is replaced with atomic counter
38     _sync_add_and_fetch( q.thCmpl, 1 ); }
```

(b) Using lock-free queues

Figure 3: Code Transformation for Queues in Dedup

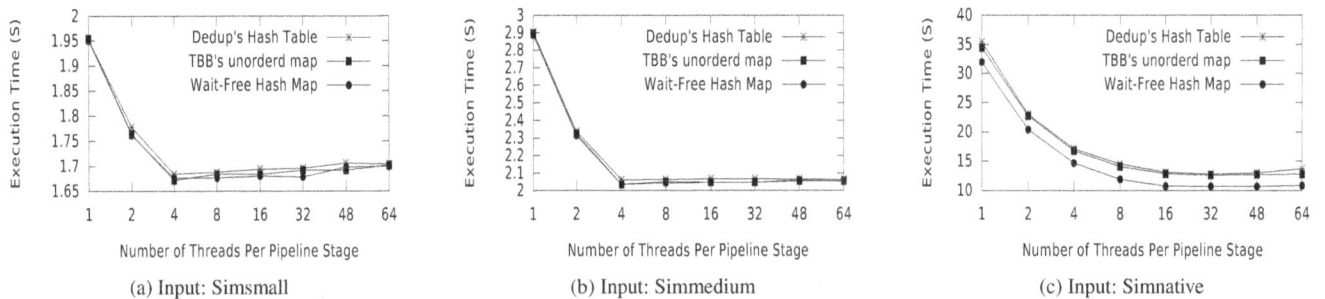

(a) Input: Simsmall

(b) Input: Simmedium

(c) Input: Simnative

Figure 5: Performance of Dedup when using different hash map implementations

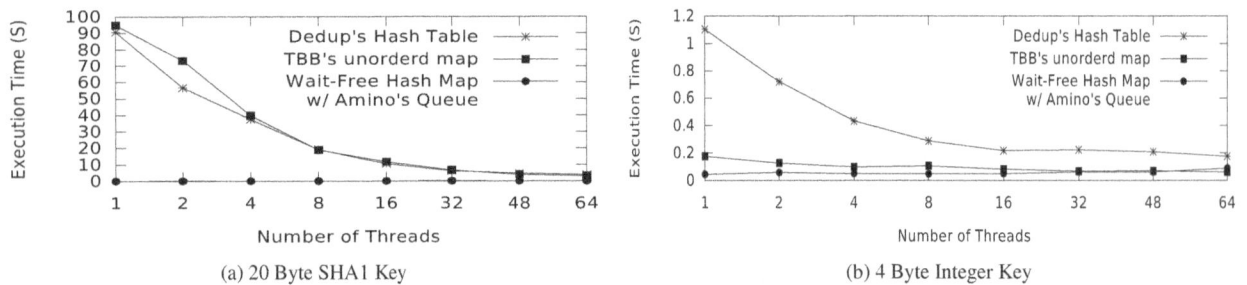

(a) 20 Byte SHA1 Key

(b) 4 Byte Integer Key

Figure 6: Synthetic Hash Map Tests

We hypothesize that the wait-free hash map performs better than *Dedup's* hash map and Intel TBB's hash map because: 1) it provides better collision management by guaranteeing a constant bound on both the search and insert operations, and 2) it supports a higher degree of concurrency when multiple threads are competing to update the hash map. To validate this hypothesis, we designed two synthetic tests and present the results in Fig. 6.

Since operations from different threads are executed sequentially only when they need to operate on a common position within the hash map (that is, when they need to operate on the same hash key or when their keys incur a collision within the hash map), our first synthetic test aims to maximize these occurrences. By artificially increasing the total number of operations to 15 million (an 18x increase), with similar distributions of search and insert operations as those in Dedup, we expect to trigger a much larger degree of contention in the hash maps and to observe their relative efficiencies of handling the contention and their ability to scale.

Fig. 6a compares the performance of the different hash map implementations when each thread uses a list of randomly generated SHA1 values (the hash key data type used by *Dedup*) to perform its share of the 15 million operations, where 16% of the operations are insert operations and 84% are search operations. Note that in *Dedup*, there is only a total of about 810,000 operations on the hash map when using the *Simnative* input. From Fig. 6a, we see the much larger number of operations indeed result in more contention, which in turn severely degrades the performance of the TBB and *Dedup* hash maps so that the wait-free hash map now performs orders of magnitude better (41.72x - 838.81x).

To isolate the effect of hash collision management from the overall scalability issues of the *Dedup* application, our next synthetic test aims to significantly reduce the chances of hash collisions in all three hash map implementations without affecting the probability of multiple threads contending to operate on the same hash key. Our study revealed that the SHA1 key data type used by Dedup imposes an artificial dependence among the different keys so that overall a much higher number of collisions results, as many keys are hashed to a small number of clustered positions within the TBB and *Dedup* hash maps. This defect in the Dedup hashing function, however, may have a much smaller impact on the wait-free hash map as it is more resilient to poor hashing functions.

To validate this hypothesis, Fig. 6b compares the performance of the hash maps when using a hash function with a more even distribution. Here, since the keys are much better distributed, the number of hash collisions is significantly reduced. Consequently, the performance differences are mostly caused by the different degrees of concurrency when multiple threads are operating on the same key. When up to 32 threads are used, the wait-free hash map outperforms the alternative approaches. In addition, both the wait-free and the TBB hash maps perform significantly better when compared to the original Dedup hash map due to their use of fine-grained synchronization. Note that the performance differences between the TBB and the wait-free hash maps are much smaller, as both of them support a high degree of concurrency when multiple threads need to work on the same data.

7. Comparing Local Queue Implementations

In contrast to the concurrent hash map, where operations with distinct hash keys can proceed in parallel independently of each other, all operations on a shared queue occur at either the head or the tail of the queue. Because of its inherently sequential First-In First-Out (FIFO) property, the degree of concurrency that a queue can support is limited. Hence, concurrent operations on a shared queue typically lead to a high degree of contention and thus performance degradations. As a result, we expect low impact on the overall performance of *Dedup* when replacing its coarse-grained lock-protected queue

with two non-blocking concurrent queues, the Intel TBB's queue and the Amino Concurrent Building Block's (CBB) queue (see Section 4.3). Fig. 7 shows our experimental results of comparing the performance impact of the different queue implementations. These results confirm that the integration of queues that support a higher degree of concurrency does not have a significant impact on the overall performance of *Dedup*.

The *Dedup* application can be reconfigured with two key parameters, the maximum number of threads per queue and the number of items to be enqueued or dequeued per operation (see Section 3.2). In particular, when the maximum number of threads operating on each queue is decreased, so is the contention on the head and tail of the queue. Increasing the number of items enqueued or dequeued per operation has two effects: the amount of work performed between calls to enqueue and dequeue is increased, and the number of times a queue operation is invoked is decreased, further reducing the contention. These two parameters can therefore be adjusted to help ameliorate any negative performance impact associated with the use of course-grained locking in the application's shared queue.

Fig. 8 shows how the application performance scales with the change of these configuration parameters when using 64 threads per pipeline stage and the *Simnative* input file. Fig. 8a confirms that as the number of threads operating on the queues increase, so does the contention among the threads, leading to a longer execution time for the whole application. Fig. 8b illustrates the importance of performing batch operations, showing a steady performance increase when more items are grouped in a single enqueue/dequeue operation, with the best performance reached when enqueuing/dequeuing 50 items at a time. By default, *Dedup* uses a batch mode of 20 items per operation, providing a performance boost of 9% compared with the non-batching mode where each operation manipulates a single item. Another observation from Fig. 8 is that the original Dedup queue has consistently outperformed the other two lock-free queues when the batch mode reaches 20 items per en/dequeue operation and when the max number of threads to share a queue is greater than 4 (the default Dedup configuration), showing better scalability than the other queue implementations.

While our evaluations in both Figs. 7 and 8 demonstrate that using the coarse-grained locking approach employed by *Dedup's* queue provides the best overall performance, we attribute this result to the fact that among the three evaluated approaches, *Dedup's* queue is the only shared queue that implements an inherent support for batching operations. As shown in Fig. 3b and discussed in Section 4.3, due to the lack of internal support for batch operations from the two alternative lock-free queues, we implemented the *Dedup* batch operations by simply invoking their single-item enqueue/dequeue operations multiple times, without taking advantage of the added concurrency.

To validate our speculation, in Fig. 9, we devised a synthetic test for the three concurrent queues by splitting all threads into two equal groups: a set of enqueuers and a set of dequeuers. Each enqueuer thread adds its share of elements, and each dequeuer attempts to dequeue until the queue is empty and the enqueuers have completed all of their work. Fig. 9a shows our results when 20 items are enqueued or dequeued at a time by each operation, and Fig. 9b shows the results when the number of elements per operation is decreased to 1.

Note that the performance of the TBB and CBB's queues did not change at all in these two graphs, while the performance of Dedup's original queue degraded significantly in Fig. 9b, where Intel TBB's queue outperformed the other approaches as the original queue of *Dedup* became a victim of lock contention and reduced parallelism due to the use of mutually exclusive locks. Compared with Amino CBB's non-blocking implementation, Intel TBB's non-blocking

(a) Input: SimSmall

(b) Input: Simmedium

(c) Input: Simlarge

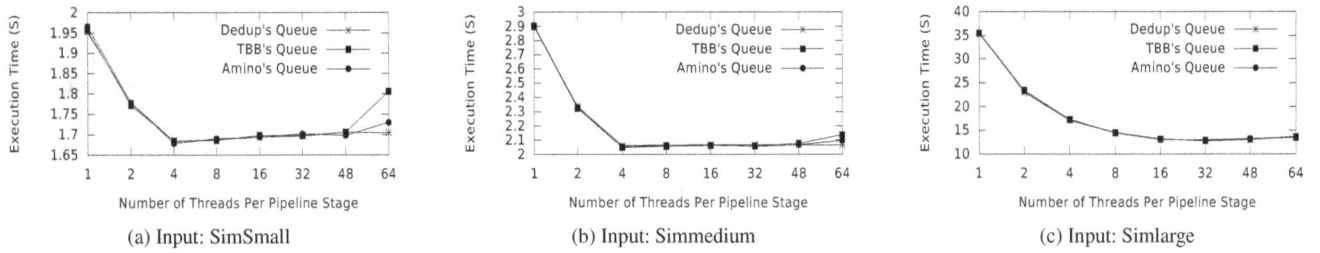

Figure 7: Performance of Dedup when using different queue implementations

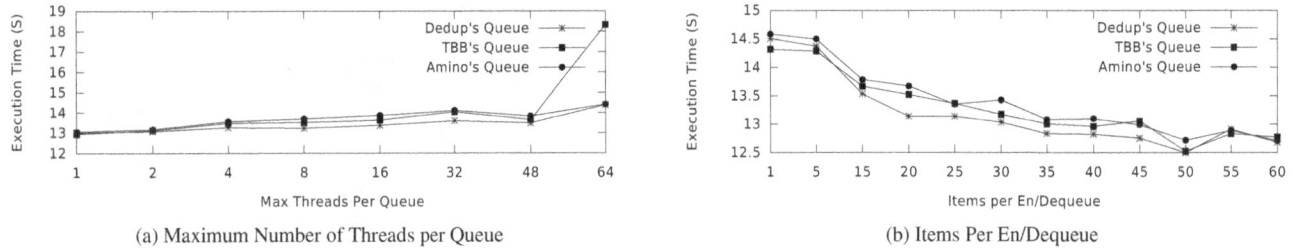

(a) Maximum Number of Threads per Queue

(b) Items Per En/Dequeue

Figure 8: Performance of different Dedup configurations. All evaluations use 64 threads per pipeline stage and the *Simnative* input file

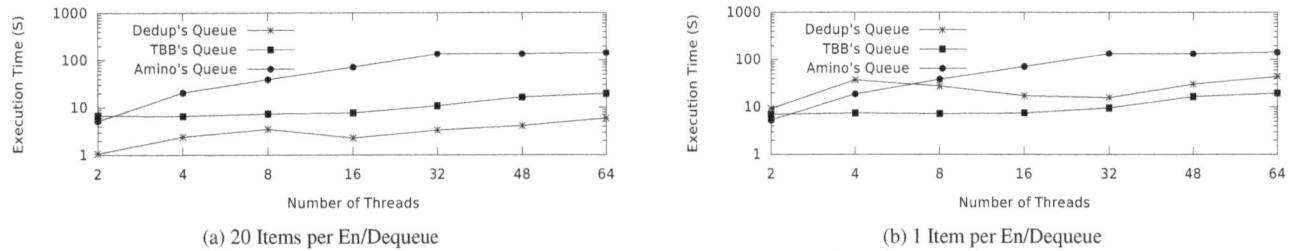

(a) 20 Items per En/Dequeue

(b) 1 Item per En/Dequeue

Figure 9: Synthetic Queue Tests

queue provides an improved and more recent design which results in higher efficiency.

In summary, our performance analysis of the shared queues shows that due to the distribution of contention to multiple queues and the batch mode of enqueueing and dequeueing, the queue's effect on the overall performance of *Dedup* is minimal. Extending the functionality of Intel TBB's queue to support a batch mode of element insertion and deletion may lead to improved performance and scalability when shared queues are used in the pipeline parallel processing model.

8. Application Scalability

Fig. 10 presents our results of studying how the overall performance of *Dedup* scales when using representative combinations of the hash map and queue implementations with varying execution configurations including the number of threads per pipeline stage, the maximum number of threads that can share a single queue (MTPQ), and the number of items per batch enqueue/dequeue operation. All evaluations use the largest input size, *Simnative*.

Most of the graphs in Fig. 10 are similar to that of Fig. 5c, as the performance impact of the hash map implementations dominates the minor performance differences caused by the varying queue implementations. However, when the maximum number of threads per queue (MTPQ) is increased in Figs. 10b, 10d, and 10f, we can

see a clear performance degradation for all hash map and queue implementations when the number of threads per pipeline stage exceeds MTPQ, where a large number of threads are competing to access a single shared queue. In spite of the fact that the shared queue operations only comprise a negligible fraction of the overall *Dedup* execution time, they could become the overall performance bottleneck as each thread spends a significant amount of time waiting to operate on the queues. As a result, the performance benefit gained from the higher degree of concurrency by the wait-free hash map can be lost, resulting in identical performance from using all hash map implementations. While the number of items per enqueue/dequeue operation can ameliorate the performance degradation to a degree, this effect is limited when contention is severe.

9. Core Utilization

In addition to measuring the execution time of the varying implementations of *Dedup*, we tracked their utilization of each CPU core using mpstat [18]. Fig. 11 presents the core utilization patterns of three representative implementations that use the *Dedup*'s original hash table and queue (Fig. 11a), TBB's hash map and queue (Fig. 11b), and the Wait-Free hash map and the Lock-Free queue (Fig. 11c) respectively. Each graph shows the percentage of utilization of each core from the third to the fifth second of execution,

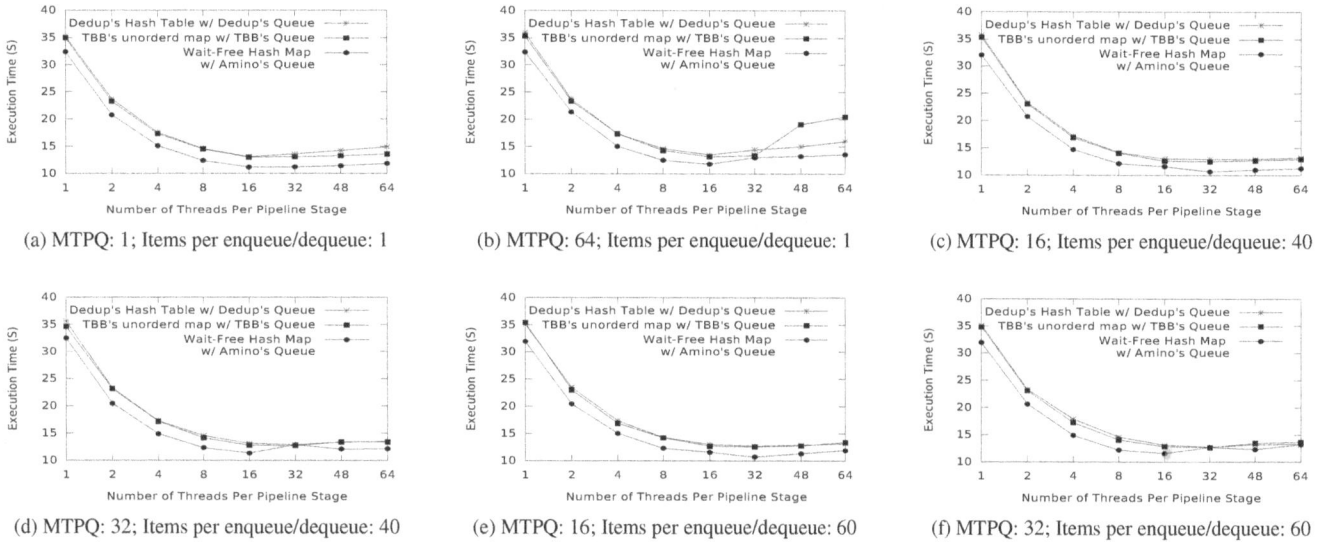

(a) MTPQ: 1; Items per enqueue/dequeue: 1

(b) MTPQ: 64; Items per enqueue/dequeue: 1

(c) MTPQ: 16; Items per enqueue/dequeue: 40

(d) MTPQ: 32; Items per enqueue/dequeue: 40

(e) MTPQ: 16; Items per enqueue/dequeue: 60

(f) MTPQ: 32; Items per enqueue/dequeue: 60

Figure 10: Scalability study of Dedup

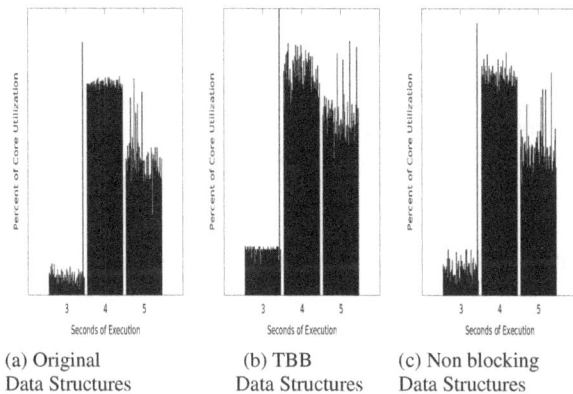

(a) Original
Data Structures

(b) TBB
Data Structures

(c) Non blocking
Data Structures

Figure 11: Core Utilization Dedup

where the majority of the utilization occurs. All three graphs use *simnative* as the input file, with the *max thread per queue* set to 4, *items per en/dequeue* set to 20, and with 64 threads executing per pipeline stage. All three graphs have similar patterns of core utilization, with the TBB configuration having the highest average utilization, followed by the non-blocking configuration, and then by original configuration. This pattern reveals that in addition to completing computation faster, the non-blocking configuration also uses less processing power to do so.

10. Related Work

In [19], Tsigas et al. present a performance study of integrating non-blocking containers into several key applications from the benchmark suites SPLASH-2 [20] and Spark98 [21]. The authors show that the use of non-blocking containers in large-scale high performance computing applications can lead to a performance increase by a factor of 24 when compared to the standard implementations. Their findings indicate that the use of non-blocking containers does not lead to performance loss in any use scenario.

Further analysis by Tsigas et al. [19] reveals that large-scale scientific applications using non-blocking synchronization generate fewer cache misses, exhibit better load balancing, and show significantly better scalability and performance when compared to their blocking counterparts. In contrast, we focus on the in-depth exploration of a single application and the process of effective and practical concurrent data structure integration and optimization in multiprocessor software. A number of prior studies explore the practical application of non-blocking containers in the context of micro-benchmarks, such as [22] and [23].

Existing research in the design of non-blocking data structures includes linked-lists [24, 25], queues [6, 26, 27], stacks [27, 28], hash maps [25, 27, 29], hash tables [30], binary search trees [31], and vectors [32]. The designs of these new concurrent data structures typically focus on reasoning about their efficiency and practicality through synthetic tests. In contrast, our work focuses on studying the practical impact and performance tradeoffs of using these concurrent data containers within real-world applications.

11. Conclusion

This paper presents a study on integrating two general-purpose concurrent data structures, hash maps and shared queues, within a multi-threaded data deduplication application from the PARSEC benchmark suite [8]. The goal is to investigate the performance trade-offs between using conventional lock-based synchronization mechanisms vs. using lock-free and wait-free synchronizations to implement these data structures and to seek a better understanding of two important issues: 1) the transformations required to modify an existing multi-threaded application from using lock-based synchronizations to using non-blocking synchronizations; and 2) the use case scenarios where non-blocking data structures provide significant performance benefits.

Our results indicate that the application often needs specialized operations, e.g., enqueueing and dequeue elements in batches, that require the standard APIs of a general-purpose concurrent data structure to be adapted for efficiency. In the case of the concurrent queue, the degree of concurrency is minimized since all of its operations are performed on the head and tail pointers. *Dedup* resolves the concurrency issues of its local queues by supporting batch enqueue/dequeue operations and allowing multiple queues to be used per pipeline stage. As a result, the lock-free queues we integrated within *Dedup* do not perform as well as the original *Dedup* queue implementation, because they cannot be easily adapted to support special batch enqueue and dequeue operations. Similar strategies need to be adopted within the non-blocking queue implementations to enhance the internal concurrency and thereby scalability of their applications.

The performance gains of using non-blocking data structures are often dictated by the distribution of operations on the data, the context within which the operations are invoked, and the degree of concurrency allowed within these operations. Within *Dedup*, the use of non-blocking hash maps produced significant performance gains, as the hash map allows a greater degree of concurrency by allowing operations on different hash keys to execute in parallel.

We did not encounter many problems while replacing traditional locking data structures with ones that provide concurrent APIs. The main diffculty was understanding the subtle implications of removing the locks, which often contain additional work that is not part of the data structure. For developers that seek to make legacy code non-blocking, these subtlies are understood, and the process of incorporating new data structures is straightforward.

References

[1] D. Dechev and B. Stroustrup, "Scalable Nonblocking Concurrent Objects for Mission Critical Code," in *OOPSLA '09: Proceedings of the ACM SIGPLAN conference on Object-oriented programing, systems, languages, and applications*, 2009.

[2] M. Herlihy and N. Shavit, *The Art of Multiprocessor Programming*. Morgan Kaufmann, March 2008. [Online]. Available: www.amazon.ca/exec/obidos/redirect?tag=citeulike09-20&path=ASIN/0123705916

[3] D. Dechev, *A Concurrency and Time Centered Framework for Autonomous Space Systems*. LAP LAMBERT Academic Publishing, August 2010.

[4] D. Dechev, P. Pirkelbauer, and B. Stroustrup, "Lock-Free Dynamically Resizable Arrays," in *OPODIS*, ser. Lecture Notes in Computer Science, A. A. Shvartsman, Ed., vol. 4305. Springer, 2006, pp. 142–156.

[5] K. Fraser and T. Harris, "Concurrent programming without locks," *ACM Trans. Comput. Syst.*, vol. 25, no. 2, p. 5, 2007. [Online]. Available: www.ddj.com/dept/cpp/184401890

[6] M. Michael, "CAS-Based Lock-Free Algorithm for Shared Deques," in *Euro-Par 2003: The Ninth Euro-Par Conference on Parallel Processing, LNCS volume 2790*, 2003, pp. 651–660.

[7] P. Tsigas and Y. Zhang, "The non-blocking programming paradigm in large scale scientific computations," in *PPAM*, 2003, pp. 1114–1124.

[8] C. Bienia and K. Li, "Parsec 2.0: A new benchmark suite for chip-multiprocessors," in *Proceedings of the 5th Annual Workshop on Modeling, Benchmarking and Simulation*, June 2009.

[9] Intel, "Intel Threading Building Blocks," threadingbuildingblocks.org/, November 2011. [Online]. Available: threadingbuildingblocks.org/

[10] M. Moir and N. Shavit, *Handbook of Data Structures and Applications*. Chapman and Hall/CRC Press, 2007, ch. Concurrent Data Structures, pp. 47–1–47–30.

[11] M. Herlihy, "Wait-Free Synchronization," in *Trans. on Programming Languages and Systems*. ACM, 1991, pp. 124–149.

[12] D. Dechev, "The ABA Problem in Multicore Data Structures with Collaborating Operations," in *Proceedings of the 7th International Conference on Collaborative Computing: Networking, Applications and Worksharing (CollaborateCom 2011)*, 2011.

[13] S. Feldman, P. LaBorde, and D. Dechev, UCF Technical Report (cse.eecs.ucf.edu/private/UCF-TechReport-HashTable.pdf). Retrieved 04/05/2013.

[14] S. Feldman, P. LaBorde, and D. Dechev, "A Lock-Free Concurrent Hash Table Design for Effective Information Storage and Retrieval on Large Data Sets," in *Proceedings of the 15th Annual High Performance Computing Workshop (HPEC 2011)*, 2011.

[15] D. Lea, "Concurrenthashmap," gee.cs.oswego.edu/dl/classes/EDU/oswego/cs/dl/util/concurrent/ConcurrentHashMap.html, May 2013.

[16] M. M. Michael and M. L. Scott, "Simple, fast, and practical non-blocking and blocking concurrent queue algorithms," in *Proceedings of the fifteenth annual ACM symposium on Principles of distributed computing*, ser. PODC '96. New York, NY, USA: ACM, 1996, pp. 267–275. [Online]. Available: doi.acm.org/10.1145/248052.248106

[17] M. M. Michael, "Hazard Pointers: Safe Memory Reclamation for Lock-Free Objects," *IEEE Trans. Parallel Distrib. Syst.*, vol. 15, no. 6, pp. 491–504, 2004. [Online]. Available: www.research.ibm.com/people/m/michael/ieeetpds-2004.pdf

[18] Linux User's Manual, "mpstat," linuxcommand.org/man_pages/mpstat1.html, May 2013.

[19] P. Tsigas and Y. Zhang, "Integrating non-blocking synchronisation in parallel applications: performance advantages and methodologies," in *Proceedings of the 3rd international workshop on Software and performance*, ser. WOSP '02. New York, NY, USA: ACM, 2002, pp. 55–67. [Online]. Available: doi.acm.org/10.1145/584369.584378

[20] S. Woo, M. Ohara, E. Torrie, J. Singh, and A. Gupta, "The splash-2 programs: Characterization and methodological considerations," in *22nd International Symposium on Computer Architectures*, June 1995, pp. 24–36.

[21] D. R. O'Hallaron, "Spark98: Sparse matrix kernels for shared memory and message passing systems," Tech. Rep. CMU-CS-97-178, October 1997.

[22] B. Lim and A. Agarwal, "Reactive synchronization algorithms for multiprocessors," in *Proceedings of the Sixth International Conference on Architectural Support for Programming Languages and Operating Systems*, October 1994, pp. 25–35.

[23] M. M. Michael and M. L. Scott, "Nonblocking algorithms and preemption-safe locking on multiprogrammed shared memory multiprocessors," in *Journal of Parallel and Distributed Computing*, vol. 51, no. 1, 1998, pp. 1–26.

[24] T. L. Harris, "A pragmatic implementation of non-blocking linked-lists," in *Proceedings of the 15th International Conference on Distributed Computing*, ser. DISC '01. London, UK: Springer- Verlag, 2001, pp. 300–314.

[25] M. M. Michael, "High performance dynamic lock-free hash tables and list-based sets," in *SPAA '02: Proceedings of the fourteenth annual ACM symposium on Parallel algorithms and architectures*. New York, NY, USA: ACM Press, 2002, pp. 73–82.

[26] H. Sundell and P. Tsigas, "Lock-free deques and doubly linked lists," *J. Parallel Distrib. Comput.*, vol. 68, pp. 1008–1020, July 2008.

[27] Microsoft, "System.collections.concurrent namespace," Microsoft, 2011, .NET Framework 4. [Online]. Available: msdn.microsoft.com/en-us/library/system.collections.concurrent.aspx

[28] D. Hendler, N. Shavit, and L. Yerushalmi, "A scalable lock-free stack algorithm," *J. Parallel Distrib. Comput.*, vol. 70, pp. 1–12, January 2010.

[29] H. Gao, J. Groote, and W. Hesselink, "Almost wait-free resizable hashtables," in *Parallel and Distributed Processing Symposium, 2004. Proceedings. 18th International*, april 2004, p. 50.

[30] O. Shalev and N. Shavit, "Split-ordered lists: Lock-free extensible hash tables," in *PODC '03: Proceedings of the twenty-second annual symposium on Principles of distributed computing*. New York, NY, USA: ACM Press, 2003, pp. 102–111.

[31] K. Fraser, "Practical lock-freedom," in *Computer Laboratory, Cambridge Univ*, 2004.

[32] D. Dechev, P. Pirkelbauer, and B. Stroustrup, "Lock-free dynamically resizable arrays," in *Principles of Distributed Systems*, ser. Lecture Notes in Computer Science, M. Shvartsman, Ed. Springer Berlin / Heidelberg, 2006, vol. 4305, pp. 142–156. [Online]. Available: dx.doi.org/10.1007/11945529_11

DevOps Patterns to Scale Web Applications using Cloud Services

Daniel Cukier

Department of Computer Science - University of São Paulo / Elo7
danicuki@ime.usp.br

Abstract

Scaling a web applications can be easy for simple CRUD software running when you use Platform as a Service Clouds (PaaS). But if you need to deploy a complex software, with many components and a lot users, you will need have a mix of cloud services in PaaS, SaaS and IaaS layers. You will also need knowledge in architecture patterns to make all these software components communicate accordingly. In this article, we share our experience of using cloud services to scale a web application. We show usage examples of load balancing, session sharing, e-mail delivery, asynchronous processing, logs processing, monitoring, continuous deployment, realtime user monitoring (RUM). These are a mixture of development and system operations (DevOps) that improved our application availability, scalability and performance.

Categories and Subject Descriptors H.3.2 [*Information Systems*]: Information Storage and Retrieval—Information Storage; H.3.5 [*Information Systems*]: Information Storage and Retrieval—Online Information Services; D.2.11 [*Software*]: Programming Techniques—Software Architectures

Keywords APIs, AWS, cloud, Cloud computing, DevOps, Elo7, email, IaaS, Load balancing, PaaS, REST, S3, SaaS, scalability, scalable, Tomcat, Web services

1. Introduction

DevOps culture and practices are still in the early stages of adoption [24], but there are already some known DevOps principles that leads to successful websites [21]. While some of these principles are more related to the human side of software development, others are to the technical aspects of software solutions [22].

In this paper, we share the experience of applying DevOps in the context e-commerce startup Elo7. Sellers expose their products in our website. We are responsible for bringing buyers to these sellers. This category of e-commerce is known as Electronic Marketplace[20].

Today, in Elo7, there are more than 105 thousand sellers exposing more than 1.7 million products in the website. There are something around 8 million visits per month, 100 million requests per day in our web servers and more than 2 thousand product search requests every minute. The numbers are even more impressive when

SPLASH '13, October 26–31, 2013, Indianapolis, Indiana, USA.
Copyright © 2013 ACM ACM 978-1-4503-1995-9/13/10...$15.00

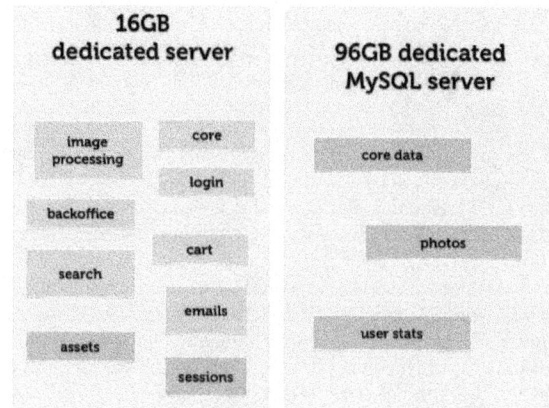

Figure 1. Our Old Architecture

we look at the past and see that they doubled every year (and we expect this growth for the next years as well).

At the beginning of 2011, we decided to move all our infrastructure to the cloud. In that time, we had a very simple and monolithic architecture. There were only two dedicated servers, one for the database and the other for the application. We did not have online backups, data redundancy, disaster recovery plan, hot deployment, or accurate monitoring. All our business data were basically stored in a single MySQL database (core, users statistics, product images, etc). User browser sessions were stored just in the application server session, as well as static application assets like images, javascripts, stylesheets, etc (Figure 1).

After one year of work, our architecture became a lot more decoupled, distributed, complex and robust. Today, we are running using more than 20 virtual servers. We use memcached servers to store user browser session data, Amazon S3 to store products photos and static assets. We also developed a brand new application, which uses a REST API. We deployed a Single Sign On solution to let users to log in once into our multiple applications. Our search data and service is detached from the web application server. We have a test and staging environment with continuous integration and deployment software. We've developed a new back-office application, to empower our customer support team with tools necessary for the daily operations (Figure 2).

These are some of many changes we have been doing. Today, Elo7 has a team of 14 software engineers. The teams are not divided based on people's skills. We do not have operations team. There

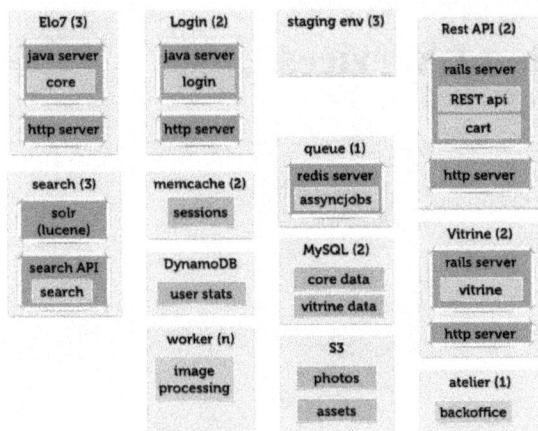

Figure 2. Elo7 new Architecture

are no *ops* guys. Actually, the *ops* **role** is performed by the same people who have the *dev* role, who also perform the *QA* role in this moment. Elo7 has a very flat hierarchy. Of course there are some specialists in each area, but normally everybody does a share of everything.

Given this context, now we would like to share some of the solutions we found trying to improve and scale our platform. Most of the solutions have some parts in the cloud, and they are profoundly based on the idea that running a successful online product is more than just writing lines of code. Furthermore, you must have knowledge of infrastructure, software architectures, product design and agile process management. In this paper we are focusing on infrastructure and software architecture patterns.

The following patterns are far from being a complete list of good DevOps solutions. They are part of something that can be transformed in a Pattern Language of DevOps practices to scale web applications using cloud services.

2. Store Big Files in Cloud Storages

2.1 Context

You have a web application that needs to deliver large files to users. These files can be documents, photos, videos, or other common binary formats.

2.2 Motivation

- Storing big quantities of large files in blob database columns can harm your database.
- Serve large data files from your own web servers consume a lot of resources.
- Large files consume a lot of disk space and you have to manage disk storage by yourself.
- Backing up your own file system can be very difficult and demand a lot of work.

2.3 Problem

Your users do not want to wait too long to download or upload files. They do not accept file corruption at all. When a file is confirmed to be uploaded, it must be safely stored and properly fetched whenever the user needs it. The user does not want to be bothered with "no disk space left" messages. Even if the number of users you serve

grows exponentially, you still must be able to have the same good level of service.

2.4 Solution

Serve large static data files using a cloud web storage like Amazon S3 or Google Cloud Storage.

2.5 Resulting Context/Consequences/Side-effects

When you use a cloud based storage, you do not need to worry with data loss. The cloud provider gives you the SLA (Service Level Agreement[1]) for that, and most of the available services have more than 99.999999999% of data durability. You won't need to worry about storage service availability either because the cloud providers SLA is at least 99.9%. Disk space will never be a problem, since storage cloud providers guarantee that you will always have enough space to store whatever you want. Storing a file is as simple as an REST API call.

2.6 Rationale

The facilities that cloud services provide today for file storage are huge. The available solutions have the following advantages:

- Service costs are very low and accessible, even for small startups
- Integration is easy and very well documented sources for doing it
- Scalable and always available by its nature

Of course, if you have a very small amount of static files and they do not grow over time, you do not need a cloud storage. For all other cases, you will have to use one, sooner or later, in your architecture.

In our company, we had a very good experience when we moved all product images from the MySQL database to Amazon S3. First of all, our database size shrunk from 100GB to 5GB. It was crashing every day and we needed a 96GB RAM server to keep the database running. After the migration, we could run our database server in a 8GB RAM server. Moreover, the server performance got a lot better. A lesson learned was: never use relational database to store large files.

We could put these files in a usual server disk, but we would certainly have problem with that since our image base grows very fast. Today we have more then 10TB of network transfer just for images, and there are more than 20 million image files. By using S3, it is also easy to process images (e.g. generate new thumbs) without impacting on website performance.

2.7 Known Uses

Today, we find more and more SaaS companies using cloud file storage to easily scale their service. It is well known that Dropbox uses S3 as it storage platform. Netflix also uses S3 to store and serve video streaming content to their users. A huge list of companies using cloud storage can be found in AWS website[5], which mentions also Airbnb (a community marketplace for people to list, discover, and book unique accommodations around the world), Mendeley (a free reference manager and academic social network).

2.8 Related Patterns / See also

If you are using your own filesystem to serve static photo files, you will need to migrate them to the cloud. If your image database is huge, this migration can take some time, and you will need to right

---

[1] The contract cloud providers have with customers, that guarantee their service will work properly. It is expected that the SLA is more than 99% in most services

software that guarantees that all photos were properly migrated. One easy way to do this is by enqueuing image copy jobs. For this, you can use the queue process system as described in Section 3.

2.9 Example

Amazon AWS provides libraries that make easy to use all of its services[18], including S3 storage system. Here is a simplified version of a Java class we created to facilitate photo transferring to S3:

```java
import java.io.*;
import java.util.*;
import com.amazon.s3.*;

public class S3Utils {
  static AWSAuthConnection amazon =
    new AWSAuthConnection("<KEY_ID>", "<ACCESS_KEY>");

  public static void createImage(String folder,
      String name, byte[] imageBytes) throws IOException {

    Map<String, List<String>> headers =
        new TreeMap<String, List<String>>();
    headers.put("Content-Type",
        Arrays.asList(new String[] { "image/jpeg" }));
    headers.put("x-amz-acl",
        Arrays.asList(new String[] { "public-read" }));

    S3Object object = new S3Object(imageBytes, null);
    amazon.put(folder, name + ".jpg", object, headers)
      .connection.getResponseMessage();
  }
}
```

3. Queue based solution to process asynchronous jobs

3.1 Context

Your web application needs to respond quickly to users, but some user requests need to perform tasks that takes some time to be processed. You want to respond to the user that you are performing these tasks and process them in background. You will publish the task results somewhere the user can fetch later and, sometimes, you will notify the user when the task is done.

3.2 Motivation

- You could perform these tasks asynchronously using *threads* inside your application server, but it does not scale in many platforms, since you would need ten thousands of concurrent threads.

- If a task fail, you would want to re-run them later. You would need to implement a re-schedule police by yourself.

- You need to monitor the tasks progress, e.g. monitoring threads inside a JVM cannot be trivial.

- If tasks consume a lot of infrastructure resources (e.g. CPU, memory), it can harm your web server performance.

- You want easily provision new infrastructure resources when you have a lot of background jobs to process.

3.3 Problem

When you run time consuming jobs synchronously, the end user have to wait for it to continue using your website. Moreover, the web server will lock a thread and a network socket for this user,

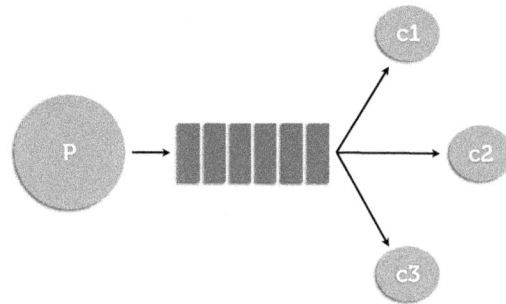

Figure 3. Producer-consumer queue

that could cause eventual unavailability problems. You could use native Java threads to run these jobs, but when they are many, it does not scale as well, since having many concurrent Java threads is limited. If one of these threads fails, you would have to manage this by re-creating it. This would overload your system, causing impact on end user response time.

3.4 Solution

Use a queue based solution to process your jobs. From you web application, you just need to create a new instance of the job in the queue server. You will have a server with the list of jobs to process; and consumer clients that will pop tasks from the server and process them (Figure 3).

The consumer has all the software needed to perform the tasks. You can create as many consumer instances you want. You can create an image of the consumer instance and replicate them using auto-scaling policies.

3.5 Resulting Context/Consequences/Side-effects

With a queue based solution for asynchronous processing, your users will not need to wait for long running tasks to be completed. With a faster response time, their navigation experience will be improved.

On your side, you will have a better control of all background processes. If one of the asynchronous jobs fails, it will be automatically re-processed. You will be able to see reports about queue sizes.

Queue processing workers can be easily configured to scale out, using auto scaling policies based on queue size or CPU usage. You can configure your infrastructure to create new instances to process queues that have accumulated too many jobs. The number of jobs can grow or have spikes, but your response time to users will not be affected by this. If long running jobs have any kind of bugs, they will not affect the user experience either.

3.6 Rationale

Our company has a partnership with Brazilian postal service. Sellers in our platform can send their craft products for at lower rates. To make this solution available to our customers, we had to integrate our system with the Brazilian postal service's. The integration was to generate a posting code, so that our users could get the discount on shipping. The problem was that the postal service did not have any web service for this integration. It only had a web site, where the user would need to fill manually many forms to get the posting code.

We created something we called HTML as a Service, using selenium-like software, that navigated the Post Office website and generated the posting code automatically. Obviously this process could take sometime to run (open Firefox browser, visit some page, fill some data, etc). In this case, a processing queue was the perfect solution. Our queue started with only this job. Today, we have more than 10 different asynchronous jobs running in the queue.

3.7 Known Uses

Well-known queue processing software include RabbitMQ, ActiveMQ, Resque and Sidekiq. The last two are based on Redis, a very light and stable key-value store database. They are both developed in Ruby but also support Java clients. RabbitMQ have support to Java, .NET and Erlang Client. ActiveMQ is an Apache project supporting integration with many programming languages besides Java such as PHP, Haskell, Ruby and Smalltalk.

3.8 Related Patterns/See also

When your platform is integrated with others through REST web services, sometimes you will not want that these third party services have influence over your end user experience. If you store customer pictures in cloud based storage (Section 2) or send notification emails using a cloud based email delivery service (Section 6), you want all these tasks to be processed by a queue, so your customer will not be affected. This pattern is very useful for all cases you need to integrate with a REST API and want to have a robust integration.

3.9 Example

In Elo7 website, when a user uploads a product photo, it must be processed to generate a optimized version of the image. Moreover, we also need to generate the image in different resolutions (e.g. thumbnails). Here is the code snipped in ruby using Sidekiq that we use to process images:

```
class ConvertImageWorker
  include Sidekiq::Worker
  sidekiq_options queue: :image_processing

  DIMENSIONS = %w(50x50 90x90 300x400 685x685)

  def perform uri_path
    @uri     = URI(URI.parse(URI.encode(uri_path)))
    download_to_temp
    DIMENSIONS.each{|dimension| process dimension}
  end
end
```

The "download_to_temp" method downloads the original image from the Internet to the local filesystem, then the "process" method call executes system calls to ImageMagick software, which converts the original file to a new one, with the new dimentions. The "process" method also uploads the new file to the cloud storage. The code example above uses the Sidekiq queue software. It is one of many open source queue solutions. You can also test Resque, RabbitMQ[27], Apache ActiveMQ[25].

4. Prefer PaaS over IaaS

4.1 Context

You have a complex application that has many architecture components. You need to deploy and maintain different pieces of software (e.g. Operational Systems, Relational Database Systems, NoSQL Databases, cache systems, firewalls, virtual machines, etc). Your companies core business is not technology, and you use infrastructure as a commodity, not as competitive differentiation.

4.2 Motivation

- It is very expensive to maintain your own low level infrastructure. Probably you will need to have staff dedicated to this task. Manage infrastructure will take you precious time. You'd rather to dedicate your engineers time to business related issues.

- You need to find professional software engineers with different skills to cover all the requirements of your systems architecture.

- Developing a highly available and scalable architecture is not trivial.

4.3 Problem

Maintaining operational system installations demands knowledge and time of your engineering team. If your engineers spend much time on these tasks, they will not give the proper attention to business related issues, that are higher priority for your customer.

4.4 Solution

Run your application using Platform as a Service (PaaS) instead of Infrastructure as a Service (IaaS)

4.5 Resulting Context/Consequences/Side-effects

When you choose to use PaaS over IaaS, you will not have to worry about a lot of aspects of the architecture, especially scalability and availability. Moreover, most of the time you won't need to monitor any low level infrastructure, focusing on monitoring just application related metrics. This is good to keep you focused on you business core.

On the other hand, when your PaaS provider has any infrastructure problem, your application will be affected out of your control. Besides this, PaaS platforms are usually more restrictive regarding to technologies or libraries that you can use. You will not be completely free to choose any software to run under PaaS. Because of security or performance issues, PaaS providers standardize what you can and what you cannot run in their platforms.

Another important aspect to consider when choosing PaaS over IaaS is cost. Obviously, the infrastructure cost still exists for PaaS providers. In the end, you will have to pay for the infrastructure plus the PaaS provider profit. Even when they have lower infrastructure costs compared to yours (because of their scale), sometimes using PaaS will be more expensive than having your own infrastructure. It is not easy to calculate the final cost of the whole solution, so you will have to spend some time to conclude what choice is better for your environment.

In conclusion, if you do not want to spend your time on infrastructure, nor your technical team has the sufficient knowledge about scalability, security, availability and other non-functional requirements of your products, you'd better choose PaaS (Table 1).

4.6 Rationale

In our company, we wrote a very small ruby application that serves to forward incoming phone calls to developers when they are working on weekends and the support team detects some anomalies in the website. We use the Twilio service as a Telecom provider. Twilio integrates very well with web services. We created a web service that has a small database with our developers phone numbers and the schedule of what developer is working on each weekend. We did not wanted to deploy this application in one of our servers and maintain it, so we deployed it on Heroku. Since the service has a very low usage, we do not even have to pay for it.

PaaS	IaaS
• Low knowledge about infrastructure • No knowledge about scalability or secutiry • Do not want to monitor infrastructure • You application does not have have any specific technology	• Want to have more control of the infrastructure • Infrastructure is core to your business • You have software components that are do not conform to PaaS providers standards

Table 1. When to use PaaS or IaaS

4.7 Known Uses

Web hosting providers are a good example of PaaS used by many companies, but examples are not restricted to them. Actually, most of providers do not offer an automatic scalable solution. But some of them do and are supposed to be very scalable and easy to use, like Heroku, CloudFoundry and Google App Engine to cite some. Examples of companies who use these services are Art.sy, ASICS, CloudApp, CareerBuilder, Gigya, Best Buy, Boo-box, etc [12][14].

4.8 Example

There are tens of examples of PaaS providers. To cite some: Amazon Web Services Elastic Beanstalk, AppFog, Cloud Foundry, Engine Yard, Force.com, Google App Engine, Heroku, Windows Azure, etc. Most of web hosting companies like Kings Host, Dreamhost, Locaweb, Linode, etc are also examples of PaaS providers. In some of them, deploying code to production is as easy as executing two or three command lines. In Heroku, you deploy an application with these commands:

```
$ heroku create
$ git push heroku master
```

Creating a Play Framework 2.0 Application and deploying to Cloud Foundry is as easy as:

```
$ play new hello-world
$ play dist
$ cf push --path=dist/hello-world-1.0-SNAPSHOT.zip
```

5. Load Balancing Application Server with memcached user sessions

5.1 Context

You run a web application over Tomcat or a similar Java web application server that needs to serve thousands of users. There is no single server that is capable to hold all your user requests. Moreover, you need to be fail proof for server outages. This means that if one of your server fails, you still need to deliver the service to your end user.

Your application is constantly changing. You need to deploy new features almost every day. You cannot stop your service while you deploy new code to your servers. There are a lot of user session information stored in the web servers and you do not want to lose them after server restarts. You could have all session information stored in cookies, but your application has a lot of legacy code, that could be difficult to change and refactor.

5.2 Motivation

• Tomcat hot deploy does not work perfectly. After a couple of hot deploys, the server usually crashes or goes to a memory leak state.

• Your will have an outage if you restart Tomcat and have only a single server.

• If you have multiple independent servers behind a Load Balancing with sticky sessions, users will lose their session data when their respective servers are out.

• Having a complete stateless application is not always possible, specially when there is a lot of legacy code.

• The cluster provided by Tomcat does an all-to-all replication which limits scalability.

• Deploying

5.3 Problem

If you do not use any persistence strategy for user session data, when your application server restarts, users lose their session information. Logins, cart items and other useful information are lost. You could store this information in cookies, but you have the downside of sending these cookies in all transactions degrades your application performance. Moreover, cookies are limited in size.

Even if you have a session storage strategy, if it is not memory based, you will fall into performance and availability issues as well. By using the Tomcat native cluster solution, you cannot scale out well, because all sessions are replicated to all servers. This means that the more users you have, the more memory you will need in each server. This obviously does not scale for millions of users.

More than the session data, you need to balance network traffic between Tomcat servers. You could do this by deploying a HAProxy or Nginx reverse proxy software over Linux instances in the cloud. But you would have to manage this server. Moreover, it would be a single point of failure in your architecture.

5.4 Solution

Use memcached session manager (MSM) software[13] to store user session data and replicate it between many tomcat servers instances. Put all servers behind a Load Balancing, preferring cloud based load balancing.

5.5 Resulting Context/Consequences/Side-effects

With many application servers running behind a Load Balancing and sharing sessions with memcached, your users will not lose their session after Tomcat restarts or fails. You will not have a single point of failure anymore. This solution handles also memcached nodes failures as well. You will be able to deploy new code in the middle of the day, with no website outage. If one of your servers fail, users will automatically be migrated to a new one, preserving all their session data.

The number of users can grow infinitely, you just need to create new Tomcat7 servers, put them behind a cloud based Load Balancing and configure the session manager to use the memcached session replication strategy.

5.6 Rationale

The Tomcat provided cluster solution DeltaManager does an all-to-all replication which limits scalability. The other Tomcat approach, BackupManager, does replication to another tomcat, that requires special configuration in the load balancer to support it. The memcached-session-manager supports non-sticky sessions (not supported by Delta/BackupManager) and provides session locking to handle concurrent requests served by different tomcats.

Moreover, DeltaManager/BackupManager use java serialization, memcached-session-manager comes with pluggable serialization strategies is based on kryo, one of the fastest serialization libs as of today (2013).

When using cloud based load balancing, you will not have to worry about availability and single point of failures. Your provider guarantees that the Load Balancer will always be there. Moreover, configuring these cloud based load balancers is as easy as navigating in the Internet. Providers offer easy-to-use user interfaces to configure load balancers.

5.7 Known Uses

Amazon Elastic Load Balancing is an example of cloud based Load Balancing. Rackspace also has its own solution for that cloud based load balancing. Some examples of companies that use these services are R7, Ci&T, Grupo El Comercio, Kununu, 36Boutiques, etc.

Tchibo, one of the biggest mail order companies and e-commerce shops in Germany, uses memcached session manager. So do GMX, one of the biggest mail service providers in germany.

5.8 Related Patterns

There are many different solutions for load balancing web servers [7]. The one cited in this paper is simple to implement, but very powerful to scale. Even if you have many servers load balanced, you still need to monitor their performance and constantly check log files in these servers. For that, we recommend taking a look at Logging (Section 7) and Real User Monitoring (Section 8)

5.9 Example

Configuring the Tomcat server to use memcached is simple. You just need to follow the setup and configuration instructions provided in the memcached session manager website[13]. Basically, you will need to have a memcached node created in your infrastructure and point your Tomcat to it with the following configuration in your context.xml file:

```
<Context>
...
 <Manager
 className=
 "de.javakaffee.web.msm.MemcachedBackupSessionManager"
 memcachedNodes="n1:host1:11211,n2:host2:11211"
 failoverNodes="n1"
 requestUriIgnorePattern=".*\.(ico|png|gif|jpg)$"
 />
</Context>
```

6. Email delivery

6.1 Context

Your application sends a lot of emails to users when they perform some specific tasks, specially transactional operations (e.g. new user registry, order confirm, payment received, etc). You need a guarantee that these emails are properly delivered, since they are an important part of your product user experience.

6.2 Motivation

- Having your own SMTP server for email delivery can cost a lot.
- If you want to have your own SMTP server, you will need a system administration with great knowledge about mail servers and the SMTP protocol.
- Programming SMTP client software is not as trivial as programming a REST Web Service client.

- Normally, when using your provider's SMTP server, you have a limit of how many emails you can send.
- You can't easily track wether the user received or clicked on a received message.
- It is not easy to guarantee that the sent email will not fall into customers SPAM box.

6.3 Problem

Email is still very important communication tool[19]. If you want to send relevant notifications to your users, it is expected that you send them emails with such notifications. If your users do not receive these emails properly, they will have their business impacted negatively, and so do your business. Moreover, if these emails do not have a clear and well presented message, users will not read them or will not be able to perform the actions you need them to do.

If you cannot track whether the users opened a given email, you cannot be sure they received the message, gave proper attention to it or received the message in their spam box.

6.4 Solution

Use cloud mail delivery services that provide easy-to-use REST API.

6.5 Resulting Context/Consequences/Side-effects

When using a cloud based email provider, you have more guarantees that your emails will be properly delivered. Furthermore, with the provider delivery reports, you will be able to understand your users behavior when receiving emails. You could, for example, re-schedule a message send if you notice that the user did not read the previous one.

Cloud based email services usually give you the possibility to reserve IP addresses for the message servers, so you can gain credibility of spam checker tools over time, avoiding your messages falling into spam boxes.

These services also provide email template tools to customize your messages to have the same user interface. This is a good way for your users to develop identification with your brand.

You will not need to maintain SMTP servers and have a highly available solution for them. Moreover, you don't need to worry about scalability either. If your demand on message sending grows, the only thing you will need to do is send more requests to the cloud email providers. They will deal with scalability for you.

Besides these advantages, you will certainly have cost reductions, because most of these services have very economic prices for email sending, varying from US$0.10/thousand emails (e.g. Amazon SES) to US$0.80/thousand emails (e.g. most expensive package in SendGrid)

6.6 Rationale

REST APIs are a very common way to integrate systems. Developers are very used to provide and consume REST APIs. There are a lot of libraries in most of programming languages that makes easy to integrate with REST Web Services with a few lines of code.

6.7 Known Uses

The known cloud services providing email delivery are:

- Amazon SES
- SendGrid
- Mandrill

Some examples of companies that use these services are Pinterest, FourSquare, Spotify, Pandora, Eyejot, Greplin, Talkbox, MediaNet/Prise, etc.

6.8 Related Patterns/See also

Even if you use a third party API for email message delivery, it is expected that these services have a variable response time. In the worst case, these services can be unavailable for some time during the day. You do not want to lose messages, nor want your end user to wait so long for a third party service. One way to avoid this problem is to use asynchronous processing, instead of calling the mail service API directly from your application. Enqueue the API call using a queue based service (Section 3). The queue will deal very well with availability, performance and stability issues presented by the third party service.

6.9 Example

SendGrid is one of the biggest email delivery service and provides both REST and SMTP. Here is the code example in Ruby of how to integrate your application with SendGrid mail delivery [23]:

```ruby
require 'mail'
Mail.defaults do
  delivery_method :smtp,
   { :address   => \smtp.sendgrid.net",
      :port       => 587,
     :domain     => \yourdomain.com",
     :user_name => \yourusername@domain.com",
     :password   => \yourPassword",
     :authentication => 'plain',
     :enable_starttls_auto => true }
end

mail = Mail.deliver do
  to 'yourRecipient@domain.com'
  from 'Your Name <name@domain.com>'
  subject 'This is the subject of your email'
  text_part do
    body 'Hello world in text'
  end
  html_part do
    content_type 'text/html; charset=UTF-8'
    body '<b>Hello world in HTML</b>'
  end
end
```

Besides mail delivery, SendGrid provides and whole set of reports about the API calls and your users behavior (email opening rates, bounce rates, delivery amount, etc).

Another easy to use service is Amazon SES. Here is a Scala code example using Amazon Simple Email Service (SES) module for Play 2.0 [8]:

```scala
Ses.sendEmail(Email(
  subject = "Test mail" ,
  from = EmailAddress("John", "john@john.com"),
  replyTo = None,
  recipients =
    List(Recipient(Message.RecipientType.TO,
        EmailAddress("Daniel",
                     "danicuki@ime.usp.br"))),
  text = "text",
  htmlText = "htmlText",
  attachments = Seq.empty))
```

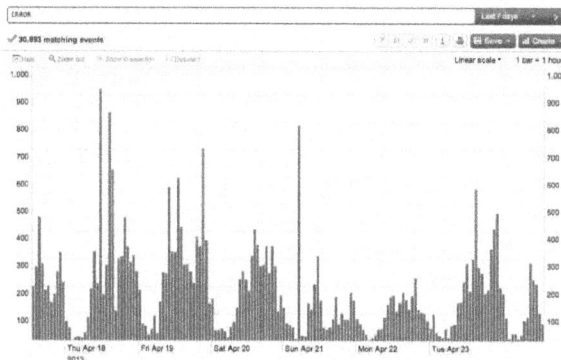

Figure 4. Errors/hours graph based on logs

7. Logging

7.1 Context

Your complex application is deployed among many servers. The application generates a lot of log files, each of them with thousands of lines. These logs have information that would be very useful for you. You don't want all members of your team logging into production servers to read logs. Moreover, you want all the logs to be consolidated in a single point. You want to find patterns in the logs, make custom searches on it and have graphs of the logs evolution along time.

7.2 Motivation

- Manually copying log files demands a lot of work
- If you will maintain all your logs, you need to take care of disk usage
- If your logs are huge, you will need to index them to make efficient searches

7.3 Problem

Your developers need to quickly check logs without losing time searching for what they need. If you have any anomaly in your system and log files indicate this, you do not want to take hours to identify the problem. You want to immediately be notified. Searching and indexing huge amount of big text files is not trivial. You do not want to develop a system for searching logs or aggregate logs from many servers into a single repository. Moreover, logs require a lot of infrastructure and you do not want to spend your time managing log files infrastructure.

7.4 Solution

Use a cloud based log service to consolidate your application logs.

7.5 Resulting Context/Consequences/Side-effects

By using a cloud based log service, you will have easy access to all your logs in a centralized system. You can make fast searches or filter your logs for specific terms. You can easily build graphs that shows trends about your system and problem hot spots (Figure 4). Moreover, you can create alerts based on thresholds (e.g. if errors log is greater than 10 items per minute for more then 5 minutes).

7.6 Rationale

In the first version of our architecture, we had to manage only two servers. When we needed to look at log files, we accessed these

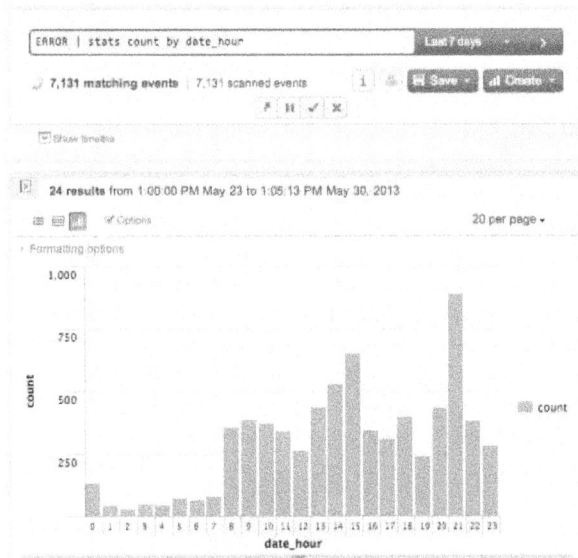

Figure 5. Graph based on logs

servers and "grep" the log files from the terminal or downloaded the files and filtered them locally. Our work with logs was limited by these simple command line operations. When log files started to rotate, we would have to join them back together when we wanted to search or group historical information.

Besides the limitation of working with raw files and bash command line tools [9], our infrastructure started to grow to more than twenty servers, each one with its own log files. Moreover, some servers would live for one or two days, and then be shut down because we did not need them anymore. We could not access log files in dead servers, so historical log data would be lost forever.

When we started to use cloud based log services, we solved all these problems. All servers now can send data to the centralized log service, and our developers can search for specific log entries from a easy-to-use web interface. And not only developers, but also product people and the customer support staff can have access to logs. Nobody needs to have access to production servers to watch relevant log information.

Sometime ago, we noticed that we were having problems with our database at specific moments of the day. We suspected that there were some background processes that were consuming a lot of database resources, but we did not know exactly at what times these processes were running. We decided to look in the log service. We did a simple query:

```
ERROR | stats count by date_hour
```

We noticed that exactly at 9pm the number of errors more than doubled compared to other hours. We found out the process that were causing these problems and optimized it to avoid the database errors (Figure 5).

7.7 Known Uses

Splunk is well known to be a very powerful log analyzing software. In the beginning, to use Splunk, you would need to install the server software in your own infrastructure and pay for a very expensive license. Today, Splunk company offers cloud based log server called Splunk Storm [15]. Other two known similar services are Loogly [3], Logentries [2] and Logstash [4].

Cloud based log services are being used to generate semi-structured time series database [6] or structured log analysis [16]. They can also be used as online visualization system for computing clusters [28].

7.8 Related Patterns/See also

Since logs are generated almost in the same time things are happening in your system, you can eventually use log graphs to monitor business metrics in realtime (Section 8). For example, in our application, when a user adds an item to a cart, we log "[INFO] item X added to cart". Our cloud based log can easily create a graph showing how many items are added to the cart per minute.

If you have a huge amount of background processing using queues, you want to monitor the progress of this processing. So, using cloud based log together with queue based processing is a good way to have control and metrics about your asynchronous jobs (see Section 3).

Some PaaS providers like Heroku offers cloud based log integration add-on. If you prefer running your application over PaaS instead of IaaS (Section 4), you can also have the benefit of using cloud based logs.

7.9 Example

Splunk [26] is a well known log aggregation software. You can use it installing a Splunk server by yourself, or by integrating with Splunk Storm Cloud Service. There are many ways to integrate your application with Splunk Storm. One of them is by configuring your rsyslogd service to send the log files to Splunk Storm [15] via UDP packages. All you need to do is to add these lines to your /etc/rsyslogd.conf file:

```
$ModLoad imfile
$InputFileName /var/log/nginx/error.log
$InputFileTag nginx:
$InputFileStateFile stat-nginx-error
$InputFileSeverity error
$InputRunFileMonitor

$InputFilePollingInterval 10

*.* @@logsX.splunkstorm.com:20000
```

8. Realtime User Monitoring (RUM)

8.1 Context

You have a complex web application being used by hundreds or thousands of users. Your need to deploy new features every day, so your system is constantly evolving. You need to make sure that every new deployment to production does not break the existing features or insert new bugs, specially for business critical operations.

Furthermore, you need to know how your users behave at specific times during the day (e.g. do people prefer buying online after lunch or after dinner). You want to know when you have an uncommon visiting pattern (e.g. why today at 10am people are adding more products to the cart then usual)

8.2 Motivation

- Complex big systems are difficult to have a 100% test coverage

- Even when having a complete test suite in staging environment, features can still fail in production environment, because creating a staging environment that is perfectly identical to production is cost prohibitive or to hard to do

8.3 Problem

Sometimes, when you deploy a bug into production, it takes a long time for you to realize that this bug is affecting your users. Moreover, you normally come to know that this bug is there from the users themselves, which is really bad for your business.

Unexpected behaviors sometimes demand you to provide extra infrastructure resources to keep your service available, without outages or performance degradation.

It is difficult to measure the impact of a marketing campaign in you business, because you cannot observe all your users behavior in realtime when the campaign is active.

8.4 Solution

Use a tool that provides you Realtime User Monitoring (RUM). Choose to monitor business metrics, instead of infrastructure resources metrics.

8.5 Resulting Context/Consequences/Side-effects

When our engineering team started to grow, the number of new features developed also increased. As we started to deploy new features every day, the chance of breaking and inserting bugs into production increased. We did not want our users to be the first to notice and report the bugs. When we started to look at *statsd* after every deploy, after no more than 5 minutes we could be able to notice any anomaly in the system for critical business operations like user logins, order submissions, user sign-ups and so on.

We started to notice web bots access peaks, user login behavior, new product creation patterns and so on. Now, we have a dashboard in the office showing these graphs. We monitor them throughout the day and we can take a quick action if someone notices any abnormal pattern in the graphs. Users are less affected by these problems and this impacts positively ii our business.

8.6 Rationale

System administrators are used to use monitoring tools like Nagios or Zabbix to monitor the servers infrastructure. This is essential for their operations, but not enough from the business point of view because sysadmins usually monitor CPU, memory, network and other low level metrics. When these low level metrics are healthy, it does not mean that the system is running properly. Sometimes a bug or an external factor can cause sales loss. This cannot be tracked by low-level infrastructure monitoring.

In the end, what means for your business is that your key business indicators are going well. That is, indicators like number of sales, successful transactions, new users registries, etc. This does not mean you will neglect your infrastructure monitoring. You should do both, since the look at your business in different granularities. Infrastructure monitoring is to Unit Tests what Real User Monitoring is to acceptance tests.

8.7 Known Uses

Etsy, well known craft marketplace platform, developed "statsd" as open source[11] software. They used it to monitor their own users. Etsy is a company that has as a principle to "Measure Anything, Measure Everything"[10].

Another very simple but powerful realtime monitoring tool is Pingdom, which is used by many famous e-commerce companies like eBay, Amazon, BestBuy, Shopify, as well as technology or communication companies like Apple, Microsoft, AT&T, etc. With Pingdom, you configure a specific service (by providing an URL) that you want to monitor. Their service is to "ping" the URL every minute and measure whether the server is responding, and also it response time. Then Pingdom records this data in graphs, so you can easily know your uptime, downtimes, and mean response time

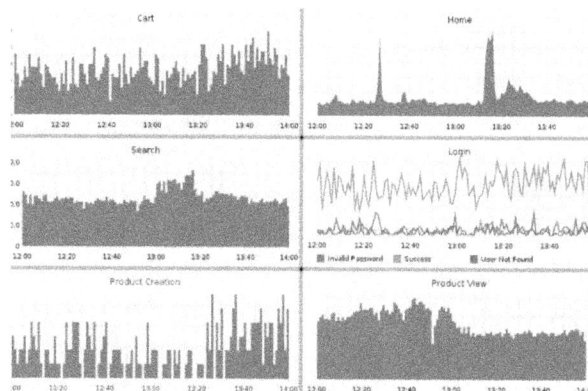

Figure 6. Realtime User Monitoring with statsd

over the month. You can use these metrics as a base for your SLA with your customers.

New Relic is a service that provides both low level infrastructure monitoring as well as end user realtime monitoring. With this tool, you can track your web server end-user response time, as well as ApDex

8.8 See also

It is possible to use log files to do real user monitoring. You can save all critical or important events from your system to log files, and then graph these log files events using a cloud based log system (See section 7).

8.9 Example

We had a good experience using statsd to monitor realtime user data. We run a e-commerce marketplace platform, so our monitoring dashboard has graphics "add to cart" actions, product searches, home visits, logins, product creation, etc (Figure 6). Statsd has client implementations for most of popular languages [17] and it has the additional advantage of using UDP to send packages, so network traffic for your monitoring does not compromise your application end user.

To deploy a statsd server, you need to install Node.js as well as a Graphing backend service like Graphite [1].

9. Conclusions

When an Internet startup starts to grow in number of users and key transactions, scaling the business online platform can be very challenging. In this article, we covered some practical aspects of how to scale an Internet application. By having a good Load Balancing strategy (Section 5) for your web servers, you guarantee that the website will remain available and with good performance. You do not want to spend time managing large amount of static files, therefore using a cloud based storage (Section 2) will facilitate your job.

Monitoring (Section 8) your business metrics is essential for the decision making process. You will also need to understand what is going on with your infrastructure, so you want to have easy access to log files data (Section 7).

Every Internet business must deliver emails in some part of its business. Have your emails in good hands by using cloud based email delivery service (Section 6). For time consuming jobs or asynchronous processing, use queues (Section 3) and you will have a very robust and scalable solution.

When infrastructure is not your strength and you want to focus your developers team on business related features, use PaaS instead of IaaS (Section 4).

This article is far from being a complete catalog of DevOps patterns to scale web applications using cloud services. But, using these solutions together is a good start point for scaling your online business. We did not cover very important topics like continuous delivery, deployment, configuration management, software quality process and tests. These are some issues that could complement this catalog to form a Pattern Language with DevOps practices to scale web based business using the cloud.

Acknowledgments

First, I would like to thank Luis Artola for his help on the shepherding process and Eduardo Guerra for his attention over this paper initial submission. All the engineers in Elo7 also deserve a big thanks, for helping me to develop and deploy rocking technologies.

References

[1] Graphite. Available at: http://graphite.wikidot.com/, 2013. Accessed in: 05/05/2013.

[2] Logentries. Available at: http://logentries.com/, 2013. Accessed in: 05/05/2013.

[3] Loggly. Available at: http://loggly.com/, 2013. Accessed in: 05/05/2013.

[4] Logstash. Available at: http://logstash.net/, 2013. Accessed in: 05/05/2013.

[5] Amazon.com. Amazon web services case studies. Available at: https://aws.amazon.com/solutions/case-studies/, 2013. Accessed in: 05/05/2013.

[6] L. Bitincka, A. Ganapathi, S. Sorkin, and S. Zhang. Optimizing data analysis with a semi-structured time series database. In *SLAML'10: Proceedings of the 2010 workshop on Managing systems via log analysis and machine learning techniques*, pages 7–7, 2010.

[7] T. Bourke. *Server load balancing*. O'Reilly Media, Incorporated, 2001.

[8] J. Brünemann. Amazon simple email service (ses) module for play 2.0. Available at: https://github.com/ Rhinofly/ play-libraries/, 2013. Accessed in: 05/05/2013.

[9] A. Chuvakin, K. Schmidt, and C. Phillips. *Logging and Log Management: The Authoritative Guide to Dealing with Syslog, Audit Logs, Events, Alerts and other IT 'Noise'*. Syngress, 2012.

[10] Etsy. Measure anything, measure everything. Available at: http://codeascraft.etsy.com/2011/02/15/measure-anything-measure-everything/, 2011. Accessed in: 05/05/2013.

[11] Etsy. Statsd. Available at: https://github.com/ etsy/statsd/, 2013. Accessed in: 05/05/2013.

[12] Google. Google cloud platform. Available at: https://cloud.google.com/customers/, 2013. Accessed in: 05/05/2013.

[13] M. Grotzke. memcached-session-manager: Tomcat high-availability clusters with memcached. Available at: https://code.google.com/p/memcached-session-manager/, 2013. Accessed in: 05/05/2013.

[14] Heroku. Heroku success. Available at: http://success.heroku.com/, 2013. Accessed in: 05/05/2013.

[15] S. Inc. Splunk storm user manual. Available at: http://docs.splunk.com/ Documentation/ Storm/, 2013. Accessed in: 05/05/2013.

[16] D. Jayathilake. Towards structured log analysis. In *Computer Science and Software Engineering (JCSSE), 2012 International Joint Conference on*, pages 259–264. IEEE, 2012.

[17] D. Josephsen. Changing the game, part 2. *;login:*, pages 55–59, Feb 2012.

[18] J. Murty. *Programming Amazon Web Services: S3, EC2, SQS, FPS, and SimpleDB*. O'Reilly Media, 2009.

[19] S. Radicati and Q. Hoang. Email statistics report, 2011-2015. *Retrieved May*, 25:2011, 2011.

[20] W. Raisch and G. Foreword By-Gartner. *The eMarketplace: Strategies for success in B2B eCommerce*. McGraw-Hill Professional, 2000.

[21] M. Sacks. Devops principles for successful web sites. In *Pro Website Development and Operations*, pages 1–14. Springer, 2012.

[22] M. Sacks. *Pro Website Development and Operations: Streamlining DevOps for large-scale websites*. Apress, 2012.

[23] SendGrid. Getting started with sendgrid. Available at: http://sendgrid.com/docs/, 2013. Accessed in: 05/05/2013.

[24] D. M. Smith. Hype cycle for cloud computing, 2011. *Gartner Inc., Stamford*, 2011.

[25] B. Snyder, D. Bosnanac, and R. Davies. *ActiveMQ in action*. Manning, 2011.

[26] J. Stearley, S. Corwell, and K. Lord. Bridging the gaps: joining information sources with splunk. In *Proceedings of the 2010 workshop on Managing systems via log analysis and machine learning techniques*, pages 8–8. USENIX Association, 2010.

[27] A. Videla and J. J. Williams. *RabbitMQ in action*. Manning, 2012.

[28] J. Xia, F. Wu, F. Guo, C. Xie, Z. Liu, and W. Chen. An online visualization system for streaming log data of computing clusters. *Tsinghua Science and Technology*, pages 196–205, April 2013.

Ultimate Architecture Enforcement

Custom checks enforced at code-commit time

Paulo Merson

Federal Court of Accounts (TCU)
Brasília, Brazil
pmerson@acm.org

Abstract

Creating a software architecture is a critical task in the development of software systems. However, the architecture discussed and carefully created is often not entirely followed in the implementation. Unless the architecture is communicated effectively to all developers, divergence between the intended architecture (created by the architect) and the actual architecture (found in the source code) tends to gradually increase. Static analysis tools, which are often used to check coding conventions and best practices, can help. However, the common use of static analysis tools for architecture enforcement has two limitations. One is the fact that design rules specific to a software architecture are not known and hence not enforced by the tool. The other limitation is more of a practical issue: static analysis tools are often integrated to the IDE or to a continuous integration environment; they report violations but the developers may choose to ignore them. This paper reports a successful experience where we addressed these two limitations for a large codebase comprising over 50 Java applications. Using a free open source tool called checkstyle and its Java API, we implemented custom checks for design constraints specified by the architecture of our software systems. In addition, we created a script that executes automatically on the Subversion software configuration management server *prior* to any code commit operation. This script runs the custom checks and denies the commit operation in case a violation is found. When that happens, the developer gets a clear error message explaining the problem. The architecture team is also notified and can proactively contact the developer to address any lack of understanding of the architecture. This experience report provides technical details of our architecture enforcement approach and recommendations to employ this or similar solutions more effectively.

Categories and Subject Descriptors D.2.11 Software Architectures; D.2.9 Management: software quality assurance.

Keywords software architecture; architecture conformance; architecture enforcement; static analysis; Java; checkstyle.

1. Introduction

Creating a software architecture is a critical task in the development of software systems because the structures in the design will dictate whether the system will exhibit good modifiability, performance, interoperability, and other qualities. Software architectures are created every day in IT departments and software companies around the world based on previous experience of the architects as well as knowledge codified as architecture patterns, design patterns, and tactics. These architectures are often discussed and reviewed with the stakeholders. Incrementally, the software architecture is handed to developers who translate the design diagrams into code. Once in place, the code becomes the main artifact of a software project ("code is king!").

In software projects of reasonable size, several people do write code. Often times, these people are geographically distributed. It's also common for new developers to join software projects when the software system is partially implemented and/or rolled out. The newcomers are readily assigned features to implement, or bugs to fix. Many times they write code before they understand the overall architecture. Developers of large software systems are like the XV century explorers who tried to "connect", say, Portugal to India, but didn't have the big picture (of Earth!) and ended up finding unexpected pathways, often not optimal.

When software development and maintenance involves several developers and spans months or years, a common phenomenon can happen: the *actual* architecture found in the source code diverges from the *intended* architecture, which was the diligent work of the architects. This problem, often introduced involuntarily by developers who write code non conformant to the architecture, is influenced by different factors:

- whether the architecture documentation is effectively communicated to developers;

- turnover among developers, since newcomers may be required to write code before they have a good understanding of the architecture;

- pressure to quickly fix bugs and deliver new features, which leads developers to take shortcuts in the code disregarding the architecture;

- size of the system (the larger the codebase, the more likely developers don't see the big picture);

- presence of sub-teams of developers, possibly outsourced; and

- degree of accountability for creating code that violates the design constraints.

The disconnect between the code and the intended architecture may also occur due to changes in the architecture itself. Long after the implementation is created, the intended architecture may be modified to tend to new requirements and technology innovations. This evolution of the architecture is natural and welcomed. However, in many cases refactoring the old code in order to comply with the new design is too expensive. The once-compliant old code is left as is and now it doesn't conform to the (new) architecture anymore.

When the discrepancy between the architecture and the source code grows uncontrolled, problems arise. First off, maintainability is impaired. The introduction of code dependencies (shortcuts) not permitted by the architecture makes the code brittle, hard to understand and to change. But consequences can go beyond that. Design decisions in the intended architecture aimed at achieving certain qualities, such as reliability, security, modifiability, performance, portability, and interoperability. If the code departs from that architecture, these qualities can be negatively affected.

This paper describes our experience creating an approach based on static analysis to watchfully check that source code is only added to the codebase if it follows the design rules and other constraints defined in the software architecture. Section 2 will discuss how to address the architecture conformance challenge in general. Section 3 briefly describes the environment where this experience took place. Section 4 is a quick introduction to the checkstyle tool and how to create custom checks using the checkstyle Java API. Section 5 gives an overview of the types of custom checks created so far in our organization. Section 6 describes how we made architecture conformance an automatically enforced requirement for source code added to our subversion repository. Section 7 describes the results and lessons learned in this experience. Section 8 provides some conclusions and final thoughts, including a discussion of the limitations of the approach.

2. How to avoid code and architecture disparity

To keep the source code compliant with the software architecture over time, there are two important things to be done: one is to properly communicate the architecture to the developers, and the other is to actively check that the source code follows the intended design.

2.1 Communicating the architecture to stakeholders

The architecture of a software system is the set of structures needed to reason about the system, which comprise software elements, relations among them, and properties of both [2]. Describing and communicating the software architecture to all stakeholders is an encumbering task. It involves: documenting the different structures as multiple views; recording information needed by the stakeholders about the software elements and their relations; describing the relevant software interfaces; creating structural design diagrams and complementing them with behavior documentation, such as UML sequence diagrams and state-machine diagrams; recording the rationale for the design decisions; and keeping the documentation up-to-date.

Creating effective software architecture documentation is important not only to avoid that developers create code that doesn't follow the architecture. The architecture documentation is the blueprints for creating the code, is the primary indicator of the quality attributes of the system (e.g., performance, availability, modifiability), and guides incremental development plans, allocation of tasks, procurement of software and hardware. However, the focus of this paper is not on documenting and communicating the architecture to developers—for that we refer the reader to the

work of Paul Clements and colleagues [2]. This paper will explore automated architecture conformance analysis, introduced next.

2.2 Automated architecture conformance analysis

One can manually review the code to check that it conforms to the intended architecture. Indeed, architecture conformance can be one of the goals of code reviews. However, manual reviews are time consuming. Also, the reviewer is not always well versed in the architecture, and the architect is not always available to participate in code reviews. Thus, architecture conformance is more often verified using automated tools.

The tools commonly used in industry for architecture enforcement employ static program analysis. Examples include: Checkstyle, FindBugs, Fortify, JDepend, Lattix, Lint, NDepend, PMD, Sonar, and Understand [12]. Some tools give you a reverse-engineered depiction of the actual architecture found in the code, so that you can visually compare it with the intended architecture. In other tools you can even indicate that a dependency between modules A and B is not allowed, and the tool will let you know whenever that dependency rule is violated.

Adding static analysis to continuous integration is important to ensure the quality of the code remains at a good level, or at least to ensure it is not deteriorating. However, the common practice of continuous conformance verification has two limitations.

One limitation of static analysis as performed in many organizations is that it is restricted to the checks available out-of-the-box in the static analysis tools. Although the tools usually give you the ability to turn on/off, configure thresholds, and change the severity of each check, these built-in checks are always generic. They are oblivious to the architecture of your software system; they are unaware of the many design constraints, infrastructure services, and idiosyncrasies specific to your software projects.

The other limitation is the fact that violations may find their way into the codebase despite the finger pointing of the tools. Sometimes the number of violations creeps up to hundreds or thousands; sometimes there is no accountability for violations added to the codebase; sometimes management does not want to allocate time and effort to fix the violations ("after all, addressing these violations doesn't represent progress towards delivering functionality to the customers"). As a result, violations tend to be ignored. This problem can be attenuated when the static analysis tool offers a classification of the violations. In such cases, the top priority or critical violations are not acceptable, but the lower priority ones may remain unheeded.

The approach presented in this paper solves these two limitations.

3. Context of our development organization

The experience described in this paper took place at the IT department of the Brazilian Federal Court of Accounts (TCU). TCU has over 50 Java EE applications and several shared libraries developed in house. The Java codebase consists of approximately 2.2 million physical LOC spread across 15 thousand source files.

The common denominator platform for all these applications is a cluster of JBoss EAP application servers and an Oracle database. Yet, some applications access different small data repositories and interact with other software systems, both internal and external to the organization.

To a great extent, these applications are built using the same frameworks and libraries, have nearly the same quality attribute requirements, offer similar data-centric functionality, and share the same runtime environment. Because of this similarity, reference architectures [4] have been established over the years. Current reference architectures prescribe a layered architecture, MVC and other architectural patterns, and constrained use of a few specific frameworks. Any application may specialize and deviate from the reference architecture if necessary, but otherwise design constraints are prescribed to all Java applications.

The development team consists of 57 full-time employees. Their development skills and experience vary tremendously, since the recruiting process does not require previous experience with Java or any specific technology. Part of the development team, there are also 24 interns working part-time. The internship program takes computer science undergraduate students for a period of six months to two years. The development work force will soon grow, since a contract is about to be signed for outsourcing some of the software development effort.

3.1 Architecture conformance undertaking

The small group within the software development organization responsible for the reference architectures has always strived to see the architecture being followed in the implementation of the various applications. This group has spent significant effort to document the reference software architectures and to communicate them to all developers, including new hires and interns, through presentations and one-on-one coaching.

In the past, this group resorted to source code lexical searches based on regular expressions and code reviews to spot architecture conformance problems. Success was very limited. In 2011, we set out to create a mechanism based on static analysis tools to enforce our own architecture constraints and coding guidelines. We evaluated four different static analysis tools for Java and chose checkstyle for its Java-based API for creating custom checks. This choice has showed to produce effective results at a low cost. The remaining of this paper describes some technical details, results of this experience, and lessons learned.

4. Checkstyle API

Checkstyle is a free open-source static analysis tool for Java [5]. Like other tools, out of the box it can analyze the source code for coding conventions and numerous programming best practices. Unlike most tools though, Checkstyle offers a Java API that allows the implementation of custom code analyses.

A *check* is a Java class that is invoked when Checkstyle is parsing a Java file. The check is given that file's AST and can inspect each token and look for constructs that represent a violation of some sort. Using the Checkstyle API, we can create *custom checks*. For example, let's say your architecture uses data access objects (DAO) [6] to access the database. Suppose in your architecture, a class could be recognized as a DAO class by the "Dao" prefix—other common options would be extending an abstract Dao class, or using a specific annotation, such as @Dao or @Repository. Now suppose your architecture dictates that only code in the "service" layer can use DAO classes, and classes in the service layer belong to a package namespace com.mycompany.service.*. **Figure 1** shows the code for the custom check that enforces that rule.

Checkstyle uses the Visitor design pattern [7] to invoke the checks while traversing a Java program AST. Each check is a visitor that has a single entry point method called visitToken. This method takes as argument the AST where the root is the token just parsed in the Java program. The visitToken method typically has an if-else-if or switch-case construct to identify what type of token it received and execute the part of the analysis logic that applies to that type of token. As an optimization, a check can declare which types of tokens it's interested in. The example in **Figure 1** is only interested in package definitions (Token-Types.PACKAGE_DEF) and references to identifiers (Token-Types.IDENT), so checkstyle only calls visitToken on this check when it parses tokens of these types.

```
/**
 * Classes prefixed by Dao can't be used
 * outside com.mycompany.mysystem.service.*
 */
public classCheckNonServiceUsesDao extends Check {
  private boolean inServiceLayer;
  @Override
  public int[] getDefaultTokens() {
    return new int[] {TokenTypes.PACKAGE_DEF, TokenTypes.IDENT};
  }
  @Override
  public void visitToken(DetailAST aAST) {
    if (aAST.getType() == TokenTypes.PACKAGE_DEF) {
      inServiceLayer = false;
      String packageName = fullyQualifiedPackage(aAST);
      if (packageName != null &&
          packageName.startsWith("com.mycompany.mysystem.service")) {
        inServiceLayer = true;
      }
    } else if (aAST.getType() == TokenTypes.IDENT && !inServiceLayer) {
      if (aAST.getText().startsWith("Dao")) {
        log(aAST.getLineNo(),
          "Classes outside the service layer can't call Dao classes");
      }
    }
  }
}
```

Figure 1. Example of a checkstyle custom check.

The checkstyle API provides several methods used in the implementation of custom checks, including:

- findFirstToken: for the current AST node, returns the first child (in pre-order) of a given token type.
- getNextSibling, getPreviousSibling, getFirstChild: allow navigation around the AST.
- branchCointains: returns true if the AST rooted at the current node contains a node of a given token type.

We have enhanced the API by creating a few other methods, which have been submitted as contributions to the checkstyle sourceforge project [5]. Two of the API methods we created are:

- findFirstAstOfType: returns the first node (in pre-order) within an AST of a given token type. Different from findFirstToken, this method searches the root node and the entire tree, not only the direct children.
- findAllAstsOfType: returns the list of all nodes of a given token type found within a given AST traversed in pre-order.

A key benefit of checkstyle over other approaches is that the custom analysis is implemented using Java—there is no need to learn another language or syntax for specifying an analysis rule. Another benefit is that checkstyle gives you the flexibility to inspect any syntactic element of a Java program, even comments. Other approaches used for architecture conformance analysis, such as AOP [8], are limited to inspecting class definitions, method definitions, method calls, and other specific points in a Java program.

5. Custom checks at TCU

We have created 40 checkstyle custom checks so far. The checks are divided into three categories: architecture conformance, coding guidelines, security constraints.

5.1 Architecture conformance checks

We have created 19 custom checks that verify design constraints defined in the reference architectures. These checks enforce: the layered architecture; specific class inheritance or interface realization that is required from certain types of modules; proper placement of business logic, data access logic, UI logic; proper use of infrastructure and "util" software elements; naming of certain types of modules as defined in the architecture; and disallowed dependencies in general.

The custom check in **Figure 1** is an example of architecture conformance check that can help to enforce a layered architecture, such as the one seen in **Figure 2**. That custom check along with similar checks can make sure usage dependencies that violate the design (shown by dashed lines in **Figure 2**) are not created. We have written several custom checks like that.

Another example of architecture conformance check is related to class inheritance. For instance, in our reference architecture, a design constraint dictates that stateless session beans [1] must be a subclass of a given abstract class. This abstract super class transparently introduces exception handling, auditing, and transaction management services in all subclasses. Thus, we created a custom check that identifies that the analyzed class is a stateless session bean and makes sure that that class is a subclass of the aforementioned abstract class.

5.2 Coding guideline checks

We created other 12 custom checks that enforce coding guidelines that are specific to our organization. These guidelines span vari-

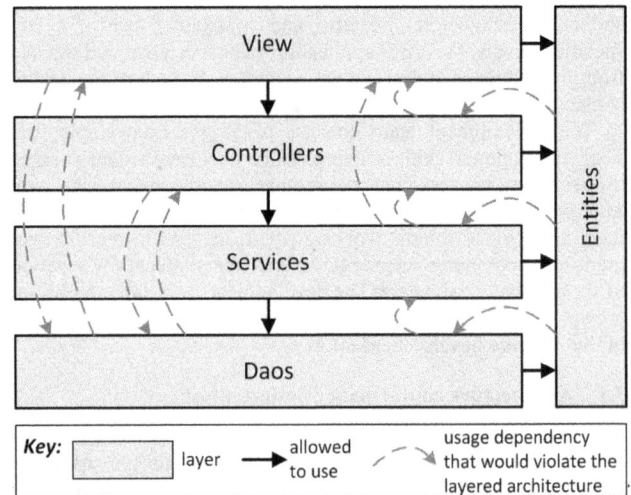

Figure 2. Layered architecture showing dependencies that could be enforced by architecture conformance checks.

ous aspects of Java programming, including: exception handling, resource release to avoid resource leaks, proper placement of JUnit tests, thread programming traps.

An example of coding guideline that we enforce using a custom check is that threads cannot work on previously created transactional objects. In our reference architecture, we identify by inheritance, Java annotation or package namespace all the objects that carry a transactional context. Some applications employ the "introduce concurrency" tactic [3] by spawning threads for background processing. We created a custom check that makes sure the constructor of a thread does not receive as a parameter an object that holds transactional context. This check prevents two threads from operating on the same transaction and causing a runtime error.

5.3 Application security checks

A couple of years ago we had the opportunity to analyze part of our codebase using a static analysis tool called Fortify, which specializes in detecting security vulnerabilities in application programs. Although Fortify is very useful to improve application security, it has the limitations discussed in Section 2.2—the security checks the tool applies are generic and unaware of specific elements in our architecture. So we decided to implement custom checks that deal with security vulnerabilities. Some are generic and others target elements of our home-grown software infrastructure that are security sensitive.

We developed 9 custom checks that enforce security constraints in Java applications. These checks prevent vulnerabilities such as: SQL injection in JDBC and Hibernate programming, execution of external programs on Java web applications, hardcoded passwords, and security critical classes or methods that can be subclassed or overridden.

6. Next step: prevent new violations

Section 2.2 discusses two limitations of the common use of static analysis tools to automate conformance checks. The second limitation is that violations reported by automated checks can be ignored by developers, and unfortunately often they are. We solved this limitation in our organization with a mechanism that runs the checks when the developer attempts to commit a source file to the code repository. This mechanism denies the operation if there are violations.

A Subversion (svn) hook is a program that can be configured in the subversion repository [13]. The hook is automatically invoked when there is a commit operation. We created a *pre-commit hook* that runs our checkstyle custom checks on the Java source files that are the subject of the commit operation. If any of the checks detects a violation, the commit operation fails and the user gets an error message indicating the source file, line number, and a description of the problem.

The svn pre-commit hook does not allow developers to ignore violations. The violations are either fixed or out of the codebase.

6.1 Notification of violations

As soon as the svn hook was in place, developers began to get error messages upon svn commit attempts. We realized we needed to keep track of these failed code commit attempts, not only to have a sense of the number of attempts, but more important to explain the enforced rule and indicate a solution to the developers.

We configured the svn hook to send an email to the architecture team whenever a developer tries to commit source code that violates the architecture. This email message allows the architecture team to pro-actively contact the developer and help address the issue. **Figure 3** shows the overall flow that takes place when a code commit attempt violates a custom check. (The diagram is a simplification, since the loop is executed for each custom check, not only one.)

7. Results and lessons learned

There are two general approaches that architecture teams follow to try to enforce the architecture. One is to act as the "architecture police" to make sure developers are following the published architecture. The other is to mentor and work closely with developers to make sure they understand and naturally follow the architec-

ture. It may look like automated checks that bar source-code commit attempts because of violations fall within the first approach. In our experience, it's the opposite. The email notifications mentioned in Section 6.1 are the answer. They expose lack of understanding of the architecture to which we can respond immediately. We contact the developer to further explain why and how does his/her code violate the architecture. These email messages have been incredibly effective in raising awareness of the architecture and coding best practices.

Today the custom checks that execute prior to any svn commit operation quite frequently deny the introduction of violations in our Java codebase. More precisely, in a period of 12 months more than 400 commit attempts resulted in an error message to the code committer due to a custom check violation. Based on the specific violation in these attempts, the architecture team has sent approximately 40 email messages to developers with further clarification; in other instances a quick chat clarified matters. A couple of times this personal follow-up with the code committer ended up in revisions to the custom checks. However, the vast majority of cases resulted in the code being fixed by the developer.

The experience has been successful. At this point, we can quickly develop a custom check when a new design constraint is devised. There were some hurdles we had to overcome that could have been avoided. Following are some recommendations based on our experience.

7.1 Recommendations

In these two years working with custom checks, we adopted some practices to make the most out of the checks. Probably the most important guideline is to adopt an architecturally-evident coding style [9], which is translated into the first three recommendations in the list.

1. Use naming conventions that define different prefix or suffix for different types of classes and interfaces. This idea is quite

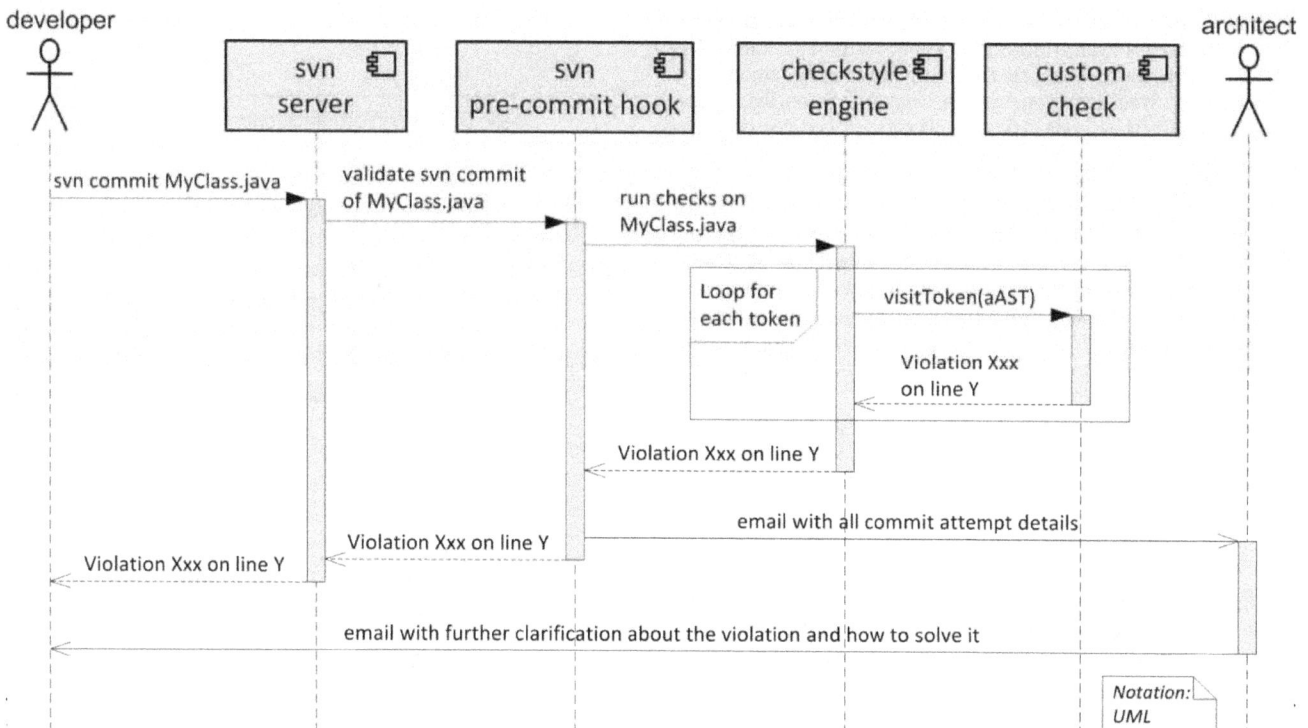

Figure 3. UML sequence diagram of a code commit attempt that has a violation and architect follow up email.

common in Java and other development platforms. For example, exception classes in Java by convention have suffix "Exception", the controller classes in applications crated with the Spring MVC framework usually use suffix "Controller".

2. When a naming convention that establishes a prefix or suffix for classes is not adequate for some reason, define a convention for the package namespace. For example, if not all classes in the presentation layer can be identified by strict name prefixes or suffixes, we could define that all of them should be in a package namespace that ends in "presentation".

3. If a naming convention is not adequate for packages either, define Java annotations that qualify the classes. For example, we could identify the classes that represent data entities mapped to relational database tables because they necessarily have the @Entity annotation.

4. Once established, divulge the existence of code verification at commit time to all developers, and then on to any newcomers. Indicate the benefits and try to get their buy-in. Make sure to open space for suggestions. Some of the checks we created were suggested by application developers.

5. Create and nourish the unit tests for your custom checks, and enhance them with new code idioms found along the way.

6. Create a mechanism for easily configuring exceptions. It should give you the ability to configure projects, packages or classes over which the custom checks should not be run.

7. Keep track of the number of violations found for each check. When you first implement it, write down the date and the total number of violations. If you are able to fix all violations, write down another checkpoint with the date that total number came down to zero. If you were not able to fix all violations, whenever you run the check over the entire codebase, take note of the number of violations, so you can assess if that number is under control. If you use the Sonar platform, you can use the time machine mechanism [10].

8. Make sure software architects understand the potential of the custom checks even if they don't understand the technical details. Then try to establish the following mindset among the architects: whenever you make a design decision that is reflected in the Java code, ask yourself whether that decision can be enforced via a custom check, and what conventions should be defined to make the custom check feasible. For example, suppose some business classes in your application need to support simple "undo" on operations that change state. The architect decides to use the Memento design pattern [7] to implement undo. Keeping in mind that a custom check can enforce the proper use of Memento, the architect just needs to define a means to identify those business classes. So, an extra decision could be that business classes that require undo must have annotation @UndoEnabled.

9. In addition to custom checks that can be executed at code commit time, enable the static analysis tool built-in checks in the developers IDE and/or in the continuous integration environment.

7.2 Process followed for each check

We have created custom checks that analyze the code for various kinds of rules. In common, all checks went through the same work process, which is described below and summarized in **Figure 4**:

1. The first step is to envision the rule and express it in terms of syntactic elements in the Java code.

2. Next the corresponding custom check is implemented using the checkstyle Java API.

3. The custom check is then executed against the entire codebase to generate an html report showing all violations. Sometimes there's only a handful, sometimes there are thousands of them. In this step we often find false positives that take us back to steps 1 and 2, that is, we refine the rule statement and its implementation as a custom check.

4. The most laborious step is to manually fix the violations in the codebase. In fact, this step involves a go/no-go decision with respect to fixing the violations. In some situations, that task is not feasible. The ideal situation is when we can take the time to fix the violations and move on to the next step.

5. Once the number of code violations for a particular custom check is down to zero (or a small number of violations in legacy code), the check is enabled in the svn pre-commit hook. As described in Section 6, the pre-commit hook will ensure that new violations will not be added to the codebase from then on.

6. Even when we can't fix all the violations, the check can still be enabled in the pre-commit hook. In this case, we either enable it only for "svn add" operations (new code) or we adapt the check to ignore the few modules with violations (they're considered exceptions to the rule).

The downside of a no-go decision for fixing the violations is step 4 is that the rule cannot be added to the pre-commit hook. Otherwise, developers will not be able to make any changes to classes that contain violations. Violations that stay in the codebase tend to creep up due to copy and paste programming [11]. To minimize this propagation of violations, our pre-commit hook treats *svn add* and *svn update* operations differently. Thus, rules that were not fixed in the overall codebase are still enforced for svn add operations. However, many developers quickly found out a trick to bypass the svn add conformance check. I will let it to the reader to find out what that trick is.

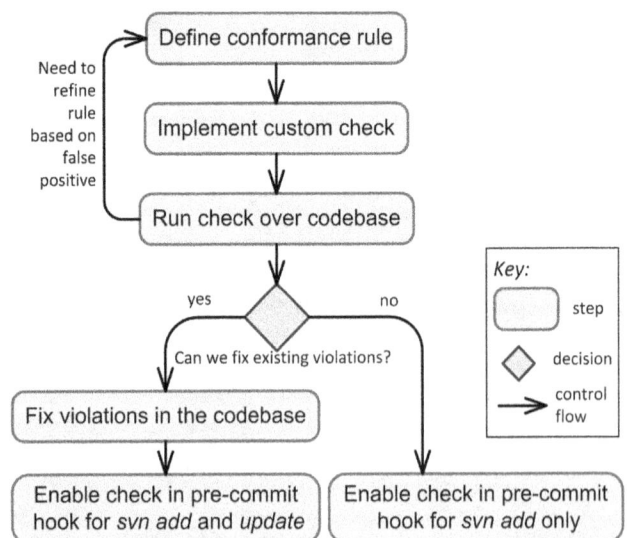

Figure 4. Process followed for defining, implementing and enabling a custom check.

8. Conclusions

The codebase of an active software project is like a shapeless, living entity that is subject to frequent, localized modifications and additions. Lack of conformance between the as-designed architecture and the as-built architecture can easily happen and indeed is a problem faced by many software development teams. For many years, I've studied and tried out various solutions to this problem. This paper described the first solution I see that is simple to implement, scales up to all codebase, allows for continuous verification, and is powerful and flexible. At TCU we have tackled the problem with static analysis of the code. To verify some design constraints in the code, a simple lexical analysis would suffice. For other constraints, contextual information (semantic information) is needed. We have created custom checks using the checkstyle tool, which offers a Java API that uses the Visitor design pattern and gives us the ability to create AST-based verifications with contextual information.

Checkstyle checks also have limitations. The most inconvenient one is that a check logic only sees the tokens within the source file being analyzed. A check can't verify, for example, that a given class is a grandchild of a specific class—it can only see the immediate superclass because of the `extends` keyword present in the type declaration. (One can use introspection to overcome this particular limitation, but that alternative incurs other limitations.) Checkstyle in particular is limited to parsing Java artifacts, so custom checks cannot verify design and implementation constraints on xhtml, jsp, wsdl, xsd, or any other non Java artifacts. Another limitation of checkstyle checks and static analysis in general is that they cannot detect patterns of interaction that rely on polymorphism, late binding, or introspection. For dynamic interactions, we would need a profiling tool, code coverage tool, or worse, code instrumentation. However, dynamic analysis is not suitable for continuous verification because the environment where the verification takes place can be set up to read source files (static analysis), but typically does not have all the infrastructure pieces required to *execute* the programs.

The pairing of checkstyle checks with the pre-commit svn hook was an important addition to the solution. The pre-commit hook not only curbs violations in the source code repository, but also (discreetly) names the developers who need further clarification about architecture or implementation rules.

In addition to architecture enforcement, we have successfully used checkstyle checks to enforce proper exception handling, use of design patterns, security guidelines for application development, and other good Java development practices. I invite the reader who works with Java development to try out the approach described in this paper.

Acknowledgments

I want to thank Jefferson da Silva and Frederico Ferreira for invaluable help in exploring the checkstyle API, implementing many different custom checks, and—the hardest task—fixing violations in the code by the thousands. I'm also grateful to Marcelo Pacote and Fabiana Ruas for the continuous support to this project.

References

[1] *Enterprise JavaBeans 3.1, Final Release*. Sun Microsystems, November 2009.

[2] Clements, P., F. Bachmann, L. Bass, D. Garlan, J. Ivers, R. Little, P. Merson, R. Nord, and J. Stafford. *Documenting Software Architectures: Views and Beyond, Second Edition*. Addison-Wesley, 2010.

[3] Bass, L., P. Clements, R. Kazman. *Software Architecture in Practice, Third Edition*. Addison-Wesley, 2013.

[4] Garland, J., and R. Anthony. *Large-Scale Software Architecture: A Practical Guide Using UML*. John Wiley & Sons, 2003.

[5] Checkstyle project: http://checkstyle.sourceforge.net/

[6] Fowler, M. *Patterns of Enterprise Application Architecture*. Addison-Wesley, November 2002.

[7] Gamma, E., R. Helm, R. Johnson, and J. Vlissides. *Design Patterns: Elements of Reusable Object-Oriented Software*. Addison-Wesley, November 1994.

[8] Merson, P. *Using Aspect-Oriented Programming to Enforce Architecture*. Software Engineering Institute, CMU/SEI-2007-TN-019, September 2007.

[9] Fairbanks, G. *Just Enough Software Architecture*. Marshall & Brainerd, 2010.

[10] Mallet, F. "Sonar Time Machine: replaying the past". Blog post available at www.sonarsource.org/sonar-time-machine-replaying-the-past. January 2009.

[11] "Copy and Paste Programming". Available at: http://c2.com/cgi/wiki?CopyAndPasteProgramming

[12] "List of tools for static code analysis". Available at: http://en.wikipedia.org/wiki/List_of_tools_for_static_code_analysis.

[13] Collins-Sussman, B., B. Fitzpatrick, and C. Pilato. "Version Control with Subversion". Available at: http://svnbook.red-bean.com/en/1.7/svn.reposadmin.create.html#svn.reposadmin.create.hooks.

Sensors, Actuators and Services - A Distributed Approach

Tiago Boldt Sousa

INESC TEC (formerly INESC Porto)
Department of Informatics Engineering, Faculty of Engineering, University of Porto
tiagoboldt@gmail.com

Abstract

Proliferation of the Internet is enabling the use of sensors and actuators to capture data and control devices remotely in a multitude of domains. Still, there is a general lack of best practices while designing such large scale real-time systems. This paper describes a generic architecture used on the implementation of a framework for deploying such systems in the cloud, enabling run-time evolution of the system with new sensors, actuators or services possibly developed by third-parties being integrated dynamically. Such architecture orchestrates the flow of information in the ecosystem and scales transparently to external components when needed, requiring no change in them. Adoption in the Portuguese nation-wide AAL project AAL4ALL is then described.

Categories and Subject Descriptors   C.1.4 [*Parallel Architectures*]: Distributed Architectures

General Terms   Design, Performance, Reliability, Security

Keywords   Distributed Systems, Software Engineering, Software Architectures, Interoperability

1. Introduction

We are living in a world of information, with the Internet playing a major role transporting it. Sensors and actuators are being deployed to capture data and control devices across a multitude of domains: weather (wind speed, temperature, precipitation), warehouses (stock information, product identification via RFID, automatic order dispatching) or even continuous healthcare monitoring (heart rate, respiration, body temperature, drug dispensing) just to name a few [3, 4, 6]. This massive deployment of sensors and actuators is commonly referred to as the *The Internet of Things* [1]. At the same time, with the reduced prices for cloud computing, service oriented business models in the cloud are becoming widespread.

While the process of building sensors and actuators as been improved in recent years, there is a general lack of knowledge on how to propagate this information from its source to the appropriate consumer, and back. This paper proposes an architecture for orchestrating information in an highly distributed system which easily scales horizontally and allows on-the-fly addition of new sensors, actua-

tors or services to monitor or control them, as well as interacting with the outside world.

This paper is organized in 7 sections. This initial section is the introduction. The next section describe what sensors, actuators and services are and how they interact with the system and each other. Section 3 describes the proposed architecture, including requirements, adopted technologies and key design decisions. Section 4 describes the adoption of the platform in a nation-wide AAL project. Section 5 elaborates on the future work for this project with the next section resuming the paper with a list of conclusions achieved considering the completed work in this project. Last section includes this work's acknowledgements.

2. Distributed Monitor and Control Framework

Monitor and control applications solve the problem of acquiring and processing information using electrical devices to interact with the physical world. Computer software is used to process and display the captured data, as well as controlling existing devices. Commonly, architectures are tightly coupled with the problem they are solving, with portability to other scenarios being impossible.

2.1 Sensors, Actuators and Services

To create a framework for monitor and control, three major components are required to interact with the system:

Sensors: Can exist in a fixed location or be attached to a machine or person, continuously capturing data from their surroundings. Sensors should be pre-configured and plug and play, meaning that they acquire and publish data in the system automatically. Additionally, these might be configured in run time with new specification, if needed. Sensors must have a way to integrate with the system, either by talking directly with it, or by communicating via a gateway [1].

Actuators: Allow the remote control of a mechanism or system. Actuators register themselves in the ecosystem of devices and wait for instructions from the remote software which knows how to control them.

Services: Manage the behavior in the ecosystem. By itself, the framework is responsible for propagating information from its origin to the right destination. Services consume captured data and compute this information, either for visualization purposes or for data analysis, which can be resent to the ecosystem (as source of information for another service or an action for an actuator).

---

[1] In sensor networks, gateways are devices to which multiple sensors and actuators can connect to, acting as a point of protocol translation. Gateways can connect directly with the framework while maintaining connection with low-level sensors (e.g. via Bluetooth or ZigBee) that are not network enabled, hence, unable to communicate via HTTP and publish their data in the system.

2.2 Publisher-Subscriber Pattern

Following the above description, sensors and actuators are able to capture data and control devices. Their behavior is controlled by external services to which these are connected, responsible for analysing the acquired data, processing it and issuing instruction for actuators or generating data for other services.

Primitive implementations could connect devices directly to the service which will handle their data, but enabling devices and services to connect with each other dynamically would allow the runtime evolution of the ecosystem, without requiring changes in the orchestration framework nor on the components themselves. This motivation lead to the adoption of the well known publisher-subscriber pattern.

Reviewing the pattern, two roles exist, described as follows:

Publishers: Generate and publish data in the system. Considering the previously described domain, publishers are sensors and services who generate data to be orchestrated by the framework.

Subscribers: Subscribe to the data they want to receive and have it delivered to them whenever it is available in the system. Subscribers then reactively act on the received data, computing it in order to provide either visualization or transformation of that data, which is injected once again into the system to be consumed by another subscriber. Any component can be a subscriber of data, e.g.: sensors can subscribe to configurations, actuators to instructions and services to any relevant data to them.

If we consider services as components that can be both publishers and subscribers of information, we acknowledge that services can be composed, easily allowing the creation of pipelines of services for data transformation, implemented using independent and possibly distributed services.

2.3 Application Domains

Research has been performed on the application of sensor and actuator networks, but there is still a general lack of good practices on how to capture and propagate data in such networks. Two scenarios can be observed in these networks. The first scenario, where the network is static, is with sensors and actuators connecting directly to known services. A second, more complex scenario, is the one where the network is dynamic, with sensors, actuators and services being added and removed at any time. While the first scenario results in a straightforward implementation, the second requires an orchestrating system to allow the ecosystem to continuously evolve with sensors, actuators and third-party services being able to join or leave at any given time.

The number of domains where sensors and actuators can be applied is clearly increasing. For better understanding the requirements of such networks, two cases where considered:

Health Monitoring: In Ambient Assisted Living projects, the author identified a set of recurrent situations where sensors are used to gather health-related information from patients during their daily lives. Information is acquired from the sensors using some sort of external gateway (usually via Bluetooth in a mobile phone), which then propagates the data to a server in the cloud [4].

Factory Automation: Apply sensor networks to a multitude of features, namely monitoring equipment to prevent failures or acquiring performance data used to evaluate and improve overall performance [2].

2.4 Framework Requirements

It is the author's belief that a generic software architecture for orchestrating data propagation could ease the process of building the previously described distributed systems. By analysing the problem at hand, we can easily assert that this is a message passing problem, with every component in the system being a potential publisher and subscriber of information.

Although it is possible to approach this problem using a common Publisher/Subscriber implementation [5], the continuous expansion of data being generated and consumed over the internet raises some engineering questions which lack a generally accepted answer. The main question can be formulated as *how can information be orchestrated, ensuring fast and secure delivery with dynamic component evolution and transparent scalability?*. Elaborating on the previous question, the following requirements can be asserted:

Performance: Monitoring and control are usually real-time systems, meaning that they should make decisions with the acquired information very fast. In health systems, a system that reacts quickly might result in saving a patient's life. In factory automation it is critical to increase productivity.

Extensibility: Components can possibly be added or removed from the system at any given time.

Scalability: Considering the previous requirement, the system should never be compromised due to excessive traffic. It should be able to scale transparently to the integrated components.

Security: Critical data might be routed through the system. In order to prevent sensitive data from being leaked to unauthorized users, there should be an authorization service that ensures that each subscriber can read only the data for which it is authorized.

Logging and billing: In order to monitor how data is being propagated in the system, either for debug or billing purposes, a logging system should be exist, keeping track of all routed messages in the system for a relevant amount of time.

3. Framework Architecture

Implementation of this framework consisted of the refined integration of a set of known proven technologies in order to answer to the stated requirements. The framework can be deployed to multiple servers, which cluster together for scaling purposes, as described later. Each server where the framework is deployed is referred to as a *network node* or simply *node*.

3.1 Communicating with Components

The framework's core functionality is to orchestrate messages between the integrated components in the system. Special care was taken when evaluating the best technologies to either receive and deliver messages to them.

3.1.1 Routing Strategy

While components adopt a role of publishers and subscribers, a node must be able to route messages from publishers to the proper subscribers. Subscribers register themselves within a node by providing the node with the set of routing keys they want to receive. A routing key is a simple text string that acts as identifier for the data being delivered in the system. As an example, a weight sensor positioned at the place *bathroom1* for an user with username *username1* could generate data with the routing key *username1.bathroom1.weight*. Routing keys can be also subscribed using wildcards. Considering the previous example, if a service would like to receive all weight data from *username1* it could simply subscribe to the routing key *username1.*.weight*.

```
{
''origin'':    ''health.device.5434'',
''date'':      ''232425326235'',
''topic'':     ''johndoe.bodypressure'',
''payload'':   {''data'': ''binary payload''}
}
```

Figure 1. Example of a message sent to a node.

3.1.2 Publishing Data

HTTP is currently one of the most widely adopted protocols for exchanging data on the WWW. Due to the maturity of the protocol and the wide availability of HTTP-based libraries in many languages, HTTP has been chosen as protocol for components to publish their messages in the node. A web service was created to which messages should be posted using the format described in section 3.1.4, using an authenticated HTTP POST request. Authentication can uniquely identify which component the message was sent from. This identity is matched against an authorization list to evaluate if that particular component has the authority to publish that information. If accepted, a 200 HTTP code is returned to the publisher, which acts as an acknowledgement of message delivery.

This server was implemented using the *Scala* programing language and an actor based concurrency model.

3.1.3 Data Propagation and Delivery

Once in the node, messages must propagate to the proper subscribers. Software exists to manage propagation of messages to clients based on the publisher-subscriber pattern. The Asynchronous Message Queue Protocol (AMQP) provides a solution for this problem, ensuring high message throughput, while managing client message queues and delivery. RabbitMQ, an implementation of AMQP, was adopted to handle message delivery. Whenever a message is published, it is internally forwarded to the AMQP server, where subscribers have registered with their routing keys.

3.1.4 Message Format

To ensure compatibility, a message format needed to be enforced to which all components should comply. JSON was the chosen format, due both to its semantic intuitivity, when compared to the know XML alternative, and to the wide range of libraries able to work with this format. Every message must contain four fields, as described below.

Origin: Represents the origin for the message. Might be used later for sending a reply to a service or device via the node.

Date: The date and time when the message was sent. Can be used for log or debug purposes. Dates relevant to the message itself, e.g. the date when a body temperature was captured, should not be included in this field, but instead be included in the payload as these are relevant only in the context of the message.

Topic: The routing key which should be used to propagate the message in the ecosystem.

Payload: The actual content of the message. This can be anything that the remote subscriber can decode, with recommendation being the adoption of a JSON dictionary as well.

Figure 1 exemplifies a possible message sent to the node. The message identifies the device where it was first created, the topic which contains the message type, and which will be used to forward it to subscribers authorized to receive messages with the specific routing key and user and finally a mock payload. Payload can either

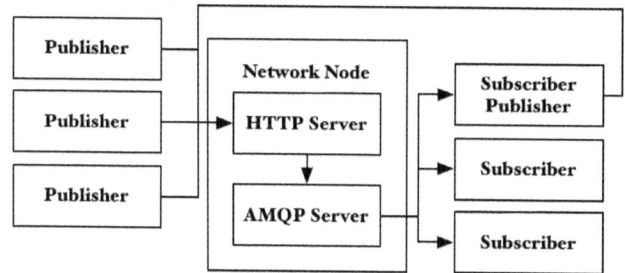

Figure 2. Network Node Representation

```
{''data'': ''binary payload''}
```

Figure 3. How message from Fig. 1 is sent to the AMQP server.

be a plain JSON or an encrypted string, as long as the encompassing JSON is still kept valid (by not using reserved JSON characters).

When a message arrives at the server, its structure and each field gets validated. Invalid messages are discarded, and an alert may be sent to notify an administrator that a specific integrated component is generating invalid messages.

3.2 Node Architecture

Figure 2 shows how a network node coexists with publishers and subscribers using the protocols described in this section.

Every publisher communicates with the node via HTTP, using the POST method to send a well formated message to the ecosystem. Once a message is validated, it get propagated to the internal AMQP server using the routing key from the message body. Figure 3 shows that all fields from the original JSON dictionary are removed and only the content of the payload field is kept. Remaining fields are used to validate the message, its origin and destination and to propagate it to the AMQP server with the proper routing key.

A node can be deployed to any machine and nodes automatically discover each other and cluster. Deploying a node consists of running a script that downloads all the necessary dependencies, configures the local machine and cluster with any other existing nodes, if at least one already exist. The main responsibility for the node is to receive and propagate data to the appropriate destination. This is achieved using an AMQP server. Producers use routing keys to categorize the information they are sending to the node with the type of data in it, as well as the data origin. While trying to contact a node, DNS is used to balance the load between them. If the producer is authorized to send the data with that routing key, the message is accepted and forwarded to destination, either an actuator or a service consuming it. Therefore, consumers must previously register themselves in the nodes by subscribe to data using routing keys, meaning that they subscribe to the information type that they want to receive from a specific origin, as far as they are authorized to do so. Authorization is an external service responsible for storing information on all components that can connect to nodes, including the routing keys they are authorized to publish and subscribe.

3.2.1 Required Services

A multitude of services can integrate the ecosystem to extend its functionality. Some of these will probably be required by any domain to which the framework is applied to, becoming an extention to the framework itself. Bellow some are described.

Authentication: Components integrated into the ecosystem must be registered and have their own login credentials to become either a publisher or subscriber in the ecosystem. An authentication service was developed, allowing an administrator to register services, actuators or sensors and their respective keys, individually providing them with the proper permissions via a browser interface. This service integrates with the node by subscribing to a specific routing key used by nodes to request for configurations. Using the reply from this service, nodes configure themselves to only allow authorized messages to propagate in the ecosystem.

Logging/Billing: To monitor the health of the ecosystem, debug messages could also be propagated by the system, being caught and permanently saved by a logging service. In commercial scenarios this service could also be used to keep a billing history for a certain user, keeping count of how many messages are being propagated in the system from him and with which destination. Such data could be paired with a business model to calculate the bill for an user based on his ecosystem usage.

Alerts: While the previous service can log issues in the system, some might be critical and administrators should be contacted directly to solve possibly critical issues. An alert service could subscribe in the node to these critical events and raise email or SMS alerts automatically.

3.2.2 Deployment

For simplifying the process of creating a new network node, a shell script was developed to automatically download and configure all the necessary dependencies in a freshly installed Ubuntu Server[2]. Furthermore, this script is configured per project and can have the necessary information to maintain node clusters.

3.3 Clustering

Using a single node for building a distributed and scalable system could result in the stoppage of the whole ecosystem. Failure can be introduced by the possible lack of capacity to scale in the number of integrated components and messages being routed, as well as possible hardware failures. Having a single point of failure is then strongly advised against.

The AMQP protocol already provides the ability to cluster servers together. The author's approach consisted of clustering the multiple AMQP servers and balancing workload across nodes by applying a DNS round-robin technique for each available server.

3.3.1 Multi-level orchestration

Parallel to clustering, a second approach to scale an ecosystem consists of the creation of multi-level nodes, hierarchically organized, which would handle different types of data on each level. By doing so, data would only propagate to the next higher-level if any service would consume it, with services deployed at the lowest possible level. Clusters could be created at a specific level to ensure the ability to handle higher loads specifically where these exist.

Consider a security system built on top of the framework with multiple houses being monitored, a service that evaluates the current security of the house based on multiple sensors deployed in windows and doors and second service that warns a security company about the possible security issue. A node could exist inside the house which would have either the monitoring service and all the house sensors integrated in it. Whenever this local service detected an issue, it would raise an alarm that would be published to the higher level *cloud* node which would deliver that information

---

2 Ubuntu is a free Linux distribution, based on Debian. Details at `http://www.ubuntu.com`

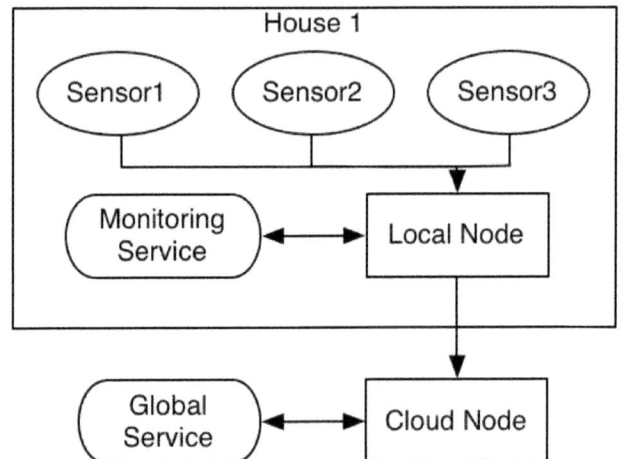

Figure 4. Multi-level organization of nodes.

to the security company monitoring service. Figure 4 exemplifies this scenario, using one node inside the house and a cloud node to where alarms get published.

This approach would greatly reduce data propagation between levels and could be used to manage load balance more thoroughly, increasing the number of nodes in the specific cluster where load is expected to be higher.

4. National AAL Ecosystem

The described architecture is currently deployed in the Portuguese AAL project AAL4ALL, consisting of a consortium of 31 partners that aim at improving the life quality of older adults through adoption of new technologies. The project expects to provide Portuguese citizens with the necessary infrastructure required to provide caretaker services remotely. Contrary to similar projects where the whole system is deployed by a set of partners, AAL4ALL encourages new partners to participate in the ecosystem by making available their own products: new sensors, actuators or services that can be certified and then freely commercialized as AAL4ALL compatible. This business model is to be adopted by the end of the research phase of the project and expect to attract partners who can increase the value of the ecosystem by contributing with their expertise with devices and services.

As an example, a patient could buy two body weight scales from different manufacturers, which would publish data under the same routing key. A remote caretaking service could be capturing data from both and display it to the patient's doctor for body weight monitoring.

Considering the scenario of a patient who is being monitored for cardiac problems, the sensor monitoring the patient could be switched at any time for another from a different manufacturer that would still publish the same information to a node through the use of the same routing key. Together with the identification of the patient and the data type, such data would be propagated to the appropriate service that it is monitoring that particular patient.

At any time it would also be possible to switch a service provider, applying routing changes that stop delivering content with a given routing key to a previously subscribed service, which starts being routed to the new service.

Multiple demonstrations have been performed using the framework for propagating data between components built by multiple partners in the project. Currently, no issue was identified in the adoption of this framework as orchestrating platform for the data in the ecosystem. Field trials are scheduled for the end of the current year.

5. Future Work

Much work is still missing before the framework is ready for a public release.

Some of the additional services required to expand the framework's functionalities are still not implemented. A prototype for the Authentication service already exists but needs to be abstracted before the framework can be applied to other domains. No work has been done in the logging and billing service yet.

Clustering could be greatly improved in order to balance load by considering the current workload for each node, being new connections always routed to the node with least load. Furthermore, clustering could be achieve at an higher level, by using Akka's cluster module [3] which could propagate messages to other nodes based on subscriptions, instead of the native RabbitMQ's approach which always propagates all messages to all nodes.

Simulated load tests will help to measure the performance and response of the clustering environment, including the message capacity per node and the message latency of the ecosystem.

6. Conclusions

This paper presented a generic architecture for deploying distributed sensor and actuator networks at any given scale. Scaling is done automatically as needed by adding new nodes to the distributed cluster. The author believes that this architecture fills a gap by providing an adaptable distributed framework, allowing sensors and actuator networks to be orchestrated via external services in an continuously evolving ecosystem.

7. Acknowledgments

This work is financed by the ERDF - European Regional Development Fund through the COMPETE programme (operational programme for competitiveness) within project AAL4ALL, *cf.* FCOMP-01-0202-FEDER-013852. Details at www.aal4all.org

References

[1] L. Atzori, A. Iera, and G. Morabito. The Internet of Things: A survey. *Computer Networks*, 54(15):2787–2805, 2010. ISSN 13891286. . URL http://linkinghub.elsevier.com/retrieve/pii/S1389128610001568.

[2] K. Islam, W. Shen, S. Member, and X. Wang. Wireless Sensor Network Reliability and Security in Factory Automation : A Survey. 42(6):1243–1256, 2012.

[3] H. B. Lim, M. Iqbal, W. Wang, and Y. Yao. The National Weather Sensor Grid: a large-scale cyber-sensor infrastructure for environmental monitoring. *Management Science*, 7(1/2):19, 2010. ISSN 17481279. . URL http://dl.acm.org/citation.cfm?id=1734150.1734152.

[4] S. Prescher, A. K. Bourke, F. Koehler, A. Martins, H. Sereno Ferreira, T. Boldt Sousa, R. N. Castro, A. Santos, M. Torrent, S. Gomis, M. Hospedales, and J. Nelson. Ubiquitous ambient assisted living solution to promote safer independent living in older adults suffering from co-morbidity. *Conference proceedings : ... Annual International Conference of the IEEE Engineering in Medicine and Biology Society. IEEE Engineering in Medicine and Biology Society. Conference*, 2012:5118–21, Jan. 2012. ISSN 1557-170X. . URL http://www.ncbi.nlm.nih.gov/pubmed/23367080.

[5] D. C. Schmidt and C. ORyan. Patterns and performance of distributed real-time and embedded publisher/subscriber architectures. *Journal of Systems and Software*, 66(3):213–223, June 2003. ISSN 01641212. . URL http://linkinghub.elsevier.com/retrieve/pii/S016412120200078X.

[6] Z. X. Z. Xiaoguang and L. W. L. Wei. The research of network architecture in warehouse management system based on RFID and WSN integration, 2008.

---

[3] Akka is the library used in Scala to provide the actor-based concurrency model. Details at http://akka.io.

Producing and Delivering a MOOC on Pattern-Oriented Software Architecture for Concurrent and Networked Software

Douglas C. Schmidt and Zach McCormick

Vanderbilt University, Institute for Software Integrated Systems, Nashville, Tennessee
{d.schmidt,zach.mccormick}@vanderbilt.edu

Abstract

A massive open online course (MOOC) is a web-based class environment aimed at large-scale global participation and open access via the Internet. MOOCs are also a disruptive trend changing how education is delivered and funded throughout the world. In the spring of 2013, we developed and taught Vanderbilt's first MOOC, entitled "Pattern-Oriented Software Architecture for Concurrent and Networked Software" (known as the POSA MOOC). This ten-week MOOC was an amalgamation of several courses on software design and programming taken by ~600 undergraduate and graduate students at Vanderbilt during the past decade. Enrollment in our POSA MOOC was more than 50 times (31,000+) that number, consisting of students with a wide range of background, interests, and expertise from scores of countries around the world.

This paper describes our experiences producing and delivering the POSA MOOC. Where possible, we ground our observations in data from statistics collected via Coursera, which was the delivery platform we used for the POSA MOOC. We also discuss the broader implications of MOOCs on life-long learning and the role they play in improving the quality and productivity of software professionals in academia and industry.

Categories and Subject Descriptors K.3.1 [*Computer Uses in Education*]: Distance learning; K.3.1 [*Computer Uses in Education*]: Collaborative learning

Keywords MOOCs; Coursera; pattern-oriented software architectures and frameworks; object-oriented design and programming

1. Introduction

Vanderbilt has been a respected institution of higher education since 1873, graduating over one hundred thousand students during the past 140 years. In a span of the past 8 months, however, Vanderbilt has more than doubled the number of students taught by its faculty. The source of this surge in exposure stems from the "Massive Open Online Courses" (MOOCs) that Vanderbilt began offering through Coursera in March of 2013 (see www.coursera.org/vanderbilt for the list of Vanderbilt MOOCs).

The MOOC we taught on the Coursera platform was called "Pattern-Oriented Software Architecture for Concurrent and Networked Software," which we refer to as the POSA MOOC (see www.coursera.org/course/posa for access to this material). This MOOC showed by example how applying object-oriented patterns and frameworks can help to alleviate many accidental and inherent complexities associated with developing and deploying concurrent and network software. The patterns and frameworks covered in this MOOC have been used successfully in many domains, including telecom and datacom, mobile devices, electronic medical imaging, network management, aerospace aviation and automation, as well as online gaming, web services, and financial systems.

By the time the POSA MOOC launched on March 4th, 2013, 31,000+ students were enrolled, hailing from a wide range of countries, as shown on the heat map in Figure 1. During the ten

Figure 1. Global POSA MOOC Student Locations

weeks of the POSA MOOC, a subset of these students accessed the on-line video lectures 464,498 times and attempted the on-line quizzes 37,817 times. Many students expended significant effort to submit 13,220 assignments—written in 6 different programming languages—and conduct 45,649 unique peer-graded assessments of these assignments. Moreover, conversations between students and course staff on the discussion forums numbered well over 7,000 unique posts, providing a highly interactive (albeit time-consuming to monitor and manage) virtual learning community.

Producing and delivering a MOOC at this scale was much different from the courses we've traditionally taught at Vanderbilt. Imagine teaching a course where the students could have the prerequisite background (or not), join the class (or not) at any time, listen to the lectures (or not) at any time, take the quizzes (or not) at any time, do the programming assignments (or not) at (almost) any time, read the archives of past discussions (or not — usually not by the way) prior to posting their questions, etc. This summary captures just part of what it's like teaching a MOOC. In addition to being a non-linear—often hectic—adventure, it's also a fascinating experiment in the democratization of learning, as well as a harbinger of things to come in higher education.

Differences between MOOCs and traditional face-to-face classes at Vanderbilt profoundly affected the preparation, presentation, and assessment of the POSA MOOC material. For example, the students we taught in the POSA MOOC had much more diverse backgrounds, interests, and expertise than traditional Vanderbilt undergraduates, which impacted both our teaching style and student learning experiences. One example of this diversity in the POSA MOOC is shown in Figure 2, which depicts enrollment by age based on a voluntary survey completed by a subset of the enrolled students. These demographics look nothing like the typical

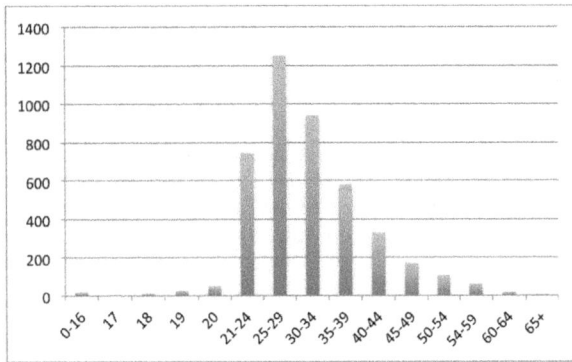

Figure 2. POSA MOOC Enrollment by Age

age profile at Vanderbilt, where the vast majority of students are 18-22 years old. Moreover, there were significant challenges associated with assessing student performance in "design-oriented" MOOCs (such as POSA) versus "fact-oriented" MOOCs (such as the Algebra or Pre-Calculus) on Coursera.

A common criticism [11] of conventional MOOCs is that they dehumanize education by neglecting or degrading interactions amongst students and teachers. There's certainly no substitute for face-to-face engagement between motivated teachers and students. We applied several innovative techniques and social media tools in our POSA MOOC, however, that enabled meaningful dialogue between students and the course staff, which helped ameliorate some noted deficiencies with conventional MOOC offerings.

The remainder of this paper is organized as follows: Section 2 summarizes the contents and structure of the POSA MOOC, emphasizing the changes we made to our face-to-face classes to handle the lack of prerequisites in Coursera MOOC offerings; Section 3 discusses our observations and lessons learned creating and presenting the POSA MOOC; Section 4 discusses our experience with the impact—both pro and con—that MOOCs are having on traditional on-campus education; and Section 5 presents concluding remarks and outlines our future plans for the POSA MOOC.

2. Structure and Contents of the POSA MOOC

This section describes the POSA MOOC structure and contents.

2.1 Summary of the POSA MOOC

Our MOOC is motivated by the advent of multi-core and distributed core processors—coupled with ubiquitous wired and wireless connectivity—which is increasing the demand for researchers and practitioners who understand how to successfully develop and deploy concurrent and network software. Despite continuous improvements in processors and networks over the past four decades, however, developing quality concurrent and network software remains hard. Moreover, developing quality *reusable* concurrent and network software is even harder.

The principles, methods and skills required to develop such software can be greatly enhanced by understanding how to create and apply *patterns* [3] and *frameworks* [7]. A pattern describes a reusable solution to a common problem that arises within a particular context. When related patterns are woven together, they form *pattern languages* [2] that provide a vocabulary and a process for the orderly resolution of software development problems.

A framework is an integrated set of software components that collaborate to provide a reusable architecture for a family of related applications. Frameworks can also be viewed as realizations of pattern languages that facilitate reuse of detailed design and source code. The POSA MOOC described how to apply patterns and frameworks to alleviate many accidental and inherent complexities associated with developing and deploying concurrent and network software in multiple domains, including mobile applications, web servers, object request brokers, and avionics control systems.

2.2 Summary of the Video Lectures

The students we teach in our courses on patterns and frameworks at Vanderbilt have the necessary background. For example, our *Intermediate Software Design* course (www.dre.vanderbilt.edu/~schmidt/cs251) focuses on object-oriented design patterns and advanced object-oriented programming techniques with C++. Students taking this course must have successfully completed introductory courses on programming and data structures, so we know they are familiar with core object-oriented programming features (such as classes, inheritance, and dynamic binding) and object-oriented programming languages (such as Java and C++). In contrast, when developing and teaching the POSA MOOC we had no idea how well/poorly prepared the students would be since there are no prerequisites in the Coursera curriculum.

We dealt with the lack of prerequisites by structuring the POSA MOOC into multiple sections. While the overall focus of the MOOC was on patterns and frameworks for concurrent and networked software, we added several introductory sections that covered the background material needed to understand core concepts in concurrency, networking, patterns, and frameworks, as well as an optional section that covered core object-oriented design, programming, and pattern concepts. The following is a summary of the topics we covered in all these sections.

2.2.1 Section Zero: Course Overview

This hour of introductory videos was designed to help students visualize the motivations for—and challenges of—concurrent and networked software. We also summarized how patterns and frameworks help to address key challenges of software, in general, as well as concurrent and networked software, in particular.

2.2.2 Section One: An Introduction to Concurrent and Networked Software

This section contained 3.5 hours of videos that provided background information related to operating systems and middleware. We discussed key design dimensions of concurrent and networked software (such as principles for partitioning systems into multiple layers and services), as well as reviewed common UNIX and Windows operating system programming mechanisms and Android programming mechanisms (which figured prominently in Section Two of the POSA MOOC).

Section One emphasized concepts, so there wasn't much discussion of patterns, frameworks, or code. Our goal was to summarize the material students needed to understand the topics covered in later sections. At Vanderbilt this material would have been covered in earlier courses, but since the Coursera curriculum enforces no prerequisites we filmed these introductory videos.

2.2.3 Section Two: An Introduction to Patterns and Frameworks

This section had 6 hours of videos that delved deeper into the POSA MOOC's main emphasis: *patterns and frameworks for concurrent and networked software*. This section focused largely on design rather than programming, with many structural and behavior elements of patterns and frameworks conveyed via UML diagrams. Although there was some example code in Java, C++, and C, expertise in these programming languages wasn't needed to understand the material in this section.

We began with an overview of patterns and frameworks in general, emphasizing key concepts, such as codifying design experience, enabling systematic reuse, and combining groups of related patterns to define a process for the orderly resolution of software development problems in particular domains. We outlined several examples of common concurrent and networked programming patterns (such as Proxy, Broker, Observer, and Command Processor) and frameworks (such as Android [10], ACE [14], and TAO [15]) written in Java and C++.

We also discussed the pros and cons of patterns and frameworks, when to use them and avoid them, and what alternatives to consider if they don't work in particular contexts. In addition, we summarized additional reference material on patterns and frameworks to guide students interested in learning more about these topics than we covered in the POSA MOOC.

2.2.4 Section Three: Applying Patterns and Frameworks to Concurrent and Networked Software

This section contained 6 hours of videos and had the most technical depth of the POSA MOOC. It focused on how to develop concurrent and networked software by applying patterns and frameworks and grouping patterns into pattern languages. To make the examples in this section concrete and relevant, we chose a case study from the domain of high-performance web servers, based on the JAWS [6] open-source web server developed in C++ using many patterns and ACE framework components. There were numerous C++ code examples in this section, so students needed a solid grounding in C++ (or an equivalent object-oriented language like Java or C#) to understand the examples.

The patterns and frameworks covered in this section covered a range of concurrent and networked software capabilities, including service access and configuration, inter-process communication, synchronous and asynchronous event handling, concurrency, and synchronization. Most patterns in this section were based on the pattern language in the *Pattern Oriented Software Architecture Volume Two* book [13], which covers patterns for concurrent and distributed objects. We also discussed how patterns from the book *Design Patterns: Elements of Reusable Object-Oriented Software* (the so-called "Gang of Four" book) [3] help simplify certain design and programming aspects of concurrent and networked software.

2.2.5 Section Four: A Case Study of "Gang of Four" Patterns

This optional (*i.e.*, no quizzes or peer-graded assignments) section provided 3.5 hours of background videos on object-oriented design and patterns that weren't directly relevant to concurrent and networked software, but which are essential to becoming an effective developer of object-oriented programs. It was organized around a case study that applied over half of the 23 patterns in "Gang of Four" book to showcase a pattern- and object-oriented design and programming techniques using C++. This case study enabled students to learn and evaluate the limitations with alternative software development methods (such as algorithm decomposition) and

demonstrate by example how patterns and object-orientation help to alleviate these limitations.

2.3 Student Assessment Mechanisms

To obtain approval from Coursera and Vanderbilt to launch the POSA MOOC, we created several methods for assessing the student performance. Moreover, we offered the course at the following two levels of engagement in recognition of the fact that not all participants have the same learning objectives or available time:

• **Normal Track**. Students at this level received a *Statement of Accomplishment* that certified proficiency with the course concepts, which we assessed via weekly auto-graded quizzes. This track was designed for students who had time/interest in taking the auto-graded quizzes and final exam, but who did not have time/interest to complete the peer-graded short essay questions and peer-graded programming assignments.

Students could fulfill the Normal Track without joining when the MOOC started, as long as they completed all auto-graded quizzes and final exam by the time the POSA MOOC ended after ten weeks. The final grade for the Normal Track was based on the weekly quizzes (90% of the final grade) and a final exam (10% of the final grade). Students who obtained 70% or more of the maximum score received a Statement of Accomplishment.

• **Distinction Track**. Students at this level received a *Statement of Accomplishment with Distinction*. In addition to completing the auto-graded weekly quizzes and final exam from the Normal Track, students in the Distinction Track also completed peer-graded short essays and peer-graded programming assignments. The programming assignments involved writing concurrent and networked software in popular pattern-oriented software architecture frameworks written in a range of languages—including Java, C++ (and C++11), C#, Python, Ruby, and Scala—using a variety of production object-oriented frameworks—including Netty (Java); Twisted (Python); and Qt, Boost, and ACE (all C++). This track was designed for students willing to invest the time to achieve mastery of the course material and apply it in structured assignments.

To fulfill the Distinction Track students needed to complete the various peer-graded assignments by their due dates (which were typically two or three weeks after the assignments were initially released on the Coursera platform). The final grade for the Distinction Track was based on the weekly quizzes (35% of the final grade), peer-graded short essays and peer-graded assignments (55% of the final grade) and a final exam (10% of the final grade). Students who obtained 70% or more of the maximum score received a Statement of Accomplishment with Distinction.

3. Observations and Lessons Learned

Although we were institutionally responsible for teaching thousands of students, by the time the POSA MOOC finished we felt like we'd learned at least as much as we'd taught. This section describes some of our observations and lessons learned while producing and delivering our POSA MOOC.

3.1 An Enormous Amount of Time was Needed to Prepare the Content Prior to MOOC Launch

Filming videos used by thousands of students as their primary exposure to the POSA MOOC content required considerably more preparation than we were accustomed to based on face-to-face courses we've taught at Vanderbilt and other universities. Below we discuss several reasons for the concentrated effort.

3.1.1 Filming High Quality Video Lectures

After teaching courses on object-oriented software patterns and frameworks for two decades, it's become second nature to present lively and inspiring lectures despite minimal rehearsal and *ad hoc* slides. This haphazard model of preparation *does not* work in a MOOC since there are no students to interact with while filming the videos in the studio. As a result, we needed to produce much tighter scripts and highly structured lecture material.

Each week of the POSA MOOC featured several hours of video lectures from one or more of the *sections* summarized in Section 2. Each section was similar to a volume in a multi-volume book series and was composed of multiple *modules*, which were akin to chapters in a book. Each module was composed of multiple *parts*, which were akin to a portion of a book chapter and were roughly 15–20 minutes long (the length Coursera recommends to keep the attention of students). Every five minutes or so, a multiple-choice "in-video" quiz popped up to check whether the student viewing the video understood the material covered thus far.

It took us two solid months of filming to produce 80+ individual videos that ran for ∼20 hours. In contrast, ∼40 hours are spent lecturing in a conventional semester-long Vanderbilt class (and the preparation time for these lectures is *much* lower since there's more opportunity for improvisation). Many POSA MOOC videos were filmed using advanced *green screen* technology (see en.wikipedia.org/wiki/Chroma_key), which provided maximal flexibility in rendering the instructor in front of various backgrounds, which were mostly Powerpoint presentation slides.

We prepared 1,200+ Powerpoint slides for the POSA MOOC videos. Many slides were new since we had to convey the material without the benefit of interactive dialogue from students in a face-to-face class, so we made the slides more explanatory than normal. Moreover, explicit permission was needed to use copyrighted images in MOOC videos, so we replaced copyrighted images in our original slides with Creative Commons licensed images that didn't require explicit permission to use.

Even with 1,200+ slides and 20+ hours of videos, the POSA MOOC just scratched the surface of patterns and frameworks for concurrent and networked software, which are much broader and deeper topics than we could possibly hope to cover in a single MOOC. The Powerpoint presentations therefore also contained extensive URL cross-references at the bottom of many slides. These URLs pointed to resources, papers, documentation, and source code that we or other experts have produced on topics related to material covered in the POSA MOOC.

Presenting the POSA MOOC material on camera was also *much* harder than giving lectures in class since there were no students to ask questions or give visual cues indicating if they comprehended the material. We therefore had to master the art of presenting slides smoothly and at an even pace, as well as maintaining enthusiasm while staring into the steely gaze of a video camera for hours at a time. A significant amount of time was also spent learning and applying screen capture and video editing tools during the post-production process to fix various glitches that inevitably crept into the videos and Powerpoint presentations.

3.1.2 Creating Student Assessment Mechanisms

In addition to the time required to develop the videos, we needed considerable time to formulate in-video quizzes (which was a tedious process we called "quizzification"), weekly quizzes (which counted towards the final grade, whereas the in-video quizzes did not), and peer-graded essays and programming assignments. In traditional classrooms, open-ended questions enable students to synthesize their knowledge in a free-form way, with instructors interpreting student responses and providing immediate feedback. Due to the infeasibility of providing individual feedback to thousands of students in a MOOC, however, we needed much more effort up front to construct questions for quizzes and rubrics for peer grading in a clear and helpful manner. Section 3.2 describes how we

leveraged crowd-sourcing to improve the POSA MOOC assessment mechanisms after the class began.

Help from experts in other areas helped to temper the increased time commitment stemming from the large amount of work involved in creating the POSA MOOC. For example, we leveraged the skills of experienced project management and video production experts at Vanderbilt, who filmed the lectures and edited/rendered the video content, thereby increasing the productivity and quality of the course production process. Having knowledgeable members of Vanderbilt's *Center for Teaching* (cft.vanderbilt.edu) and *Associate Provost for Undergraduate Education* to (1) answer our numerous questions about using Coursera platform, (2) help create and review supplementary course material, and (3) assist in the review process was also invaluable. In addition, the Coursera course operations specialists did a masterful job of supporting our needs both before and during the POSA MOOC.

3.2 An Even Larger Amount of Time is Needed to Manage a MOOC After Launch

After finishing the rendering and quizzification of the final POSA MOOC videos we had a great sense of relief since we thought the hard part of the project was over. Little did we know that the most demanding aspects of our work was just beginning. After the POSA MOOC went live at 2pm GMT on March 4th, the online discussion forums were immediately inundated with questions from students around the world, who wanted answers to questions ranging from what programming languages were allowed to clarifications about how the MOOC grading policies affected their chances of receiving Statements of Accomplishment. We each spent 40+ hours per week attempting to answer every question posed by the students.

In addition to enjoying our interaction with motivated students on topics associated with patterns and frameworks for concurrent and networked software, we spent so much time in the discussion forums for the following reasons:

• **Accelerate and amplify the learning process**. We quickly realized that the discussion forums were essential to the learning process. In particular, these forums helped transform the course from passively watching "lecture-oriented" videos to actively engaging in "learning-oriented" dialogue between us and the students. It was fascinating to watch students evolve and deepen their understanding of the course material based on the types of questions and resulting conversations that occurred in the discussion forums.

• **Dispel common misconceptions**. Our heavy involvement in the discussion forums was essential in dispelling common misconceptions resulting from "folk lore" that's accrued over time in the software community. For example, many students initially thought that (1) patterns were only applicable to object-oriented programming languages, (2) the only purpose of patterns was to compensate for deficiencies in mainstream languages (particularly C++ and Java), and (3) object-oriented frameworks incurred too much time/space overhead for use in resource-constrained systems. These types of misconceptions rarely arise in face-to-face courses at Vanderbilt since few undergraduates have sufficient experience with alternative programming languages and design methods to raise these issues. In the MOOC environment, however, there were many spirited debates on these topics.

• **Build good will**. Maintaining a continuous course staff presence in the discussion forums also built up good will that paid off in various ways throughout the POSA MOOC. For example, many students contributed back to the MOOC by crowd-sourcing the programming assignment specifications beyond C++ to different programming languages (including Java, C#, Python, Ruby, and Scala) and different frameworks beyond ACE (including Netty, Twisted, Qt, and Boost). Students also crowd-sourced the entire contents of POSA MOOC wiki site (share.coursera.org/wiki/index.

php/posa:Main), which ultimately provided a detailed glossary of technical terms used in the videos, as well as a comprehensive list of all URL cross-references to other technical literature we embedded in the Powerpoint slides.

• **Reward constructive student participation**. Based on our involvement in other MOOCs, we noticed that the tone and content of discussion forum postings often tended to devolve into frustration and *ad hominem* attacks without the consistent presence of course staff. In general, the conversations that occurred in the POSA MOOC discussion forums were civil and technically focused. The most active participants were also quite knowledgeable and thoughtful in their postings, which we explicitly encouraged through our heavy engagement in the forums.

Although it was time consuming to engage with all students posting on the discussion forums, this investment yielded significant improvements in course material, better understanding for course staff and students, and a greater camaraderie in the POSA MOOC "virtual classroom." Ideally, the time commitment required for future offerings of the POSA MOOC will be reduced by codifying our answers to frequently asked questions into a "FAQ" database and leveraging the assistance of "Community TAs" drawn from the pool of students who did well in the initial offering.

3.3 The POSA MOOC Student Diversity was Both Challenging and Rewarding

Students in our Vanderbilt courses come from diverse socio-economic and national backgrounds, but are uniformly smart (their average SAT scores asymptotically approach perfection) and generally well-prepared (having successfully completed the prerequisites). In contrast, student background, expertise, and interests in the POSA MOOC were *much* more diverse, as discussed in Section 1, which yielded the following challenges:

• **Much greater level of skepticism from experienced students**. Undergraduates at Vanderbilt rarely have much programming experience when they arrive. In contrast, many POSA MOOC students—especially those posting frequently in discussion forums—had 20+ years of experience as software professionals. They manifested this experience by stating much stronger preferences for particular programming languages, runtime platforms, software tools, and development methods. They also asked *much* harder and more probing/skeptical questions about the pros and cons of different technical approaches relative to typical students in undergraduate courses at Vanderbilt.

Instructors benefit from being challenged to communicate clearly and justify their positions, just like students. We therefore found it was tremendously educational (and exhilarating) to engage in discussion forum debates on many topics in the POSA MOOC. Moreover, most students eventually came to appreciate the benefits of patterns and frameworks as a result of our discussions. We spent substantially more time, however, motivating and justifying the topics and techniques covered in the lectures than we'd expected based on our prior experience at Vanderbilt.

• **Increased workload to fill knowledge gaps**. At the other end of the spectrum were POSA MOOC students who lacked the necessary background since Coursera enforces no prerequisites, as noted in Section 2.2. We therefore filmed over eight hours (*i.e.*, nearly half the videos) of supplemental material to prepare less experienced students for the key topics of the POSA MOOC. Likewise, we spent a great deal of time in the discussion forums explaining basic concepts of object-oriented design and programming to inexperienced students. In contrast, our Vanderbilt students would have had these prerequisites, which greatly reduces the time required for course preparation and delivery.

In hindsight, a better solution than filming supplemental material would have been to create a group of related MOOCs that students could take as a sequence. As with the curricula offered in conventional on-campus Computer Science and Computer Engineering programs, the goal of sequenced MOOCs is to introduce students to the material in the right order and at the right level. Section 5 describes the sequenced MOOCs we are creating together with the University of Maryland for the spring of 2014.

• **Generalizing from limited perspectives impedes learning**. Vanderbilt students are generally well-rounded, *e.g.*, they are trained—and predisposed, given the rigorous admissions process that emphasizes a range of scholastic and extracurricular activities—to think critically from multiple (holistic) perspectives and are equally facile at verbal, written, and quantitative skills. Moreover, the Computer Science and Computer Engineering programs at Vanderbilt expose undergraduates to a wide range of programming languages, development environments, operating systems, middleware, development methods, and application domains.

In contrast, judging from the comments and questions on the discussion forums, many of the POSA MOOC students tended to express themselves from much more narrow (and reductionist) perspectives. For example, if they developed one-off end-user apps they thought everyone just developed one-off end-user apps (and thus had no use for developing frameworks that encouraged systematic reuse). Likewise, if they worked in an organization that didn't appreciate the value of software design they assumed everyone worked in an environment that doesn't appreciate software design (and thus there was no point in learning about design patterns). Helping to broaden student perspectives was an essential role we played in the POSA MOOC discussion forums.

• **Overly narrow focus on programming**. A point related to the limited perspectives discussed above was how students reacted to different types of assignments. It's not unusual for Computer Science and Computer Engineering courses at Vanderbilt to have short-essay questions, either as homework assignments or quizzes, since instructors (and most students) recognize the strategic value of communicating effectively via technical and persuasive writing. As shown in Figure 2, however, most POSA MOOC students did not fit the profile of university students who've recently taken courses in writing or other non-technical subjects. Many of these students were highly averse to the short-essay questions we assigned in the early part of the MOOC.

We originally intended these short-essay questions as a means to assess the students' ability to codify/convey their understanding of the software *design*, which formed the bulk of the Section Two videos (outlined in Section 2.2.3). Design knowledge isn't adequately assessed by having students write programs that are assessed for functional correctness. Although functional correctness is necessary, it's not sufficient to demonstrate the application of good design practices and patterns.

Based on feedback we got on the discussion forums, however, we quickly realized that the bulk of the POSA MOOC students wanted to write programs, not essays. We therefore adapted our assignments after the first several weeks and updated the rubrics used to assess the essays to downplay the weighting of grammar and correctness based on concerns voiced by non-native English speakers from the wide range countries shown in Figure 3. We also rapidly switched to programming assignments instead of short essays for the remainder of the MOOC.

Rewarding aspects of the POSA MOOC diversity included:

• **Highly stimulating discussions with expert software developers**. As noted above (and in Section 3.2) we engaged in many informative conversations (and intense debates) on common misconceptions about patterns and object-oriented frameworks in the POSA MOOC discussion forums. These discussions rarely occur in our classes at Vanderbilt, where most students lack the experience of expert practitioners, and thus the same (few) students typ-

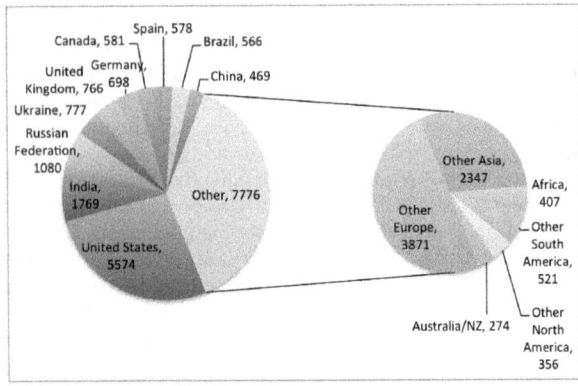

Figure 3. POSA MOOC Enrollment by Country

ically answer most questions. Getting other students to engage is often hard, which makes the class less interesting for both instructors and students. In contrast, we had extensive student engagement in the POSA MOOC. Although the relative anonymity of a MOOC certainly helped encourage greater student participation, it was also clear that expert practitioners were eager to share their experience.

- **Greatly improved course structure and content**. Another benefit of the diversity in the POSA MOOC student population was the vast amount of feedback given by the students on the discussion forums. Students in our on-campus courses rarely provide detailed feedback on the course contents. Again, this lack of feedback likely stems from the fact that 18-22 year-olds have limited experience with developing production software, so they aren't attuned to subtle problems with the material.

In contrast, many students in the POSA MOOC had decades of experience developing software and were eager to share their knowledge in the discussion forums. Moreover, they quickly found and reported mistakes or ambiguities in the POSA video slides/lectures, quizzes, and peer-graded assignments. This crowd-sourcing feedback enabled us to support multiple programming languages in assignments, as well as helped us improve course material, *e.g.*, fixing typos in slides, repairing broken links, and improving peer-graded assignment rubrics.

Such a rapid, iterative course improvement process is rare in conventional Vanderbilt classes, which are much smaller (typically 10-20 students), so there's less critical mass for crowd-sourcing. There are also fewer opportunities for students to provide structured feedback on course material. For example, by the time this feedback is solicited in a post-course survey, students may have forgotten their earlier concerns.

In addition to improving POSA MOOC content, student feedback also improved MOOC structure and logistics. For example, we released videos over weekends so students could watch them outside of work. We also moved all quiz deadlines to the end of the MOOC, so students could finish these auto-graded quizzes at their own pace. In general, we found that being responsive to diverse student needs helped us built a more effective learning environment for the POSA MOOC.

3.4 Assessing Student Performance in a "Design-oriented" MOOC is Harder than in "Fact-oriented" MOOCs

In our experience, the POSA MOOC students wanted meaningful ways to assess their progress, *i.e.*, they didn't just want to watch videos, they want to actually apply what they'd learned into practice. For example, after we started releasing peer-graded programming assignments there was an explosion of participation in the discussion forums, with students posting their questions/solutions

and generating many interesting analyses and comments on each others solutions. Our challenge was to assess their solutions in a realistic and scalable manner.

Assessing student performance in the software design and programming courses we teach at Vanderbilt involves a significant amount of manual scrutiny. For example, we personally review and comment upon every line of software written by our students. While that level of personalized scrutiny may work for a small class in a private (and expensive) university, we couldn't afford to assess thousands of solutions from MOOC students (who generally pay nothing to the course staff).

Ideally, scaling up POSA MOOC assessments would apply auto-grading tools. Despite being an active field of research, however, the auto-grading tools available to assess students in a design-oriented MOOCs (such as POSA) aren't as mature as in a "fact-based" MOOC (such as Algebra or Pre-Calculus). The problem stems from the lack of useful tools for auto-grading software *designs* in terms of (relatively subjective) quality attributes, such as reusability, understandability, and evolvability.

We evaluated these quality attributes in the POSA MOOC via Coursera's two-phase peer-assessment feature. In phase one, students uploaded their submissions to the Coursera platform by the deadline. In phase two, students automatically received an anonymized set of submissions from other students. The Coursera web interface guided students through a grading rubric and they scored each submission and entered free-form comments. They had to finish grading their assigned submissions (we had them grade four submissions each) before the grading deadline or they received a 20% penalty for their own submission). After this deadline passed, students could see their final grade, which was an average of the grades they were given by their four peer graders.

Although Coursera's peer-assessment feature is scalable, the wide range of student abilities, motivations, and time constraints made peer assessment problematic. In the POSA MOOC, we started with simple rubrics that gave students significant freedom in assigning grades. We met with resistance almost immediately since some students were lax graders and others were strict, so we switched to providing more detailed rubrics.

Although we had better success with detailed rubrics, the lack of expert judgement was evident, regardless of the specificity of the prompts and rubrics. In our future MOOC offerings, therefore, we plan to use more systematic assessments by calibrating the peer review process [9] with videos that walk through our solutions and compare them against the rubrics.

The limitations with peer-assessment and auto-grading in MOOCs underscore the invaluable role that expert judgment plays in fostering critical thinking by—and experienced evaluation of—students in on-campus courses at immersive educational institutions like Vanderbilt. In other words, you get what you pay for..

3.5 The Coursera Platform is a Work-in-Progress

Bugs, kludges, workarounds, and missing features are realities in all the existing MOOC platforms. While none of the problems we encountered with the Coursera platform used for the POSA MOOC were show-stoppers, we did encounter the following limitations, some from our perspective and some from the students' viewpoint.

- **Lack of an integrated view of their progress**. We were initially overwhelmed by students' obsessions with their scores on various quizzes and peer-graded assignments. These obsessions were manifested by the volume of questions about how grades were calculated and complaints from students who didn't know their current grades. Moreover, there was simply no single place in the Coursera platform for students to get a sense of completion status or due dates for assignments.

We repeatedly answered the same questions on the discussion forum to help students attain a bird's-eye view of their status since the Coursera platform did not support this capability. Obviously, this could be very different for different courses, so a one-size-fits-all solution would not work, but we managed to adapt one case at a time. Eventually, we created a semi-automated grading calculator (discussed in Section 3.6.3), but what's really needed is a standard solution provided by the Coursera platform itself.

- **Information overload on the discussion forums**. In addition to repetitive questions from students about their grades on the discussion forums, many students didn't look for existing answers before posting their questions. After answering the same questions several times, we decided to keep a running list of links to common questions that we'd answered before, so that we could efficiently guide them to the information they needed. While this practice wasn't too time-consuming for us, it indicates something that Coursera should emphasize in future platform releases to help students find the resources they need quickly, *e.g.*, some type of automated FAQ capability.
- **Lack of scalability as a MOOC progresses**. Many POSA MOOC students requested the programming assignment specifications be provided in languages beyond Java and C++. We agreed to do this as long as students themselves crowd-sourced the appropriate changes to the specifications. While this enhanced the breadth of the POSA MOOC by allowing students to program in the language of their choice, it introduced quite some confusion due to limitations with the Coursera platform.

For example, there was no way to put different peer-graded assignments into subfolders under "Peer Assessments." Since each assessment was a unique combination of programming language, (optional) framework, and assignment number, the number of assignments on the page skyrocketed as the MOOC progressed. Moreover, Coursera provided us with no automated means to help students who submitted to an incorrect link (*e.g.*, submitted a Java solution to the Python version of the assignment) after the submission period closed. There was also no easy way for students who submitted assignments in multiple programming languages to see their grades since they had to open each submission and calculate the highest score from all their submissions (which became their final grade for that assignment).

- **Limited hardware/software support for the Coursera platform**. Since MOOCs are intended for students around the world, MOOC delivery platforms should ideally be compatible with a wide range of browsers and devices. When we taught the POSA MOOC in the spring of 2013, however, the Coursera platform primarily supported Chrome, Firefox, and Internet Explorer. Other common hardware/software combinations, such as Android and iPhone/iPad, weren't well supported.

When our students encountered issues with different phones, tablets, and browsers they complained to us via the discussion forums. Occasionally, we could suggest a quick fix, but more often our only recourse was to point them to the official Coursera technical support portal. To their credit, the Coursera technical support staff quickly fixed many problems we reported.

For example, it's now possible for the course staff to edit typos and mistakes in video subtitles. Originally, course staff could not perform these edits, which meant that non-native English speaking students were often confused when they tried to read the nonsensical subtitles (mis)transcriptions. Likewise, Coursera added support for "permalinks" (see en.wikipedia.org/wiki/Permalink) to discussion forum postings, which allowed us to post links to common questions that we'd answered before.

In general, we were pleased with the scalability of the Coursera platform and the responsiveness of the Coursera operations staff.

3.6 Innovations Helped Make the POSA MOOC More Like a "Real" Course

Despite the limitations with the Coursera platform discussed in Section 3.5, our goal was to make the POSA MOOC seem like a "real" course. The following is a summary of the innovations we devised for the POSA MOOC that went beyond conventional usage scenarios for the Coursera platform. Some of these innovations have become standard practice in other MOOCs.

3.6.1 Virtual Office Hours

Learning involves much more than watching videos—it requires meaningful dialogue between students and teachers to clarify doubts and deepen collective understanding of the material. A common criticism [11] of conventional MOOCs is that they dehumanize the learning experience by neglecting or degrading interactions between students and teachers. To address this limitation, we used two social media tools—discussion forums (discussed in Section 3.2 above and webcasting (discussed in the following paragraph)—to engage in continuous interactive dialogue with our POSA MOOC students.

We used Google Hangout and a YouTube channel (see www. youtube.com/user/vuposa) to hold weekly "virtual office hours," where students asked questions about assignments and videos via instant messaging and we broadcast answers to them live. Google Hangout automatically recorded the office hours, which we uploaded to the POSA Coursera website so students could view them offline. Roughly 70–100 students participated live for virtual office hours each week, but well over ten times that number viewed the archived videos of the virtual office hours (nearly as many as those who watched the higher-quality videos lectures).

These viewing statistics are particularly noteworthy since we recorded the virtual office hours on a laptop webcam connected to a YouTube channel. This technology was *much* less sophisticated than the green screen technologies we used in the video lectures, which indicates MOOC students are attracted to more than flashy visuals. As social media technology matures it should become feasible (albeit potentially time consuming) for MOOC professors to communicate with students in ways similar in quality and quantity to those found in large lecture courses at many universities.

3.6.2 Crowd-sourced Programming Assignments

Our use of crowd-sourced programming assignment specifications was particularly effective at broadening the scope of the course and engaging more students. Although the videos largely focus on C++ and Java (*i.e.*, the programming languages with which we are most fluent), the peer-graded programming assignment descriptions were crowd-sourced to include C#, Ruby, Python, and Scala. Incidentally, the total number of programming assignment submissions for each programming language was Java (2,205), C++ (869), C# (450), Python (382), Ruby (100), and Scala (75).

Supporting this diversity of programming languages is impractical in a course at Vanderbilt, due to the effort needed to understand and assess assignments written in many different languages. The Coursera peer assessment system, however, enabled students to complete assignments in programming languages that were foreign to the course staff. Students could therefore tailor the course to meet their needs/interests, while still enabling us to teach common architecture and design structures and behaviors via patterns.

3.6.3 Grading Calculator

The Statements of Accomplishment discussed in Section 2.3 conferred no course credit at Vanderbilt. Despite this lack of college credit, many students in the POSA MOOC were quite concerned with the grading policies. For example, many non-native English speakers were frustrated by the short-essay assignments because they feared they would be penalized for poor grammar or language skills, as discussed in Section 3.3. We didn't anticipate this much concern with grading—in fact, students in the MOOC seemed as concerned with grades as undergraduates in our credit-bearing courses at Vanderbilt.

Not surprisingly, therefore, many students requested an easy-to-use, bird's-eye view of their progress in the course relative to the criteria needed for attaining a "Statement of Accomplishment". In response to these requests, We built a simple calculator in JavaScript and attached it to a wiki page. Our solution, however, still required students to navigate to several different pages to figure out their individual assignments scores to feed into the calculator. This capability therefore should really be part of the Coursera platform so it's available to all students in all MOOCs.

3.7 Interpret MOOC Enrollment Statistics Carefully

Although 31,000+ students enrolled in the POSA MOOC, only ~20,000 ultimately ever logged in and participated in some way, such as by watching videos or reading/posting in the discussion forums (Figure 3 provides a breakdown of the countries these ~20,000 students hailed from). Moreover, only ~1,600 of these participants actually received some form of Statement of Accomplishment, as shown in Figures 4 and 5)

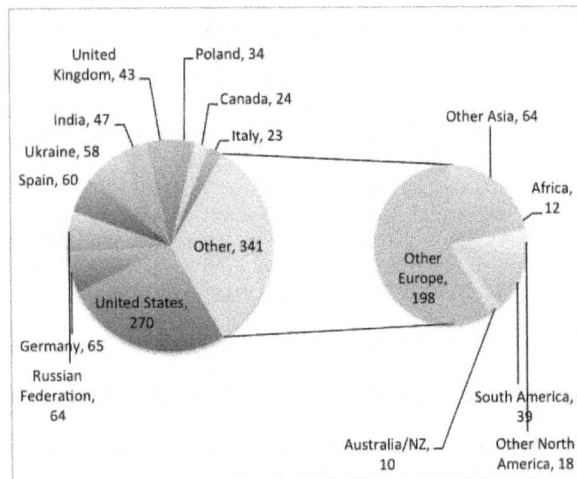

Figure 4. Normal Track Completions by Country

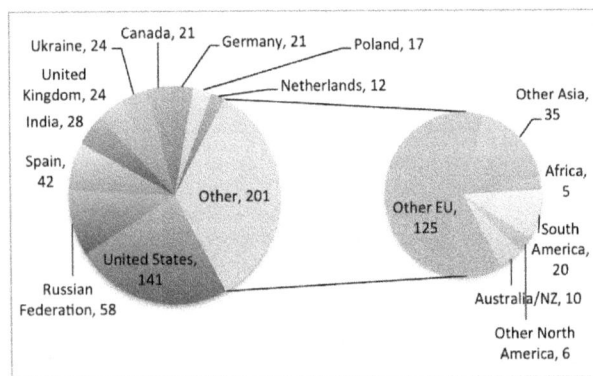

Figure 5. Distinction Track Completions by Country

A completion rate of 5-10% (which is consistent with other published studies [5]) may seem less impressive than the original 31,000+ enrollment figure suggests. Even having ~1,600 students complete the POSA MOOC is notable, however, since it would take us 20+ years to teach that many undergraduates at Vanderbilt. Moreover, it's clear from numerous conversations in the discussion forum and virtual office hours that students learned a great deal from the POSA MOOC, even if they didn't have time to obtain a Statement of Accomplishment.

Some intriguing findings are suggested by the statistics collected from the Coursera platform. For example, the 4.2% completion rate for students from India (1,769 started and 75 finished) versus the 11.3% completion rate for students from the Russian Federation (1,080 started and 122 finished). We have not yet identified the cause for such differences, but our future work will examine the correlations between completion rate and various diversity related factors (such as broadband penetration, English proficiency, age, and types of software jobs available in various countries) discussed in Section 3.3.

3.8 MOOCs Can Enhance Student-centered Learning Opportunities

As educational researchers and teachers have preached for years, every person learns differently, and MOOCs open up new opportunities for learning to happen in a more student-centric way, especially at scale. The remainder of this section describes several ways we predict that MOOC platforms will impact student-centered learning based on our experience with the POSA MOOC.

3.8.1 Increasing Asynchrony in Courses

A traditional university course might begin at 8am on Mondays, Wednesdays, and Fridays, with some students in the room wide-eyed and ready to learn, while others are barely awake. Likewise, many students may have avoided that particular course because it did not fit in their schedule. MOOCs can thus provide students—even those who live on a college campus—increased opportunities for taking courses they otherwise would not be able to take due to scheduling conflicts.

During the POSA MOOC, students could watch videos, take quizzes, and complete programming assignments at their own pace. Although students needed to finish certain parts at certain times, they were not restricted to completing their work by a certain day or time. This freedom granted by MOOC platforms allows students to tailor their learning to match their schedules.

3.8.2 Location-agnostic Learning

We found that MOOCs enhanced the virtual classroom model used by other online learning systems in unique ways. For example, one of the POSA MOOC discussion forums was dedicated to students forming study groups, both online and offline. Some students simply exchanged e-mails throughout the course, or explored topics on the discussion forum. Other students got together in face-to-face meetup groups (both at Vanderbilt and elsewhere) to discuss various aspects of the MOOC. While this real-life interaction is not a guarantee, it's a benefit that some MOOC students realize compared with conventional online courses.

4. The Impact of MOOCs on Traditional On-campus Education

This section describes the impacts of MOOCs on traditional on-campus education based on our POSA MOOC experience.

4.1 Benefits of MOOCs

Some benefits of MOOCs were relevant to instructors and others were relevant to Vanderbilt, as discussed below.

4.1.1 Benefits to Faculty

Several benefits that we observed as instructors for the POSA MOOC include the following:

• **Significantly better on-campus courses**. The lecture material for our on-campus courses is now much better than before due to (1) the months we spent preparing for the POSA MOOC (described in Section 3.1) and (2) the many contributions from students, who provided extensive feedback on the correctness, completeness, and clarity of the material. Eager students would often fix glitches in material the moment it was released, which helped all students who accessed the updated content later. These crowd-sourced improvements are a return on the investment spent preparing for a MOOC. As MOOCs grow in popularity, it is likely that several iterations of the same course will provide decreasing start-up costs with a constant rate of improvement, thus amortizing the initial time commitment, thereby yielding better on-campus courses *and* MOOCs.

Improvements in the POSA MOOC material not only benefitted the students in the *Intermediate Software Design* course taught on-campus in the spring of 2013, but also helped ensure the consistency of future offerings across semesters and instructors. For example, the availability of the high-quality videos on the "Gang of Four" patterns produced for the POSA MOOC enable Vanderbilt students to personalize their learning, *e.g.*, they watch the videos before and/or after class at their own pace, read transcripts of the videos provided by Coursera, and learn from the in-depth conversations in the discussion forums. Moreover, the *Intermediate Software Design* course we're offering in the fall of 2013 is applying "flipped" and "blended" classroom models [4], using POSA MOOC videos to shift some lecture content outside of class time. As a result, more class time is available to interact with and mentor our Vanderbilt students.

• **Fostering global life-long learning communities that connect students who possess a range of experience**, which helps compensate for the lack of critical mass in a local learning community. For example, there isn't much demand in the Nashville IT community for pattern-oriented concurrent and networked software beyond our research group at the *Institute for Software Integrated Systems* (www.isis.vanderbilt.edu). Teaching a conventional face-to-face continuing education course on these topics in Nashville would therefore be of limited value.

Beyond Nashville, however, there's significant global interest in understanding patterns and frameworks for concurrent and networked software, as indicated by the POSA MOOC enrollment statistics discussed in Section 3.7. The MOOC format is ideally suited for disseminating this type of information and building a global life-long learning community around these topics. Moreover, Vanderbilt students benefit from being part of discussions with experienced software professionals from around the world, which provides them with a glimpse of both the global competitiveness and collaborative possibilities that they will face after graduation.

Related digital learning opportunities stemming from the POSA MOOC also help foster a global life-long learning community on patterns and frameworks for concurrent and networked software. For example, Professor Schmidt is creating a spinoff course on *Design Patterns in Java* for Pearson's "LiveLessons" training series as a result of the POSA MOOC.

4.1.2 Benefits to Vanderbilt

We observed several benefits to Vanderbilt that stemmed from our pilot project with the POSA MOOC, including the following:

• **Expanding the brand value of a Vanderbilt education**. The role that top-tier universities like Vanderbilt play in education goes well beyond lecturing to students in person or via videos. The classic method of determining the quality of education at a university is manifested in listings of degrees and honors conferred, grants awarded, and publications accepted by instructors and researchers. In a short span of time, MOOCs have doubled the number of students who have been taught by Vanderbilt professors, as discussed in Section 1. This wide-reaching visibility is helping Vanderbilt expand its brand value by providing a more transparent window into its classrooms, as well as demonstrating its interdisciplinary strengths in teaching, research, entrepreneurship, and innovation.

• **Better opportunities for engagement with alumni and prospective students**. The material produced for our MOOCs is being applied to better connect and (re)engage our alums with the intellectual life of Vanderbilt. Likewise, quality of a Vanderbilt education is now visible to thousands of students around the world, which encourages them to apply to Vanderbilt and partake in the immersive on-campus learning culture.

4.2 Drawbacks of MOOCs

The following were some drawbacks we observed based on our POSA MOOC experience.

4.2.1 Potential for "Deskilling" Education and Educators

A common concern with MOOCs [11] is that they will replace quality face-to-face education with impersonal delivery of information via digital media. While many of these concerns are being ameliorated via advances in MOOC technologies (such as the POSA MOOC innovations discussed in Section 3.6), it's likely that administrators at some institutions will reduce costs by "deskilling" their faculty positions, *e.g.*, combining content from MOOCs from top universities with for-credit courses at their institutions that are proctored by untenured lecturers.

Based on the trends reported thus far [12], it appears that the institutions most impacted by MOOCs will be state universities and community colleges that (1) lack large endowments and research programs and (2) are committed to educating large numbers of students, despite cuts in funding from state legislatures. The positions affected at these institutions will most likely be tenured (or tenure-track) teaching faculty, who typically don't receive significant external funding.

Universities with large endowments, robust research funding, and sufficient income from tuition and other sources (such as alumni donations) will continue (for now) to provide traditional immersive education. Even faculty at these institutions, however, may need to (and ideally *want* to) adapt their pedagogy to leverage digital learning methods and tools since it's essential to justify the value of an immersive college education in today's rapidly changing and globally competitive environment. In our experience, the effective use of digital learning techniques help amplify other value-added mentoring opportunities, such as undergraduate research, entrepreneurship, and collaborations with industry, in addition to enhancing traditional college learning experiences [1].

4.2.2 MOOCs Require Substantial Institutional Investment and the Payoff Isn't Clear (Yet)

Producing and delivering a high-quality MOOC requires a substantial commitment from course staff, as discussed in Section 3.1. Likewise, input from a plethora of campus administrators and staff is needed to review MOOC content, as well as address financial and legal concerns necessary to produce high-quality MOOCs that don't infringe on intellectual property rights. Finding qualified people to conduct all these MOOC-related activities is hard, especially if there's no clear economic benefit to the faculty and university.

Quantifying the return on investment (ROI) from MOOCs is tricky since their impact on the mission of most universities is not yet well understood. Top universities are rationalizing their investment in MOOCs primarily as outreach, *e.g.*, to help achieve the benefits mentioned in 4.1.2. It's not clear, however, the extent to which MOOCs actually improve on-campus course quality, strengthen relations with alumni, and help recruit the best and brightest students. Over time, high levels of institutional time commitment—along with money spent and resources used—will be hard to sustain without a clear ROI, even for a university like Vanderbilt with extensive human and financial resources.

4.2.3 Detecting and Dealing with Plagiarism is Tedious

Plagiarism is a chronic issue with online courses, including non-MOOC online courses. For example, it's easy to copy-and-paste answers found online into the Coursera submission form, which happened surprisingly often in our POSA MOOC, despite the fact that we weren't offering "official" Vanderbilt credit for successfully completing the MOOC. Since we didn't offer our MOOC for "real" college credit, our (admittedly limited) solution to plagiarism we encountered was simply to instruct students to cite their work and/or submit a comment with links if they posted their solutions in a blog post or online. These references enabled other students grading their work to do a cursory check to see if the work was plagiarized. With systems such as TurnItIn.com and Grammarly, we expect that Coursera and other MOOC platforms will soon integrate more effective and meaningful plagiarism detection.

5. Concluding Remarks

During a five month period in the winter and spring of 2013 we devoted hundreds of hours to producing and delivering a Coursera-based MOOC on patterns and frameworks for concurrent and networked software. Our experience was generally positive—and at times exhilarating—albeit exhausting. For a variety of reasons—not the least of which is that it would have taken us ∼500 years to teach 31,000+ students at Vanderbilt—the POSA MOOC differed significantly from our previous experience teaching software design and programming courses to Vanderbilt undergraduates.

MOOCs are particularly relevant to software professionals in academia and industry because future researchers and practitioners will likely receive much of their education through MOOCs and associated digital learning methods and tools [8]. The ability of MOOCs to connect experienced software professionals with motivated novices is a potent pedagogical combination. MOOCs also have the potential (not yet fully realized) to help students personalize their learning experiences at a reasonable cost.

Based on our experiences with the POSA MOOC, we are expanding our Coursera offerings in the spring of 2014. The next POSA MOOC will be an intentionally-coordinated, trans-institution *sequence* of MOOCs that focus on patterns and frameworks for mobile device programming. These sequenced MOOCs will showcase how intentionally-coordinated MOOCs can create life-long learning communities that (1) cross-cut traditional institutional/disciplinary boundaries and (2) would not be feasible without the MOOC paradigm and MOOC platforms like Coursera.

Our sequenced MOOCs will be organized as follows:
• Professor Adam Porter at the University of Maryland, College Park will focus his MOOC on the GUI/client portions of the Android platform starting in January 2014 and
• Professors Doug Schmidt and Jules White at Vanderbilt will focus their MOOC on the patterns/frameworks for the server portions of Android and services in computing clouds in March 2014 at the conclusion of Porter's MOOC.

Coordinated programming assignments will span both MOOCs to integrate material covered in the videos. Students in Porter's MOOC will build GUI/client portions of an app using server modules provided as "blackboxes" by Schmidt and White. Likewise, students in Schmidt and White's MOOC will build server portions of the app using client modules provided as "blackboxes" by Porter. These coordinated assignments will yield a complete solution that demonstrates the pattern-oriented integration of Android mobile devices with cloud computing platforms.

Despite our enthusiasm about the POSA MOOC, we recognize that MOOCs pose many social, economic, and technical challenges. For example, it's not clear yet how to prevent administrators at some cash-strapped institutions from diminishing the quality of higher education via wanton replacement of experienced faculty with MOOCs and inexpensive lecturers. Other discussions of our experiences with the POSA MOOC—and our observations about the MOOC paradigm—can be found at `www.dre.vanderbilt.edu/~schmidt/Coursera.html`.

Acknowledgments

Thanks to Dennis Mancl for his feedback on our initial drafts and to Vanderbilt for supporting our production and delivery of the POSA MOOC. In particular, Richard McCarty, Cynthia Cyrus, Derek Bruff, Michael Martin, Jeff Shoop, John Brassil, Doug Fisher, Melanie Moran, Jesse Badash, Katie McEwen, Sarah Collier, David Owens, Jay Clayton, and Jamie Pope provided invaluable assistance and helped position Vanderbilt for a leadership role in using MOOCs and other digital learning technologies effectively. Finally, we'd like to thank our Coursera liaisons—Ryan George and Pang Wei Koh—who patiently guided us through the mysteries of the Coursera platform. We look forward to seeing how they and the other MOOC innovators will enable affordable student-centric learning via digital learning methods and technologies.

References

[1] Bruff, D., D. Fisher, K. McEwen, B. Smith, "Wrapping a MOOC: Student Perceptions of an Experiment In Blended Learning," Accepted to the *Journal of Online Learning and Teaching*.

[2] Buschmann, F., et al. *Pattern-Oriented Software Architecture, Volume 5: Patterns and Pattern Languages*, Wiley, 2007.

[3] Gamma, E., et al. *Design Patterns - Elements of Reusable Object-Oriented Software*, Addison-Wesley, 1994.

[4] Fisher, D., "Warming Up to MOOC's," *Chronicle of Higher Education*, November 6, 2012.

[5] Hill, P., "The Most Thorough Summary (to date) of MOOC Completion Rates," *e-Literate*, February 26th, 2013.

[6] Hu, J., and D. C. Schmidt. "JAWS: A Framework for High Performance Web Servers," Domain-Specific Application Frameworks: Frameworks Experience by Industry (1999).

[7] Johnson, R. "Documenting Frameworks Using Patterns," Proceedings of the ACM OOPSLA Conference, Vancouver, British Columbia, October 1992.

[8] Meister, J., "How MOOCs Will Revolutionize Corporate Learning And Development," *Forbes*, August 13, 2013.

[9] Morrison, D., "Why and When Peer Grading is Effective for Open and Online Learning," Online Learning Insights, March 9, 2013.

[10] Murphy, M. *Busy Coder's Guide to Android Development*, CommonsWare, 2013.

[11] Rees, J., "The MOOC Racket," *Slate*, July 25th, 2013.

[12] Rosenberger, J., "John L. Hennessy on 'The Coming Tsunami in Educational Technology'," *Communications of the ACM Blog*, July 23, 2012.

[13] Schmidt, D. C., et al. *Pattern-Oriented Software Architecture, Volume 2: Concurrent and Distributed Objects*, Wiley, 2000.

[14] Schmidt, D. C., and S. Huston, *C++ Network Programming: Systematic Reuse with ACE and Frameworks*, Addison Wesley, 2002.

[15] Schmidt, D. C., D. Levine, and S. Mungee, "The Design of the TAO Real-time Object Request Broker," *Computer Communications*, 21.4 (1998): 294-324.

SPLASH'13 Workshops Summary

Stephanie Balzer

CMU

balzers@cs.cmu.edu

Ulrik Pagh Schultz

University of Southern Denmark

ups@mmmi.sdu.dk

Categories and Subject Descriptors   D.0 [*Software*]: GENERAL

Keywords   AGERE!, DSM, FOOL, FOSD, FlexiTools, ITSLE, MARC, MobileDeLi, PLASTIC, PLATEAU, PROMOTO, Parsing@SLE, REM, SBLE, SMAC, SPLASH-E, TD, VMIL, WOSC, WRT

1. Overview

Following its long-standing tradition, SPLASH 2013 will host 19 high-quality workshops, allowing their participants to meet and discuss research questions with peers, to mature new and exciting ideas, and to build up communities and start new collaborations. SPLASH workshops complement the main tracks of the conference and provide meetings in a smaller and more specialized setting. Workshops cultivate new ideas and concepts for the future, optionally recorded in formal proceedings.

We invite you to explore the workshops program online at http://splashcon.org/2013/program/workshops. This paper contains brief summaries of each of the accepted workshops, grouped by topic. The SPLASH-E workshop is separate from the regular workshop program, and its program is available at http://splashcon.org/2013/program/educator-symposium.

2. Software Language Engineering

Software Language Engineering (SLE) is one of the SPLASH topics this year. Four workshops are dedicated to this topic. *FOSD 2013* (5th International Workshop on Feature-Oriented Software Development) concerns feature orientation, an emerging paradigm of software development that supports the automatic generation of large-scale software systems from a set of units of functionality called features [7]. *ITSLE 2013* (Industrial Track of Software Language Engineering) is dedicated to industrial research on and application of SLE-based techniques, including industry oriented work done in universities and research organizations [19]. *Parsing@SLE* invites the authors of parser generation tools and parsers for programming languages and other software languages to come together, in order to explore open questions and possibly forge new collaborations [20]. *SBLE* (Workshop on the Interface between Synthetic Biology and Language Engineering) aims to bring together language designers and synthetic biologists with the

goal of analyzing the different programming paradigms that have been or could be explored to write these biological programs more effectively [15].

3. Programming Languages and Tools

Programming languages and tools are of key interest to seven workshops, ranging from foundations to applications within specific problem areas. *AGERE!* (Programming based on Actors, Agents, and Decentralized Control) focuses on programming systems, languages and applications based on actors, agents and other programming paradigms, promoting a decentralized-control mindset in solving problems and developing software [9]. *DSM* (Domain-Specific Modeling) concerns the use of domain-specific languages to raise the level of abstraction beyond coding, making development faster and easier. In Domain-Specific Modeling (DSM), the models are constructed using the concepts occurring in the application domain, rather than the concepts of a given programming language [18]. *FOOL* (20th International Workshop on Foundations of Object-Oriented Languages) aims to provide a forum for discussing new ideas in the foundations of object-oriented languages, including integration with other paradigms and extensions, such as aspects, components, and meta-programming [17]. *PLATEAU* (Evaluation and Usability of Programming Languages and Tools) aims to discuss methods, metrics and techniques for evaluating the usability of languages and language tools, by gathering an intersection of researchers in the programming language, programming tool, and human-computer interaction communities to share their research and discuss the future of evaluation and usability of programming languages and tools [14]. *PLASTIC* (Workshop on Programming Language and Systems Technologies for Internet Clients) focuses on innovative solutions in the area of Internet client software that improve on the current state-of-the-art while respecting the confines dictated by interoperability, as well as bold, new ideas that break with the status quo [16]. *PROMOTO 2013* (Programming for Mobile and Touch) brings together researchers who have been exploring new programming paradigms, embracing the new realities of always connected, touch-enabled mobile devices. This year's focus is on educational aspects, approaches, and insights [2]. *REM* (Workshop on Reactivity, Events and Modularity) serves as a conduit for novel work in the context of reactive software design and implementation broadly construed, i.e., implicit invocations, aspects and joinpoints, asynchronous methods, first-class events, purely functional reactive frameworks and design and architectural patterns such as subject/observer and publish/subscribe [12].

4. Program Execution and Optimization

Execution with emphasis on virtual machines, optimizations, and many-core platforms is investigated by three workshops. *VMIL'13* (7th Workshop on Virtual Machines and Intermediate Languages) is a forum for research in virtual machines and intermediate languages, dedicated to identifying programming mechanisms and constructs that are currently realized as code transformations or implemented in libraries but should rather be supported at VM level [3]. *WOSC* (Workshop on Optimizing Stencil Computations) aims to create a discussion between the many efforts to optimize stencil computations as well as the various domains that could benefit from these efforts, in order to evaluate the current state-of-the-art as well as pushing new research ideas influenced by the target domains [10]. *MARC* (Many-core Applications Research Community Symposium) focuses on the overlap between software systems, programming languages, and many-core architectures, bringing together diverse research interests ranging from power consumption to programming language support, from message passing to software-managed coherence, all with a common tie to many-core platforms [5].

5. Software Engineering

Software engineering is covered by five workshops, with topics ranging from processes and tools to concerns that are specific to a particular application domain. *TD* (Technical Debt) explores the sources of technical debt and some of the best practices for keeping technical debt under control. Of particular interest is the question: "If we believe that technical debt is an important issue in long-term software product development, do we have ways to keep the technical debt from causing development gridlock [11]?" *FlexiTools* (5th International Workshop on Flexible Modeling Tools) has as its goal to identify a foundational set of challenges and concerns for the field of flexible modeling, as well as emerging promising directions for addressing them, by bringing together people who understand tool users' needs, usability, user interface design and tool infrastructure [8]. *SMAC 2013* (Software Engineering for Social-Mobile-Analytics-Cloud) provides a forum for discussion and exploration of the software engineering challenges in the domain of customized analytics and analytics-based applications, for example for cloud-hosted datat [6]. *MobileDeLi* (Mobile Development Lifecycle) concerns practices and tools suitable for development of mobile applications, e.g., architecture techniques that relate to the complexity at hand, improved refactoring tools for hybrid applications using dynamic languages and polyglot development and applications, and testing techniques for applications that run on different devices [1]. *WRT* (Workshop on Refactoring Tools) brings together researchers and developers of refactoring tools to share new ideas and practical insights, discuss challenges and solutions, and together shape the future of refactoring. Topics of interest include, but are by no means limited to, refactoring tools for new domains, novel interface paradigms, and refactoring for previously unsupported languages [13].

6. Education

Education is the topic of the *SPLASH-E* workshop, which is designed to reboot the focus on education at SPLASH. While many education-focused meetings tend to segregate educators from computer science researchers and practitioners, this symposium has as an explicit goal of bringing together these communities to discuss educational issues. There are a number of items that are currently of active interest in this area that will be explored this year in the symposium. Examples include the impact of the new ACM/IEEE CS Curriculum 2013, experience with MOOCs, test-driven design, working with school-age children, and discussions on teaching other aspects of computer science [4].

Acknowledgments

We would like to thank the workshops evaluation committee for their responsive and valuable reviews of workshop proposals: Ademar Aguiar (U Porto), Dave Thomas (Bedarra Research Labs), Eric Van Wyk (U Minnesota), Erik Ernst (U Aarhus), Frank Tip (U Waterloo), Gavin Bierman (Microsoft Research), Robert Hirschfeld (U Potsdam).

References

[1] A. Abadi, R. Prikladnicki, and Y. Dubinsky. SPLASH'13 Workshop: Mobile Development Lifecycle, 2013. http://sysrun.haifa.il.ibm.com/hrl/mobiledeli2013/.

[2] J. Bishop, N. Tillmann, and A. Puder. SPLASH'13 Workshop: PROMOTO 2013: Programming for Mobile and Touch, 2013. http://pear.sfsu.edu/promoto2013/.

[3] C. Bockisch, M. Haupt, H. Rajan, and S. M. Blackburn. SPLASH'13 Workshop: 7th Workshop on Virtual Machines and Intermediate Languages, 2013. http://design.cs.iastate.edu/vmil/2013.

[4] K. Bruce. SPLASH-E 2013: Splash-Education, 2013. http://www.cs.pomona.edu/splashe/SPLASH-E2013/SPLASH-E_2013.html.

[5] D. Brylow and C. Liu. SPLASH'13 Workshop: Many-core Applications Research Community Symposium, 2013. http://www.mscs.mu.edu/~brylow/SPLASH-MARC-2013/.

[6] J. Caverlee, C. Williams, and E. Khabiri. SPLASH'13 Workshop: Software Engineering for Social-Mobile-Analytics-Cloud, 2013. http://research.ihost.com/smac2013/.

[7] A. Classen and N. Siegmund. SPLASH'13 Workshop: Fifth International Workshop on Feature-Oriented Software Development, 2013. http://www.fosd.de/2013/.

[8] F. Correia, A. Aguiar, L. Rose, A. van der Hoek, A. Egyed, D. Wüest, and M. Glinz. SPLASH'13 Workshop: 5th International Workshop on Flexible Modeling Tools, 2013. http://softeng.fe.up.pt/flexitools/2013/.

[9] N. Jamali, A. Ricci, G. Weiss, and A. Yonezawa. SPLASH'13 Workshop: Programming based on Actors, Agents, and Decentralized Control, 2013. http://agents.usask.ca/agere2013.

[10] S. Kamil, S. Amarasinghe, K. Yelick, and P. S. Sadayappan. SPLASH'13 Workshop: Workshop on Optimizing Stencil Computations, 2013. http://people.csail.mit.edu/skamil/wosc/.

[11] D. Mancl, S. D. Fraser, and B. Opdyke. SPLASH'13 Workshop: Technical Debt, 2013. http://mysite.verizon.net/dennis.mancl/splash13/.

[12] W. D. Meuter, P. Eugster, K. Pinte, G. Salvaneschi, M. Südholt, and L. Ziarek. SPLASH'13 Workshop: Reactivity, Events and Modularity, 2013. http://soft.vub.ac.be/REM13.

[13] E. Murphy-Hill and M. Schaefer. SPLASH'13 Workshop: Workshop on Refactoring Tools, 2013. http://refactoring.info/WRT13/.

[14] E. Murphy-Hill, C. Sadowski, and S. Markstrum. SPLASH'13 Workshop: Evaluation and Usability of Programming Languages and Tools, 2013. https://sites.google.com/site/workshopplateau.

[15] J. Peccoud and E. V. Wyk. SPLASH'13 Workshop: Workshop on the Interface between Synthetic Biology and Language Engineering, 2013. http://planet-sl.org/sble-at-sle2013/.

[16] G. Richards, M. Miller, and K. Palacz. SPLASH'13 Workshop: Workshop on Programming Language and Systems Technologies for Internet Clients, 2013. http://plastic.host.adobe.com/.

[17] J. Siek, J. Aldrich, and S. Krishnamurthi. SPLASH'13 Workshop: 20th International Workshop on Foundations of Object-Oriented Languages, 2013. http://fool2013.cs.brown.edu/.

[18] J. Sprinkle, J. Gray, and S. Kelly. SPLASH'13 Workshop: Domain-Specific Modeling, 2013. http://www.dsmforum.org/events/DSM13/.

[19] M. van den Brand, R. Schiffelers, I. Goodsell, and N. Brouwers. SPLASH'13 Workshop: Industrial Track of Software Language Engineering 2013, 2013. http://planet-sl.org/itsle2013/.

[20] J. Vinju and E. V. Wyk. SPLASH'13 Workshop: Parsing @ SLE, 2013. http://www.planet-sl.org/parsing-at-sle2013.

Author Index

179

www.ingramcontent.com/pod-product-compliance
Lightning Source LLC
Chambersburg PA
CBHW081528220326
41598CB00036B/6364